PRACTICAL DCE PROGRAMMING

Hewlett-Packard Professional Books

Blinn	Portable Shell Programming: An Extensive Collection of Bourne Shell Examples
Costa	Planning and Designing High Speed Networks Using 100VG-AnyLAN, Second Edition
Fristrup	USENET: Netnews for Everyone
Fristrup	The Essential Web Surfer Survival Guide
Grady	Practical Software Metrics for Project Management and Process Improvement
Grosvenor, Ichiro, O'Brien	Mainframe Downsizing to Upsize Your Business: IT-Preneuring
Gunn	A Guide to NetWare® for UNIX®
Helsel	Graphical Programming: A Tutorial for HP VEE
Kane	PA-RISC 2.0 Architecture
Knouse	Practical DCE Programming
Lewis	The Art & Science of Smalltalk
Malan, Letsinger, Coleman	Object-Oriented Development at Work: Fusion In the Real World
Madell, Parsons, Abegg	Developing and Localizing International Software
McMinds/Whitty	Writing Your Own OSF/Motif Widgets
Phaal	LAN Traffic Management
Poniatowski	The HP-UX System Administrator's "How To" Book
Poniatowski	HP-UX 10.x System Administration "How To" Book
Thomas	Cable Television Proof-of-Performance: A Practical Guide to Cable TV Compliance Measurements Using a Spectrum Analyzer.
Witte	Electronic Test Instruments
Witte	Spectrum & Network Measurements

PRACTICAL DCE PROGRAMMING

Charles Knouse

GSY Early Adopter Program
Hewlett-Packard

Prentice Hall P T R
Upper Saddle River, New Jersey 07458

Library of Congress Cataloging-in-Publication Data

Knouse, Charles.
Practical DCE programming / Charles Knouse
p. cm.
Includes index.
ISBN 0-13-324419-9
1. Client/server computing. 2. Electronic data processing–
–Distributed processing. 3. Electronic digital computers–
–Programming. I. Title.
QA76.9.C55K56 1995 95-25643
005.2--dc20 CIP

Editorial /production supervision: Betty Letizia
Cover design director: Jerry Votta
Cover design: Defranco Design
Manufacturing manager: Alexis R. Heydt
Acquisitions editor: Karen Gettman
Page layout/formatting: Bear Type & Graphics
Manager, Hewlett-Packard Press: Pat Pekary

Published by Prentice Hall P T R
Prentice-Hall, Inc.
A Simon & Schuster Company
Upper Saddle River, NJ 07458

The publisher offers discounts on this book when ordered in bulk quantities. For more information, contact:

Corporate Sales Department
Prentice Hall P T R
One Lake Street
Upper Saddle River, New Jersey 07458
Phone: 800-382-3419
FAX: 201-236-7141
E-mail: corpsales@prenhall.com

Printed in the United States of America

10 9 8 7 6 5 4 3 2 1

ISBN 0-13-324419-9

Prentice-Hall International (UK) Limited, *London*
Prentice-Hall of Australia Pty. Limited, *Sydney*
Prentice-Hall of Canada, Inc., *Toronto*
Prentice-Hall Hispanoamericana S.A., *Mexico*
Prentice-Hall of India Private Limited, *New Delhi*
Prentice-Hall of Japan, Inc., *Tokyo*
Simon & Schuster Asia Pte. Ltd., *Singapore*
Editora Prentice-Hall do Brasil, Ltda., *Rio de Janeiro*

Table of Contents

Preface

The Distributed Computing Environment (DCE), from the Open Software Foundation (OSF), is becoming an important standard for developing open, cooperative client-server applications. There are DCE implementations on almost all major computing systems, ranging from personal computers and workstations to powerful multiuser systems, mainframes, and supercomputers. (See Table 1.1 in Chapter 1 for a list of implementations.)

If you will be developing a distributed application, you should consider using DCE. It provides solutions to many problems inherent in distributed processing, including management of network communications, location of resources, enforcement of security, and many others.

But DCE is both powerful and complex. There are many DCE calls with which you must contend to write a client-server application. You will find a guide to the features and facilities of DCE most helpful.

This book is entitled *Practical DCE Programming* because it seeks to provide practical guidelines and examples to aid in the development of client-server applications using DCE. Guidelines are given for writing Remote Procedure Calls (RPCs) from clients to servers, including specification of the remote calls using the Interface Definition Language (IDL). Examples are given of working clients and servers, including the DCE calls you will need to develop your application. Particular attention is given to the new facilities in the OSF DCE 1.1 release that ease the development and management of application servers.

Audience

This book is written for application programmers who will be writing clients and servers that use DCE. The programming language used is C, so you will need the ability to read simple C code to understand the concepts and examples.

Book Organization and Topics

After an introductory chapter, each chapter of this book introduces a new DCE programming topic. In addition, the chapters contribute new features to the *Room Schedule* application, a sample application that illustrates the use of DCE concepts and calls.

Several of the chapters include detailed discussions on how DCE features have been implemented. This knowledge is not essential to developing applications with DCE, so if you are not interested in the internals of DCE, you can skip these sections. Also, several chapters end with an examination of how DCE features affect application performance. Topics covered in each chapter are listed below.

Chapter 1: The Distributed Computing Environment

- an overview of client-server models
- the Open Software Foundation and its process for developing DCE
- components of DCE (threads, RPC, CDS, security and so on)
- the sample Room Schedule application.

Chapter 2: Remote Procedure Calls

- review of procedures and procedure calls in local programs
- the concept of remote procedure calls between clients and servers
- details of the DCE RPC mechanism and protocols
- performance of remote calls

Chapter 3: Interface Definition

- the Interface Definition Language (IDL) used to define remote calls
- the IDL compiler and the IDL-generated client and server stubs
- data types supported by IDL
- use of arrays, pointers, pipes, and context handles
- UUIDs (Universal Unique IDs) that identify various things in DCE
- ACFs (Attribute Configuration Files) that control the generation of IDL-related files.

Chapter 4: Basic Client and Server Setup

- setting up server bindings for protocol sequences
- registering interfaces with the server's RPC Runtime
- setting up to execute remote calls
- use of string bindings by a client to locate and use a server.
- RPC endpoint mapping

Chapter 5: Client and Server Setup Using CDS

- organization of the Cell Directory Service
- RPC Name Space (RPC server, group, and profile entries)

- tools for viewing CDS entries (**cdsbrower**, **rpccp**, and **dcecp**)
- exporting bindings from the server using CDS
- importing bindings into the client using CDS
- implicit, explicit, automatic, and custom binding
- operation of CDS components
- performance implications of using CDS

Chapter 6: Security

- security requirements for distributed applications
- DCE Security Registry objects (principals, groups, etc.)
- tools for managing the Registry (**rgy_edit** and **dcecp**)
- establishment of client and server identities using principals
- authentication between clients and servers
- data protection using encryption techniques
- server key management techniques
- details of Kerberos and DCE authentication
- the impact of security on performance

Chapter 7: Server Management in DCE 1.1

- server configuration using **dcecp**
- integrated server registration
- server management operations

Chapter 8: Objects and Managers

- object definition in DCE
- object types and manager routines
- object registration with the RPC Runtime and with CDS

Chapter 9: Access Control

- access control lists (ACLs) for authorization of requests
- types of ACLs
- DCE 1.1 ACL management library
- ACL setup
- ACL storage
- ACL evaluation algorithm
- tools for managing ACLs (**acl_edit** and **dcecp**)
- the `rdacl` interface

Chapter 10: Threads

- the concept of multithreaded applications
- thread creation and termination

- concurrency problems with multithreaded applications
- mutual exclusion (mutex) facilities for concurrency control
- thread coordination facilities (condition variables)
- thread initialization and thread-specific data
- the CMA Threads package

Appendix A: Hints for Debugging DCE Applications

Appendix B: Room Schedule Application
- room interface IDL and ACF files
- room server source
- room manager source
- room client source
- common utilities source and header files
- security and CDS setup scripts
- makefile

Topics Not Covered in This Book

Given the sheer size of DCE, it is not possible to cover all areas of DCE in detail in this one book. I have tried to cover those topics that are required to start writing production client-server applications based on DCE. Other topics that I have omitted are

DCE Administration

The administration of DCE is in itself a suitable topic for an entire book. Some bits of DCE administration that are necessary to get a DCE application operating will be included in this book.

Other DCE services

Chapter 1 gives an overview of the services provided by DCE. But only services that are central to the development of client-server applications are discussed in detail. Other DCE services that are not covered in this book:

- the Distributed File Service (DFS),
- the Distributed Time Service (DTS),
- the Global Directory Service (GDS), and
- non-RPC use of the Cell Directory Service (CDS).

Conventions

Since this book is about programming, its conventions concern programming elements and examples.

Programming elements

Procedure names, parameters, variables, and defined types are represented in Courier font, for example: `room_name`. Procedure names, following established C convention, end in `()`: `room_description()`.

Files, programs, and commands

File names are also represented in Courier font: `room_server.c`. Program names and commands are in bold Courier font: **`room_server`** and **`rpccp show mappings`**.

Code and output samples

Code samples are presented as excerpts from the sample application files. All code samples are in Courier font and are labeled with the relevant example directory, file and procedure name. Code that is omitted in a code sample is replaced by ellipses (. . .). Sample output is shown in a similar fashion, but using a smaller Courier font to fit within the margins of this book. An example of a code sample:

```
 rpc_server_use_all_protseqs(
    rpc_c_protseq_max_reqs_default, &status);
  CHECK_DCE(status,
    "Cannot get bindings for all protocols");
```

Code Sample 4.1
`schedule/room_server.c main()`: Using all protocol sequences

A note on the word "the"

DCE documentation seems to be split on whether to use the article "the" in front of acronyms like DCE and CDS. *The* Distributed Computing Environment certainly sounds correct, but *the* DCE seems a bit awkward. So I have chosen to omit the *the* before acronyms.

Source Files on the Book Diskette

The source files for the sample applications are included on the diskette that accompanies this book. The diskette is in MS-DOS format and contains a file named `tarfile`, in Unix **`tar`** format. `tarfile` contains these directories:

- `delegation`
- `get_file`
- `get_file/custom_handle`
- `perf`
- `schedule`
- `schedule/auto_handle`
- `schedule/exp_handle`

- `schedule/imp_handle`
- `schedule/obj`
- `schedule/obj/thread`

There are `README` files in each directory describing how to build and use the sample applications. To retrieve the source files:

- On an MS-DOS system that is networked to the target Unix system, insert the book diskette. Transfer `tarfile` from the diskette to the target directory on the Unix system, using `ftp` or another appropriate file transfer program. Use binary mode for the transfer.
- On the target Unix system, restore the directories using the command **`tar -xvf tarfile`**. You should have restored the directories listed above under the directory to which you transferred and unpacked `tarfile`.
- Follow the directions in each directory's `README` file to compile and try out the sample applications.

If you do not have access to a networked MS-DOS system from which you can restore the source files, you can also obtain these files by sending me an e-mail request at `cwk@cup.hp.com`.

Code Examples

The sample application clients and servers were compiled and tested in this environment:

- Computer: HP9000/847
- Operating System: HP-UX 9.04
- DCE Version: HP DCE/9000 1.4 (beta version)

I have tried to verify that the programming presented in this book is correct and accurate. However, as every programmer knows, no piece of software can be certified to be completely defect-free. The sample application has not been used in a production environment, so it has not been subjected to the level of usage that will disclose hidden defects.

HEWLETT-PACKARD MAKES NO WARRANTY OF ANY KIND WITH REGARD TO THIS MATERIAL, INCLUDING, BUT NOT LIMITED TO, THE IMPLIED WARRANTIES OF MERCHANTABILITY AND FITNESS FOR A PARTICULAR USE.

Acknowledgments

I would like to thank the following people for their help and support during the writing of this book. The management of the General Systems Division Early Adopter Program, including April Brake, Dave Stevens, and Richard Webber, allowed me the time and resources to write it. The book's reviewers, including John Dilley, Deborah Caswell, and Julian Thomas, provided many valuable and insightful comments. The DCE experts in the Chelmsford Systems Software Lab have always been helpful in answering questions and resolving problems. Working with all of my colleagues in the Early Adopter Program has been an educational experience. I am indebted to Bob Joslin for the loan of a PowerBook during a crucial phase. Finally I would like to express my appreciation for the encouragement and understanding I received from my wife, Anita, during the long process of writing this book.

About the Author

I have been a software developer at Hewlett-Packard for 17 years. I am currently in the Early Adopter Program in the General Systems Division, where I have been working on distributed application security solutions for DCE and other environments. Prior to that I was in the Information Networks Division, where I ported DCE and the Network Computing System (NCS) to the HP3000/MPE-iX environment and worked on the Network Services/3000 product.

I graduated from the University of Iowa with an M.S. in computer science and Coe College (Cedar Rapids, IA) with a B.A. in mathematics and physics.

I can be reached via e-mail at `cwk@cup.hp.com`. I look forward to any comments or corrections you might send me.

About This Book

This book was written using FrameMaker 4.0 on an HP 9000/730 and Apple Macintosh Performa and PowerBook computers. Graphs were plotted using ClarisWorks 2.3.

CHAPTER 1

The Distributed Computing Environment

Before taking the plunge into the world of DCE programming, let's first look at the concepts and history behind the Distributed Computing Environment. This chapter answers the questions:

- What is client-server and what client-server models exist?
- Where did DCE come from and what are its major components?
- What is this Room Schedule example application that will appear throughout the book?

1.1 Client-Server Models

"Client-server" is one of the major buzzwords of current information technology, and consequently it is used to describe a number of different approaches to solving the same problem. That problem is: How do users (the clients) use resources (the services) when the users and resources are distributed across a network of computers? To simplify the discussion here, let's consider the important class of OLTP (On-line Transaction Processing) applications. In OLTP, the clients are users who need to look at and modify data concerning the enterprise in which they work. For instance, order entry clerks need to enter and retrieve customer and order information.

There are three primary components to be considered in an OLTP application.

Presentation Management

The user interacts with the application through some sort of presentation interface. This may be anything from command lines on an ASCII terminal, to screen panels on a 3270 terminal, to graphical windows on an intelligent workstation. The Presentation Management (PM) portion of the application is responsible for sending data to and receiving data from the user's interface device (terminal, screen, or window). It may also enforce minor correctness checks on input data, like numeric only fields. There are many commercial software packages available for presentation management with all manner of terminals, workstations, and personal computers.

Application Logic

The heart of the application is its Application Logic, which decides what to do with data and user actions based on programmed business rules. The Application Logic interfaces with the user through Presentation Management and with the data through Data Access.

Data Access

The application uses and controls data through a file system or database management system (DBMS). File and database systems are either provided with the operating system or are a commercial add-on to the system. They provide a defined, frequently standardized interface for data access and manipulation and efficient techniques for organization, storage, and retrieval of data on the computer's mass storage subsystem.

The four client-server models to be discussed here differ in how they split up these components of the application.

Monolithic Application

In a monolithic application, all components reside in one system, as shown in Figure 1.1. Since all components are on a single system, this cannot be considered a true client-server model. But it is included here for comparison, and because most existing, so-called *legacy*, applications conform to this model. This is particularly true in the host mainframe world.

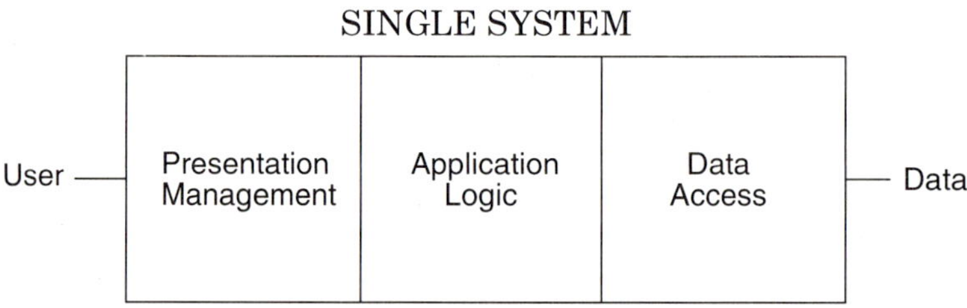

Figure 1.1
Monolithic Application Model

The user usually sits in front of an ASCII or 3270 terminal directly attached to the host system or connected through a terminal concentrator or modem link for remote access. Presentation Management means input and output of characters or screen panels. Examples of host PM software include

- On IBM MVS hosts: CICS Basic Mapping Support (BMS)
- On Unix systems: JAM screen manager
- On the HP 3000: V-PLUS screen manager

Each of these Presentation Managers provides a set of commands or calls that the application uses to read and write data to the user's terminal.

There are a wide variety of Database Management systems available on host systems, including

- On IBM MVS hosts: VSAM files, IMS and DB2 databases
- On Unix systems: Oracle, Sybase, and Informix databases
- On the HP 3000: KSAM files, and TurboIMAGE databases

The advantages of the monolithic model are that host-based applications are well understood and host systems have been tuned to maximize performance. The disadvantage is that monolithic applications are not distributed and so cannot exploit the dramatic increase in power and flexibility on the desktop and in the network.

Distributed Presentation

In the Distributed Presentation model, shown in Figure 1.2, the application is split between the Presentation Manager and the Application Logic. The Presentation Manager resides in an intelligent desktop system, such as a PC, a Macintosh, or a Unix workstation. The PM can then take advantage of the display capabilities of the client system like multiple windows and graphics. The Application Logic and Database Management remain on the host system.

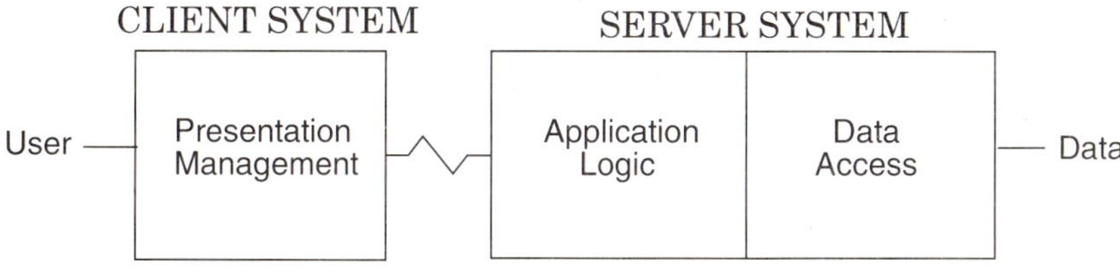

Figure 1.2
Distributed Presentation Model

Virtual Terminals

In this simplest form of distributed presentation, the client logs onto the host system using **telnet** or **rlogin** (on Unix), **:REMOTE HELLO** (on the HP 3000) or a 3270 emulator (on an IBM host) and runs the application on the host. Character or screen data are directed to the user's display on the client system. The host application need not be modified to be used from a remote system over a virtual terminal.

Screen Scrapers

Screen scrapers are the next level of distributed presentation. These are software packages, running on the client systems, that intercept the terminal traffic from the host application and transform it into a better looking, more versatile interface on the client system. The host application need not be modified to be used through a screen scraper. Examples of commercially available screen scrapers include Choreographer (from GUIdance), Easel (from Easel Corp.), and Enfin (from Software Productivity International).

X-Windows and Motif

An application on a Unix system can be written to use the X-Windows presentation manager, or more commonly, a higher-level package like OSF Motif. X/Motif allows the applications windows to be displayed on any suitable workstation or X-terminal on the network. (PCs and Macintoshes with the appropriate software can also display X-Windows.) This can usually be done by running the application on the host and specifying the target system in the DISPLAY environment variable. Note that from X's perspective, the application is the X client, and the workstation displaying the windows is the X server. X allows the application, with considerable programming effort, to control the full range of graphical objects on the display.

World Wide Web Browsers

Browsers for the World Wide Web, for example, Mosaic and Netscape, can be thought of as a form of distributed presentation. The server application displays documents written in the HyperText Markup Language (HTML) on the client system. HTML and the Web browsers provide superb graphics and other multimedia output like sound and video. They can also accept input in forms displayed by the server.

The advantage of distributed presentation is that the existing applications need not be modified to be used from remote systems. The disadvantage is that the remote user may still have to log on to the host and have to execute access to the host application. Also, the application does not take advantage of the processing power on the desktop beyond handling the presentation.

Distributed Data

In the Distributed Data model, shown in Figure 1.3, the application runs primarily on the client system. Both the presentation management and the application logic reside on the client. The server system is a back-end for access to data.

Remote File and Database Access

The simplest form of distributed data access is remote file. Each file or database operation is directed from the client to the server system. The entire file or database must reside on one server system. If there are many access operations, such as in reading and writing individual records in a file, performance over the network can be slow. Another drawback is the client and server need to share common data access operations, restricting the interoperability of proprietary clients and servers. Examples of remote file access include function shipping in IBM CICS and Network Systems RFA/RDBA on the HP 3000.

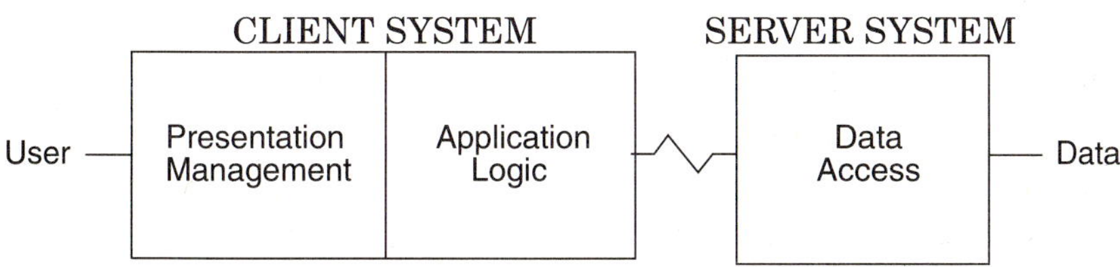

Figure 1.3
Distributed Data Model

Distributed File Systems

The next step up from remote file access are distributed file systems. Here the distribution of data occurs at a lower level than remote file operations. Distributed file systems have the ability (or at least the potential) to cache data to improve performance and to use tokens to maintain integrity of distributed data. Examples of distributed file systems are the Network File System (NFS) from Sun Microsystems, the Andrew File System (AFS) from Transarc Corporation, and OSF's DFS (of which more later).

Distributed Databases

A distributed database management system allows a client to make database queries and updates against a database distributed across a number of servers. The location of the data is transparent to the client. The performance of distributed databases can be slow, especially for browsing operations that generate a lot of network traffic. Examples of distributed database products that run on client workstations are SQL Windows (from Gupta Technologies) and SQL-Forms (from Oracle).

The advantages of distributed data access include transparency for the application developer and more utilization of the power of the client. The disadvantages are poor performance for some types of access, and database management software must reside on every client accessing the data. Also, the application is dependent on the security (or lack of security) of the database manager.

Cooperative Processing

The final client-server model to be considered is cooperative processing. In this model, shown in Figure 1.4, the application logic is split between the client and the server. The client contains the logic for specific user tasks, while the server contains the logic for business transactions relating to the enterprise data on the server. This split permits enforcement of business rules, including access control, by the server while hiding those rules from the client.

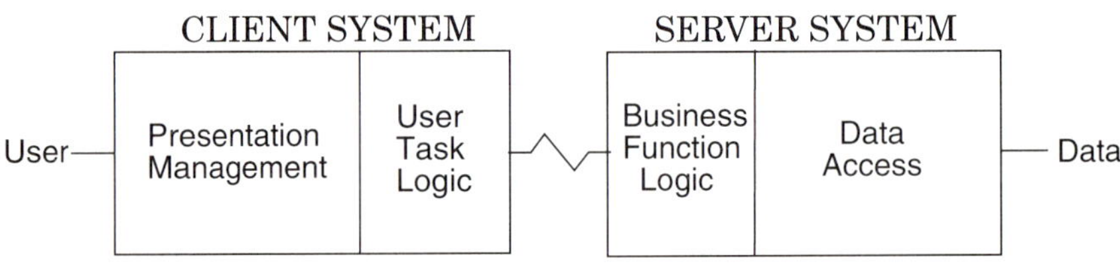

Figure 1.4
Cooperative Processing Model

For cooperative processing, some form of communication is required between the client and server. A wide range of communication mechanisms are available, including the following.

Direct Message Delivery

With direct messages, the client sends a request message to the server and the server (which must be active) receives and processes the request and sends a response message back to the client. The client and server are both responsible for managing the communications channel and for formatting messages. Examples of this method include the ever popular BSD sockets on Unix, NS NetIPC on the HP 3000, and IBM APPC (LU6.2).

Queued Message Delivery

In this method, the client can send a request message to a queue, and the server receives the message from the queue at a later time. This allows asynchronous processing between the client and server, and so it is quite useful for applications like electronic mail. Examples include the HP Software Integration Sockets product and the MQ product from IBM.

Remote Procedure Calls (RPC)

With RPC, the client makes a procedure call with input and output parameters. The RPC mechanism packages the input parameters into a request message and sends the message to the server. The server unpackages the input parameters, executes the indicated procedure, packages the output parameters in a response message, and sends the response back to the client. The client RPC unpackages the output parameters and returns to the client. The application need not be aware of the management of the communications channel and the formatting of the messages. Examples of RPC include DCE RPC (much more about this later), Open Network Computing (ONC) RPC from Sun Microsystems, and Netwise RPC from Netwise, Inc.

The advantages of cooperative processing include maximum flexibility in the design of distributed applications, the potential for tuning for critical performance, and the ability to separate user tasks and business transactions. The disadvantage is the need to write to the communication mechanism, especially for messaging.

Two-Tier and Three-Tier Models

The client-server models presented so far have been *two-tier* models with the application split into a client piece and a server piece. Another possibility is the *three-tier* model, which divides the application into three parts: a client, a business server, and a data server. As in the cooperative (two-tier) model, the client contains presentation management and user task logic. But in the three-tier model, shown in Figure 1.5, the business transaction logic and data access reside in separate servers. The business server then becomes a client of the data server.

The advantage of the three-tier model is that the data access interface is encapsulated in the data server. The business server need not be concerned with the implementation of the database.

RPC is well suited for the three-tier model. The user task logic in the client calls a set of procedures defined for business transactions in the business server. The business transactions then call a set of procedures for data access defined by the data server.

The three-tier model can be generalized to an arbitrary number of tiers by further dividing the business function logic. A complex application may consist of many levels of interacting servers.

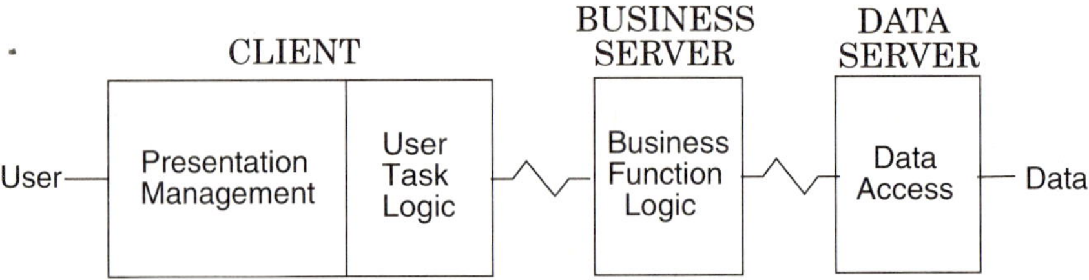

Figure 1.5
Three-Tier Model

1.2 An Overview of DCE

Next, let's take a brief tour of the Distributed Computing Environment. First, let's find out what OSF is and how it works, and how DCE came into existence. Then, we will look at each of the major DCE components: threads, RPC, the CDS and GDS directory services, security, the DTS time service, and the DFS file system.

OSF and Its Technology Process

The Open Software Foundation is a non-profit organization with the mission of "bringing open, distributed, mixed-vendor computing from concept to reality" (from the OSF Challenge '93 brochure). OSF was founded in 1988; its founding members included IBM, HP, and DEC. It now has over 350 member companies, including many computer system vendors along with many computer users.

OSF follows an open process for specifying, integrating, and distributing base technologies. OSF first decides on an area for investigation, such as operating systems or distributed computing. Working with its member Special Interest Groups (SIGs), OSF produces a Request for Technology (RFT). The RFT is a specification of the requirements in the area and an invitation to companies to submit their technology for consideration. Prospective technology suppliers respond by submitting proposals for their technology. For example, 32 companies submitted technology proposals for the DCE RFT. OSF convenes a panel of its experts, augmented by outside industry and academic consultants, to evaluate the proposals. The evaluation team selects the technology components that best meet the requirements of the RFT. The winning suppliers then submit the actual technologies (i.e., source code for software) to OSF. OSF integrates the technology components into a vendor-neutral product, which OSF tests by porting to several reference computer platforms. (The process where OSF integrated and tested the products was changed in 1994.

OSF now contracts out the integration and testing to vendors.) OSF then distributes the source for the integrated product to vendors who have acquired licenses for the product. These vendors port, test, and market the software product on their own platforms. A company like HP may be both a technology supplier and a product vendor. This is an iterative process, with the technology suppliers submitting new versions of their technology, OSF producing and distributing regular releases of the integrated software, and vendors incorporating new OSF releases into their products. Figure 1.6 diagrams the OSF technology process.

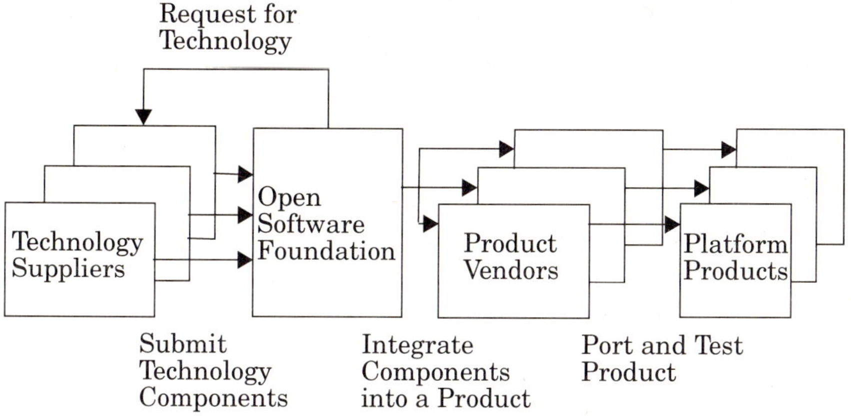

Figure 1.6
OSF Technology Process

Products that OSF has produced include

- Motif: a graphical user interface (GUI) based on X-Windows,
- OSF/1: an operating system based on Unix, and
- DCE: the Distributed Computing Environment.

DCE Components

The Distributed Computing Environment consists of a number of components from various technology vendors. An implementation of DCE may provide some or all of these components, and a distributed application may use some or all of the components. Figure 1.7 shows a typical arrangement of the DCE components and services. This diagram does *not* express all of the interrelationships between the DCE components.

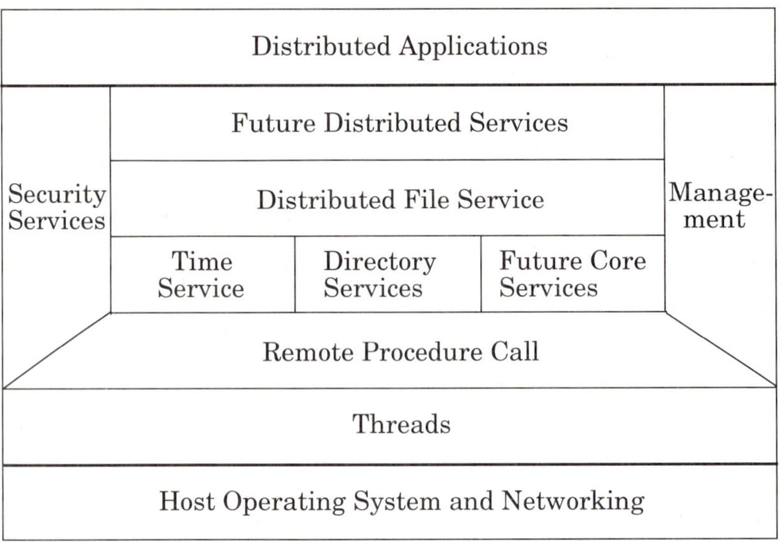

Figure 1.7
DCE Components

Threads, RPC, Security, Directory and Time Services are called the *DCE Core* or *Secure Core*. Most DCE implementations will provide these components for the development of distributed applications. The Distributed File Service uses the DCE Core components and is not available in all DCE implementations.

Threads

The DCE Threads facility provides multiple threads of execution within a process of the host operating system. Each thread has code to execute (starting with a base procedure) and a private data stack for local procedure variables and execution markers. All the threads in a process can share global variables and other objects like opened files and network connections. The DCE Threads facility schedules and dispatches execution of the threads. Figure 1.8 shows a sample of threads in a process.

Threads are very useful for programming asynchronous operations within a process. For example, if the process needs to perform a blocking operation like a receive on a network connection, it can create a separate thread to wait for the operation. Other threads can continue to execute while that thread is blocked. All of the DCE components use threads for this and for other purposes. Most of the DCE thread usage is invisible to the distributed application. However, applications may have to use DCE concurrency control features discussed in Chapter 10.

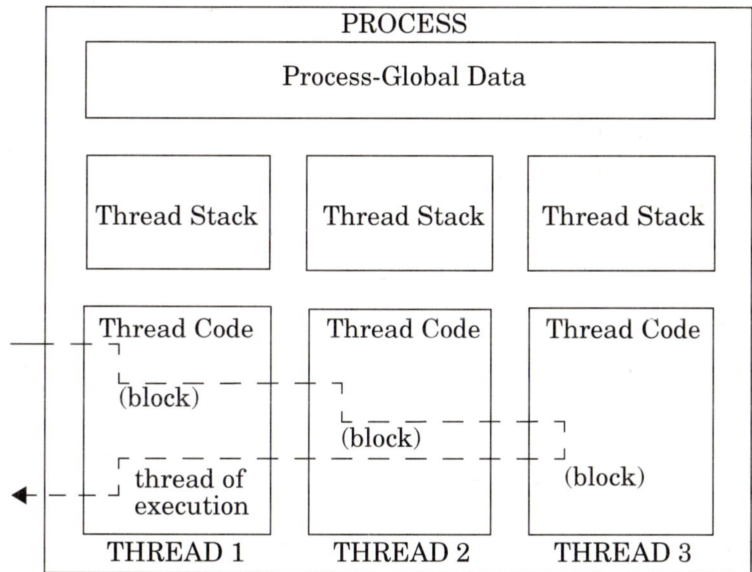

Figure 1.8
DCE Threads

DCE Threads were derived from the DEC CMA (Concert Multithread Architecture) package. CMA provides so-called *user-space threads* that are implemented within the existing host operating system process structure. Some operating systems, including OSF/1, OS/2, Microsoft NT, MPE/iX, and Solaris, provide *kernel threads* as an integral part of the operating system. A DCE implementation on these platforms may or may not use the operating system's kernel threads.

Remote Procedure Call

Remote procedure calls are at the heart of client-server applications built with DCE. The interaction between the client and server is defined in terms of procedure calls. The client calls a remote procedure with input and output parameters. The RPC mechanism intercepts and sends the call and its input parameters to a server. The server executes the procedure, and sends the result and output parameters back to the client. Remote procedure calls will be discussed in Chapter 2. Figure 1.9 illustrates a remote call between a client and a server.

When developing a DCE application, the application designer uses the Interface Definition Language (IDL) to describe a collection of remote procedure calls called an *interface*. The IDL definition is used by the RPC mechanism to correctly package and transmit the remote call and its parameters. Chapter 3 describes how to use IDL to build interfaces for DCE applications.

A client and server must make a number of DCE setup calls, for actions such as specifying which network protocols and which remote procedures to use. Chapters 4 and 5 discuss these setup calls.

DCE RPC was derived from the Network Computing System (NCS) developed by Apollo Computers (now part of HP) in the mid 1980s. HP-Apollo and DEC worked together on the RPC submittal to DCE, with DEC adding enhancements for connection-oriented communication.

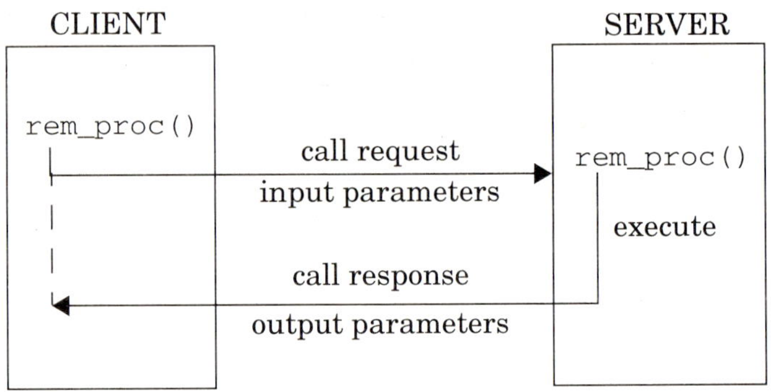

Figure 1.9
DCE Remote Procedure Call

Cell and Global Directory Services

Finding objects in the network is important for distributed computing. For example, a client needs to find which servers can execute a remote procedure interface. The DCE provides two directory services for this purpose: the Cell Directory Service (CDS) and the Global Directory Service (GDS).

A *cell* is a group of computers on a network defined by DCE for administrative and performance reasons. For example, all of the systems at a particular site might form a cell. All the computers in a cell share the same CDS name space. This name space is organized in a top-to-bottom hierarchy of directories and objects in the same fashion as the usual Unix file system paths. The top of a cell name space is `/.../`*`cell_name`*`/`. The top of the local cell can be abbreviated `/.:/`. A full name space entry may include a number of directories and an object name, for example, `/.:/subsys/sch/room_group`. The Cell Directory Service manages the cell name space directories and entries. There are one or more CDS servers in a cell for this purpose, and the cell directory can be replicated for high availability. Chapter 5 discusses how servers can be named and how clients can locate servers using CDS.

Sometimes it may be necessary to find an object in another cell. The Global Directory Service is available to locate objects in foreign cells. GDS is based on the CCITT X.500 directory standard, which defines a worldwide name space. An example of a GDS-style cell name is /.../C=US/O=HP/OU=CUP (where C is the country name, O is the organization name, and OU is the organization unit name).

The Internet Domain Name Service (DNS) style of naming can also be used for a cell, for example, /.../cup.hp.com. In this case, the Internet DNS is used to resolve the name of the cell.

The Global Directory Agent (GDA) is the intermediary between a cell's CDS and the rest of the world. If an object is in a foreign cell, GDA will contact GDS or DNS, based on the cell name syntax, to find the foreign cell. Figure 1.10 shows two cell name spaces and the interface of the Cell and Global Directory Services.

The Cell Directory Service is derived from the DECdns (Distributed Name Service) product. The Global Directory Service comes from the Siemens-Nixdorf X-DIR X.500 product.

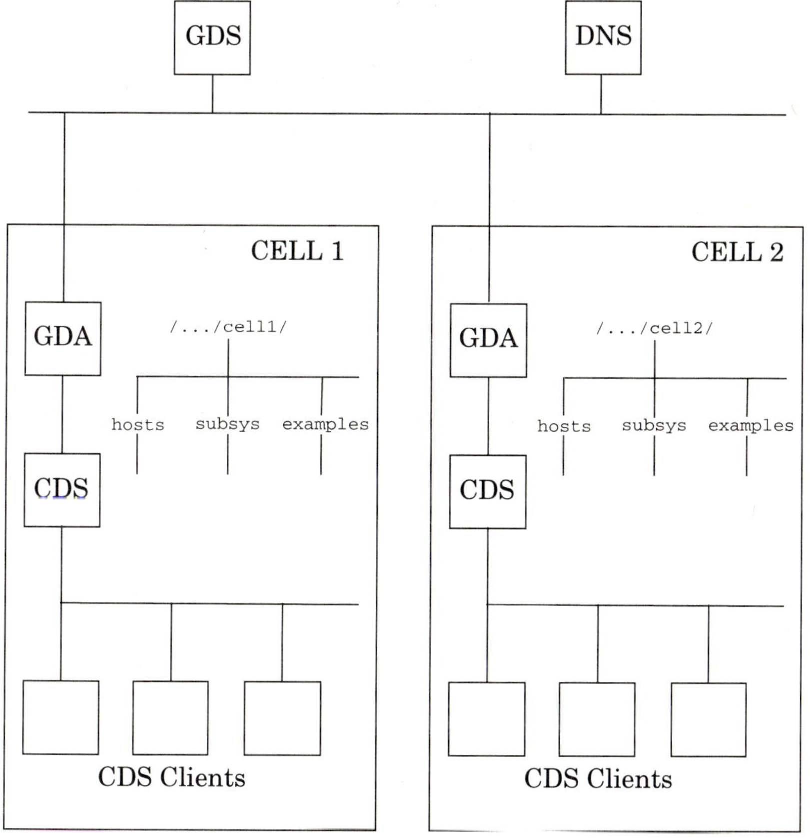

Figure 1.10
DCE Directory Services and Name Spaces

Security Services

Distributed computing opens up information resources to the widest range of access by users on the network. This also opens the resources to a wide range of attack. So security becomes more important, and more difficult to enforce than in a non-distributed environment. DCE includes a number of state-of-the-art security facilities.

A DCE *principal* is a user, program, or system that is assigned an identity in the DCE *Security Registry.* The principal has various attributes, including a secret password, that are stored in the Registry. Principals are defined within the context of a cell (see the Cell Directory Service above). Users establish their principal identities by executing the **`dce_login`** command (which might be integrated into their local system login). DCE uses the *Kerberos authentication protocol* to securely verify that the user has supplied the correct password.

The Kerberos protocol can also be used for authentication between a client and a server. The client and server principals (and their secret passwords) are recorded in the Security Registry. When a client wants to communicate with a server, it requests a *ticket* for the server from the cell's Security Server. This ticket securely encodes the client's identity, along with other information. When the client makes a remote procedure call to the server, the ticket is included. The server can then use the ticket information to identify the client. (The actual workings of DCE authentication are much more complex. Chapter 6 will go into more detail on authentication.)

DCE also provides an authorization mechanism based on Access Control Lists (ACLs), which associate access permissions with principals. The ticket passed from the client to the server includes a secure indication of the client's identity. The server can compare the client's identity to its ACLs to determine what access permissions a client has. ACLs are discussed in Chapter 9. Figure 1.11 illustrates the interaction among an application client and server and the DCE Security Service for authentication and authorization.

Another aspect of security is secure communications. Sensitive data transmitted over the network between a client and a server should not be altered by an attacker or even intelligible to an eavesdropper. DCE RPC includes several levels of data protection. The highest levels provide encryption using DES (the Data Encryption Standard) to ensure data integrity and privacy. Chapter 6 will discuss the RPC protection levels and encryption.

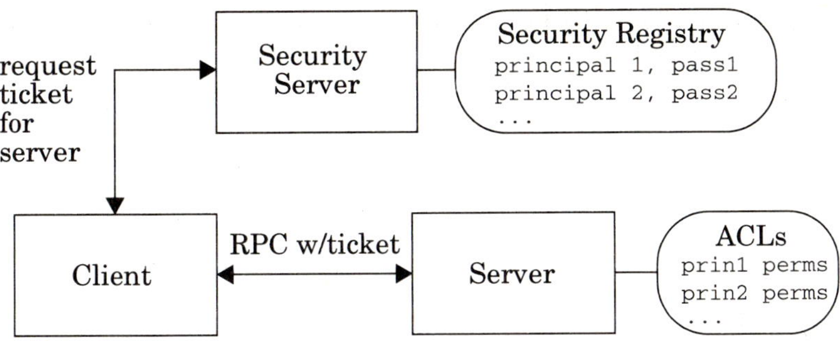

Figure 1.11
DCE Client-Server Authentication and Authorization

Kerberos was developed at the Massachusetts Institute of Technology. It has become a defacto standard for network authentication. Many vendors are adding Kerberos to network products like **ftp** and **telnet**. The DCE Security Registry was derived from the HP/Apollo Password- Etc product. DES is a standard encryption method developed under the auspices of the National Institute for Standards Technology (NIST) and the National Security Agency (NSA).

Distributed Time Service

Synchronizing time across the network is important for distributed applications. Each system has its own local clock, but these clocks can drift at different rates and become out of synchronization with each other (and the operator of the system may set the wrong time to begin with). The DCE Distributed Time Service (DTS) ensures that systems in a cell have a consistent view of the time. There must be at least three time servers in a cell and each system has its own time client. Periodically, the time clients poll the time servers for the correct time. Each time server responses with a *time interval*, a UTC (Universal Coordinated Time) time with an estimated range of inaccuracy. The time client compares each of the server's time intervals to come up with a mean time and inaccuracy. The time client may (gradually) change its system clock to match the mean time. Figure 1.12 shows a DTS client polling three DTS servers. The servers respond with time interfaces that the client combines into a mean time interval.

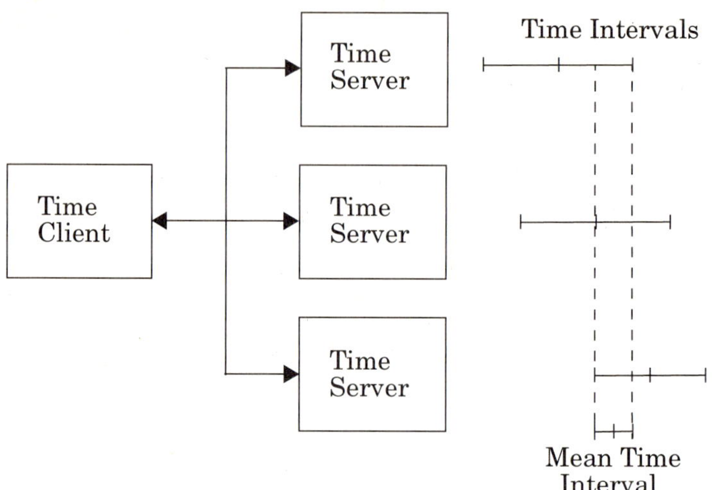

Figure 1.12
DCE Distributed Time Service

The DCE Distributed Time Service was derived from the DECdts (distributed time service) product.

Since most applications do not need to use the Time Service directly, DTS will not be covered elsewhere in this book. However, be aware that time stamps used by the DCE Security Service require reasonable synchronization of time on client and server systems.

Distributed File Service

The DCE Distributed File Service allows users and programs to access and share files, without having to know the actual location of the files. A file has a global name, starting with `/.:/fs` (or `/.../`*`cell_name`*`/fs` if it is in another cell). A DFS client can open, read, and write such a file using the normal file operations for its host operating system. For Unix systems, these are `open()`, `read()`, `write()`, and so on. DFS intercepts the file operations and directs them to the appropriate DFS file server. To improve performance, DFS caches recently used portions of the file on the client's system. To ensure consistency between the file and its caches, DFS uses a scheme with read and write tokens. Figure 1.13 shows an example of DFS.

The DCE Distributed File Service was derived from the Andrew File System (AFS), originally developed by Carnegie-Mellon University. AFS was commercialized (and submitted to OSF) by Transarc Corporation. DFS will not be discussed further in this book.

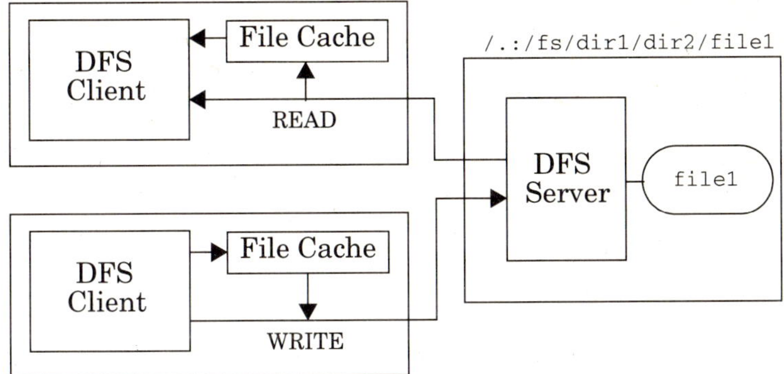

Figure 1.13
DCE Distributed File Service

Management

DCE management is provided by tools and control programs from each of the DCE components. For example, the Security Service provides the **rgy_edit** tool to create principals and their passwords.

In general, DCE management is outside the scope of this book. (See the *OSF DCE Administration Guide* and the *OSF DCE Administration Reference* manual for more information.) Some management tools will be discussed when needed to build applications and examples.

The DCE management tools and features continue to evolve with new releases of DCE. For example, the DCE 1.1 release introduces a control program, **dcecp**, that combines management functions for all of DCE components.

DCE Products

DCE products are available from many vendors on the widest range of platforms, from personal computers to mainframes and supercomputers. Table 1.1 shows vendors with available or announced DCE products in 1995 (from the *OSF DCE Product Catalog*). All of these DCE implementations provide the DCE Secure Core. Some also provide GDS and DFS.

Table 1.1

DCE Products				
Vendor	Platform	Operating System	GDS	DFS
AT&T	Intel	SRV4 MP-RAS		
Bull	DPX/20		X	X
	DPS 7xxx/9xxx	GCOS		
	Intel	Windows		
Cray	Cray	UNICOS		
Data General	AViiON	AViiON	X	
Digital Equipment	Alpha AXP	OSF/1		X
	VAX, Alpha AXP	OpenVMS		
	VAX	Ultrix		
	Alpha AXP, Intel	Windows NT		
	Intel	Windows		
Fujistu	DS/90 7000	UXP/DS		
Gradient Technology	Intel	PC/DOS, Windows		
	Intel	Unix SVR4		
Hewlett-Packard	9000/700,800	HP-UX	X	X
	3000/900	MPE/iX		
Hitachi	HI-OSF/1-MJ	HI-OSF/1		
	3050,3500	HI-UX/WE2		
IBM	RS/6000	AIX	X	X
	Intel	OS/2, Windows		
	AS/400	OS/400		
	ES/9000	MVS/ESA		
	ES/9000	VM/ESA		
Kapsh	IBM/370, /390	VM/SP, /XA, /ESA		
NEC	EWS/UP4800			
Olivetti	LSX 5000			
Pyramid Technology	Intel MP	DC/OSx (SVR4)		
Santa Crux Operation	Intel	Open Desktop/ Server	X	
Siemens-Nixdorf	BS2000/OSD			
	Intel, MIPS	SINIX (SVR4)	X	X

Table 1.1 (Continued)

DCE Products				
Vendor	Platform	Operating System	GDS	DFS
	Intel	Windows		
Silicon Graphics	SGI/MIPS	IRIX		
Sony	NEWS	NEWS-US		
Stratus	XA/R	FTX		
Tandem	Himalaya, Integrity	NonStop		
Transarc	Sun SPARC	SunOS, Solaris		X

DCE Versions and Vendor Releases

OSF has released a number of versions of DCE. Vendors in turn have taken the OSF versions and produced new releases of their DCE products. Vendors have differed in the pace at which they add new OSF releases to their products and in the features they have chosen to support. To add to the potential for confusion, each vendor has numbered their product releases differently, making it difficult to know which product versions correspond to which OSF releases. To try to avoid more confusion, I will refer to the OSF DCE versions as simply "DCE" (e.g., DCE 1.1) and vendor DCE versions by the vendor name (e.g., HP-UX DCE 1.4).

This book is based on the HP-UX DCE 1.4 product, which corresponds to the OSF DCE 1.1 version. This version contains new features to ease the development of servers and an integrated tool, **dcecp**, for managing objects of interest to DCE.

Both the pre-DCE 1.1 calls and commands and the new DCE 1.1 calls and commands will be discussed so that you may choose whichever is appropriate to your DCE version and your tastes.

1.3 The Room Schedule Application

The concepts discussed in this book will be illustrated through a sample client-server application called the Room Schedule application (or just Room for short). This application manages the scheduling of meeting rooms. The requirements for the Room Schedule application are

- People must be able to use the application from whatever they have on their desktops, including Unix workstations, PCs, and terminals connected to multiuser systems.
- People must be able to use the application without having to know the actual location of the database involved. As a corollary of this requirement, the database should be free to be moved.

The Room Schedule application will be implemented as a cooperative application. The communication method used will be DCE RPC. Through RPC, other DCE features like CDS and Security will be employed as needed to meet the application's requirements. A brief description of the Room client and server follows. Figure 1.14 shows the relationships between these application components

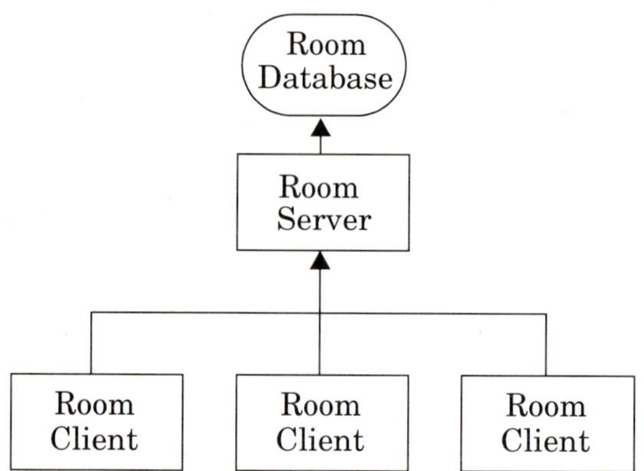

Figure 1.14
The Room Schedule application clients and server

Room Server

The room server keeps track of meeting rooms at a site. It maintains a database with entries for each room, containing information about the room and its reservations. The room server performs these tasks:

- provides a description of a room (location, capacity, features),
- reserves a room for a specified date and time,
- cancels a room reservation,
- provides a list of rooms available at a specified date and time, and
- provides a list of reservations for a room within a specified time interval.

The room server enforces controls on who can make and cancel reservations.

Room Client

The room client allows a person to make and cancel room reservations and to inquire about rooms. It uses the interface to a room server to perform these tasks. In a production version of the Room application, the room client would offer an attractive graphical user interface based on Motif (for Unix clients) or Windows (for PC clients). But to keep things simple, the room client in this book provides only a character interface.

Room Schedule Application Examples

The Room Schedule application will be constructed gradually throughout this book. Each chapter will build on the application, as shown in Table 1.2.

Table 1.2

Schedule Application Examples	
Chapter	Examples
2	uses some of the room remote procedure calls as examples.
3	defines the room interface, using the DCE Interface Definition Language (IDL).
4	presents an initial implementation of the room client and server using string bindings.
5	enhances the application to use CDS for location of the room server.
6	adds security to the application, including authentication of room clients to the room server and RPC protection levels.
7	adds **dcecp** configuration and management of the room server.
8	adds room location objects to the server, with multiple servers for different locations.
9	adds authorization of client requests using ACLs.
10	adds multiple call threads and mutex data protection.

CHAPTER 2

Remote Procedure Calls

The key to developing distributed applications with DCE is mastering the remote procedure call (RPC). Clients and servers in a DCE application interact through RPC. Many of the DCE features and facilities used by the application, including directory and security services, will be used through RPC. In fact, writing to the RPC paradigm shapes the way an application is designed. This chapter will begin the discussion of DCE RPC, starting with a review of local procedure calls.

2.1 Local Procedure Calls

All modern high-level programming languages provide some form of procedures: functions in C and C++, procedures and functions in Pascal, subprograms in COBOL, functions and subroutines in FORTRAN, and so on. These procedure-calling mechanisms are termed local in that they work within one computer, one process, and one address space. There are many similarities and some important differences between local procedure calls and remote procedure calls.

Let's look at the elements of a local procedure call, using the program shown in Code Samples 2.1 and 2.2. This is the **`room_desc_loc`** program, a simple subset of the Room Schedule application. When run with a room name as its argument (e.g., **`room_desc_loc Landmark`**), the **`room_desc_loc`** program will look up the room associated with that name and report the location and description of the room.

```
typedef char sch_loc_name_t [20];
typedef char sch_room_desc_t[30];
typedef char sch_room_name_t[20];
typedef long int sch_status_t;

typedef struct {
   sch_loc_name_t  loc;
   sch_room_name_t name;
   sch_room_desc_t desc;
   long int        max_people;
} sch_room_t;

#define sch_status_ok             0
#define sch_status_loc_not_found  1
#define sch_status_room_not_found 2
```

Code Sample 2.1
`sch_loc.h`: Definition of room record and status for **room_desc_loc** programs.

```
#include <stdio.h>
#include "sch_loc.h"

#define MAX_ROOMS 25
sch_room_t rooms[MAX_ROOMS];
long int n_rooms;

#define ROOM_NAME_EQUAL(n1, n2) \
  (strncmp(n1, n2, sizeof(sch_room_name_t)) == 0)

void room_open()
{
  /* not shown */
}

void room_close()
{
  /* not shown */
}
```

Code Sample 2.2
`room_desc_loc.c`: **room_desc** program implemented using a local procedure call.

```
void room_description(
    /* [in ] */ sch_room_name_t room_name,
    /* [out] */ sch_room_t      *room,
    /* [out] */ sch_status_t    *status)
{
   long int i;

   for (i = 0; i < n_rooms; i++)
   {
      if (ROOM_NAME_EQUAL(rooms[i].name, room_name))
      {
        memcpy(room, rooms[i], sizeof(sch_room_t));
        *status = sch_status_ok;
        return;
      }
   }
   *status = sch_status_room_not_found;
}

int main(int argc, char *argv[])
{
   sch_room_t   room;
   sch_status_t st;

   room_open();

   room_description(argv[1], &room, &st);
   switch (st)
   {
   case (sch_status_ok):
      printf("Location    : %s\n", room.loc);
      printf("Name        : %s\n", room.name);
      printf("Description : %s\n", room.desc);
      printf("Max people  : %i\n", room.max_people);
      printf("\n");
      break;
```

Code Sample 2.2 (continued)

```
   case (sch_status_room_not_found):
       printf("Room not found.\n");
       break;
    default:
       printf("Unexpected status %i\n", st);
    }

    room_close();
}
```

Code Sample 2.2 (continued)

Procedure Definition

In ANSI C, a procedure (also called a *function* or a *routine*) is defined using this syntax:

```
return_type procedure_name(parameter_list)
{
procedure_body
}
```

where

- `return_type` is a data type of a value to be returned by the procedure after a call. The special type `void` is used for procedures that do not return a value.
- `procedure_name` is an identifier containing alphanumerics and underscores. The procedure name is bound by the compiler and the linker to the entry point for the procedure body code. The procedure name in the room example is `room_description`. Henceforth we will use the usual C convention of referring to a procedure as `procedure_name()`, for example, `room_description()`.
- `parameter_list` is zero or more parameters, separated by commas. This is also known as the *signature* or *formal parameter list* of the procedure. Each parameter is of the form

  `parameter_type parameter_name`,

  where

  `parameter_type` is the data type of the parameter, and
  `parameter_name` is an alphanumeric identifier representing the parameter in the procedure body.

  The parameter list for `room_description()` is

```
sch_room_name_t room_name,
sch_room_t      *room,
sch_status_t    *status
```

These parameters will be discussed shortly in the Input and Output Parameter sections.

- `procedure_body` is a sequence of statements that will be executed when the procedure is called. If the procedure has a non-void return type, it must have at least one statement of the form `return expression`, where *expression* evaluates to the return type.

A complete procedure definition does not have to exist in each source program file that calls the procedure. The procedure may be compiled separately or may reside in a library and be linked into the program later. In these cases, the program should include a definition of the procedure's signature so that the compiler can check that calls to the procedure have the right number and types of parameters, and that the return type is correctly used. In ANSI C, the procedure signature is declared by a *function prototype*, a procedure definition without the procedure body:

```
return_type procedure_name(parameter_list);
```

Function prototypes are often included in header (`.h`) files that are included at the beginning of the program source. This way the procedure signature is officially defined in one place and imported by all the calling programs.

Procedure Call

A procedure call in ANSI C looks like

```
procedure_name(parameter_value_list)
```

where

- `procedure_name` is the name of the procedure assigned in the procedure definition. The compiler and linker resolve the procedure name to the address of the entry point for the procedure body.
- `parameter_value_list` is a list of values, separated by commas. This is sometimes call the *actual parameter list*. There are exactly as many values as in the parameter list in the procedure definition. Each parameter value must have the same type as the parameter type in the definition (or at least can be cast to that type).

  The parameter value list for the call to `room_description()` in `main()` is `argv[1], &room, &st`. These parameter values will be discussed in the Input and Output Parameter sections below.

If the procedure is declared with a non-`void` return type, it can be called from within an expression. The value returned by the procedure is set by a `return` statement in the procedure body. If a non-`void` procedure is used as a stand-alone statement, the return value is discarded. A procedure with a `void` return type can only be used as a stand-alone statement, as is the case with `room_description()`.

When a procedure is called, program execution is transferred from the calling program to the entry point of the procedure. The procedure body executes until it encounters either a `return` statement or the end of the procedure body. Then program execution is transferred back to the point in the calling program immediately after the procedure call.

Program Address Space and Parameters

Local procedure calls execute within the same address space as the calling program. Addresses that are valid in the calling program are also valid in the called procedure. This feature can be exploited by using pointers as parameters and global variables.

Input Parameters

Parameters that are used to pass values from a calling program into a procedure are *input parameters*. In C, an input parameter can be a simple data value (say, an integer or a floating-point number) or an address (pointer) of a simple or compound data item (like an array or a structure). An input parameter has to be allocated and have a meaningful value when the procedure is called.

There is one input parameter in the `room_description()` procedure: `room`, which is of type `sch_room_name_t`, defined in `sch_loc.h` to be a character string of up to 20 characters. In the call to `room_description()` in `main()`, the value of the parameter is `argv[1]`, a pointer to the first program argument.

Output Parameters

Parameters that are used to pass values from the procedure back to the calling program are *output parameters*. In C, an output parameter must be an address of a data area that can receive the output value(s). If the target of the output parameter is a simple variable or a structure, a pointer to the data item must be specified using the `*` notation in the parameter list and the `&` notation in the parameter value list. An example is the `status` parameter of `room_description()`: The parameter type is `sch_status_t *` (a pointer to an integer variable), and the parameter value in the call is `&st` (a pointer to the integer variable `st`).

But if the target of the output parameter is an array or string, the type is already a pointer. When to use or not to use the `*` and `&` notations in parameter declaration and passing can be confusing and error-prone. This problem is exacerbated by parameter types defined by `typedef` statements, where it is not immediately clear whether the actual type is an array or a structure.

Some programming languages, like Pascal and C++, make the distinction between parameters passed *by value* and *by reference*. A value parameter is used for input and a reference parameter is used for output. In FORTRAN and COBOL, all parameters are normally passed by reference.

Storage for an output parameter must be allocated either by the calling program before the call or allocated by the called procedure. An output parameter need not have a meaningful value prior to the call; any value it has will be replaced by the output from the procedure. (But see Input/Output Parameters next.)

Input / Output Parameters

A parameter can be used for both input and output. As an input parameter, it must have a meaningful value at the call to the procedure. As an output parameter, it must be a pointer to storage allocated by the calling program to receive the output from the procedure. Consequently, an input/output parameter must follow the same declaration rules as an output parameter.

Return Value

A non-void return value of a procedure can be considered a form of output parameter. But since the procedure call is embedded in an expression which uses the return value, the calling program does not provide a pointer to a target data area.

Local Variables

Any variables declared within the body of the procedure are *local* to the procedure. Local variables do not exist outside the scope of the procedure; hence they cannot be used by the calling program. There is one local variable in `room_description()`: the integer `i`, used as the index for searching the `rooms[]` array.

Global Variables

Variables that are declared outside the scope of any procedure are *global* and can be used by all of the procedures within the program. If procedures are compiled separately from the program source, C allows the global variables to be declared `extern`. The linker resolves the addresses of global variables when it links the program.

In `room_desc_loc.c`, the global array `rooms[]` holds the room records, and the global variable `n_rooms` keeps track of the number of records in the array. The `room_description()` procedure reads the `rooms[]` array when it searches for the room information. Note that the calling program (`main()`) does not use these global variables—a good design decision that hides the implementation of the database.

It is possible (but not a good design) to implement the room program where `main()` does use the global variables. Such an implementation is shown in Code Sample 2.3. Here, the procedure `room_index()` returns the index into the `rooms[]` array for the room record with the specified name. The calling program then uses the returned index to retrieve the room record from the array.

```
#include <stdio.h>
#include "sch_loc.h"
#define MAX_ROOMS 25
sch_room_t rooms[MAX_ROOMS];
long int n_rooms;

#define ROOM_NAME_EQUAL(n1, n2) \
  (strncmp(n1, n2, sizeof(sch_room_name_t)) == 0)

void room_open()
{
  /* not shown */
}

void room_close()
{
  /* not shown */
}

long int room_index(
  /* [in ] */ sch_room_name_t room_name)
{
   long int i;

   for (i = 0; i < n_rooms; i++)
   {
      if (ROOM_NAME_EQUAL(rooms[i].name, room_name))
      {
        return(i);
      }
   }
   return(0);
}
```

Code Sample 2.3

`room_desc_loc2.c`: **room_desc** program using an index into a global variable.

```
int main(int argc, char *argv[])
{
    long int i;

    room_open();
    i = room_index(argv[1]);
    if (i > 0)
    {
        printf("Location    : %s\n", rooms[i].loc);
        printf("Name        : %s\n", rooms[i].name);
        printf("Description : %s\n", rooms[i].desc);
        printf("Max people  : %i\n", rooms[i].max_people);
        printf("\n");
    }
    else
    {
        printf("Room not found.\n");
    }
    room_close();
}
```

Code Sample 2.3 (continued)

Own Variables

An *own variable* is a cross between a local variable and a global variable. Like a local variable, it is declared within the scope of the procedure and is not accessible outside the procedure. But like a global variable and unlike local variables, the value of an own variable persists after the procedure returns to the calling program. The next time the procedure is called, the own variable will retain its value from the previous call. To accomplish this, an own variable is typically allocated in the process global storage area but is hidden from everything except the procedure in which it is declared.

In C, own variables are declared with the attribute `static`. Code Sample 2.4 shows how a static variable could be added to `room_description()` to count the number of times the procedure is called. The initialization of `count` is performed before the first execution of the procedure, and then `count` is incremented by 1 on each procedure call.

```
void room_description(...)
{
  ...
  static long int count = 0;
  count++;
  ...
}
```

Code Sample 2.4
Example of an own variable in `room_description()`.

Faults

An invalid execution condition, like division by zero or dereferencing an invalid pointer, will cause a hardware or software *fault* to occur. Usually this results in the abrupt termination of the program. On Unix systems, a fault raises a *signal*, which can be caught by a signal handler in the program. A signal handler for the division by zero signal might print "Division by zero in such-and-such procedure," and then try to work around the problem, if possible. If a signal is not caught, it may abort the program.

Faults are often programming errors. A common programming error is to pass a value instead of an address to an output parameter. An example of this would be the call

```
room_description(argv[1], &room, st);
```

where the & was omitted from the `st` parameter. Normally, an ANSI C compiler will flag this as an error. But if `room_description()` was separately compiled, and there is no prototype (or worse, an incorrect prototype) for the procedure in the calling program, this error would not be detected until the program is run. Then, the value of `st` will be passed instead of its address. When the statement

```
*status = sch_status_ok;
```

is executed in the procedure body, the value instead of the address of `st` will be deferenced, causing an invalid address error. On Unix systems, this is translated into the informative "Bus error" message and the process is aborted.

2.2 Remote Procedure Calls

To illustrate the similarities and differences between local and remote procedure calls, let's split the **room_desc_loc** program into a client and a server using RPC. The server portion is shown in Code Sample 2.5 and the client in Code Sample 2.6. These examples concentrate on the remote procedure definition in the server and the remote procedure call in the client; important setup is omitted in both. Client and server setup will be discussed extensively in later chapters.

```
#include <stdio.h>
#include "room.h"

#define MAX_ROOMS 25
sch_room_t rooms[MAX_ROOMS];
long int n_rooms;

#define ROOM_NAME_EQUAL(n1, n2) \
  (strncmp(n1, n2, sizeof(sch_room_name_t)) == 0)

void room_open();
void room_close();

int main(int argc, char *argv[])
{
  /* main variables not shown */

  room_open();

  /* server setup code not shown. */

  room_close();
}

void room_open()
{
  /* not shown */
}
void room_close()
{
  /* not shown */
}

void room_description(
    /* [in ] */ handle_t        h,
    /* [in ] */ sch_room_name_t room_name,
    /* [out] */ sch_room_t      *room,
    /* [out] */ sch_status_t    *status)
{
```

Code Sample 2.5
`schedule/room_server.c`: Server for a remote procedure.

```
    long int i;

    for (i = 0; i < n_rooms; i++)
    {
       if (ROOM_NAME_EQUAL(rooms[i].name, room_name))
       {
         memcpy(room, rooms[i], sizeof(sch_room_t));
         *status = sch_status_ok;
         return;
       }
    }
    *status = sch_status_room_not_found;
}
```

Code Sample 2.5 (continued)

```
#include <stdio.h>
. . .
#include "room.h"

int main(int argc, char *argv[])
{
  . . .
  sch_room_t room;
  sch_status_t st;
  /* Client setup code not shown. */
  room_description(h, (unsigned_char_p_t) argv[1],
                   &room, &st);
   switch (st)
   {
     case (sch_status_ok):
        printf("Location    : %s\n", room.loc);
        printf("Name        : %s\n", room.name);
        printf("Description : %s\n", room.desc);
        printf("Max people  : %i\n", room.max_people);
        printf("\n");
        break;
```

Code Sample 2.6
`room_desc.c`: Client using a remote procedure call.

```
        case (sch_status_room_not_found):
            printf("Room not found.\n");
            break;
        default:
            printf("Unexpected status %i\n", st);
            break;
    }
}
```

Code Sample 2.6 (continued)

Procedure Definition

Procedures to be called remotely by clients exist as local procedures within a server program. Hence each remote procedure has a normal procedure definition in the server source program, or in a separately compiled source that is linked into the server program. The definition includes the procedure name and return type, parameter list, and procedure body as described for the local procedure case. When the server is compiled and linked, the procedure name will be bound to the procedure's entry point in the server code.

The procedure `room_description()` is a local procedure within `room_server.c`. The definition is the same as in `room_desc_loc.c`, except for the addition of the parameter `h`, which will be explained in a bit.

Remote procedures appear as external procedures to client programs. Instead of the complete function definition, a client just includes a function prototype defining the remote procedure's signature. With DCE RPC, the remote procedure prototypes are contained in an *interface header file* that the client includes. For `room_desc.c`, this header file is `room.h`. (`room.h` also includes definitions for the `sch_` data types and constants). Interface header files are automatically generated by the IDL compiler, as will be discussed in Chapter 3.

Procedure Call

Remote procedures are called from clients. Each remote procedure call looks like a normal procedure call, with a procedure name and a parameter value list. The procedure name is the same as the name defined in the server, and the parameter values match the number and types defined in the procedure's parameter list. The DCE RPC mechanism gives the appearance that the remote procedure is being called locally. How this actually happens will be described in Section 2.3.

In `room_desc.c`, the remote call to `room_description()` looks just like the original local call in `room_desc_loc.c`, except for the addition of the parameter `h`.

Client and Server Address Spaces and Parameter Passage

A crucial difference between local procedure calls and remote procedure calls is the address spaces involved. In the local case, both the calling program and the called procedure exist in the same process address space and so can share addresses. In the remote case, the client and the server processes execute in different addresses spaces, which are likely to be on different systems. Consequently clients and servers cannot share addresses. If data is to be passed by reference between a client and a server, a copy of the data must be transmitted. Figure 2.1 shows the address spaces for the **room_desc** and **room_server** program.

Input Parameters

In a remote procedure call, the values of input parameters are passed from the client to the server. As in the local case, all input parameters must have valid values in the client. The RPC mechanism ensures that the input parameters have valid values in the server when the procedure is executed.

In the remote call to `room_description()`, the input parameter values are supplied by `h` and `argv[1]`. (The casting of `argv[1]` to the `unsigned_char_p_t` data type is required due to the way the IDL compiler defines character data, as discussed in Chapter 3.) RPC on the client passes the value of `argv[1]`, a character string terminated by a null character, to the server. In the server, RPC allocates and initializes a character string with the value to be passed into `room_description()`.

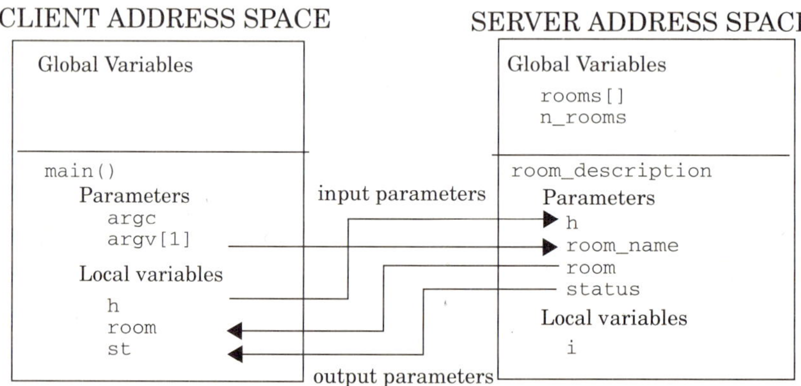

Figure 2.1
Client and Server Address Spaces

The parameter `h` is a special input parameter for RPC, called the *binding handle*. The purpose of the binding handle is to associate a client with a server, so that the RPC mechanism knows where and how to make the remote procedure call. The binding handle is set up by various DCE calls in the client, which are not shown in `room_desc.c`. These calls will be the subject of extensive discussion in future chapters.

Output parameters

Since the address space is not shared between a client and a server, pointers cannot be used directly to pass output parameters from the remote procedure back to the calling program. Instead, the values of the output parameters must be explicitly passed from the server to the client; the RPC mechanism must take care of copying the values to the appropriate targets in the calling program.

In `room_description()`, the output parameters are `room`, a structure, and `status`, an integer. When the server calls the procedure, it allocates storage in the server address space as targets for these parameters. When the remote call completes, the server passes the values from these parameters back to the client. RPC on the client copies the structure and integer values to the original output parameters, `room` and `st`, in the client's address space.

Note that the RPC mechanism must know whether a parameter is used for input or output to determine in which direction to pass the parameter value. Parameter usage cannot be determined from ANSI C procedure signatures or procedure calls. As an example, you cannot determine whether the `room_name` parameter is used for input or output by just looking at the `room_description()` signature or call—you need to analyze how `room_name` is used within the procedure to know that it is an input parameter. Consequently, DCE RPC needs more information about the procedure than just the standard C signature. This is supplied in the Interface Definition Language, the subject of Chapter 3.

Input/output Parameters

As in the local case, a parameter can be used for both input and output in a remote procedure call. In that case, the input value is passed from the client to the server, and the output value is passed from the server back to the client. The RPC mechanism must know that the parameter is used for both input and output.

Return Value

The return value of a remote procedure call is passed from the server back to the client in a manner similar to that of output parameters. The RPC mechanism ensures that the value is available for use in any expression the remote call was embedded.

Local Variables

Just as in the local case, remote procedures can have local variables that are known only within the scope of the procedure. The procedure body can use local variables without any special programming. Even if there is more than one instance of the procedure executing concurrently within the server (which can happen with multiple server call threads, discussed below), the local variables of each instance are accessible only from that instance.

Global Variables

Since the client and server have separate address spaces, the calling program (the client) and the called remote procedure (in the server) cannot share global variables. Each side has its own distinct globals. Global variables cannot be used to implicitly pass data between the calling program and the remote procedure. This is an important difference from local procedure calls.

In the room client and server example, the global variables `rooms[]` and `n_rooms` are located in the server address space and are accessible from within the `room_description()` procedure. They do not exist in the client address space and are not accessible from within the client `main()`.

Consider again the **`room_desc_loc2`** program shown in Code Sample 2.3. Both the calling program `main()` and the called procedure `room_index()` share the `rooms[]` array: The procedure searches the array and returns an index into the array, and the calling program uses the returned index to get the room information out of the array. This implementation cannot be split between a client and a server, since the `rooms[]` array cannot be shared between the client and the server. This is another reason why this implementation is not a good design.

Global variables present another challenge due to potential concurrency in the server. The threads within a server process that execute remote procedure calls on the behalf of clients are called *call threads*. The number of call threads in a server is set by the `rpc_server_listen()` call, as described in Chapter 4. As long as there is only one call thread within a server (and no other threads created by the application), global variables in the server address space can be used in the remote procedures without special programming. However, if there is more than one thread, global variables may have to be protected from improper access by two or more threads concurrently executing remote calls. DCE provides the *mutex* facility for this purpose. Mutex protection will be discussed in Chapter 10. Until then we will restrict the number of call threads to one, to simplify the server examples.

Own Variables

Own variables can be used by remote procedures within a server, but care must be taken to ensure that they are used as intended. The static variable `count` used in Code Sample 2.4 could also be used in a remote procedure to count the number of times it is called. However, it would count all calls for all clients, not just the calls for one client as did the original code fragment. If there is more than one call or application-created thread, own variables require mutex protection just like global variables. In general, own variables should be avoided within remote procedures.

Faults

Faults present a special problem for RPC. Normally, if a procedure encounters a fault like an address error or a division by zero, the fault is raised in the calling program. The calling program can trap the fault, or it will be aborted. This behavior should also be exhibited by remote procedure calls that cause faults. But the fault will occur in the server program, while the signal and possibly the abort should occur in the client program. Moreover, a fault caused by one client should not cause the server to abort and become unavailable to other, better behaved clients.

DCE solves the RPC fault problem as follows: A fault that occurs while executing a remote procedure within a server is trapped and not allowed to abort the server. The fault is then relayed back to the client which called the offending procedure, and a corresponding fault is raised in the client. The client can then trap the fault or be aborted. Details of how the fault is transmitted from the server to the client will be covered in the RPC Protocol discussion later in this chapter.

In addition to the usual faults that can occur in single processes, new faults can happen with RPC, due to the underlying network communications between the client and the server. The most common situation is a communications error, which can be reported if the server crashes, the network connection to the server is lost, or (in some cases), the network or server is heavily loaded. Remote procedures calls that are coded correctly may still experience these types of faults, and the calling program should be prepared to recover from them.

DCE Exceptions

When a fault or a communications error occurs in a remote call, DCE *raises an exception*. If no special preparation is made, the client will be aborted, most probably with a cryptic error. DCE includes a mechanism to *catch* exceptions. Code Sample 2.7 shows how the exception handling is coded.

The `TRY` and the first `CATCH` delimit the scope of the exception handling. If an exception is raised by the call to `room_description()`, it will be caught by `CATCH` blocks. If a communications failure occurs, the first `CATCH` block will be executed. If any other exception is raised, the `CATCH_ALL` block will be executed. The `ENDTRY` demarks the end of the exception handling.

```
TRY
  room_description(h, (unsigned_char_p_t) argv[1],
                   &room, &st);
CATCH(rpc_x_comm_failure)
  printf("Cannot communicate with server.\n");
CATCH_ALL
  printf("Unexpected exception.\n");
ENDTRY;
```

Code Sample 2.7
`TRY-CATCH` exception handling around a remote call.

The `TRY`, `CATCH`, `CATCH_ALL`, and `ENDTRY` constructs are implemented in C as macros, defined in the DCE header file `exc_handling.h`. The `TRY` macro calls `setjmp()` to record the location of the `CATCH` blocks. When DCE raises an exception, it calls `longjmp()` to the `CATCH` blocks, if any exist.

Fault Status Parameters

As an alternative to the TRY-CATCH-ENDTRY constructs, an additional output parameter can be added to a remote procedure call to be used to return a fault status to the calling program. Code Samples 2.8 and 2.9 show the **room_desc** and **room_server** implemented using a fault status parameter.

```
void room_description(
  /* [in ] */ handle_t         h,
  /* [in ] */ sch_room_name_t room_name,
  /* [out] */ sch_room_t      *room,
  /* [out] */ sch_status_t    *status,
  /* [out] */ error_status_t *call_status)

{
    ...
    *call_status = rpc_s_ok;
    ...
}
```

Code Sample 2.8

Error status parameter in the room server.

```
int main(int argc, idl_char *argv[])
{
    ...
    error_status_t call_st;
    ...
    room_description(h, (unsigned_char_p_t) argv[1],
                     &room, &st, &call_st);
    switch (call_st)
    {
      case rpc_s_ok:
         switch (st)
         { . . .
         }
         break;
      case rpc_s_comm_failure:
         printf("Cannot communicate with server.\n");
         break;
      default:
         printf("Unexpected exception.\n");
         break;
    }
}
```

Code Sample 2.9

Error status parameter in the room_desc client.

The `call_status` parameter of `room_description()` is declared to be a pointer to a variable of type `error_status_t`, defined by DCE for reporting error values. `call_status` is initialized to `rpc_s_ok`, a DCE-defined constant for successful completion. If a communications error or fault occurs during the remote call to `room_description()`, `call_status` will be set to the corresponding DCE error number. The client can then inspect the returned `call_status` to see if the call was successful.

The error and fault status parameter is declared using an Attribute Configuration File, as described in Chapter 3.

2.3 DCE RPC Stubs and Runtime

Now let's look at the DCE RPC mechanism in more detail. There are two major components to this mechanism: the RPC stubs and the RPC Runtime. The *RPC Runtime* handles communications over the network between the client and the server. The *RPC stubs* handle the interface between the application code (in the client and the server) and the RPC Runtime.

The RPC Runtime is a library (in HP-UX, part of the DCE library `libdce.sl`) that is linked with each client and server. The primary task of the RPC Runtime is to manage the network facilities used by RPC and to send and receive data packets over the network. *Request packets* are sent from the client to the server and carry input parameter values. *Response packets* are sent from the server back to the client and carry output parameter and return values. The way in which the network facilities are used and the packets transmitted by the Runtime depends on the network protocols used. These will be discussed in more detail in the RPC Protocols section.

The RPC stubs are customized for each remote procedure. *Client stubs* provide the interface between the client calling the remote procedures and the client's RPC Runtime. *Server stubs* handle the interface between the server's RPC Runtime and the actual remote procedures. Client and server stubs are generated automatically by the DCE IDL compiler, discussed in Chapter 3. The resulting object files for the stubs are linked into the client and server programs.

Marshaling and Unmarshaling

A major responsibility of RPC stubs is the marshaling and unmarshaling of parameter values. *Marshaling* is the action of copying values from one or more locations in an address space into a packet or sequence of packets that can be transmitted over the network. (This borrows from the original meaning of marshaling: "to arrange in a line.") The inverse operation is *unmarshaling*, where data values are copied from one or more packets into locations in an address space. The client stub marshals input parameters into request packets, and the server stub unmarshals the input parameters from the request packets. After the remote call completes, the server stub marshals output parameters into response packets, and the client stub unmarshals the output parameters from the response packets. This is illustrated in Figure 2.2.

To marshal and unmarshal parameters, RPC stubs must know the type of each parameter, and whether it is used for input, output, or both. This information is supplied in a description of each remote procedure in the Interface Definition Language (IDL) and is used by the IDL compiler to generate the required code in the stubs. IDL is discussed in Chapter 3.

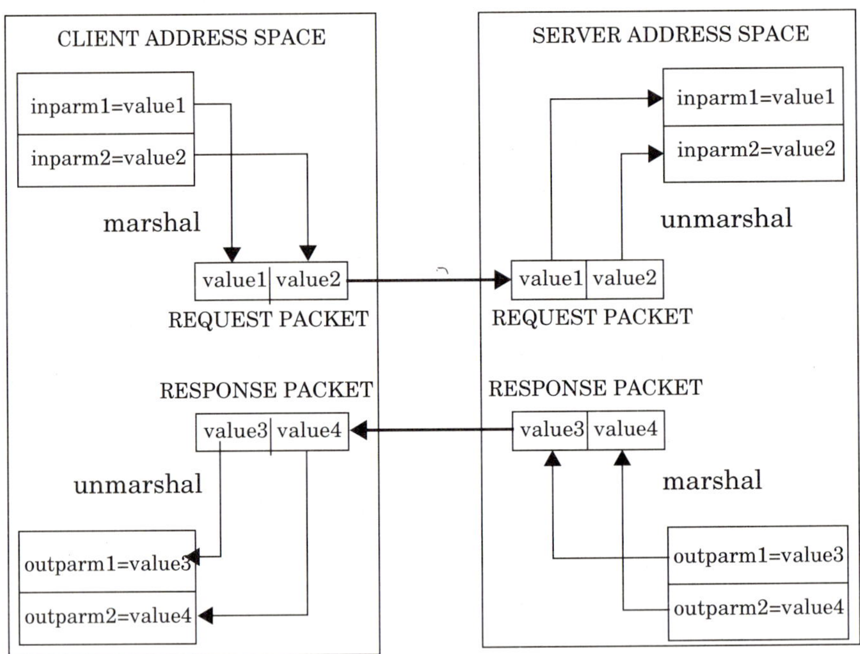

Figure 2.2
Marshaling and Unmarshaling of Parameter Values

Data Conversion

Another important responsibility of RPC stubs is *data conversion*, which is necessary when the client and server execute on machines with different data representations. To resolve this, DCE RPC uses the "receiver makes it right" concept: The *sender* of a data item sends it in its own data representation, and the *receiver* of the data item must convert it from the sender's representation to its own if it is different from the sender's representation. For example, the client stub sends input parameters in its own representation, while the server stub receives and converts the input parameters.

The "receiver makes it right" concept requires the receiver to be able to convert any data representation it might receive. With many possible data formats, this could be a daunting task. To help lessen this task, DCE RPC defines a small number of common data representations to which the sender must conform, called the Network Data Representation (NDR). NDR is a *multicanonical* data scheme. It was inherited from the HP/Apollo Network Computing System (NCS).

An alternative to the multicanonical scheme is a *single-canonical* arrangement, where there is just one data representation used for transmitting data. All senders must convert from their own data format to the canonical format, and all receivers must convert from the canonical format to their own representation. The ISO OSI protocols use this approach, with the Basic Encoding Rules (BER) canonical representation. In the future, DCE may support the ISO BER format as well as its existing multicanonical scheme. ONC RPC also uses a single-canonical approach with a canonical representation called XDR (eXternal Data Representation).

The advantages of "receiver makes it right" are that data conversion usually has to be done only at one end and can be omitted entirely if the sender and receiver share the same data representation. The advantage of the single-canonical approach is that only one type of data conversion—to the canonical form—is required by each sender and receiver.

Table 2.1

Network Data Representation (NDR) for Common Architectures

Architecture	Integer	Character	Floating Point
Motorola 68000	big-endian	ASCII	IEEE
HP PA-RISC	big-endian	ASCII	IEEE
Sun SPARC	big-endian	ASCII	IEEE
Silicon Graphics MIPS	big-endian	ASCII	IEEE
IBM PowerPC (RS/6000)	big-endian	ASCII	IEEE
Cray	big-endian	ASCII	CRAY
IBM Mainframes	big-endian	EBCDIC	IBM
DEC VAX	little-endian	ASCII	VAX
DEC Alpha	little-endian	ASCII	VAX or IEEE
Intel x86,Pentium	little-endian	ASCII	IEEE

Integer Order

Integer data representation varies in the ordering of the bytes of a multi-byte integer value. Architectures where the bytes are ordered from the most significant to the least significant are called *big-endian*. Conversely, architectures where the bytes are ordered from the least significant to the most significant are *little-endian*. Figure 2.3 shows an example of big- and little-endian integers. Data conversion between the two formats is done by swapping bytes.

As Table 2.1 shows, most modern architectures are big-endian. Notable exceptions are the DEC and the Intel architectures. Because of the prevalence of Intel-based PCs, much of the data in the world is stored in the little-endian format. (In recognition of this, recent HP PA-RISC processors are *bi-endian*, able to process both big- and little-endian integers.)

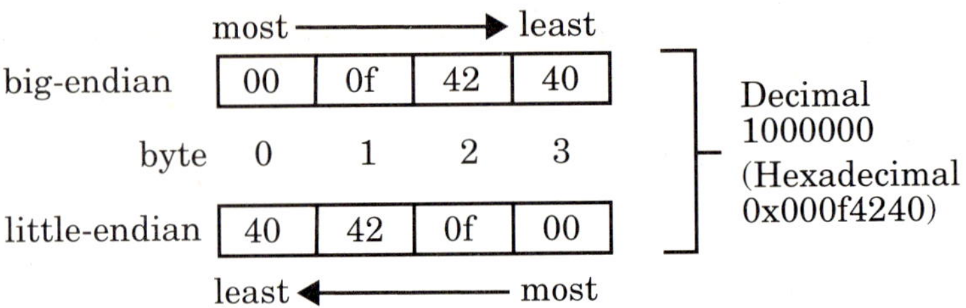

Figure 2.3
Big- and Little-Endian Integer Ordering

Character Code Sets

A character code set maps a byte value (or a sequence of bytes) into a character graphic for display or storage. There are two major (8-bit) character code sets: EBCDIC, used by IBM, and ASCII, used by everyone else. Both of these code sets can be used with DCE RPC.

Data conversion between character codes is done by table lookup. The RPC Runtime library contains routines and mapping tables for ASCII-to-EBCDIC and EBCDIC-to-ASCII conversions.

DCE 1.1 provides some support for applications using multiple-byte character sets, like those used for Japanese and Chinese graphics. This is discussed in Chapter 3, Section 3.5.

Floating-Point Formats

DCE provides four floating-point representations: the standard IEEE format, and the formats used by the VAX, Cray, and IBM mainframe architectures. Most modern architectures conform to the IEEE floating-point standard.

Conversion between floating-point formats involves computation and is done by routines in the RPC Runtime library.

Operation of the Client and Server Stubs and the Runtimes

Figure 2.4 shows the operation on an RPC client and an RPC server. Steps in the operation are listed below.

1. The client calls the "remote" procedure, which is in actuality a procedure in the local client stub.

   In the **room_desc** example, the local client stub contains a procedure named `room_description()`.

2. The client stub procedure marshals all input parameters from the client address space into one (or more) request packet(s). The client stub invokes the client's RPC Runtime.

   In the example, the value of `argv[1]` is marshaled for the `room_name` parameter.

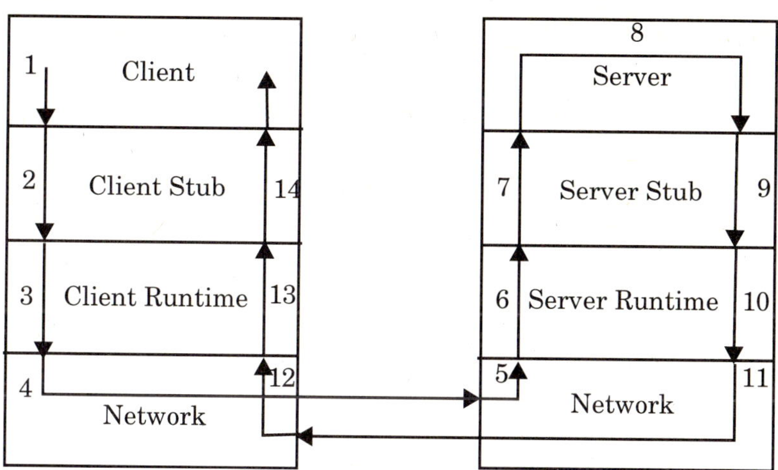

Figure 2.4
Operation of the RPC Stubs and Runtime

3. The client's RPC Runtime identifies the target server from the binding handle parameter and invokes the network software to send the request packet(s) to the server.
4. The client's network software transmits the request packet(s) over the network to the server.
5. The server's network software receives the request packet(s) and passes it (them) onto the server's RPC Runtime.
6. The server's RPC Runtime identifies the target remote procedure and calls the corresponding server stub procedure.
7. The server stub procedure unmarshals the input parameters from the request packet(s) into the server's address space, performing any necessary conversions between the client (sender) and the server (receiver) data representations. The server stub also allocates any data areas to be used for output parameters. Then the server stub calls the actual remote procedure, passing in the input parameters and supplying addresses for the allocated output parameters.

   In the example, the server stub for the `room_description()` procedure allocates a character string for `room_name`, a structure for `room`, and an integer for `status`. It unmarshals the input value for `room_name` and calls the actual `room_description()`, passing the `room_name`, `room`, and `status` parameters.

8. The remote procedure executes, with the input and output parameters supplied by the server stub. When it completes execution, it returns to the server stub.

   In the example, `room_description()` searches the `rooms[]` array for a match to `room_name`. If one is found, the room information is returned to `room` and `status` is set to `sch_status_ok`. Otherwise `status` is set to `sch_status_room_not_found`.

9. The server stub marshals the output parameter values returned by the remote procedure into one (or more) response packet(s). The server stub procedure then returns to the server's RPC Runtime.

   In the example, the values for room and status are marshaled into a response packet.

10. The server's RPC Runtime invokes the network software to send the response packet(s) to the client.
11. The server's network software transmits the response packet(s) over the network to the client.
12. The client's network software receives the response packet(s) and passes it (them) onto the client RPC Runtime.
13. The client's RPC Runtime returns to the client stub procedure.
14. The client stub procedure unmarshals the output parameters from the response packet(s) into the original call's output targets. Since the client is now the receiver, the client stub will perform any needed data conversion from the server's data representation. The client stub then returns to the client program.

    In the example, the `room` and `status` values are unmarshaled from the response packet into the `room` and `st` variables.

The next two sections of this chapter discuss the RPC protocols and RPC's use of threads. Knowledge of these topics is not required when writing distributed applications with the DCE. In fact, most of the protocol and thread operation is not visible to application developers. You may skip to Chapter 3 if you like. However, it is useful to know some of the underlying behavior of DCE RPC to understand how errors like communications faults occur, and how the choice of RPC protocol can affect application performance.

2.4 RPC Protocols

A *protocol* is a set of rules governing the interaction between two communicating entities, including diplomats and computers. In computer communications, protocols specify how data is transmitted between computers and how the computers should respond to various conditions that might arise. In modern networking, there are layers of protocols controlling different aspects of communication.

The DCE defines a set of *protocol sequences* that specify the type of RPC protocol and the underlying networking protocols to use. Protocol sequence names are character strings used in several of the DCE RPC setup calls that will be discussed in later chapters. There are two protocol sequences we will use: `ncadg_ip_udp` and `ncacn_ip_tcp`. These are the most common DCE protocol sequences. They will be examined in the datagram and connection protocol sections next.

RPC Datagram Protocol

The RPC datagram protocol (abbreviated `dg`) is used with network datagram protocols, such as the UDP (User Datagram Protocol) of the ARPA Internet Protocol (IP) suite. The salient characteristics of a datagram network protocol are

- *Independent packets*

  Data are transmitted in packets, each independently routed from the source to the destination.

- *Unreliable delivery*

  Packets may be *lost*, *duplicated*, or delivered *out of order*. Unreliable delivery may be a very rare occurrence, as on a single segment of a LAN, or it may be common, as across an internet connected by heavily loaded routers. A program using a datagram protocol must compensate for these conditions.

- *Maximum packet length*

  Packets have a maximum length defined by the network protocol. For UDP/IP, this maximum length is typically 8192 bytes. If the data to be transmitted is longer than the maximum packet length, it must be broken into multiple packets.

- *Low overhead*

  Little or no setup is required to transmit a packet, and resources are not required to maintain state between packet transmissions.

The only datagram protocol currently implemented by OSF is for the UDP/IP network protocol: Its protocol sequence is `ncadg_ip_udp`. Most DCE RPC implementations use the BSD (Berkeley Standard Distribution) Sockets calls to transmit data over the network. These calls operate on sockets bound to socket addresses. Each socket address consists of an IP address that identifies a computer in the network and a port number that identifies the socket on the computer. The relevant Sockets calls for UDP are

- `sendto()` - send a packet to a destination socket
- `recvfrom()` - receive a packet sent from a source socket

Most of the ncadg_ip_udp protocol in DCE RPC was inherited from the Network Computing System (NCS) RPC protocol. The original NCS protocol is defined in the *Network Computing Architecture* document published by HP/Apollo. The DCE RPC dg packet formats are backwards compatible with NCS, so that an NCS client (or server) can interoperate with a DCE server (or client). For backwards compatibility with NCS, the protocol sequence ip is accepted as a synonym for ncadg_ip_udp. (NCS also provided another RPC datagram protocol for the Apollo DDS network. There is a DCE protocol sequence, ncadg_dds, defined for this but not implemented by OSF.)

Request-Response Operation

Figure 2.5 shows the normal operation of the dg protocol. (The following protocol diagrams use these conventions: p is a remote procedure name or its equivalent; ins refers to zero or more input parameters; outs refers to zero or more output parameters and possibly a return value; and p(ins,outs) is a full procedure call. *Type [contents]* refers to a packet of a given type with selected contents. These elements will be numbered when there is more than one remote call in a diagram.)

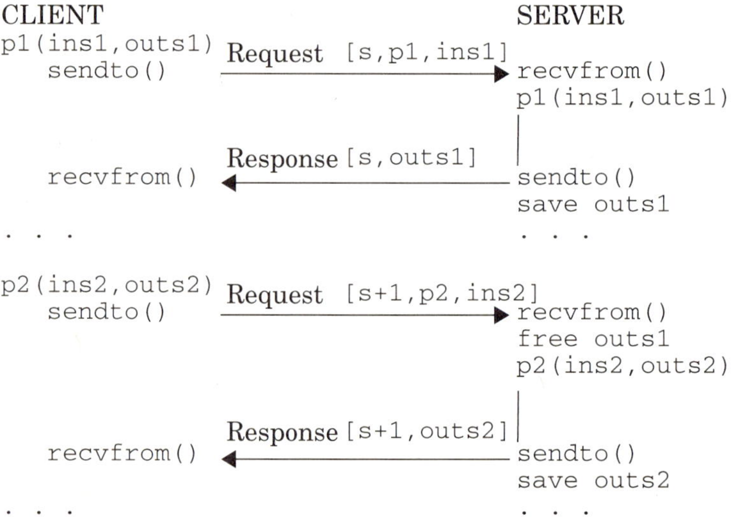

Figure 2.5
ncadg_ip_udp: Request-Response-Implicit Acknowledgment

In the client's first call to p1, RPC builds a *request* packet with a sequence number s, an identifier for the procedure p1, and the ins1 input parameters. The server receives the request packet and calls p1 with the ins and outs parameters. After the call completes, RPC builds a *response* packet with the sequence number and the outs1 values and sends the packet back to the client.

The server also saves the outs1 values for recovery purposes (discussed later) until it knows that the client has received the response packet. There are two ways this can happen. One is an RPC *implicit acknowledgment*, where the next request packet from the client (in this case, for call p2, with sequence number s+1) implies that the client has successfully received the response for the preceding call.

But there may not always be another request from the client, or the next request may not come for a long time. In this case, the client is responsible for sending an *explicit acknowledgment* to the server. When the client makes a remote call, the RPC Runtime sets up an *acknowledgment timeout* (typically three seconds) for the call. If the client has not executed another remote call to the server when the acknowledgment timeout expires, the client RPC Runtime sends an *ack* packet to the server, with the sequence number s of the last request. When the server receives the ack, it knows that it can release the retained outs for the last call. This is diagrammed in Figure 2.6.

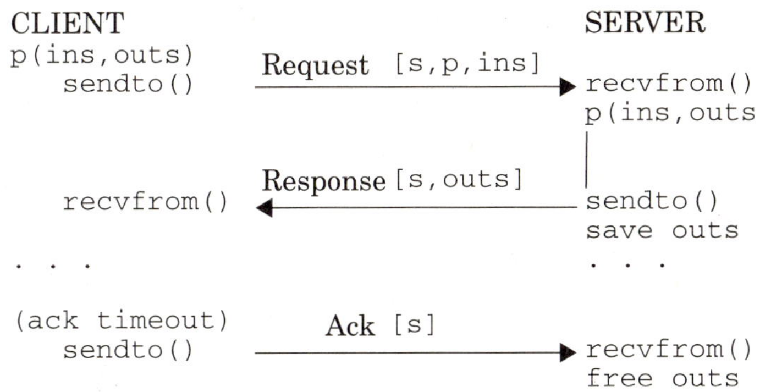

Figure 2.6
ncadg_ip_udp: Request-Response-Explicit Acknowledgment

Subsequent protocol diagrams will assume that either another call or an explicit acknowledgment is made by the client after it successfully receives a response.

Recovery from Lost Packets

Since a datagram network protocol is unreliable, the RPC dg protocol must recover from either a lost request or lost response packet. This is done using the *ping* packet, which is an inquiry from the client to the server about the status of a remote call in progress. When the client initiates a remote call, its RPC Runtime sets up a *wait timeout* (typically starting at one second). If the client has not received a response before the wait timeout expires, it will send a ping to the server. The server will respond in one of several ways, depending on the state of the call.

Figure 2.7 shows the case where the request was received by the server, the procedure was executed, but the response was lost. When the server receives the ping, with a sequence number s, it will retrieve the outs for the call associated with that sequence number, build a new response packet, and send the packet back to the client.

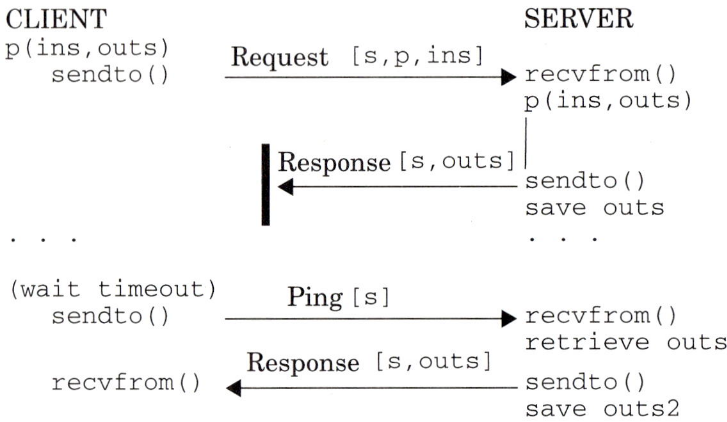

Figure 2.7
ncadg_ip_udp: Recovery from Lost Response

Figure 2.8 shows the case where the request from the client was lost. When the server receives a ping for a request with sequence number s, it notes that it never received that request and replies with a *nocall* packet to the client. The client then rebuilds the request packet and sends it to the server.

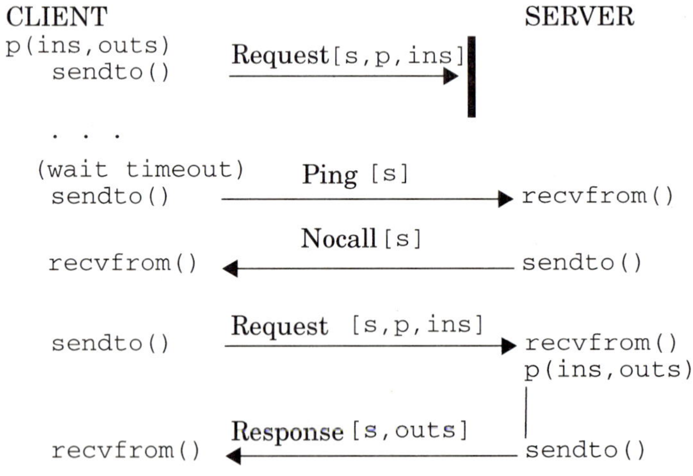

Figure 2.8
ncadg_ip_udp: Recovery from Lost Response

Long Running Calls

It is possible that the server has not responded to the client by the ping timeout, not because a request or response packet was lost, but because the server is still executing the remote call. In this case, the server responds to a ping with a *working* packet, as shown in Figure 2.9. This tells the client that everything is OK (so far). The client will then wait until it receives the response or until another ping timeout expires.

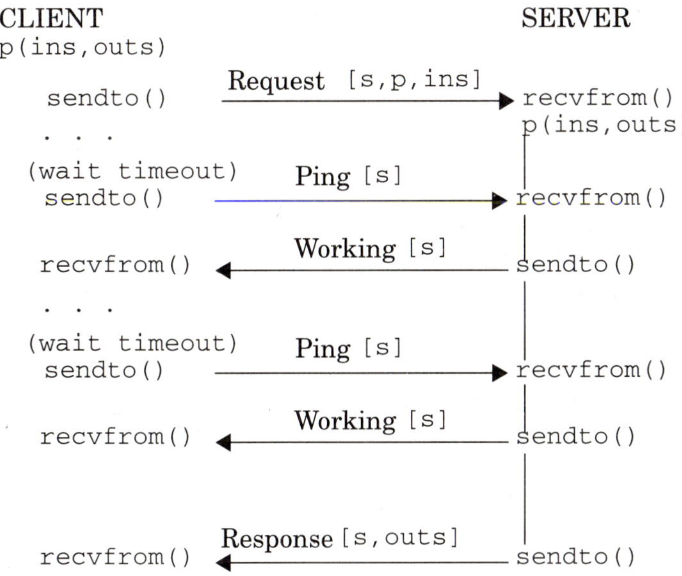

Figure 2.9
ncadg_ip_udp: Long Running Call

When the server responds to a ping with a working packet, the client RPC Runtime will *back off* the wait timeout to a longer value. This way the client will not inundate the server with pings that would delay the server from completing the remote call. But if the server fails to respond with a working packet, the client will snap back to more frequent pings (see Non-responding Servers next.)

Note that the server must have at least two threads to respond with a working packet: one thread that is executing the remote call and one thread that receives the ping and responds with the working packet. This will be discussed in the RPC Threads section.

Non-Responding Clients and Servers

Figure 2.10 illustrates what happens when a server does not respond. This may happen because the server program has aborted (or was not started), the server's system has crashed, or the network path between the client and the server's system has been broken. In some very extreme cases, the server system or the network may just be heavily loaded, and the server has not been able to respond quickly enough. There is no way for the RPC dg protocol to tell which of these situations has occurred; all it knows is that the server is not responding. (There are other ways outside of DCE to distinguish the failure conditions. For example, you can use the **ping** command to determine if the server's system is up and the network path between the client and the server is functioning. If you can log in remotely to the server's system, you can use the **ps** command to see if the server is running.)

When the client sends a ping, it sets a *ping timeout*, typically starting at one second. If the server does not respond before the ping timeout expires, the client will send another ping and set another ping timeout. If the server fails to respond to any pings over a period of time, the client will send one or more *quit* packets to the server to let it know that the client is giving up. Then the client RPC Runtime raises the `rpc_x_comm_failure` exception. If the call has an `error_status` parameter, the `rpc_s_comm_failure` error will be returned in that parameter.

Since the client must go through a number of ping timeouts, it can take some time—the default is 30 seconds—for a client to report that a server is not responding. A user of a client program may see a noticeable (and possibly annoying) pause in the operation of the program. The client can control the length of time it will wait for a server response by calling the DCE routine `rpc_mgmt_set_com_timeout()`. Care must be taken to select a timeout interval that balances quick reporting and possibly recovery from a non-responding server against possible network and server loads that affect response time. Also, you must consider whether the client and server communicate over a high- or a low-speed network.

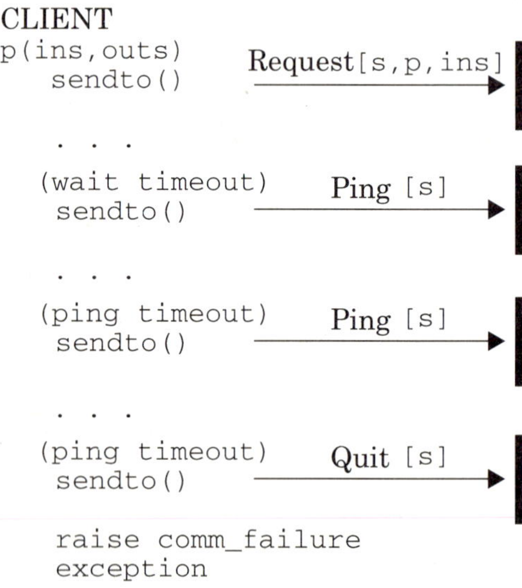

Figure 2.10
`ncadg_ip_udp`: Non-responding Server

It is also possible for a client to stop responding to a server. This is shown in Figure 2.11. The client could be aborted after it has sent its request but before it has acknowledged the response from the server. If the server did not detect this condition, it could retain the outs for the call indefinitely. When the server sends a response, it sets a *resend timeout*, typically three seconds. If the client has not acknowledged the response when the resend timeout expires, the server will resend the response. The server will do this over a period of time similar to the client's ping period (and with a typical default of 30 seconds). If after that time none of the responses have been acknowledged, the server will give up and free the retained outs values and any other state for the call.

There is a common case where this occurs—when the client terminates before the acknowledgment timeout for the last remote call has expired. Then the last response is not acknowledged by the client and the server will resend the response, wasting network bandwidth. There is really no good way to solve this problem. The client can delay its termination long enough for the acknowledgment timeout to expire, but that delay may not be acceptable to the user of the client program. There is no way for the client to *force* an acknowledgment to be sent, even if it knows it is making its last remote call to the server.

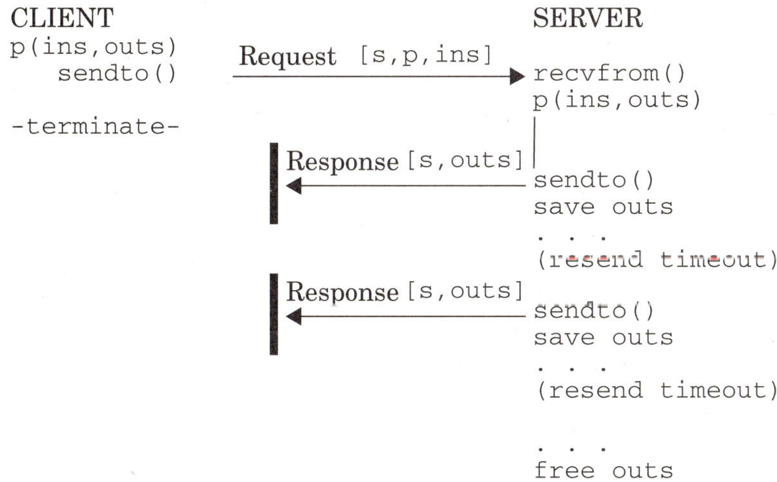

Figure 2.11
ncadg_ip_udp: Non-Responding Client

Recovery from Duplicate and Out-of-Order Packets

The sequence number in each dg packet is used to detect duplicate and out-of-order packets. The sequence number is established on the first call from the client to the server and incremented for each subsequent call. If a request packet arrives with an unexpected sequence number, it could be a duplicate or a misordered packet, so the server discards it. Duplicate and misordered packets may be produced by the underlying (unreliable) datagram transport, or they may be produced by RPC's own recovery procedures under certain timing conditions.

Idempotent Calls

The dg protocol includes optimizations for a certain class of remote calls, which are designated as *idempotent*. This curious word means that a procedure can be repeated (with the same parameters) without undesired side effects. An idempotent procedure should not change the state of the server or its data. Procedures that read data are typically idempotent, while procedures that update data are typically non-idempotent. The classic example is a bank application with balance inquiry, deposit, and withdrawal. A balance inquiry can be done more than once without affecting an account's balance and so is an idempotent operation. But each deposit and withdrawal has a definite effect on an account balance. The bank certainly would not want one actual deposit to be credited more than once to an account, nor would a customer want one withdrawal to be debited more than once.

The optimization for idempotent calls eliminates the acknowledgment step in the datagram protocol. The server does not retain any outs for a remote call to an idempotent procedure. The client does not send an implicit or an explicit acknowledgment of the server's response, as shown in Figure 2.12.

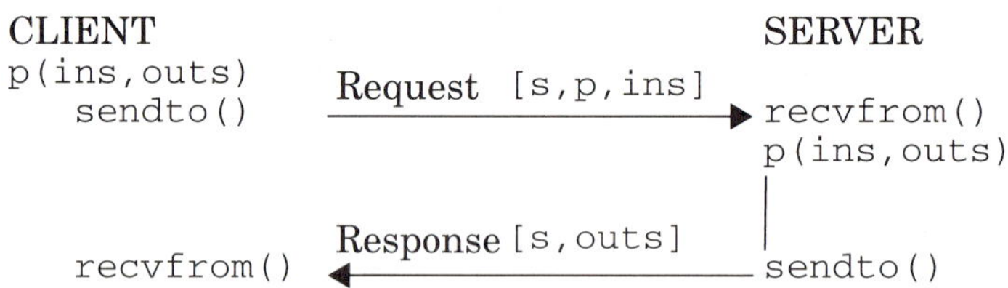

Figure 2.12
ncadg_ip_udp: Idempotent Request-Response

Recovery from lost packets during an idempotent call uses the fact that the procedure can be repeated without ill-effect. Consider Figure 2.13. Here the server has executed an idempotent procedure p but has not retained the outs. The response is lost, and in due time the client sends a ping to the server asking about the call. The server has not saved the state of the call, so it returns a nocall packet to the client. The client then resends the request packet. The server executes p again and sends back another response packet. Since the procedure is idempotent, the second execution is acceptable.

Remote procedures can be given the idempotent attribute in their definition in the Interface Definition Language. If a remote procedure is not so declared, it is assumed to be non-idempotent.

Maybe and Broadcast Calls

The dg protocol includes other specialized classes of remote calls. A *maybe* call, shown in Figure 2.14, can be used if the client does not need any results returned from the server. A maybe procedure must be idempotent and can have only input parameters. When a maybe procedure is called, only a request packet with the procedure's ins is sent. Since there can be no outs, the server does not send a response packet back to the client. The client cannot then know if the server ever received the request and executed the remote call.

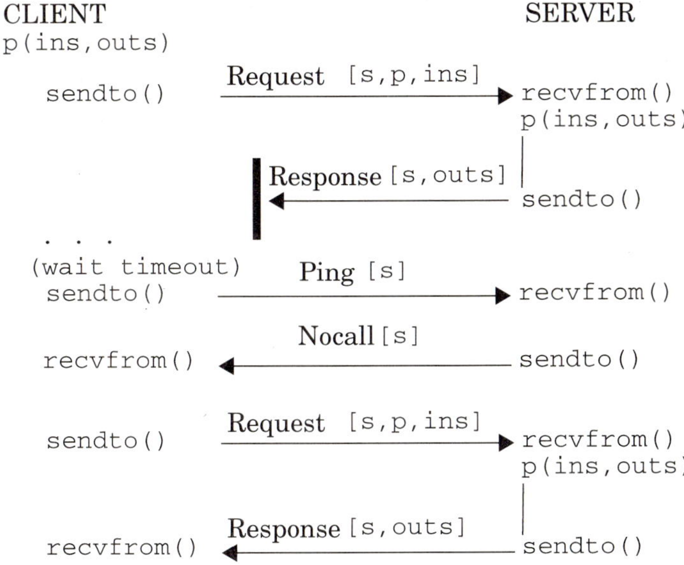

Figure 2.13
ncadg_ip_udp: Idempotent Recovery from Lost Response

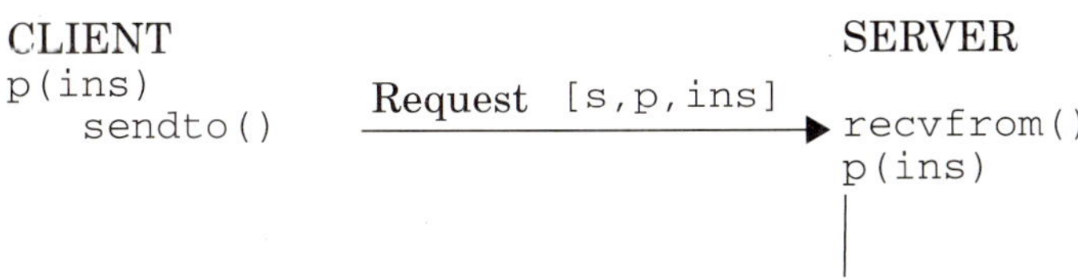

Figure 2.14
ncadg_ip_udp: Maybe Request

Datagram protocols have the ability to broadcast packets to all systems on the network (or at least, all systems on a local network segment). The dg protocol allows *broadcast* calls to be sent to all servers listening to a particular port. Broadcast calls must be idempotent.

The client broadcasts a request packet over the network. Any server can respond to the request by sending a response packet back to the client's socket address. The client will accept the first response it receives and discard any subsequent responses. The client sets a *broadcast timeout*, typically five seconds. If no responses are received when the broadcast timeout expires, the client RPC Runtime will raise the `rpc_x_comm_failure` exception.

A broadcast call can also be a maybe call. In this case the client broadcasts the request packet and does not wait for any responses.

Since broadcasts affect all systems on the network, they should be used sparingly and with care. Too frequent use of broadcasts can interfere with the transmission of other data in the network.

Procedures can be declared with the `maybe` and `broadcast` attributes in the Interface Definition Language. These attributes imply `idempotent`.

Fragmentation

If the length of the data to be transmitted in a request or response packet is longer than the maximum packet size of the datagram protocol, the RPC Runtime will *fragment* the data into two or more packets and send the packets in sequence. The receiver receives each fragment packet and reassembles the complete data from the fragments.

Fragment packets are susceptible to loss, duplication, or out-of-order delivery just like other datagram packets. To recover from these problems, the RPC `dg` protocol again uses acknowledgment with retransmission. The sender sends a *blast* of fragment packets (typically starting at two). Each packet has a fragment number indicating its position in the sequence. When the receiver has received the packets in the burst, it sends back a *fack* packet, indicating which fragments it has received. If a fragment was not received, the sender will retransmit it. If fragments are received out of order (as indicated by their fragment numbers), the receiver will reassemble them in order. If a duplicate fragment is received, it will be discarded.

The fragment acknowledgment algorithm used by the `dg` protocol can adjust itself to the reliability of the underlying datagram transport. If there are few retransmissions due to packet loss, the RPC Runtime will increase the size of the fragment bursts to cut down on the number of facks. Conversely, if many packets are being retransmitted, the Runtime will decrease the burst size to cause more frequent acknowledgments.

Figure 2.15 shows a request and a response, each consisting of a number of fragments. Note that fack packets are sent by both the server and the client to acknowledge request and response fragments, respectively.

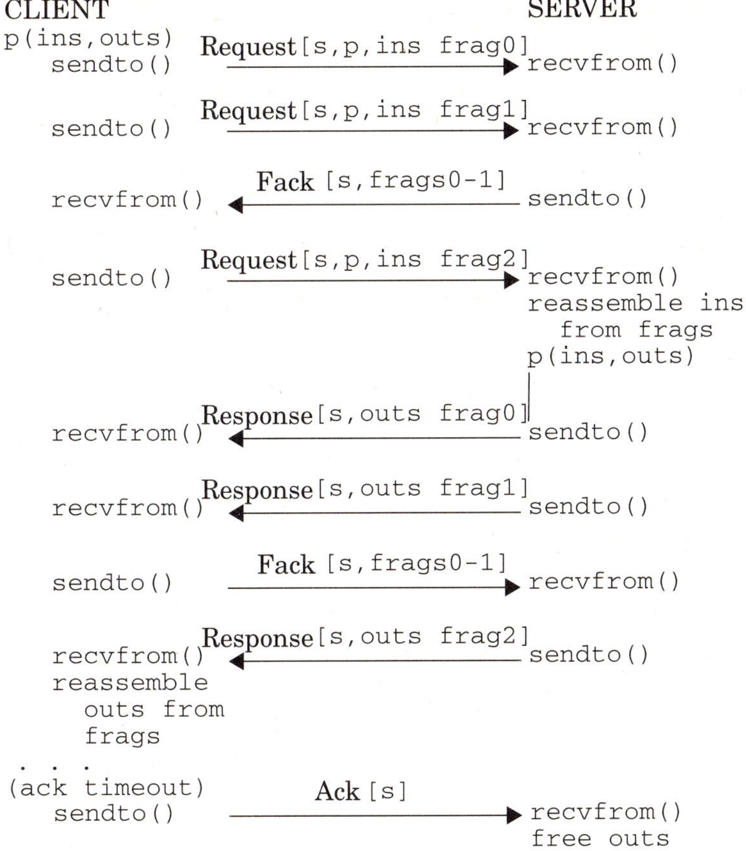

Figure 2.15
ncadg_ip_udp: Fragmentation

Faults and Rejects

If a fault occurs during the execution of the remote call within the server, the server will trap the fault and send a *fault* packet back to the client. The fault packet indicates the type of fault (for example, division-by-zero or an address error). The client RPC Runtime receives the fault packet and raises an exception that corresponds to the fault (for example, exc_intdiv_e or exc_illaddr_e). If the client program set up exception handling for the call (either a TRY-CATCH block or an error_status parameter), it will trap the exception. Otherwise the exception will abort the client. Figure 2.16 illustrates a fault.

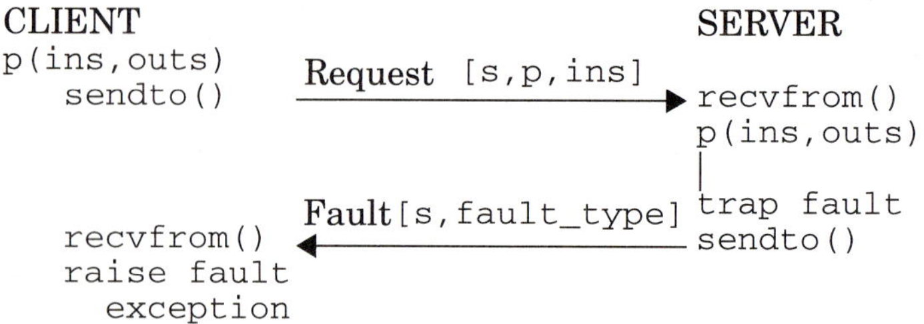

Figure 2.16
ncadg_ip_udp: Fault

When the server receives a request, its Runtime performs a number of checks on the request to ensure that it is valid. If the server finds the request to be invalid, it will send a *reject* packet to the client containing the reason for the rejection. In this way the server protects itself from inadvertent or malicious tampering with the RPC protocol. Rejects should not occur during normal operation of RPC. Figure 2.17 shows a reject.

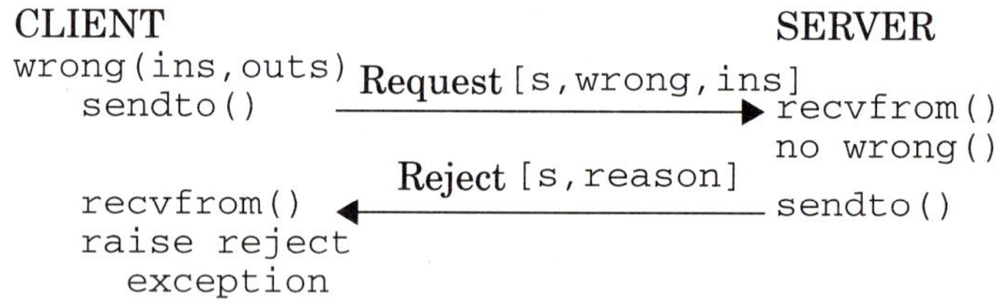

Figure 2.17
ncadg_ip_udp: Reject

The dg packet types are summarized in Table 2.2.

Table 2.2

ncadg_ip_udp: Packet Types		
Packet Type	Direction	Purpose
Request	client->server	Sends procedure call with ins
Response	server->client	Returns procedure call result with outs
Ping	client->server	Inquires about the status of a call in progress
Working	server->client	Indicates the call is still being executed

Table 2.2 (Continued)

ncadg_ip_udp: Packet Types		
Packet Type	Direction	Purpose
Nocall	server->client	Indicates the call state is unknown
Ack	client->server	Acknowledges receipt of a response
Fack	both directions	Acknowledges receipt of fragments
Fault	server->client	Indicates the call caused a fault
Reject	server->client	Indicates the call was rejected for a given reason
Quit	client->server	Indicates the client is abandoning the call
Quack	server->client	Acknowledges receipt of a quit

RPC Connection-Oriented Protocol

The RPC connection-oriented protocol (abbreviated `cn`) is used with network connection-oriented protocols, such as the TCP (Transmission Control Protocol) of the ARPA Internet Protocol (IP) suite. The salient characteristics of a connection-oriented protocol are

- *Connection between sender and receiver*

  Before data can be transmitted, one process (the initiator) establishes a connection to another process (the acceptor). Once the connection is established, both processes can send and receive data using the connection.

- *Reliable delivery*

  A connection-oriented protocol guarantees that data sent on a connection is delivered in order, with no loss or duplication. The protocol itself takes care of recovery from network transmission problems. Also, the protocol will fragment data itself to fit into network packets.

- *Connection overhead*

  Connection establishment usually requires one or more packets to be exchanged between the requestor and the responder. Once the connection has been established, both sides must keep track of the state of the connection during its lifetime. This requires buffer space and state tables to be allocated by the network software.

The only connection-oriented RPC protocol currently implemented by OSF is on the TCP/IP network transport protocol: Its protocol sequence is `ncacn_ip_tcp`. As with UDP/IP, DCE RPC uses the BSD Sockets calls to interface to TCP/IP. The sockets calls for TCP are

- `connect()` establish a connection to a target socket address
- `accept()` respond to a connection establishment request
- `listen()` set max number of queued connection requests
- `send()` send data through the connection to the partner
- `recv()` receive data through the connection from the partner

An important feature of TCP/IP is *stream transmission*. Data is sent as a stream of bytes, without message or packet boundaries. A sometimes undesirable side effect of this is that several `send()` calls may be needed to send a particular buffer of data, and several `recv()` calls may be necessary to receive a buffer of data. Programmers using sockets learn to enclose the calls in loops to make sure all of the intended data is transmitted. Fortunately, the RPC Runtime handles this for remote calls.

The `ncacn_ip_tcp` protocol was developed by HP/Apollo and Digital Equipment Corporation for DCE RPC. The original Network Computing System (NCS) did not include a connection-oriented protocol.

Someday DCE RPC may support other connection transport protocols. Candidates include the TP4 protocol from the ISO (International Standards Organization) OSI (Open Systems Interconnect) standards, and the IBM SNA (Systems Network Architecture) protocols.

DCE for Microsoft NT includes a number of additional connection-oriented protocols that are important in the PC world, including `ncacn_np` (for Microsoft LAN Manager named pipes) and `ncacn_spx` (for the Novell NetWare SPX protocol). Note that these protocol sequences cannot be used between the NT DCE and other DCE implementations, including HP-UX.

Normal Operation

Because the underlying transport protocol is reliable, the RPC `cn` protocol is much simpler than the `dg` protocol. In general, the client just sends a request to the server, and the server sends a response back to the client. But on the first call from a client to a server, the RPC Runtimes must establish a connection between them prior to sending the request. The client Runtime calls `connect()` and the server Runtime calls `accept()`. TCP has a three-way connection establishment handshake, with request, accept, and acknowledgment packets. Figure 2.18 shows the normal operation of the `cn` protocol.

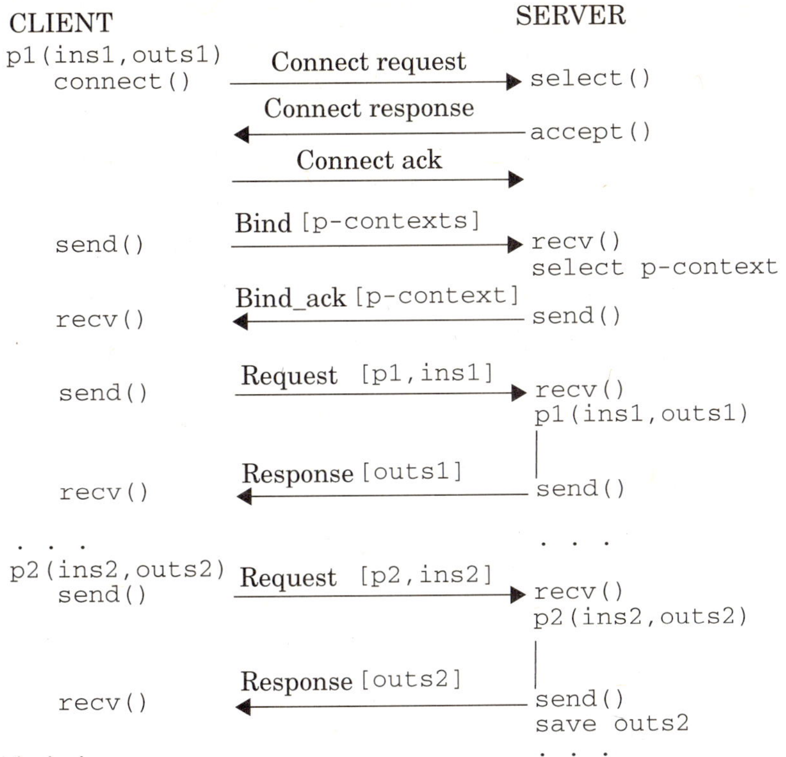

Figure 2.18
ncacn_ip_tcp: Bind-and-Request Response

Once the connection is set up, the client and server must negotiate a *presentation context* to be used between them. This is an ISO OSI concept related to data conversion, put in place in case DCE RPC ever supports the OSI protocols. The client sends a *bind* packet with a list of *transfer syntaxes* (data representation formats) that it can understand. The server selects one of these and sends back a *bind_ack* packet indicating the selected transfer syntax. Currently, only one transfer syntax is allowed—the NDR data formats originally defined for the dg protocol and described earlier in the Data Conversion section. The presentation context also includes one other important piece of information—the identification of the interface (that is, the set of remote procedures) that the client intends to call. All calls over the connection will refer to the interface indicated in the bind, and so requests need only indicate the procedure within the interface. If the requested interface is not available, the server will send a *bind_nak* to reject the first call.

New Interface

Suppose, after establishing a connection to a server for one interface, the client later calls a remote procedure from another interface in the same server. Since the interface has changed, the presentation context must be renegotiated. To do this, the client will send an *alter_context* packet indicating the new interface. The server sends back an *alter_context_resp* packet, accepting or rejecting the new presentation context. The alter_context exchange is shown in Figure 2.19.

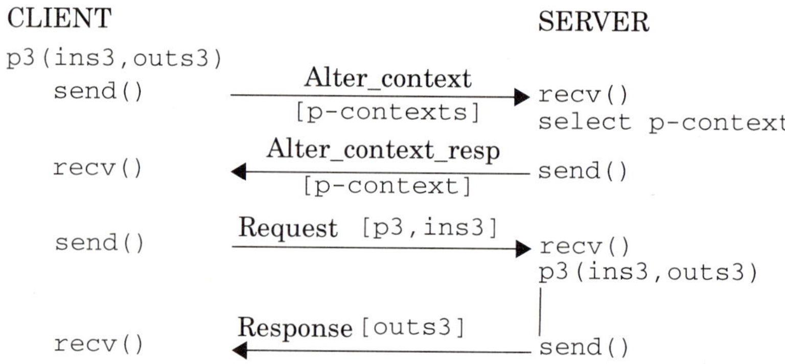

Figure 2.19
ncacn_ip_tcp: Alter_context for a New Interface

Failures

If the server crashes or the network path between the client and the server fails, the client will receive a connection failure error on its `recv()`. Then the client RPC Runtime raises the `rpc_x_connection_aborted` exception. This may be handled by a `TRY-CATCH` block or an `error_status` parameter. If not, this exception will abort the client. Figure 2.20 illustrates this.

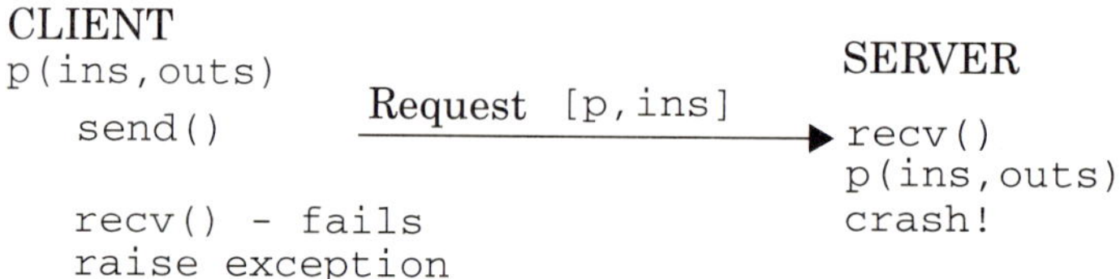

Figure 2.20
ncacn_ip_tcp: Connection Failure

Connect Shutdown

If the connection between a client and a server is not used for some period of time (the *client disconnect timeout*, typically 10 seconds), the server sends a *shutdown* packet to the client. This asks the client to gracefully shutdown the connection. In this way unused connection resources are eventually reclaimed. If the client later makes another remote call to the server, a new connection will be established and bound as described above. Figure 2.21 shows a connection shutdown.

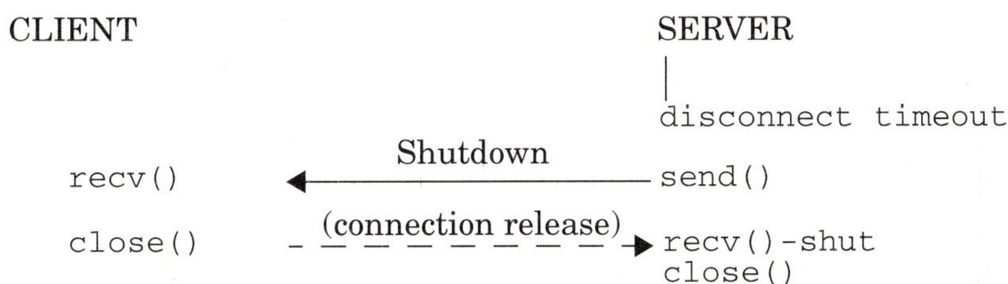

Figure 2.21
ncacn_ip_tcp: Connection Shutdown

The packet types for the cn protocol are summarized in Table 2.3

Table 2.3

ncacn_ip_tcp: Packet Types		
Packet Type	Direction	Purpose
Request	client->server	Sends procedure call with ins
Response	server->client	Returns procedure call result with outs
Bind	client->server	Offers initial presentation contexts
Bind_ack	server->client	Accepts an offered presentation context
Bind_nak	server->client	Rejects offered presentation contexts
Alter_context	client->server	Offers change in presentation contexts
Alter_context_resp	server->client	Accepts/rejects new contexts
Auth3	client->server	Not currently used
Fault	server->client	Indicates the call caused a fault
Shutdown	server->client	Requests that a client close a connec-
Remote_alert	client->server	Propagates a thread cancel
Orphaned	client->server	Indicates the client abandoned the call

Loopback

A client and a server on the same system can communicate using the *loopback* mode of the UDP or TCP transport protocol. With UDP loopback, the sender calls `sendto()` specifying a datagram socket that exists on the local system. With TCP loopback, the sender calls `connect()` specifying a call socket on the local system. In both cases the receiver works the same as with remote senders. There really isn't anything special about loopback at the socket level. There also isn't anything special about loopback at the RPC level—the remote calls and setup are done in exactly the same manner as when the client and server are on different systems. The client and server may not even be aware that they are on the same system. This provides location transparency: There is no difference between a client using a local and a remote server.

Loopback is particularly useful when developing and testing DCE applications. Both the client and the server can be run on one system.

2.5RPC Threads Implementation

The RPC Runtime creates a number of threads within each client and server process to manage remote calls and the associated protocol. Normally these threads are not visible to the application programmer. They are described here for general interest.

A general principle of threads is to use a thread for each operation that may block, such as waiting for an incoming packet. While the operation blocks the thread, other threads in the process can execute. Threads can signal one another when significant events, such as an arrival of a packet, occur.

The RPC Runtime maintains many tables that record the bindings between clients and servers, the states of remote calls in progress, and retained parameter data. These tables are shared among the RPC threads. Mutex locking and unlocking (described in Chapter 10) are used extensively to coordinate thread access to these data.

Client Main/Call Threads

When a process is created, it has one thread, called the *main* or *initial thread*. In processes written in C, the main thread executes the program's `main()` procedure. When the main client thread executes remote procedure calls, it becomes a *client call thread*. The remote call's client stub executes in the call thread, as does part of the RPC Runtime. The operation of the call thread is as follows.

- The main thread makes a remote call `p(ins, outs)`.
- The client stub for `p()` marshals the `ins`.
- If the `dg` protocol is used, the RPC Runtime

  Builds the request packet and calls `sendto()` to send the request packet to the server.

  Waits for the listener thread to signal reception of the response packet.
- Else if the `cn` protocol is used, the RPC Runtime:

  If a connection does not yet exist to the server,

    Calls `connect()` to establish a connection to the server.

    Creates a receiver thread for the connection.

    Calls `send()` to send the bind packet to the server.

    Waits for the receiver thread to signal reception of bind_ack.

  Builds the request packet(s) and calls `send()` to send the request packet(s) to the server.

  Waits for the receiver thread to signal reception of the response packet(s).
- The client stub unmarshals the `outs` and returns to the main thread.

In advanced DCE applications, the client main thread may create additional threads for various purposes. Each of these client threads may make remote calls, becoming client call threads. The RPC Runtime will coordinate the calls so that one thread making a remote call does not block other client threads.

Server Main/Call Threads

The main thread of the server makes the initialization calls to set up the server to process remote calls (as described starting in Chapter 4). To start servicing clients' calls, the server main thread makes the call

```
rpc_server_listen(n_concurrent_calls);
```

This call turns the main thread into a *server call thread*. If *n_concurrent_calls* is greater than one, `rpc_server_listen()` will create *n_concurrent_calls*-1 additional server call threads. Each server call thread can execute incoming remote calls. The sequence of operations in a server call thread is

- The RPC Runtime waits to be signaled that a request for a call, say `p(ins,outs)`, has arrived.
- The RPC Runtime decodes the request packet and calls the server stub for `p()`.
- The server stub unmarshals the `ins` and calls the `p()` procedure.
- `p(ins,outs)` executes and returns to the server stub.
- The server stub marshals the `outs` and returns to the RPC Runtime.
- The RPC Runtime builds the response packet(s) and
  - If using the `dg` protocol, calls `sendto()` to send it (them) to the client.
  - Else if using the `cn` protocol, calls `send()` to send it (them) to the client.
- The RPC Runtime waits for the next incoming call.

In advanced DCE applications, the server main thread or the other call threads can create other application threads for various purposes. These threads can execute independently of the RPC threads within the server.

Listener Thread

Each client and server has one *listener thread*, created by the RPC Runtime during RPC initialization. This thread calls the `select()` procedure to wait for events on a set of sockets. The sockets can be datagram sockets for receiving UDP packets or call sockets for establishing TCP connections.

Datagram sockets

For a datagram socket, `select()` returns when a packet has arrived. The listener thread calls `recvfrom()` to receive the packet. Based on the packet type, the listener thread performs the appropriate `dg` protocol processing:

- Request: (server)
  - Select an available server call thread.
  - Signal the call thread that a call request has arrived.

- Response: (client)

  Match the response with the client call thread making the call.
  Signal the call thread that a response has arrived.

- Ack: (server)

  Release the retained data for the acknowledged call.

- Ping: (server)

  Locate the call referenced by the ping.
  If the call is completed, resend the response packet.
  Else if the call is still in progress, send a working packet.
  Else if no call was found, send a nocall packet.

- Working: (client)

  Adjust the ping time-outs and wait some more.

- Nocall: (client)

  Match the nocall with the client call thread making the call.
  Signal the call thread that the call has been lost.

- Fack: (either)

  Retransmit any unacknowledged fragments.
  Adjust the fragment window, if necessary.

- Quit: (server)

  Release any retained data for the abandoned call.

- Quack: (client)

  Complete abandoning call.

Connection Call Sockets

For a call socket, `select()` returns when a connection request has arrived. The listener thread calls `accept()` to accept the connection request and create a connection socket. Then the listener thread creates a receiver thread to manage the connection.

Receiver Threads

There is one receiver thread for each connection used by a client or server. A receiver thread is created when a connection is established and exists as long as the connection is open. The receiver thread fulfills the same role for the `cn` protocol as the listener thread does for the `dg` protocol: It receives and processes packets. Each connection has its own receiver thread so the thread can block on a `recv()` without blocking other threads. Packet processing for the `cn` protocol includes

- Request: (server)

  Select an available server call thread.
  Signal the call thread that a call request has arrived.
- Response: (client)

  Match the response with the client call thread making the call.
  Signal the call thread that a response has arrived.
- Bind: (server)

  Select a presentation context from the set offered in the bind.
  If one is selected, send a bind_ack back to the client.
  Else send a bind_nak back to the client.
- Bind_ack: (client)

  Use the presentation context returned from the server.
  Signal the client call thread that the bind is completed.
- Bind_nak: (client)

  Signal the client call thread that the bind failed.
- Alter_context: (server)

  Select a new p-context from the set offered.
  Send an alter_context_resp with the selected p-context, or failure, back to the client.
- Alter_context_resp: (client)

  Use the presentation context returned from the server.
  Signal the client call thread that the alter_context is done.
- Auth3: (server)

  (This is available for use by three-way authentication protocols. It is not currently used.)
- Shutdown: (client)

  Call `close()` to gracefully shut down the connection.
- Remote_alert: (server)

  Signal the server call thread executing a call for the client to raise a thread cancel exception.
- Orphaned: (server)

  Release call data for the orphaned call.

A receiver thread also handles errors on the connection, such as connection aborted. If a connection fails, the receiver thread signals the corresponding call thread to raise an exception.

Timer Thread

Each client and server has an RPC *timer thread*, created during RPC initialization. The timer thread manages the various protocol timeouts and performs processing required if a timeout expires. RPC threads insert timer events into a list that the timer thread reads. The timer thread sleeps until the next event on the list is to be processed. Timer events include

- Ack (client)

  Send an ack packet to the server.
- Wait (client)

  Send a ping packet to the server.
  Set the initial ping timeout.
- Ping (client)

  If the maximum number of pings have been sent
    Signal the call thread that a comm_failure has occurred.
  Else
    Send another ping packet.
    Set the next ping timeout.
- Resend (server)

  If the maximum number of resends have been sent
    Release the retained call information.
  Else
    Resend the response packet(s).
    Set the next resend timeout.
- Broadcast (client)

  Signal the call thread that the broadcast failed.
- Connect inactive (client)

  Send a shutdown packet to the client.
  (The client will close the connection and the server receiver
    thread will detect the connection close.)

The thread interactions for the dg and cn protocols are summarized in Figures 2.22 and 2.23, respectively

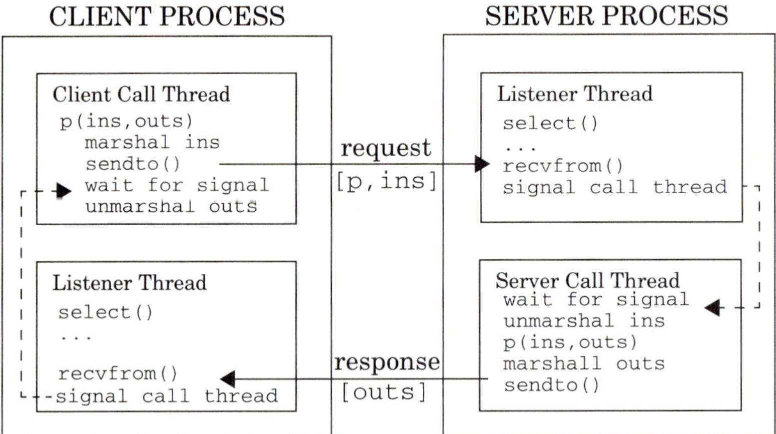

Figure 2.22
RPC Threads for the ncadg_ip_udp Protocol

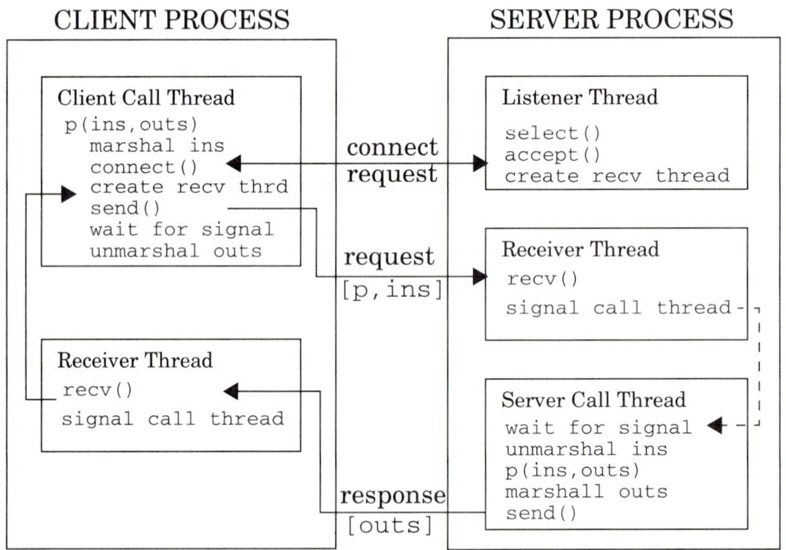

Figure 2.23
RPC Threads for the ncacn_ip_tcp Protocol

2.6 RPC Performance

Developers of distributed applications using DCE RPC should have an idea of how RPC performs so they can make informed choices in their design. Two measures of RPC performance will be discussed here:

- *call time*: How much elapsed time (in milliseconds) it takes to execute a remote call, and
- *transfer rate*: How much data can be transferred (in kbytes/second) in input and output parameters of a remote call.

First, you should recognize that remote calls are not the same as local procedure calls within a process address space. The time to make a remote call will be tens to thousands of times greater than a local call. Remote calls cannot be substituted for local calls without some performance impact. You should design distributed applications to make judicious use of remote calls.

RPC Performance Factors

Many factors influence the performance of an RPC-based application. Some are listed here.

Client and Server Processor Speed, Memory, and Load

As with all computation, the speed, available memory, and load of a processor affect RPC performance. But with RPC, there are two processors involved—the client and the server system. If the power of either of the client or server is insufficient, RPC performance will suffer.

Network Transmission Rate, Load and Reliability

The performance of the network has a strong influence on RPC call time and transfer rates. Obviously, RPC cannot transfer data faster than the peak network transmission rate, so a slow network will result in slow remote calls. If the network is heavily loaded or it drops many packets, RPC performance will be adversely affected.

Threads Creation and Context Switching

As we have seen in the preceding section, RPC makes extensive use of threads. New threads are created on the first RPC operation and, for the `ncacn_ip_tcp` protocol, when a connection is established. Each remote call involves a number of thread switches between the call threads and the listener or receiver threads. The standard DCE Threads package is designed to create and switch threads quickly. The performance of a platform's implementation of DCE Threads, or its native threads package, will affect RPC performance.

Initial Call Overhead and Call Distribution

There is some initial overhead when a client makes its first remote call to a server. This overhead is greater for the `ncacn_ip_tcp` protocol, which has to set up a connection, than for the `ncadg_ip_udp` protocol. The initial call overhead is amortized over all of the calls made by the client to the server, so the impact of the overhead is less if many calls are made. If only a small number of calls are made between a client and a server, the dg protocol may perform better than the cn protocol.

Size of Parameter Data

The amount of data in in and out parameters in a remote call affects the call time and transfer rate. In fact, the transfer rate of a call can be defined as the amount of data divided by the call time. Obviously, more data requires more time for marshaling, unmarshaling, sending, and receiving the data over the network. On a network with sufficient bandwidth, the RPC transmission rate generally increases as the amount of data per remote call increases. This is because the RPC Runtime can make more efficient use of the network's transmission capacity.

Complexity of Parameter Data and Data Conversion

The amount of work done by the client and server stubs in marshaling and unmarshaling in and out parameters depends on the complexity of the parameters. For example, marshaling arrays and structures with pointers takes more time than marshaling simple integers. Also, if the client and server systems have different data representations, there will be additional overhead for data conversion on the receiving system.

Computation Time for Remote Procedures

Each remote procedure requires time to execute. The computation time for a procedure is of course application dependent. It may be small or it may dwarf the other overhead of the remote call.

Concurrent Server Load

When a server executes more than one remote call concurrently, each call will run slower than if it had exclusive use of the server. Concurrency itself introduces overhead in thread context switching and thread mutex locking and unlocking. The server should be sized to handle the expected peak call load.

RPC Performance Data

This section gives you an example of actual RPC performance. The data cited here was obtained with the **perf_client** and **perf_server** programs, included in the sample programs for this book. The client executes and times a series of remote calls against the server. Each call transmits an in, out, or in/out buffer of character, integer, or floating- point data. The client measures the call time and transfer rate for each measured call. The client and server also measure the time it takes to set up for RPC. These measurements will be discussed in future chapters. These measurements are raw data and have not been subjected to statistical analysis. They should be considered as samples of RPC performance and not as a definite benchmark.

The **perf_client** was run on an HP9000/730 workstation and the **perf_server** was run on an HP9000/826 server. Use of the ncadg_ip_udp and ncacn_ip_tcp protocols was measured. No other applications were running on the test systems, and network traffic was minimal. Table 2.4 provides further information on the test systems.

Table 2.4

Performance Test Systems

	Client	Server
Model	HP9000/730	HP9000/826
Processor	66 MHz PA-RISC	80 MHz PA-RISC
Memory	64 Mbytes	128 Mbytes
Operating System	HP-UX 9.05	HP-UX 9.04
DCE Version	HP DCE/9000 1.4	HP DCE/9000 1.4
Network	10 Mbit/sec IEEE 802.3 LAN	

Table 2.5 shows RPC performance measurements for null calls and for character in/out calls, averaged over 100 calls. Note that, while the ncacn_ip_tcp protocol has a longer initial call time, it performs slightly better than the ncadg_ip_udp protocol for subsequent calls. Figure 2.24 provides a graphical comparison of the call times and transmission rates for the two RPC protocols.

Table 2.5

RPC Performance Over a Local Area Network

		ncadg_ip_udp		ncacn_ip_tcp	
Call	Bytes	CallTime (millisec)	TransRate (kbyte/sec)	CallTime (millisec)	TransRate (kbyte/sec)
Initial null		8.71		43.51	
Null		2.17		1.78	
Char in/out	10	2.70	7.41	2.36	8.46
	100	2.90	69.03	2.38	83.91
	1000	4.50	444.14	4.09	488.79
	10000	25.78	775.65	21.01	952.08

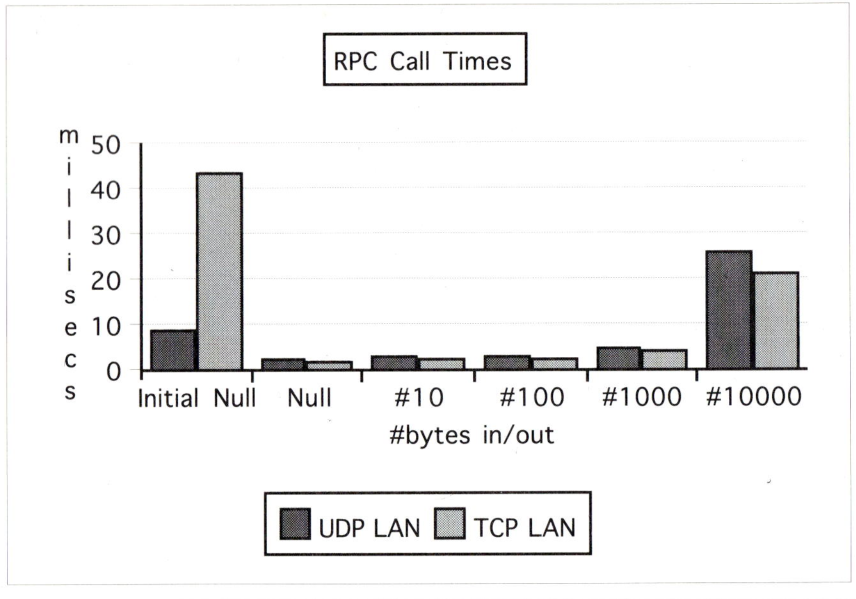

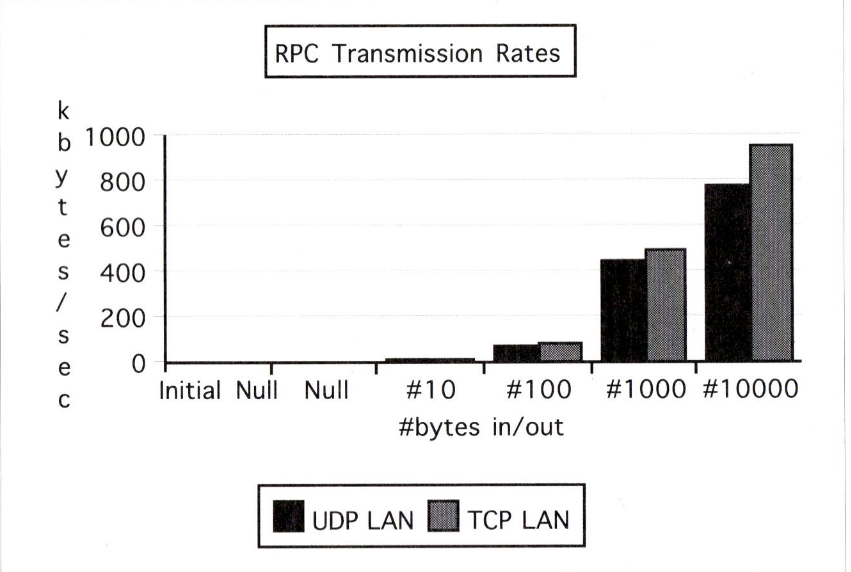

Figure 2.24
RPC Call Times and Transmission Rates

CHAPTER 3

Interface Definition

An *interface* is a collection of related procedures that a server can execute on behalf of its clients. The interface is a basic organizational unit of DCE RPC. Interfaces are described using the DCE *Interface Definition Language (IDL)*. Each interface used by a client or server is defined by one or more IDL files. These IDL files are processed by the DCE *IDL compiler* to produce client and server stubs for the remote procedures in the interface. Fluency in IDL is one of the major skills you will need to learn to develop DCE-based applications. This chapter introduces you to the IDL language and compiler.

The DCE Interface Definition Language and its IDL compiler were derived from the NCS Network Interface Definition Language (NIDL) and the NCS NIDL compiler. DCE IDL includes some features (labeled `v1` features) that provide backwards-compatibility with NCS NIDL. There is also a DCE tool, **`nidl_to_idl`**, which converts NIDL files to IDL files.

3.1 A Simple Interface Definition

To start our discussion of interfaces and IDL, let's look at two simple IDL files for the `room` interface that was introduced in Chapter 2. The first file `sch.idl`, shown in Code Sample 3.1, defines data types and constants used in the interface. The second file `room.idl`, shown in Code Sample 3.2, defines the actual interface.

```
interface sch
{
typedef char sch_loc_name_t [10];
typedef char sch_room_desc_t[30];
typedef char sch_room_name_t[20];

typedef long int sch_status_t;

typedef struct {
   sch_loc_name_t  loc;
   sch_room_name_t name;
   sch_room_desc_t desc;
   long int        max_people;
} sch_room_t;

const sch_status_t sch_status_ok             = 0;
const sch_status_t sch_status_room_not_found = 1;
}
```

Code Sample 3.1
`schedule/sch.idl`: Definition of data types and constants for the `room` interface.

```
[uuid(6101efd0-89fc-11cd-be27-080009307c01),
version(0.0)]
interface room
{
import "sch.idl";

[idempotent] void room_description(
   [in ] handle_t        h,
   [in ] sch_room_name_t room_name,
   [out] sch_room_t     *room,
   [out] sch_status_t   *status);
}
```

Code Sample 3.2
`schedule/room.idl`: Definition of the `room` interface (Version 1.0).

Interface Attributes

Let's look at `room.idl` first. The first three lines define general attributes of the interface. The general syntax for the IDL file is

```
[interface_attributes] interface interface_name
{
   idl_body
}
```

Interface UUID

The first line assigns a UUID (short for *Universal Unique IDentifier*) to the `room` interface. This UUID will be used to identity the interface throughout DCE. What UUIDs are, and where they come from, will be covered in more detail in Section 3.3. The UUID assigned to the room interface is `6101efd0-89fc-11cd-be27-080009307c01`.

Interface Version

The second line of `room.idl` specifies a version number of `0.0` for the `room` interface. A server can support multiple versions of the same interface. The version number is used to distinguish the version and so appears in a number of places. An interface version number is of the form *`major_version.minor_version`*. There are rules determining when the major and minor versions must be changed. In general, any change that is backwards-compatible with the previous version requires the increment of the minor version number. An example would be adding a new procedure at the end of the IDL file. Any change that is not backwards-compatible with the previous version requires the major version number be incremented. An example would be changing the signature of an existing procedure in the interface. The version number of the `room` interface will be changed as the interface is augmented in this book.

Interface Name

The interface name is used to construct various data elements created for the interface by the IDL compiler. To keep things consistent, the interface name and the IDL file name (minus the `.idl` suffix) should be the same, as in our example: `interface room` in `room.idl`. But note that this convention is not mandatory. Another useful but not mandatory convention that will be followed in this book is to prefix each interface operation name with the interface name, for example, `room_description()`.

Data Definition

The file `sch.idl` defines data types and constants used by the `room` interface. No interface attributes (no UUID nor version) need be defined in this kind of IDL file. The `import` statement in `room.idl` makes these definitions available for use within the `room` interface.

Typedefs

Data types are defined in IDL using `typedef` statements very similar to those in C. For instance, the statement

```
typedef char sch_loc_name_t[10];
```

defines a type `sch_loc_name_t` that is an array of 10 characters. Other types defined in `sch.idl` include `sch_status_t`, a long integer, and `sch_room_t`, a structure of four fields. (Note that we are following the usual C convention of adding the suffix `_t` to defined types.) Like C defined types, these types can be used in the definition of other types and as the parameter types for procedures.

Constants

Constants are defined in IDL using the `const` statement, with the syntax

```
const type name = value;
```

Each constant must have both a value and a type, which is used if the constant is marshaled. This differs from the usual C method of defining constants as preprocessor symbols using the `#define` statement. Constants defined in IDL are available for use in client and server programs. They are useful for defining values that will be passed between clients and servers. For the `room` interface, constants are defined for the `status` parameter passed back to the client from the server.

Operation Definition

Each remote procedure defined in an IDL file is called an *operation*. An operation definition looks very much like an ANSI C function prototype, with additional information required by DCE RPC. The general syntax of an operation definition is

```
[operation_attributes] return_type operation_name(
  [parm_attributes_1] parm_type_1 parm_name_1,
  [parm_attributes_2] parm_type_2 parm_name_2,
  . . .
  [parm_attributes_n] parm_type_n parm_name_n);
```

Operation Attributes

Operation attributes provide information to RPC about the semantics of the operation—that is, how the operation behaves. RPC can use this information to optimize the way it executes remote calls for the operation. In `room.idl`, the `room_description()` operation has one attribute, `idempotent`. This declares that the operation execution can be repeated without ill effect and that the idempotent version of the RPC datagram protocol can be used (see the RPC Protocol section in Chapter 2 for more information). Other possible operation attributes are `maybe` and `broadcast` (also described in the RPC Protocol section).

Return Type

The return type of the operation is either an IDL data type or a data type defined within the IDL file (and its imports). Any value returned by the operation must be of this type. Since `room_description()` does not have a return value, its return type is `void`.

Operation Name

The operation name defines the remote procedure name used in calls by clients of the interface. The remote procedure definition in the server may also use the operation name. (But not always: With the object type manager feature of RPC, the server's manager name may be different than its corresponding operation name. An example of this will be given in Chapter 8.)

Within RPC, an operation is identified not by its operation name, but by the order in which it is declared in the IDL file. In true computer fashion, the first operation is numbered 0, the second 1, and so on. An operation is fully identified by the combination of interface UUID, interface version, and operation number. The `room_description()` operation is identified by

```
6101efd0-89fc-11cd-be27-080009307c01,0.0,0
```

Parameters

Each parameter of an operation has attributes, a type, and a name. The attributes provide information needed by RPC to correctly marshal and unmarshal the parameter data. The most common parameter attributes are `in`, for an input parameter, and `out`, for an output parameter. A parameter used for both input and output has both of these attributes. The parameter type is an IDL data type or a type defined in the IDL file (and its imports). The parameter type and name follow the same syntax as in ANSI C function prototypes. An example from the `room_description()` operation is

```
[in] sch_room_name_t room_name,
```

which defines an input parameter `room_name` of the defined type `sch_room_name_t`.

3.2 IDL Compilation

Now that we have an interface definition, we need to process it with the IDL compiler. This will produce an interface header file and the client and server stubs for the interface that are needed to complete the client and server programs.

Compilation Steps

The IDL compiler is invoked by the **idl** command, with the syntax

idl *idl_options IF*.idl

where

- *idl_options* are zero or more options for the IDL compiler, and
- *IF*.idl is the IDL file for an interface.

The steps in the IDL compilation are diagrammed in Figure 3.1 and described below.

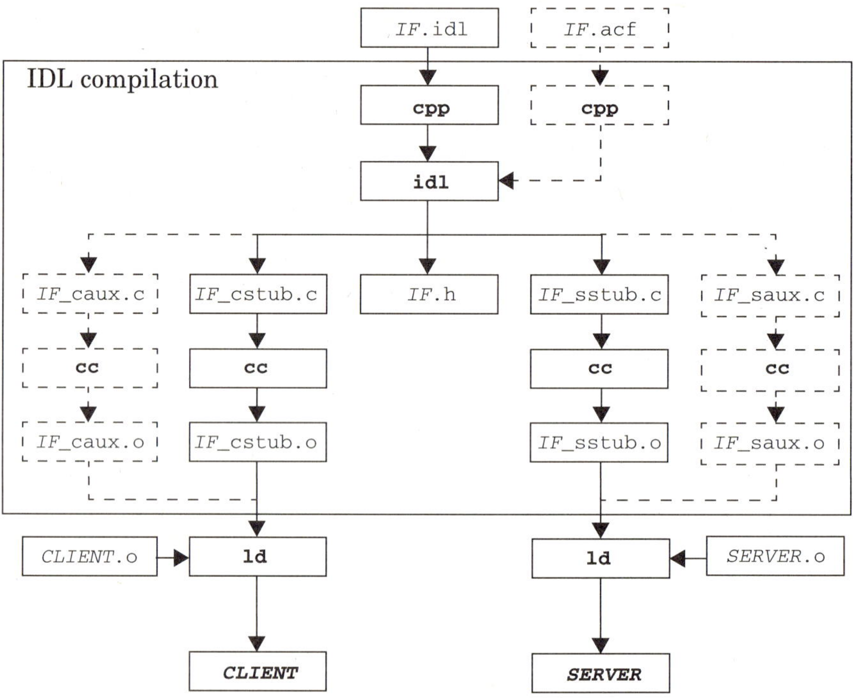

Figure 3.1
Compilation of IDL File and Stubs for an interface *IF*.

Note that if the client and server programs are on different platforms, the IDL compiler must be run on each platform to produce suitable stubs for each program.

Preprocessing of IDL File

The first action performed by the IDL compiler is to run the interface's IDL file through the C Preprocessor **cpp**. This allows the IDL file to contain the following C-style constructs:

- `/* ... */` comments
- `#include` files
- `#define` macro definitions
- `#ifdef ... #else ... #endif` conditional compilation

IDL options that affect preprocessing are

• **-no_cpp**	suppresses preprocessor phase
• **-I***directory*	directory to search for include files
• **-cpp_cmd** *'command'*	command to use instead of **cpp**
• **-cpp_opt** *'options'*	options to pass to **cpp**
• **-D***name[=definition]*	defines symbol with optional definition
• **-U***name*	undefines symbol

If the interface has an ACF file (see Section 3.5), the ACF file will also be run through the C Preprocessor

Compilation of IDL File

The next step in the IDL compilation is the processing of the IDL file (and ACF file, if it is present) by the IDL compiler itself. The IDL compiler parses the IDL statements, checking for correct syntax. As output, the IDL compiler produces three (or more) files of C source. These files are described in more detail below. IDL options that affect the IDL compilation phase are

• **-client** *file_type*	determines client files to generate
• **-server** *file_type*	determines server files to generate *file_type* is **none**, **stub**, **aux**, or **all**
• **-cstub** *file_name*	file name to use for client stub file(s)
• **-sstub** *file_name*	file name to use for server stub file(s)
• **-caux** *file_name*	file name to use for client aux file(s)
• **-saux** *file_name*	file name to use for server aux file(s)
• **-header** *file_name*	file name to use for header *file_name* omits any file extension
• **-out** *directory*	directory to put generated files
• **-I***directory*	directory to search for imported files
• **-no_def_idir**	search only current directory
• **-no_mepv**	suppress generation of manager EPV
• **-cepv**	generate client EPV
• **-syntax_only**	checks syntax only; suppresses stubs
• **-keep** *file_type*	specifies generated files to retain *file_type* is **none**, **c_source**, **object**, or **all**.
• **-v**	verbose compiler operation

Compilation of Stub Files

The final step of the IDL compilation is the C compilation of the stub (and possible auxiliary) files generated by the IDL compiler. The IDL compiler does this automatically by executing the C compiler. The result of this step is stub object files (and possibly auxiliary object files) that can be linked into the client and server programs. IDL options that affect the C compilation phase are

- **-cc_cmd** *'command'* command to use instead of **cc**
- **-cc_opt** *'options'* options to pass to **cc**
- **-keep c_source** suppresses production of object files

Interface Header File

The interface header file generated by **idl** contains information that is used by clients and servers of the interface in various DCE calls. Each client using the interface and each server providing the interface will include the interface header file. The interface header file is named *IF*.h, where *IF* is the interface name derived from the name of IDL file, *IF*.idl. (Note that this interface name may not necessarily be the same as the interface name defined *within* the IDL file by the interface statement. If at all possible, you should strive to keep these two interface names the same to avoid confusion.) For the room interface, the interface header file is room.h.

Included Files

The interface header file brings in, through C #include statements, the data types, constants, and function prototypes defined in a set of RPC header files installed in /usr/include/dce on HP-UX. A client or server that includes an interface header file also includes the RPC header files needed to call RPC-related DCE procedures. The included RPC header files are

- idlbase.h defines basic data types used by IDL
- rpc.h defines RPC functions and includes other RPC files

(Actually, the rpc.h file is itself an interface header file derived by **idl** from rpc.idl. If you are curious about what is in this file, you should look at the original.idl files, also in /usr/include/dce. It is easier to read.)

If the interface's IDL file imports any .idl files, its interface header file will include the corresponding .h files. (This implies that any imported .idl files must have been previously processed by **idl** to generate the necessary .h files.) Then any definitions from the imported IDL files will be available to the client and server that include the interface header file. Since room.idl imports sch.idl, room.h will include sch.h (and **idl sch.idl** must be executed before **idl room.idl**). So any program that includes room.h will be able to use the sch_ types and constants defined originally in sch.idl.

Data Types and Constants

Any data types and constants defined in an IDL file will be translated into their equivalent C definitions in the interface header file. For example, the IDL definition for the sch_room_t struct shown in Code Sample 3.3 becomes the C typedef in Code Sample 3.4.

```
typedef struct {
    sch_loc_name_t  loc;
    sch_room_name_t name;
    sch_room_desc_t desc;
    long int        max_people;
} sch_room_t;
```

Code Sample 3.3
schedule/sch.idl: sch_room_t definition

```
typedef struct  {
sch_loc_name_t loc;
sch_room_name_t name;
sch_room_desc_t desc;
idl_long_int max_people;
} sch_room_t;
```

Code Sample 3.4
schedule/sch.h: sch_room_t typedef

Note that the long int type becomes idl_long_int. This mapping will be explained in more detail in the Basic Data Types section.

Constant definitions in an .idl file are translated into #defines in the .h file. The statement

```
const sch_status_t sch_status_ok = 0;
```

in sch.idl becomes

```
#define sch_status_ok (0)
```

in sch.h.

Operation Prototypes

For each operation defined in an IDL file, the interface header file contains a function prototype that defines the operation's signature—the number and types of parameters it uses. These prototypes enable an ANSI C compiler to check that clients and servers for the interface use the correct signatures for remote procedures and their calls. Code Sample 3.5 shows a function prototype from the room.h header file.

```
extern void room_description(
#ifdef IDL_PROTOTYPES
    /* [in] */ handle_t h,
    /* [in] */ sch_room_name_t room_name,
    /* [out] */ sch_room_t *room,
    /* [out] */ sch_status_t *status
#endif
);
```

Code Sample 3.5
schedule/room.h: room_description() prototype

The IDL_PROTOTYPES symbol is defined (in idlbase.h) if the basic C compiler on a system can handle ANSI C function prototypes. If IDL_PROTOTYPES is not defined, the function prototype does not include the parameter information.

Operation Entry Point Vector Type

An *entry point vector* (EPV) is an array of pointers to procedures. EPVs are used in a number of situations in DCE RPC. An example is the manager EPV that is defined in the server stub file (which will be discussed in a bit). The header file for an interface contains a type definition for an EPV for the operations in the interface. This type definition is used in clients and servers when EPVs for the interface are set up. There is one entry point for each operation in the interface. The naming convention for the EPV type is

*INTERFACE*_v*MAJOR*_*MINOR*_epv_t

where *INTERFACE* is the interface name defined by the interface statement in the IDL file, and *MAJOR* and *MINOR* are the major and minor version numbers defined by the version attribute. Including the version in a defined element is a standard tactic in DCE RPC. This allows more than one version of an interface to be included in a client or server. For version 0.0 of the room interface, the EPV type defined is room_v0_0_epv_t and is defined as shown in Code Sample 3.6. There is one entry, for the room_description() operation, with parameters as specified in a function prototype.

```
typedef struct room_v0_0_epv_t {
void (*room_description)(
#ifdef IDL_PROTOTYPES
    /* [in] */ handle_t h,
    /* [in] */ sch_room_name_t room_name,
    /* [out] */ sch_room_t *room,
    /* [out] */ sch_status_t *status
#endif
);
} room_v0_0_epv_t;
```

Code Sample 3.6
`schedule/room.h: room` EPV definition

Client Stub File

The client stub file generated by **idl** contains the stub procedures that the client calls to initiate remote calls to operations in the interface. The client stub object file must be linked with each client that uses the interface. The client stub source file is named *IF*_cstub.c, and the client stub object file is named *IF*_cstub.o, where *IF* is the interface name derived from the name of IDL file, *IF*.idl. For the room interface, the client stub source file is room_cstub.c and the client stub object file is room_cstub.o.

Included Files

The client stub source file includes the interface header file, so it has access to all of the standard RPC header file definitions and definitions specific to the interface, such as the interface EPV type. For pre-DCE 1.1 products, the client stub also includes the standard file stubbase.h, which brings in data types, constants, and macros that are used in the generated stub code. This file contains the macros used for marshaling and unmarshaling data, tailored by ifdefs to the platform on which the client will be compiled. For DCE 1.1 and later, the client stub includes idldefs.h, which defines things needed with interpretive marshaling.

Client Interface Specification

An *interface specification* is a data structure that contains information about an interface. The data type rpc_if_rep_t (defined in stubbase.h or idldefs.h) defines these fields for an interface specification:

- interface specification version
- number of operations in the interface
- interface version
- interface UUID

- stub routine version number
- well-known endpoint vector
- presentation syntax vector (currently always the NDR syntax)
- server EPV (not used for a client)
- manager EPV (not used for a client)

A client interface specification is a global variable defined in the client stub and initialized with the appropriate interface information. It is named

`INTERFACE_vMAJOR_MINOR_c_ifspec`

where *INTERFACE* is the interface name and *MAJOR* and *MINOR* are the version numbers defined in the IDL file. The client interface specification is used when a client binds to a server providing the interface, as discussed in Chapter 4. For the `room` interface, it is `room_v0_0_c_ifspec`.

Data Structures for Interpretive Marshaling (DCE 1.1)

In DCE 1.1, the client stub also includes some large data structures, `IDL_offset_vec[]` and `IDL_rtn_vec[]`, that encode information about parameters and types for the interpretive marshaling code (discussed next).

Client Stub Procedures

For each operation in the interface, there will be one client stub procedure in the client stub file. These procedures are invoked when the client makes remote calls to operations in the interface. They handle the marshaling and unmarshaling of parameter values and the interface to the RPC Runtime, as described in Chapter 2. Each client stub procedure normally has the same name and signature as its corresponding operation.

The client and server stub procedure code generated by **idl** is not intended for easy comprehension. Prior to DCE 1.1, the stub routines contained massive amounts of inline marshaling code, in the form of macros that marshaled each data item. Even the client stub for the simple `room_description()` operation was over 300 lines long! DCE 1.1 introduced *interpretive marshaling,* which uses library routines and a description of the parameters instead of the inline code. This shrinks the stub routines considerably. The DCE 1.1 `room_description()` client stub is about 80 lines long.

Since the stub procedures are generally incomprehensible, modification of the stub procedure source after it is generated by **idl** is dangerous.

Client Entry Point Vector

Normally, the client stub procedures can be invoked directly from the client using the operation names. However, if the **-cepv** IDL option is used, **idl** will generate a client entry point vector with pointers to the client stub procedures. Each client stub procedure will be named `opi_csr()`, where *i* is the operation number defined by the ordinal position of the operation in the IDL file. The client entry point vector will be defined using the operation entry point type from the interface header file and initialized to the client stub entry pointers. The client EPV for version 0.0 of the `room` interface is shown in Code Sample 3.7.

```
room_v0_0_epv_t room_v0_0_c_epv = {
    op0_csr
};
```

Code Sample 3.7
`schedule/room.h: room` client EPV definition

The client stub procedure for `room_description()` can be invoked through the client EPV, as illustrated in Code Sample 3.8.

```
room_v0_0_c_epv.room_description(
    h, (unsigned_char_p_t) argv[1], &room, &st);
```

Code Sample 3.8
Calling `room_description()` through the client EPV

By selecting the `room_description` field of `room_v0_0_c_epv`, this calls the `op0_csr()` stub procedure. Also, the `room_v0_0_epv_t` type is used to check for the correct parameter types in the call. While this may seem an unnecessarily complicated way of calling a procedure, there are occasionally situations where this is useful (see Code Sample 6.16).

Server Stub File

The server stub file generated by **idl** contains the stub procedures that the server calls to execute remote procedure calls for clients. The server stub object file must be linked with each server that provides the interface. The server stub source file is named `IF_sstub.c`, and the server stub object file is named `IF_sstub.o`, where `IF` is the interface name derived from the name of IDL file, `IF.idl`. For the `room` interface, the server stub source file is `room_sstub.c` and the server stub object file is `room_sstub.o`.

Included Files

The server stub source file includes the same files as does the client stub source: the interface header file and the standard file `stubbase.h`. or `idlddefs.h`. Like the client stub, it uses the marshaling and interface information defined in these files.

Data Structures for Interpretive Marshaling (DCE 1.1)

Like their client counterparts, server stubs generated by DCE 1.1 include data structures for interpretive marshaling.

Server Stub Procedures

For each operation in the interface, there will be one server stub procedure in the server stub file. These procedures are invoked when the server receives remote calls for operations in the interface. They handle the marshaling and unmarshaling of parameter values and the interface between the RPC Runtime and the actual remote procedure, as described in Chapter 2.

The server stub procedures are named `opi_ssr()`, where *i* is the corresponding operation number from the IDL file. Every server stub procedure has the same fixed signature, which enables the RPC Runtime in the server to call the server stubs without knowledge of the operation parameters. The server stubs call the actual remote procedures (known as *managers*) using the manager EPV discussed next.

Like the client stub procedures, the pre-DCE 1.1 server stub procedures include massive amounts of inline marshaling code. The DCE 1.0 version of the server stub procedure for the simple `room_description()` operation is almost 300 lines long. DCE 1.1 server stub procedures use the interpretive marshaling calls, so they are considerably shorter in length. The DCE 1.1 version of the server stub for `room_description()` is around 115 lines long.

Server Interface Specification

The server interface specification, defined at the end of the server stub, is very similar to the client interface specification. It provides information about the interface (UUID, version, and so on), plus the server and manager EPVs, described below. The name of the server entry point is

`INTERFACE``_v`*`MAJOR`*`_`*`MINOR`*`_s_ifspec`

where *`INTERFACE`* is the interface name and *`MAJOR`* and *`MINOR`* are the version numbers defined in the IDL file. The server interface specification is used when the server declares that it will provide the interface (also called *registering* or *exporting* the interface). This will be covered in Chapter 4. Information about the interface is stored in the server's RPC Runtime for future use. For version `0.0` of the `room` interface, the server interface specification is `room_v0_0_s_ifspec`.

Server Entry Point Vector

The server entry point vector (EPV) is the link between the server's RPC Runtime and the interface's server stub procedures, as illustrated in Figure 3.2. It is declared at the end of the server stub, after the stub procedures have been defined. It uses a fixed EPV type and includes the `opi_ssr()` procedure names. The server EPV in the DCE 1.1 version of `room_sstub.c` is shown in Code Sample 3.9.

```
static rpc_v2_server_stub_proc_t IDL_epva[] =
{
(rpc_v2_server_stub_proc_t)op0_ssr
};
```

Code Sample 3.9
`schedule/room_sstub.c`: `room` server EPV

The same data structure prior to DCE 1.1 is named `NIDL_epva`, where the `NIDL_` prefix in the EPV was a legacy of the NCS NIDL compiler.

Manager Entry Point Vector

The manager entry point vector (EPV) is the link between the server stub procedures and the actual procedures (the managers) to be executed. This is also shown in Figure 3.2. At the end of the server stub there is usually a definition for the default manager EPV, using the operation entry point vector type and the names of the operation as the managers. The default manager EPV in `room_sstub.c` is shown in Code Sample 3.10.

```
static room_v0_0_epv_t IDL_manager_epv = {
room_description
};
```

Code Sample 3.10
`schedule/room_sstub.c: room` manager EPV

A pointer to the manager EPV is then stored in the server interface specification. Prior to DCE 1.1, this data structure is named `NIDL_manager_epv`. The server stubs call through the manager EPV to invoke the managers. Code Sample 3.11 shows the server stub `op0_ssr()` call to `room_description()`.

```
(*((room_v0_0_epv_t *)IDL_mgr_epv)->room_description)(h,
  room_name_,
  room_,
  status_);
```

Code Sample 3.11
`schedule/room_sstub.c:` Call to `room_description()` through the manager EPV

Again, this would seem to be an overly complicated way to make a procedure call. However, there are situations where this is necessary. With the RPC object type manager feature, there can be more than one set of manager routines for an interface. In this case there will be more than one manager EPV, and the server's RPC Runtime will decide which manager EPV to use when executing the remote procedure.

If the **`-no_mepv`** option of **`idl`** is used, no manager EPV will be defined in the server stub. The manager EPV field of the server interface specification will then be `NULL`, and the application developer must provide a manager EPV in the server source. This must be done if the manager routines have different names than their corresponding operations.

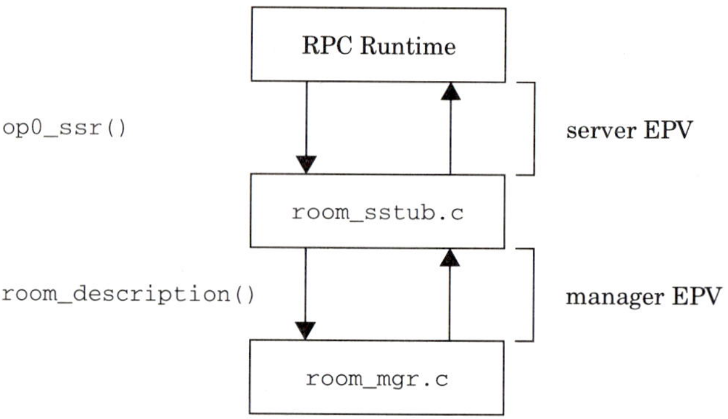

Figure 3.2
Relation between the Server and Manager EPVs

Auxiliary Files

In addition to the client and server stubs, the IDL compiler may generate auxiliary files to handle certain types of marshaling. The auxiliary files are named `IF_caux.c` and `IF_saux.c`, for the client and server sides of the marshaling. These auxiliary files contain routines that are called by the client and server stubs. Consequently the auxiliary object files (`IF_caux.o` and `IF_saux.o`) need to be linked into the client and server. It is easy to overlook this; your first clue about the existence of auxiliary files may be an unresolved external in a client or server linked without them. So when you use the more esoteric features of IDL, be on the lookout for auxiliary files. This book will try to point out which features cause auxiliary files to be generated. With the interpretive marshaling feature of DCE 1.1, auxiliary files are not used.

3.3 UUIDs

UUIDs (Universal Unique IDentifiers) are used to identify many things in DCE. Some of these are visible to application developers and users:

- interfaces
- principals and groups for security (Chapter 6)
- objects and object types (Chapter 8)
- ACL manager types (Chapter 9)

Other things assigned UUIDs are internal to DCE:

- activities (threads) identified by the RPC `dg` protocol (Chapter 2)
- presentation contexts used by the RPC `cn` protocol (Chapter 2)
- context handles (Chapter 3)

UUID Structure

UUIDs, when written in their conventional string notation, appear to be random 32-digit hexadecimal numbers. However random UUIDs may appear, they actually have an internal structure that guarantees that each of them is unique, not only on a local system but also on any system on any network, anytime. To accomplish this, the structure of a UUID encodes the time and place where it was created. Figure 3.3 shows the structure of the UUID.

```
6101efd0-89fc-11cd-be27-080009307c01
  low     mid V hi clock   node ID
```

Figure 3.3
UUID Structure

Version

The *version* field of the UUID (marked V in Figure 3.2) provides four bits to indicate the format of the DCE UUID. Currently there is only one version extant: version 1. There is another quasi-version field hidden in reserved bits of the clock sequence field. This field can distinguish between DCE UUIDs, and UUIDs for the Network Computing System (NCS) and for Microsoft RPC.

Time and Clock Sequence

The time of the creation of the UUID is encoded in four fields in the structure. The *low*, *mid*, and *hi* fields are the low 32 bits, middle 16 bits, and high 12 bits of a 60-bit integer counting the number of 100 nanosecond "clunks" since October 15, 1582 (the start of the Gregorian calender). The time is obtained from the system clock with adjustments to make it relative to the Gregorian starting date and time. It is possible that the system clock is not monotonic, that is, the clock may have been reset at some point so that it appears to have gone backwards. To take this into account, the UUID structure includes a *clock sequence* field that is incremented if the clock is not monotonic.

Node ID

The location where the UUID was created is in the *node ID* field, which contains the 802.3 or Ethernet address of the network interface card for the host system. If there is more than one network interface card, the address of the first card found by a platform-specific routine is used.

Nil UUID

There is a distinguished UUID called the *nil UUID* that is used in certain situations to indicate no interface or object is specified. The nil UUID is somewhat analogous to the `NULL` pointer in C. But unlike the `NULL` pointer, a nil UUID is an allocated variable set to a special value.

UUID Generation

Humans cannot effectively create UUIDs in the proper format, so DCE provides a command and some routines to create and manipulate UUIDs.

uuidgen

The **uuidgen** command will write a newly created UUID to `stdout`. The UUID will encode the current time when and the host node on which the command was executed. More than one UUID can be generated with the command **uuidgen -n** *number_of_uuids*. Since a UUID is commonly used in the IDL file for an interface, the **-i** option will generate a template for the IDL file, as shown in Output Sample 3.1. The output from this command can be directed into an IDL file, for example, **uuidgen -i > room.idl**.

```
:uuidgen -i
[
uuid(3bff08b0-8ec2-11cd-b8d0-080009307c01),
version(1.0)
]
interface INTERFACENAME
{

}
```

Output Sample 3.1
IDL File Template Generated by uuidgen.

With DCE 1.1, UUIDs can also be created by **dcecp**. The command is **dcecp -c uuid create.**

UUID Library Routines

The RPC Runtime library (which is part of the HP-UX DCE library `libdce.sl`) provides a number of routines for the creation and manipulation of UUIDS. These are documented in the *DCE Application Development Reference Manual* and in online reference pages.

- `uuid_create()` create a UUID
- `uuid_create_nil()` create a nil UUID
- `uuid_to_string()` convert a UUID to its string form
- `uuid_from_string()` convert a string to a UUID
- `uuid_equal()` determine if two UUIDs are equal
- `uuid_is_nil()` determine if a UUID is nil
- `uuid_compare()` lexically compare two UUIDs
- `uuid_hash()` compute a hash index from a UUID

3.4 IDL Data Types

In this section we will go into more detail on the data types available in IDL, starting with the basic data types and then moving on to constructed data types like arrays, strings, structures, and pointers.

Basic Data Types

Table 3.1 shows the basic data types that are defined in IDL for integer, floating point, character, and boolean data, plus some special data types used by IDL. IDL intends that each of these data types have the same size and value on all implementations of DCE (although the exact representation of the value may be different on different architectures).

Table 3.1

IDL Basic Data Types

IDL Data Type	Size (bits)	Macro Data Type	Default Target Types
small int	8	idl_small_int	signed char
short int	16	idl_short_int	short int
long int	32	idl_long_int	long int
hyper int	64	idl_hyper_int	struct {...}
unsigned small int	8	idl_usmall_int	unsigned char
unsigned short int	16	idl_ushort_int	unsigned short int
unsigned long int	32	idl_ulong_int	unsigned long int
unsigned hyper int	64	idl_uhyper_int	struct {...}
float	32	idl_short_float	float
doublc	61	idl_long_float	doublc
char	8	idl_char	unsigned char
boolean	8	idl_boolean	unsigned char
byte	8	idl_byte	unsigned char
void	N/A	idl_void_p_t	void * or char *
handle_t	N/A	handle_t	struct {...} *
error_status_t	32	error_status_t	unsigned long int

The *IDL data type* is the name used for the data type in IDL files. The *size* is the number of bits that values of the data type will occupy; all sizes are multiples of eight bits. When the IDL compiler generates code using an IDL data type, it uses the *macro data type*. For example, the sch_room_t structure defined in sch.idl contains a field

```
long int max_people;
```

In the sch.h file generated by **idl** this field becomes

```
idl_long_int max_people;
```

The macro data types are then defined (in idlbase.h) to map to the correct data types for the target platform. Using the default mapping (which is appropriate for PA-RISC systems and the HP ANSI C compiler), idl_long_int is defined as long int.

When you write procedure definitions for remote procedure managers, you should use the macro data type names for parameters to ensure that the correct data types are used on different platforms. Some compilers will issue warnings about type mismatches if the macro type names are not used in procedure definitions.

Integer

IDL provides eight integer types: signed (the default) and unsigned types in four sizes: small, short, long, and hyper. The first three sizes map directly into normal integer types for most C compilers. However, the hyper types need to be defined as structures for many platforms:

```
struct idl_uhyper_int_rep
   {idl_ulong_int  low; idl_ulong_int high;};
struct idl_hyper_int_rep
   {idl_ulong_int low; idl_long_int high;};
```

Data declared using the IDL integer types are subject to data type conversion by the data receiver. For integers, this is byte swapping between different sending and receiving representations.

Floating point

IDL defines two sizes of floating point numbers: float (32 bits) and double (64 bits). Data conversion is applied to floating point data if a sender and receiver have different floating point formats.

Character

The IDL char data type maps to the C type unsigned char. On many platforms (including PA-RISC), the char type defaults to signed char, and the C compiler will emit warnings when parameters of type idl_char (which is unsigned) are matched with data of the native char type (which is signed). These warnings can be suppressed by judicious use of type casting. Since all of the character string parameters to DCE calls are defined using unsigned characters, the cast to the type `unsigned_char_p_t` (pointer to `unsigned char`, defined within the RPC header files) must be used extensively. The first example of this was the remote procedure call in Code Sample 2.6, where the `argv[1]` value (of type `char *`) had to be cast to match the `idl_char` pointer required by the `sch_room_name_t` type generated by **idl**:

```
room_description(h, (unsigned_char_p_t) argv[1],
                 &room, &st);
```

Data declared using the IDL `char` type are subject to data type conversion between a sender and receiver with different character codes. As discussed in Chapter 2, the two character codes known to DCE are ASCII and EBCDIC.

Byte

The IDL `byte` data type also maps to `unsigned char`, but, unlike the other data types, is not subject to data conversion. If you wish to send raw data without conversion, you can use the `byte` type.

There are some types for multi-byte international character sets that are defined (in `nbase.idl`) using the basic `byte` type. Since `byte` is not subject to data conversion, the international character types will not be converted. Table 3.2 shows these types, their sizes, and definitions. DCE 1.1 provides additional facilities for international character sets. See the discussion on Character Sets in Section 3.5.

Table 3.2

International Character Types

Data Type	Size (bits)	Definition
`ISO_LATIN_1`	8	`typedef byte ISO_LATIN_1;`
`ISO_MULTI_LINGUAL`	16	`typedef struct{ byte row, col; } ISO_MULTI_LINGUAL;`
`ISO_UCS`	32	`typedef struct{ byte group, plane, row, column; } ISO_MULTI_LINGUAL;`

Boolean

The IDL `boolean` type is used for logical true and false values. IDL defines `true` as `1` and `false` as `0`.

Void

The IDL `void` type is used for untyped pointers. It is defined as `void *` for platforms with ANSI C compilers and `char *` otherwise.

Handle

Binding handles (discussed in Chapter 4) are used by a client to specify the server for a remote call. They are declared in IDL definitions using the special type `handle_t` and typically appear as the first parameter for an operation. This data type is a pointer to an opaque structure used by DCE RPC.

Error Status

The special type `error_status_t` is defined in `nbase.idl` for 32- bit unsigned integer status values returned by DCE. Error status codes may seem to be large random values, but they actually have an internal structure, with fields for a facility ID (bits 0-3), component ID (bits 4-23), and component status value (bits 24-31). For example, the error status for a communication failure (`rpc_s_comm_failure`) is determined by

```
facility = DCE =          1 x 0x10000000= 0x10000000 +
component= RPC =     0x6c9a x 0x00001000= 0x06c9a000 +
status value   =     0x0017 x 0x00000001= 0x00000017 =
                                          0x16c9a017 =
                                           382312470
```

An error status of zero is interpreted as success. There are several `error_status_t` constants defined to be zero, including `error_status_ok`, `rpc_s_ok`, and `uuid_s_ok`.

Each DCE component defines a number of status codes in header files in `/usr/include/dce` (on HP-UX). Status codes for RPC are defined in `rpcsts.h`. Each RPC status code constant is prefixed by `rpc_s_`.

The DCE routine `dce_error_inq_text()` maps an error status code to a character string with a (short) description of the error. Use of this routine will be illustrated in Chapter 4.

Arrays

An *array* is a sequence of *elements* of a specified data type. Each element is identified by an *index*. (At this point, we will be discussing only arrays of one dimension. Later we will discuss multidimensional arrays.) In IDL, array indices are integers and array elements are sequentially numbered, starting at 0. IDL array type declarations follow C syntax:

```
typedef element_type array_type_name[array_bounds];
```

where

- *`element_type`* specifies the IDL type for each array element,
- *`array_type_name`* defines the name of the array type, and
- *`array_bounds`* specifies the number of array elements and how they are indexed.

There are some variations on *array_bounds*.

- [0..*upper*]
  This variation specifies the first (0) and last (*upper*) indices of the array. The array is then numbered 0, 1, 2, ... *upper*, and the number of array elements is *upper*+1. [0..*upper*] is equivalent to [*upper*+1].
- [*size*]
  This case specifies that the number of array elements is *size*, and that the array is numbered 0, 1, 2, ... *size*-1. [*size*] is equivalent to [0..*size*-1].
- [0..*], [*] or []
  Here the size and upper bound of the array are unspecified. The array is then termed *open* and can be *conformant*, *varying*, or both, as discussed later. Further information must be provided in various array attributes for RPC to manage the array.

In a local procedure call, an array is passed as an address or pointer to the beginning of the array. (In fact, in C the array type *element_type name*[] is the same as the pointer type *element_type *name*.) The called procedure can then index off of the array address to access an array element.

Since the client and server do not share address spaces, array addresses cannot be passed between the client and server during a remote procedure call. Instead, the RPC stub code must marshal and unmarshal a copy of some or all of the contents of the array. IDL provides three classes of arrays—fixed, conformant, and varying—that determine how the RPC stub code marshals, transmits, and unmarshals an array.

Fixed Arrays

In the simplest class of arrays, sizes and upper bounds are fixed by their IDL definition. Fixed arrays use either the [0..*upper*] or [*size*] array bounds declarations, where *upper* or *size* are integer constants. An example is definition of the sch_room_name_t array type in sch.idl:

```
typedef char sch_room_name_t[20];
```

In the room_description() definition in room.idl, the room_name parameter, declared by

```
[in] sch_room_name_t room_name,
```

is an array of 20 characters. All of the elements of a fixed array are marshaled and unmarshaled. For room_name, all 20 characters will be transmitted between a client and a server, even if the room name is less than 20 characters long.

Conformant Arrays

When an array or array type is declared with an unspecified size and upper bound, the size and upper bound need to be determined at run time. Such an array is called *conformant*. IDL provides some array attributes that can be used to specify how the array's size or upper bound can be determined. These are

- `max_is(n)` upper bound is the value of *n*
- `size_is(n)` size is the value of *n*

At runtime, *n* must have an integer value that determines the upper bound or size of the array. If the array appears in an operation definition, *n* must be an input parameter of the operation. If the array appears in a structure (see Structures later), *n* must be a field in the structure. The `max_is` and `size_is` attributes are mutually exclusive; you will get an error if you specify both for the same array. The parameter can also be a pointer to an integer value; then the notation `*n` is used in the `max_is` or `size_is` attribute.

All of the elements of a conformant array are transmitted between a client and a server. The number of elements in the array is determined at runtime by the value of the *n* parameter or field.

Varying Arrays

Sometimes only part of an array needs to be transmitted between a client and a server. This class of array is called *varying*. Array attributes are used to specify what part of the array is to be transmitted. These are:

- `first_is(n)` lower bound to transmit is the value of *n*
- `last_is(n)` upper bound to transmit is the value of *n*
- `length_is(n)` transmit *n* elements, `0` through `n-1`

As with the `max_is` and `size_is` attributes, *n* is an integer input parameter or structure field. A pointer to an integer can be specified as `*n`. The bounds of a varying array can be specified using `first_is` or `last_is` or both, or the size of the varying array can be specified using `length_is`. But `length_is` cannot be used with either `first_is` or `last_is`; an IDL error will be reported.

Only the elements in a varying array between the first and last indices will be transmitted. Other elements of the array will be unaffected. They will retain their previous values, which might have been uninitialized.

An array can be both conformant and varying, with both the size and the transmitted elements determined at runtime. The following example will show a conformant varying array.

Array Example

An example from the `room` interface will help illustrate the different array concepts. The definition of a new operation, `room_avail()`, is given in Code Sample 3.12.

```
void room_avail(
  [in ] handle_t        h,
  [in ] sch_date_time_t date_time,
  [in ] long int        n_people,
  [in ] long int        n_pref_locs,
  [in,  size_is(n_pref_locs)]
        sch_loc_name_t  pref_locs[],
  [in ] long int        max_avail_rooms,
  [out] long int       *n_avail_rooms,
  [out, size_is(max_avail_rooms),
        length_is(*n_avail_rooms)]
        sch_room_t      avail_rooms[],
  [out] sch_status_t   *status);
```

Code Sample 3.12
`schedule/room.idl`: `room_avail()` operation using conformant and varying arrays

This operation returns a list of rooms that are available for a meeting at given date and time, ordered by preferred room locations. The input parameters for `room_avail()` are

- `h` the binding handle
- `date_time` the date and time to check for availability
- `n_people` the number of people attending the meeting
- `n_pref_locs` the number of preferred locations
- `pref_locs` an array listing the preferred locations
- `max_avail_rooms` the maximum acceptable available rooms

The output parameters are

- `n_avail_rooms` the actual number of available rooms
- `avail_rooms` an array listing the available rooms
- `status` the status of the operation

The `pref_locs` parameter is a conformant array. The `size_is` attribute of `pref_locs` specifies that the size of the array is supplied by the parameter `n_pref_locs`. The client must set `n_pref_locs` to the size of the array supplied for the `pref_locs` parameter.

The avail_rooms parameter is a conformant varying array. The size of the array is specified by the size_is attribute to be max_avail_rooms, and the part of the array returned from the server to the client is specified by the length_is attribute. This allows the client to supply an array that can hold max_avail_rooms, and for the server to return the actual n_avail_rooms. Note that, since n_avail_rooms is an output parameter, a pointer to a target integer variable (long int *n_avail_rooms) is passed. The length_is attribute then uses *n_avail_rooms to deference the pointer to get the integer value. It is important that the server always set n_avail_rooms to a valid value, since it is used to marshal the avail_rooms[] array. If there are no elements being returned, say, because an error was detected in the call, n_avail_rooms should still be set to 0. Otherwise, an invalid bounds exception may be raised.

Code Sample 3.13 shows an example of a room_avail() call. The client is requesting the available rooms for 10 people in locations 44L, 44M, and 43U on 94-06-30 between 10:00 and 11:00. The client is prepared to accept a maximum of 20 rooms returned in the avail_rooms array. The actual number of rooms is returned in n_avail_rooms. Figure 3.4 diagrams the marshaling and transmission of the array parameters in this example.

```
sch_loc_name_t pref_locs[3];
sch_room_t     avail_rooms[20];
idl_long_int   n_avail_rooms;
sch_status_t   st;
. . .
strcpy((char *)pref_locs[0], "44L");
strcpy((char *)pref_locs[1], "44M");
strcpy((char *)pref_locs[2], "43U");

room_avail(h,
    (idl_char *) "94-06-30 10:00-11:00",
    10,                  /* n_people        */
    3,                   /* n_pref_locs     */
    pref_locs,
    20,                  /* max_avail_rooms */
    &n_avail_rooms,
    avail_rooms,
    &st);
```

Code Sample 3.13
An example of a remote call using conformant and varying arrays.

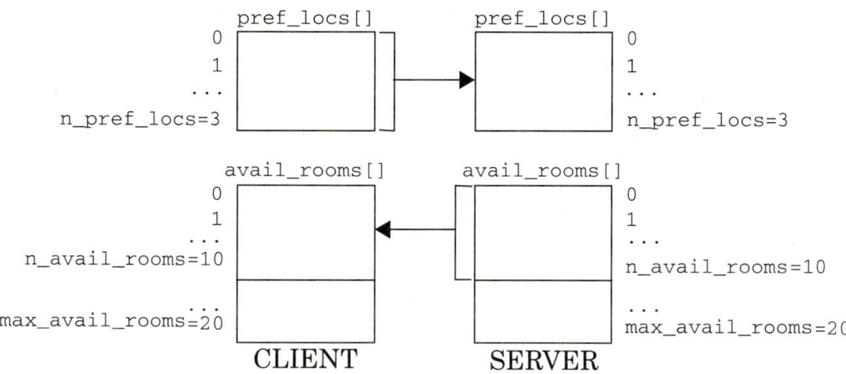

Figure 3.4
Marshaling and Transmission of Conformant and Varying Arrays

Multidimensional Arrays

The arrays that we have been discussing so far have all been one-dimensional; that is, they all have had one index. IDL also provides multidimensional arrays that have more than one index. The syntax for declaring a multidimensional array follows the C syntax

```
typedef element_type array_type_name[b1][b2]...[bn];
```

where

- *element_type* specifies the IDL type for each array element,
- *array_type_name* defines the name of the array type, and
- *b1, b2, ... bn* are the array bounds for dimensions 1, 2, ... n.

All of the array bounds can use the `[0..upper]` or `[size]` forms. But only the first array bound can be open, using the `[0..*]`, `[*]` or `[]` forms. A multidimensional array with an open first array bound can be conformant, varying, or both. Code Sample 3.14 shows a conformant two-dimensional array with an open first dimension (number of rows). Code Sample 3.15 is an invalid attempt to use a conformant two-dimensional array with an open second dimension (number of columns). The IDL compiler reports the error `Arrays can be conformant in the first dimension only` when Code Sample 3.15 is compiled.

```
[uuid(70040286-99f4-11cd-aa47-080009307c01)]
interface table
{
const long int n_cols = 10;

void table_op(
    [in ] handle_t h,
    [in ] long int n_rows,
    [in, size_is(n_rows)]
          long int table[][n_cols]);
}
```

Code Sample 3.14
A legal conformant two-dimensional array, with an open number of rows.

```
[uuid(4c7f9976-99f7-11cd-b64a-080009307c01)]
interface bad_table
{
const long int n_rows = 10;

void table_op(
    [in ] handle_t h,
    [in ] long int n_cols,
    [in, size_is(n_cols)]
          long int table[n_rows][]);
}
```

Code Sample 3.15
An illegal conformant two-dimensional array, with an open number of columns.

Structures

A *structure* consists of a sequence of *fields*. Each field can hold a value of a specified type. In C, a struct definition provides a list of field types and names. IDL uses the C struct definition, adding optional field attributes. The general syntax for a struct typedef is

```
typedef struct {
    [field_attributes_1] field_type_1 field_name_1;
    [field_attributes_2] field_type_2 field_name_2;
    . . .
    [field_attributes_n] field_type_n field_name_n;
} struct_type;
```

where

- *field_attributes* are zero or more attributes for the field,
- *field_type* is a basic or constructed IDL data type, and
- *field_name* is an alphanumeric identifier.

An example of an IDL structure is shown in Code Sample 3.16. This defines a structure type sch_room_t with four fields, named loc, name, desc, and max_people. The first three fields use types that are also defined in sch.idl. These types define fixed size arrays for character strings. The fourth field uses the basic IDL data type long int, a 32-bit signed integer.

```
typedef struct {
    sch_loc_name_t  loc;
    sch_room_name_t name;
    sch_room_desc_t desc;
    long int        max_people;
} sch_room_t;
```

Code Sample 3.16
schedule/sch.idl: sch_room_t structure definition

Field attributes are used when IDL requires more information about a field than just its type and name. Most simple fields do not need additional attributes. Fields containing arrays or pointers may require field attributes.

Open Arrays in Structures

An open array can appear only as the last field of a structure. Also, another field in the structure must provide the actual bound for the open dimension of the array. The array then has an appropriate attribute using the bound field. Note that the **n* form of the array bound cannot be used within a structure.

A common example of a structure with an open array is a *vector* type, which includes a count and the elements of a vector. This can be declared in IDL as shown in Code Sample 3.17. The C declaration for this type generated by **idl** includes an array of length 1, as in Code Sample 3.18.

```
typedef struct {
    long int n_elements;
    [size_is(n_elements)] long int element[];
} vector_t;
```

Code Sample 3.17
Example of a vector definition in IDL

```
typedef struct  {
idl_long_int n_elements;
idl_long_int element[1];
} vector_t;
```

Code Sample 3.18
Generated C type for a vector

To use the `vector_t` type, you must allocate a structure that is big enough to hold the number of elements you anticipate to be in the vector. Code Sample 3.19 illustrates this. A vector with 10 elements is allocated, where `sizeof(vector_t)` is the size of the `n_elements` field and the first element, and `(N-1)*(sizeof(idl_long_int))` is the size of the remaining elements.

```
#include "vector.h"
#define N 10

  vector_t *vector;
  long int  i;

  vector = (vector_t *) malloc(sizeof(vector_t) +
                      (N-1)*(sizeof(idl_long_int)));
  vector->n_elements = N;
  for (i = 0; i < N; i++)
  {
     vector->element[i] = i;
  }
```

Code Sample 3.19
Allocation and initialization of a vector structure.

Strings

In C, character strings are represented by a sequence of bytes terminated by a null (zero) byte. Commonly, character strings are stored in `char` arrays that are declared large enough for some maximum string length. In IDL, a character string can be declared using the `string` attribute. For example

```
typedef [string] char sch_name_t[20];
```

declares the type `sch_name_t` as a null terminated character string with a maximum length of 20 (*including* the null byte). When this type is used, as in the `sch_room_t` structure, 20 bytes will be allocated to hold the maximum string. However, only the bytes in the character string (before the null byte) will be marshaled and transmitted. If an array has the `string` attribute, it cannot have the `first_is`, `last_is`, or `length_is` attributes. The amount of data marshaled and transmitted in a string is determined solely by the null byte and the maximum string length (20, in the case of sch_name_t).

The v1_string attribute specifies that a character string is to be marshaled and transmitted using the string format used by NCS. It can be used for backwards-compatibility with NCS. It should not be used for DCE applications.

Enumerations

An *enumeration* is a sequence of identifiers assigned constant integer values. IDL enumerations follow the same syntax as C enumerations

```
enum {identifier0, identifier1, ... identifierN}
```

This is equivalent to

```
constant int identifier0 = 0;
constant int identifier1 = 1;
. . .
constant int identifierN = N;
```

In the sch.idl file, an enumeration could be used to define the sch_status_t type, as shown in Code Sample 3.20.

```
typedef enum {
    sch_status_ok,
    sch_status_loc_not_found,
    sch_status_room_not_found,
    sch_status_room_unavail,
    sch_status_bad_date_time
} sch_status_t,
```

Code Sample 3.20
sch.idl: sch_status_t enumeration type

The C code generated by **idl** for an enumeration is syntactically identical to the IDL enumeration.

Unions

Sometimes it is necessary for a variable, a field in a structure, or an element in an array to hold more than one type of data. This can be accomplished with a *union*. Let's suppose you have a field that can be an integer, a floating-point number, or a character string. Code Sample 3.21 shows how this field can be defined and used in C. The variables v1, v2, and v3 are allocated to hold the largest possible field in union_field_t (which is field_string). The actual type of the field is determined by the field selected when the variables are used.

```
typedef union {
  long int field_int;
  float field_float;
  char field_string[20];
} union_field_t;

union_field_t v1, v2, v3;

v1.field_int = 1;
v2.field_float = 1.5;
strcpy(v3.field_string, "Hi Mom!");
```

Code Sample 3.21
Example of a C Union

For IDL and DCE RPC, the C union definition is inadequate. For marshaling and data conversion, RPC must know the actual data type of a union value in cases when there are no selector fields, for example, when marshaling a union parameter. To solve this problem, IDL uses *discriminated unions*, which include an indication (the *discriminator*) of the actual data type of the union value. The discriminator must be set when the union value is initialized. The syntax for the IDL union looks like a cross between a `struct` and a `case` statement:

```
union switch (discriminator_type discriminator){
    case constant1: member_type_1 member_name_1;
    case constant2: member_type_2 member_name_2;
    ...
}
```

The discriminator can be an integer, character, boolean, or an enumerated value. Each constant must be a value of the discriminator type. The member types can be any basic type, fixed array (but not conformant or varying arrays) or structure not containing a conformant or varying array. Some IDL data type attributes, for example `string`, can precede appropriate member types.

The IDL compiler translates an IDL union to a C structure in the interface header file. This structure contains the discriminator and a C union equivalent to the IDL union.

```
struct {
    discriminator_type discriminator;
    union {
        member_type_1 member_name_1;
        member_type_2 member_name_2;
        ...
    } tagged_union;
}
```

Code Sample 3.22 shows the C union example from Code Sample 3.21 expressed as an IDL union, using an enumerated type for the discriminator type. Code Sample 3.23 shows how this union can be used.

```
typedef enum {
  field_is_int,
  field_is_float,
  field_is_string
} field_is_t;

typedef union switch(field_is_t field_is) {
  case field_is_int:    long int field_int;
  case field_is_float: float field_float;
  case field_is_string:[string]char field_string[20];
} union_field_t;
```

Code Sample 3.22
IDL Union Example: Definition of the union.

```
#include "union_example.h"
union_field_t v1, v2, v3;

v1.field_is = field_is_int;
v1.tagged_union.field_int = 1;

v2.field_is = field_is_float;
v2.tagged_union.field_float = 1.5;

v3.field_is = field_is_string;
strcpy(v3.tagged_union.field_string, "Hi mom!");
```

Code Sample 3.23
IDL Union Example: Usage of the union.

The discriminator (`field_is`) for each union variable is initialized to reflect the value stored in the variable. Because the IDL union is translated into a C structure in `union_example.h`, each union member must include the field `tagged_union`.

Pointers

A *pointer* is an address of a data item of a particular type. Pointers are declared, in both C and IDL, using the * notation. In C, pointers can be initialized to point to a data item using the & notation. *Dereferencing* is the action of following a pointer to the data item to which it points. In C, a pointer is deferenced using the * notation, or using -> for a pointer to a field in a structure. Code Sample 3.24 shows examples of pointer declaration and usage in C.

Pointers look innocuous, but they can require quite complex code for marshaling and unmarshaling. Remember that address spaces are not shared between a DCE RPC client and server. A pointer cannot just be passed between a client and a server; a pointer's value in one address space is meaningless in the other. The contents of the data item pointed to by a pointer must be marshaled (and possibly converted). IDL defines two classes of pointers: *reference* and *full*. (The DCE 1.1 IDL provides a third class: *unique*.) By choosing the appropriate pointer class, you can optimize the marshaling code for performance or flexibility.

```
typedef struct {
   long int field1;
   long int field2;
} struct_t;

struct_t s;
long int i;
struct_t *s_p;     /* pointer to a structure     */
long int *i_p;     /* pointer to an integer      */

s_p = &s;        /* initialize pointer to structure s      */
i_p = &i;        /* initialize pointer to integer i        */

s_p->field1 = 1; /* deference pointer to field 1 in
                    structure s                            */
s_p->field2 = 2; /* deference pointer to field 2 in
                    structure s                            */
*i_p = 3;        /* deference pointer to integer i         */
```

Code Sample 3.24
Examples of pointer declaration and usage in C.

Reference Pointers

Reference pointers are the simplest class of pointers provided by IDL. Pointers in parameters are by default reference or can be explicitly declared to be reference using the `ref` attribute. A reference pointer must follow these rules:

- It always points to allocated storage; it is never `NULL`.
- Its value cannot change during a remote procedure call. It must point to the same storage after a call as before.
- It cannot point to the same data as any other pointer used in the same remote procedure call; that is, a reference pointer cannot be an *alias* for any other pointer.

We have already seen reference pointers as output parameters. Consider the status parameter from the `room_description` operation defined in Code Sample 3.2.

```
[out] sch_status_t *status
```

Here status is a reference pointer. It must always point to allocated storage that will not change during the course of the room_description() call, namely, a variable of type sch_status_t that will receive the returned status value. There are no other pointer parameters in room_description() that could also point to the status variable.

Marshaling and unmarshaling of reference pointers is relatively simple. Since a reference pointer always points to allocated storage that does not change, the client and server stubs do not have to allocate new storage. Since aliasing is not allowed, the pointed-to data can be marshaled and unmarshaled in the same way as other input and output parameters.

Full Pointers

Reference pointers are too restrictive for many uses of pointers, such as building linked data structures. Consider a doubly linked list, where each list element has pointers to the previous and next elements in the list. (See Figure 3.5 for an illustration of a doubly linked list.) The next pointer of the final element needs to be NULL to indicate the end of the list, as does the previous pointer of the first element. Elements of the list typically are pointed to by two pointers—the previous pointer of the next element, and the next pointer of the previous element. These requirements conflict with the restrictions placed on reference pointers. Instead, full pointers must be used.

Full pointers are specified using the ptr attribute. Full pointers can also be declared the default pointer class by specifying pointer_default(ptr) in an interface header, as shown in Code Sample 3.25.

```
[uuid(bb6c96cc-a587-11cd-89ed-080009307c01),
 pointer_default(ptr), version(1.0)]
interface full_pointer_example
{
    . . .
}
```

Code Sample 3.25
Example of full pointer default in an IDL file.

Full pointers have these properties:

- A full pointer need not point to allocated storage; it can be NULL.
- A full pointer can change during the execution of a remote procedure call. It can be set to point to storage allocated during the call.
- Full pointers allow aliasing. Two or more full pointers can point to the same storage.

Marshaling and unmarshaling of full pointers can be quite complex. The client and server stubs may have to allocate new storage. If a full pointer points to a linked data structure, each element of the structure needs to be marshaled and the links between elements need to be represented. When the data structure is unmarshaled, new storage needs to be allocated for each element and the links need to be reconstituted. Prior to DCE 1.1, the IDL compiler creates auxiliary files (*IF*_caux.c and *IF*_saux.c) with marshaling and unmarshaling code for full pointers.

If a server allocates new storage for a full pointer, it must call the RPC routine rpc_ss_allocate(). This routine has the same purpose and calling signature as the C library malloc() call

```
idl_void_p_t rpc_ss_allocate(unsigned long size);
```

where *size* is the number of bytes to be allocated, and the return value is a pointer to the allocated storage. In addition to allocating the requested storage, rpc_ss_allocate() keeps track of the allocation. After the pointed-to data has been marshaled, the server stub will automatically deallocate the storage.

Unique Pointers (DCE 1.1)

Pointers declared to be unique fall between reference and full pointers. Like full pointers, they can be NULL and can point to data allocated in a remote call. But like reference pointers, they cannot point to any data that is pointed to by other pointers; that is, they cannot be aliased. Unique pointers requires less work for marshaling and unmarshaling than full pointers.

Pointer Example

Now let's look at an example in the room interface that uses reference and full pointers. The room_events() operation returns a doubly linked list of events for which a specified room has been reserved, between a beginning and ending time. Code Sample 3.26 shows the data types defined in sch.idl for the event list record and pointer. Code Sample 3.27 shows the definition of the room_events() operation in room.idl.

```
typedef struct SCH_EVENT_REC_T {
    [ptr] struct SCH_EVENT_REC_T *prev;
    [ptr] struct SCH_EVENT_REC_T *next;
    sch_event_t  event;
} sch_event_rec_t;

typedef [ptr] sch_event_rec_t *sch_event_rec_p_t;
```

Code Sample 3.26
schedule/sch.idl: Event list record and pointer types.

```
void room_events(
    [in ] handle_t              h,
    [in ] sch_room_t            room,
    [in ] sch_short_date_time_t begin_date_time,
    [in ] sch_short_date_time_t end_date_time,
    [out] sch_event_rec_p_t    *room_event_list,
    [out] sch_status_t         *status);
```

Code Sample 3.27
schedule/room.idl: room_events() operation.

Each list element is a structure of type sch_event_rec_t. The prev field is a pointer to the previous element and the next field is a pointer to the next element in the list. (The pointers must be declared using struct SCH_EVENT_REC_T * instead of sch_event_rec_t * because sch_event_rec_t is not yet defined within the structure declaration.) They are declared to be full pointers by the [ptr] attribute, so they can be NULL. Also, an element can be pointed to by both the prev pointer of its next element, and the next pointer of its previous element. The type sch_event_rec_p_t defines a pointer to an element of the list. Figure 3.5 illustrates how these records are linked.

When a pre-DCE 1.1 IDL compiler processes sch.idl, it produces two auxiliary files, sch_caux.c and sch_saux.c, containing routines to handle sch_event_rec_t records. They are called from room_cstub.c and room_sstub.c. The corresponding object files sch_caux.o and sch_saux.o that are also generated by IDL must be linked into the room client and server, respectively. Note that the DCE 1.1 IDL compiler does *not* produce these auxiliary files; it uses built-in interpretive marshaling routines instead.

In the room_events() operation, the list of events is passed back in the room_event_list parameter. This is by default a reference parameter. The caller must supply a variable to receive a pointer to the head of the event list. The event list pointer is itself a full pointer. It can be NULL, if there were no events for the room between the beginning and ending date and time, or it can point to the first element of an event list. Figure 3.5 shows an example of an event list.

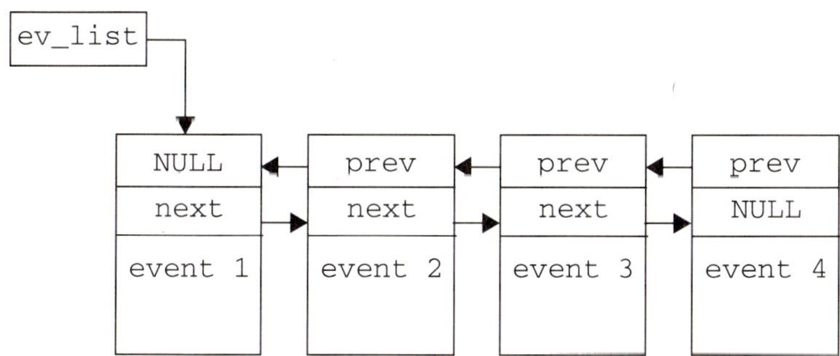

Figure 3.5
Event List Example

Code Sample 3.28 is an excerpt from room_mgr.c that shows how the room_events() operation is implemented. First, room_events() will locate the specified room and scan the list of events for the room until it finds the first event that is within the requested range. Then, for each event within the range, it will allocate and initialize a sch_event_rec_t element and link the element at the end of the room event list. It uses rpc_ss_allocate() to allocate the element. Note that, unlike malloc(), rpc_ss_allocate() does not return NULL if it cannot allocate memory. Instead, it raises the exception rpc_x_no_memory, which will be propagated back to the client.

```
#define LINK_NEW(new_p, prev_p, head) \
  if ((prev_p) != NULL) \
     (prev_p)->next = (new_p); \
  else \
     (head) = (new_p); \
  (new_p)->prev = (prev_p); \
  (new_p)->next = NULL;

void room_events(...)
{
  ...
  sch_event_rec_t *prev_ev_p;
  sch_event_rec_t *new_ev_p;

  *room_event_list = NULL;
  *status = sch_status_ok;

  /*
   * Find room, and scan room's event list for last
   * event earlier than beginning time.
   */
  prev_ev_p = NULL;
  for ( /* each event not later than end time */)
  {
     new_ev_p=rpc_ss_allocate(sizeof(sch_event_rec_t));
     LINK_NEW(new_ev_p, prev_ev_p, *room_event_list);
     memcpy(&(new_ev_p->event), &(/* event record */),
              sizeof(sch_event_t));
     prev_ev_p = new_ev_p;
  }
}
```

Code Sample 3.28
schedule/room_server.c: room_events() manager implementation.

The output parameter room_event_list is initialized to NULL, which will be returned if no events are found for the room within the requested time range. Otherwise, room_event_list is set to the head element of the list by the LINK_NEW macro.

When the room_events() manager returns, its server stub will marshal the event list pointed to by the room_event_list parameter. The data in each event record will be copied into the marshaling buffer, and the pointer relationships between the records will be recorded in the buffer. The marshaled data will then be sent back to the client in one or more response packets. Once all of the list elements have been marshaled, the server stub will deallocate the `sch_event_rec_t` records allocated by the manager.

Code Sample 3.29 is an excerpt from the `room` client that shows how `room_event()` can be called. The address of the variable `ev_list` (`&ev_list`) is passed as the `room_event_list` parameter. This points to storage allocated in the stack, so it is acceptable for a reference parameter. The server will execute the `room_events()` call and return the events list in response packets, as described earlier. The client stub for `room_events()` will unmarshal the list elements and allocate a `sch_events_rec_t` record for each element. It will also link the records together to reproduce the original `prev` and `next` links for the event list. However, the new pointers will be meaningful in the client address space. The `ev_list` pointer will be set to point to the first allocated record. After the call to `room_events()`, the client displays the event information in each record by following the `next` pointers. It also deallocates each record.

The client must be prepared to handle the case where the value returned to `ev_list` is `NULL`. This means that the server found no events for the room between the beginning and ending date and time.

```
sch_room_t             room;
sch_short_date_time_t  begin_date_time;
sch_short_date_time_t  end_date_time;
sch_event_rec_p_t      ev_list;
sch_status_t           status;
sch_event_rec_p_t      ev_p;
sch_event_rec_p_t      next_ev_p;

/* input values for room and date times */

room_events(h, room, begin_date_time, end_date_time,
            &ev_list, &status);
if (status == sch_status_ok)
{
    if (ev_list != NULL)
    {
      for (ev_p = ev_list;
            ev_p != NULL;
            ev_p = next_ev_p)
```

Code Sample 3.29
`schedule/room.c`: Use of `room_event()` operation and event list.

```
            {
                printf("%-20s %-20s %-20s\n",
                        ev_p->event.date_time,
                        ev_p->event.desc,
                        ev_p->event.reserver);
                next_ev_p = ev_p->next;
                free(ev_p);
            }
        }
        else
        {
            printf("No events in specified period.\n");
        }
    }
```

Code Sample 3.29 (continued)

Comparison of the Array and Pointer Examples

The array example, with the `room_avail()` operation, and the pointer example, with the `room_events()` operation, are two different solutions to the same problem: how to receive a variable amount of information from the server. The `room_avail()` operation could have been defined using a linked list, and the `room_events()` operation could have be defined using a varying array. There are some important differences between these two techniques:

- Maximum amount of data

  In the array example, the client controls the maximum amount of data that it will receive through the `size_is` attribute. In the pointer example, the amount of data that the server can pass back is limited only by the available memory on the client (and the server).

- Allocation and deallocation of storage

  In the array example, the storage to hold the returned data is automatically allocated as a local array and automatically deallocated when the calling procedure exits. In the pointer example, the storage is allocated by the client stub and must be deallocated by the client application code. If the client does not explicitly deallocate the storage when it is no longer needed, a *memory leak* would result that could affect later operation of the client.

- Marshaling complexity

  While marshaling of both arrays and pointers is complex, pointer marshaling is more involved and may add auxiliary files to the client and server.

Pointers and Strings

The string examples shown earlier used character arrays to hold the strings. It is also possible to use pointers to strings. Code Sample 3.30 shows how some of the data types in `sch.idl` could be defined using string pointers.

```
typedef [ptr, string] char *sch_loc_name_t;
typedef [ptr, string] char *sch_room_desc_t;
typedef [ptr, string] char *sch_room_name_t;

typedef struct {
   sch_loc_name_t    loc;
   sch_room_name_t   name;
   long int          max_people;
   sch_room_desc_t   desc;
} sch_room_t;
```

Code Sample 3.30
sch_ptr.idl: String pointer example

This makes the string fields in sch_room_t full pointers. They can point to a null-terminated character string of any length, or they can be NULL. The character strings must be allocated separately from the sch_room_t record. If the record is an output parameter in a remote procedure call, the strings must be allocated using rpc_ss_allocate() so they can be properly marshaled and deallocated by the server stub. Figure 3.6 shows an example of a sch_room_t record using string pointers.

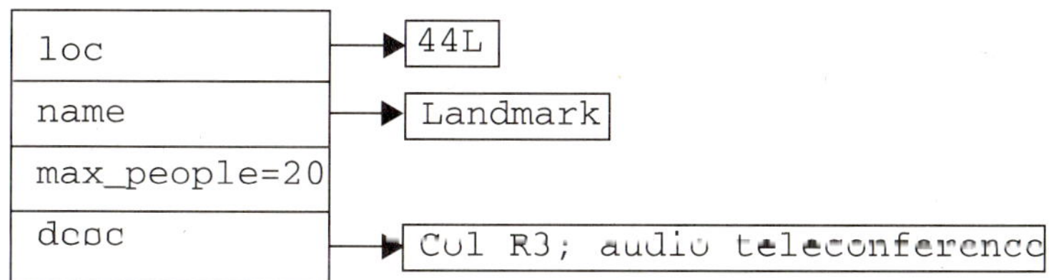

Figure 3.6
A sch_room_t record with string pointers.

Let's compare strings using arrays and strings using pointers. There are advantages and disadvantages to each.

- Maximum string length

  With array strings, the maximum length of the string is limited to the declared size of the array. With string pointers, a string can be an arbitrary length limited only by available memory.

- Storage utilitization

  With array strings, the entire declared size of the array is allocated. If typical string sizes are smaller than the maximum size, some memory will be wasted. With string pointers, only the memory required to hold the string is allocated.

- Programming complexity

  Array strings are typically allocated automatically within procedures and by the IDL generated stubs. Pointer strings must be explicitly allocated by the application. A record that contains array strings can be easily copied. When a record containing pointer strings is copied, each string must be allocated and copied. So in general, programming complexity is greater using string pointers.

For the room application, we will continue to use array strings. The increased programming complexity does not outweigh the slight savings (in this case) in storage efficiency and string size flexibility.

Pipes

The DCE pipes facility provides a way to efficiently transfer large amounts of data between a client and a server. (Note that DCE pipes are not the same as, nor particularly similar to, Unix pipes.) A pipe can be considered a data conduit between the client and the server. Data of a particular type is pushed into one end of the pipe or pulled out of the other. The direction of the pipe data flow can be in (from the client to the server), out (from the server to the client) or in,out (both ways). Data is transmitted through a pipe in chunks of one or more base type elements.

To use a pipe, the application must provide some routines specific to the pipe type. The *pipe push* routine receives a chunk of data that has been pushed through the pipe. The *pipe pull* routine sends a chunk of data that will be pulled through the pipe. The *pipe alloc* routine allocates a buffer to hold a chunk of the pipe data. These routines are called by the application client or server code to transfer chunks of data through the pipe. The actual transmission of the data is controlled by RPC to make efficient use of network connection between the client and the server.

Get File Example using Pipes

A new sample application, the get_file client and server, will be used to illustrate the use of pipes. In this application, the client requests that a file be transferred from the server. One way this can be done is with an out pipe, with the server pushing the file data into the pipe for the client to receive. Code Sample 3.31 shows the definition of the file_pipe_t type and the get_file_pipe() operation.

```
typedef pipe byte file_pipe_t;

void get_file_pipe(
   [in ] handle_t        h,
   [in,string] char     *file_name,
   [in ] long int        bufsize,
   [out] file_pipe_t    *file_pipe,
   [out] long int       *file_status);
```

Code Sample 3.31
get_file/get_file.idl: pipe definition

The input parameters of the `get_file_pipe()` operation are the binding handle, the name of the file to be transferred, and the size of the buffer to be used during the transfer. The output parameters are the file pipe and a status.

The IDL compiler transforms the `file_pipe_t` type into a structure with the same name, as shown in Code Sample 3.32. This structure includes fields for the pipe's push, pull, and alloc routines, along with a state variable to keep track of the pipe. The **`get_file`** client will fill in these fields later.

```
typedef struct file_pipe_t {
void (* pull)(
#ifdef IDL_PROTOTYPES
rpc_ss_pipe_state_t state,
idl_byte *buf,
idl_ulong_int esize,
idl_ulong_int *ecount
#endif
);
void (* push)(
#ifdef IDL_PROTOTYPES
rpc_ss_pipe_state_t state,
idl_byte *buf,
idl_ulong_int  ecount
#endif
);
void (* alloc)(
#ifdef IDL_PROTOTYPES
rpc_ss_pipe_state_t state,
idl_ulong_int bsize,
idl_byte **buf,
idl_ulong_int *bcount
#endif
);
rpc_ss_pipe_state_t state;
} file_pipe_t;
```

Code Sample 3.32
`get_file/get_file.h`: `file_pipe_t` structure

```
void get_file_pipe(
   /* [in ] */ handle_t       h,
   /* [in ] */ idl_char      *file_name,
   /* [in ] */ idl_long_int   bufsize,
   /* [out] */ file_pipe_t   *file_pipe,
   /* [out] */ idl_long_int  *file_status)
{
   int       fd;
   idl_byte *buffer;
   long int ecount;

   fd = open((char *) file_name, O_RDONLY);
   if (fd == -1)
   {
      *file_status = get_file_status_not_found;
      (*(file_pipe->push))(file_pipe->state, buffer, 0);
      return;
   }

   buffer = (idl_byte *) malloc(bufsize);
   if (buffer == NULL)
   {
      *file_status = get_file_status_no_memory;
      (*(file_pipe->push))(file_pipe->state, buffer, 0);
      return;
   }

   do
   {
      ecount = read(fd, buffer, bufsize);
      (*(file_pipe->push))(file_pipe->state, buffer,
                           ecount);
   }
   while (ecount > 0);

   free(buffer);
   *file_status = get_file_status_ok;
}
```

Code Sample 3.33

get_file/get_file_mgr.c: get_file_pipe()

Code Sample 3.33 shows the manager implementation for the get_file_pipe() operation. The manager does the following:

- Opens the source file for reading.
- Allocates the transfer buffer to the size specified in bufsize.
- Reads bufsize chunks of the file and pushes them into the file pipe.

The pipe push call (*(file_pipe->push))() appears to call the push routine associated with the pipe. In reality, this call invokes an RPC marshaling routine that fills the pipe with chunks of data.

When all chunks of the file have been pushed into the pipe, a zero-length chunk must be pushed to indicate the end of the data. Note that when the end of the file is reached, read() will return a zero count and the push call will push a zero-length chunk. Explicit zero-length pushes are included for error returns to keep DCE happy. Otherwise, a pipe discipline error can be reported to the client.

Code Sample 3.34 shows the client's get_file_pipe() call. The client must set the alloc and push fields of the file_pipe structure to application-supplied routines. The file_pipe structure also includes a state variable that is not used here. For each chunk of data the server pushes into the pipe, the client stub for get_file_pipe() will call pipe_alloc() to allocate storage for the chunk, and pipe_push() to process the received chunk. When all of the chunks have been processed, the get_file_pipe() call will return.

```
file_pipe_t           file_pipe;
rpc_ss_pipe_state_t   file_pipe_state;

file_pipe.alloc = pipe_alloc;
file_pipe.push  = pipe_push;
file_pipe.state = &file_pipe_state;

get_file_pipe(h, file_name, bufsize, &file_pipe,
            &file_status);
```

Code Sample 3.34
get_file/get_file.c main():get_file_pipe() call

The client pipe_alloc() and pipe_push() functions are shown in Code Sample 3.35. pipe_alloc() simply returns a pointer to, and the fixed size of, a static buffer to be used to receive each pipe chunk. pipe_push() writes each received chunk to the target file. It closes the target file when it receives the final zero-length chunk.

```
#define    DEFAULT_BUFSIZE 4096
long int   bufsize = DEFAULT_BUFSIZE;
idl_byte *buffer[DEFAULT_BUFSIZE];

void pipe_alloc(
   rpc_ss_pipe_state_t state,
   idl_ulong_int        bsize,
   idl_byte            **buf,
   idl_ulong_int        *bcount)
{
   *buf = buffer;
   *bcount = bufsize;
}

void pipe_push(
   rpc_ss_pipe_state_t state,
   idl_byte             *buf,
   idl_ulong_int        ecount)
{
   if (ecount > 0)
   {
      write(fd, buffer, ecount);
   }
   else
   {
      close(fd);
   }
}
```

Code Sample 3.35
`get_file/get_file.c`: `pipe_alloc()` and `pipe_push()`

Advantages of pipes are:

- The processing of the pipe data is overlapped with its transmission. In the `get_file` example, it is not necessary for the client to wait until it has received all of the source file data before it starts to write the data to the target file. Another example of where this is beneficial is a client that receives graphic data from a server over a slow transmission link. The client can display segments of the picture as it is received.
- Only enough memory for each pipe chunk is required to process the pipe. The size of the file transferred between the `get_file` client and server is limited only by available disk space, not by the sizes of the client and server processes.

Context Handles

Context handles provide a way for a server to retain state information about a client between the client's remote calls. An example of such information is a file that the server has opened on behalf of a client. A context handle has the appearance of a `void *` pointer to a data structure in the server that holds the client's state information. An initial remote call allocates the context data area and returns the context handle as an `out` (or `in,out`) parameter to the client. In subsequent remote calls, the client passes the context handle as an `in` (or `in,out`) parameter, and the server uses the context handle to retrieve the context data area.

Since pointers in the server's address space have no meaning in the client's address space, a context handle parameter transmitted between the client and server cannot be represented by an address. Instead, the RPC Runtime of the server generates a UUID to represent the context handle. The server RPC Runtime maintains a table that maps context handle UUIDs to pointers for context data areas in the server's address space. The client RPC Runtime maintains a similar table that maps the client's context handle to its UUID. When the client makes a call with an `in` context handle, the client stub routine maps the context handle to its UUID and marshals the UUID to send to the server. The server stub routine unmarshals the context handle UUID, maps it to the pointer for the context data area, and passes the pointer to the manager. The manager can then dereference the context handle pointer to get to the client's saved state information.

A typical use of a context handle is as a *cursor* that keeps track of the client's position in a sequence of data. In an initial call, the cursor is initialized to the beginning of the data. Each subsequent call advances the cursor through the data, until either the desired data is found or the end of the data is reached. A final call usually releases any resources used by the cursor. DCE itself frequently uses cursors of this type in its call; we will see one such cursor in the `rpc_ns_binding_import` calls in Chapter 5.

Get File Example using Context Handles

The `get_file` application can also be implemented using a context handle. We will use three operations, defined in Code Sample 3.36, to do this.

```
typedef [context_handle] void *file_handle_t;

void get_file_begin(
   [in ] handle_t        h,
   [in,string] char     *file_name,
   [out] file_handle_t *file_h,
   [out] long int       *file_status);
```

Code Sample 3.36
`get_file/get_file.idl`: `get_file_begin()`, `_next()`, and `_end()`

```
void get_file_next(
    [in ] file_handle_t  file_h,
    [in ] long int        max_chunk_size,
    [out] long int       *chunk_size,
    [out, size_is(max_chunk_size),length_is(*chunk_size)]
          byte            file_chunk[],
    [out] long int       *file_status);

void get_file_end(
    [in ] file_handle_t  file_h,
    [out] long int       *file_status);
```

Code Sample 3.36 (continued)

- `get_file_begin()` opens the source file and allocates and returns a context handle of type `file_handle_t`. This context handle retains the open source file descriptor in the server. It will be used as a cursor pointing at the next data in the file to be read.
- `get_file_next()` uses the file context handle to read the next chunk of data from the source file into the `file_chunk` output parameter. The `chunk_size` amount of data read is the minimum of the input parameter `max_chunk_size`, and the remaining unread data in the file. When the end of the file has been reached, this call returns a `chunk_size` of zero.
- `get_file_end()` deallocates the file context handle and closes the source file.

An important point to note is that, in `get_file_next()` and `get_file_end()`, the context handle takes the place of the normal binding handle. Part of the information associated with the context handle on the client side is the binding handle to the server, so RPC can extract the binding handle from the context handle in these calls. It is possible to include both a binding handle and an `in` context handle in a call. But then it is possible to use a binding handle that points to a different server than the one that is maintaining the context handle. This would result in an invalid context handle error. It is safer, then, to omit the binding handle and to rely on the binding in the context handle.

Code Sample 3.37 shows the manager routines for these operations. The context data area is represented by a record of type `file_desc_t`. The only field in this record is the file descriptor for the open source file. `get_file_begin()` allocates a `file_desc_t` record, opens the source file for reading, saves the file descriptor in the record, and sets the context handle to point to the record. Note that if there is an error, the context handle is set to `NULL` for proper marshaling.

`get_file_next()` casts the input file context handle into a pointer to the corresponding `file_desc_t` record. Then this routine reads a chunk of data from the file, using the file descriptor in the record.

Finally, `get_file_end()` deallocates the `file_desc_t` record pointed to by the context handle and closes the source file.

```
typedef struct {
   int  fd;
} file_desc_t;

void get_file_begin(
   /* [in ] */ handle_t       h,
   /* [in ] */ idl_char      *file_name,
   /* [out] */ file_handle_t *file_h,
   /* [out] */ idl_long_int  *file_status)
{
   file_desc_t *file_desc;

   file_desc = (file_desc_t *)
      malloc(sizeof(file_desc_t));
   if (file_desc == NULL)
   {
      *file_status = get_file_status_no_memory;
      *file_h = NULL;
      return;
   }

   file_desc->fd = open((char *) file_name, O_RDONLY);
   if (file_desc->fd == -1)
   {
      *file_status = get_file_status_not_found;
      *file_h = NULL;
      return;
   }

   *file_h = (file_handle_t) file_desc;
   *file_status = get_file_status_ok;
}
void get_file_next(
   /* [in ] */ file_handle_t  file_h,
   /* [in ] */ idl_long_int   max_chunk_size,
   /* [out] */ idl_long_int  *chunk_size,
   /* [out] */ idl_byte       file_chunk[],
```

Code Sample 3.37
`get_file/get_file_mgr.c`: `get_file_next()` and `get_file_end()`

```
   /* [out] */ idl_long_int  *file_status)
{
   file_desc_t *file_desc = (file_desc_t *) file_h;

   *chunk_size =
     read(file_desc->fd, file_chunk, max_chunk_size);
   *file_status = get_file_status_ok;
}

void get_file_end(
   /* [in ] */ file_handle_t  file_h,
   /* [out] */ idl_long_int  *file_status)
{
   file_desc_t *file_desc = (file_desc_t *) file_h;

   close(file_desc->fd);
   free(file_desc);
   *file_status = get_file_status_ok;
}

void file_handle_t_rundown(
   /* [in ] */ file_handle_t  file_h)
{
   file_desc_t *file_desc = (file_desc_t *) file_h;

   close(file_desc->fd);
   free(file_desc);
}
```

Code Sample 3.37 (continued)

If a server loses contact with a client for which it is maintaining a context handle, the server will call an application-supplied *context rundown routine*. This routine is responsible for cleaning up the orphaned context and must be named *context_handle_t*_rundown(), where *context_handle_t* is the defined type for the context handle. A context rundown routine must be supplied for each defined context handle type. The rundown routine for the file_handle_t context handle is shown in Code Sample 3.37. This routine closes the open source file and deallocates the file descriptor record for the context handle.

The **get_file** client calls using the file context handle are shown in Code Sample 3.38. First, get_file_begin() is called to open the source file and establish the context handle. Then get_file_next() is called for each file chunk, and each file chunk is written to the target file. When the end of the file is reached, get_file_done() is called to release the context handle and to close the source file.

```
file_handle_t file_h;
idl_long_int  chunk_size;

get_file_begin(h, file_name, &file_h, &file_status);
while (file_status == get_file_status_ok)
{
    get_file_next(file_h, bufsize, &chunk_size,
        buffer, &file_status);
    if (chunk_size == 0)
    {
        break;
    }
    write(fd, buffer, chunk_size);
}
if (file_h != NULL)
{
    get_file_end(file_h, &file_status);
}
close(fd);
```

Code Sample 3.38
get_file/get_file.c: Use of get_file_begin(), _next(), and _end()

Comparison of Pipes and Context Handles for Get File

The implementations of the get file example using a pipe and a context handle are similar in structure. However, the pipe implementation performs better because there is only one (extended) remote call between the client and the server, which results in a stream of file chunks from the server to the client. In the context handle implementation, there is a full remote call for each file chunk transferred. For a chunk size of 4096 bytes, the pipe version transfers a large file twice as fast as the context handle version.

3.5 Attribute Configuration Files

So far, we have seen how the IDL file defines the data types and operations for an RPC interface. The IDL file can be viewed as defining all of the aspects of the client and server interaction over the network, or "on the wire" as it is commonly called. This includes the interface UUID and version, the number and order of operations, and the input and output parameters for each operation.

In addition to the IDL file, an interface can have *Attribute Configure Files* (ACFs), which define aspects of the interface between the application and the RPC stubs and Runtime library. For an interface `IF` defined in `IF.idl`, the ACF is `IF.acf`. An ACF is not explicitly specified during IDL compilation; the IDL compiler will automatically find an ACF if it exists.

ACFs are optional; an application need not include an ACF for the IDL compilation to be successful. A client and a server can have separate ACFs. Indeed, a typical usage for ACFs is to modify how a particular client or server interacts with its local RPC. However, to use separate ACFs for clients and servers you must organize the client and server files in separate directories. Figure 3.7 shows the relationship between the IDL files and the ACFs.

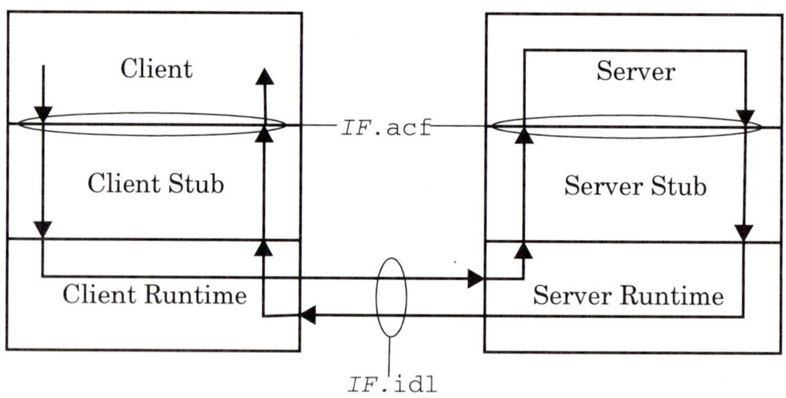

Figure 3.7
IDL and ACF Files

The structure of Attribute Configuration Files is similar to IDL files:

```
[acf_interface_attributes] interface interface_name
{
    acf_body
}
```

where *acf_body* can contain one or more of the following items.

- `include "filename";`

  Adds additional header files to IDL-generated stub files. IDL appends `.h` onto *filename*, so *filename* should not include an extension.
- `typedef [acf_data_type_attributes] data_type_name;`

  Adds additional attributes to a type defined in the interface's IDL file.

- [*acf_operation_attributes*] *operation_name*(
  [*acf_parameter_attributes*] *parameter_name_1*,
  [*acf_parameter_attributes*] *parameter_name_2*,
  ...
  [*acf_parameter_attributes*] *parameter_name_n*);

  Adds additional attributes to an operation defined in the interface's IDL file and, optionally, some or all of the operation parameters.

The following sections discuss the RPC features that can be controlled or modified using ACFs.

Status Reporting

Fault status parameters for remote operations were introduced in Chapter 2. Recall that various conditions during a remote call can cause exceptions to be raised in the client. If no special preparation were made for such an exception, it would normally cause the client to abort. Using ACF attributes, these exceptions can be turned into DCE status values of the type `error_status_t` that are returned from the remote call to the client. Then the client can inspect the returned status values and take appropriate action. There are two types of exceptions that can be handled in this manner:

- `comm_status`

  Communication exceptions occur because the client and the server cannot communicate over the network. The most common communications exceptions are `rpc_x_comm_failure`, which occurs when the client using a RPC Datagram (`dg`) protocol times out waiting for a server response, and `rpc_x_connection_aborted`, which occurs when using an RPC Connection-oriented (`cn`) protocol and the connection between the client and server fails. The corresponding status values for these exceptions are `rpc_s_comm_failure` and `rpc_s_connection_aborted`.

- `fault_status`

  Fault exceptions occur because the client or server has detected an invalid condition during the execution of a remote call. Examples of fault exceptions include `exc_e_illaddr`, which occurs when the server tries to deference an invalid pointer, and `rpc_x_invalid_bound`, which is raised when the client or server attempts to marshal a conformant or varying array with an invalid or uninitialized array bound. Faults are typically caused by programming errors.

Status Return Values

An operation can be coerced into returning the communications and/or fault status values as its return value by using `comm_status` and/or `fault_status` as an operation attribute in the ACF:

```
[comm_status] operation_name(...)
[fault_status] operation_name (...)
[comm_status, fault_status] operation_name(...)
```

The return type of the operation in the IDL file must be declared to be `error_status_t`. The server must return a valid status value, usually `error_status_ok`. If there is a fault detected, the return value will be changed to the appropriate status value.

Status Parameters

One or more operation parameters can be designed to receive communications or fault status values by including `comm_status` and/or `fault_status` as parameter attributes in the ACF:

```
[comm_status] parameter_name,
[fault_status] parameter_name,
[comm_status, fault_status] parameter_name,
```

If the parameter was previously defined for the operation in the IDL file, it must be an `out` parameter and its type must have been declared to be `error_status_t *` (a pointer to an error status variable). If the parameter was not previously defined in the IDL file, it will be added as the last parameter, of type `error_status_t *`, to the operation signature. The client will pass a pointer to a variable of type `error_status_t` as the existing or added status parameter. The server must initialize the status parameter to a valid value, usually `error_status_ok`. If there is a fault detected, the parameter value will be changed to the appropriate status value.

Using separate ACFs for the client and server, it is possible to add the status parameter to only the client's calls. The server can continue to use the original operation signatures. However, as noted earlier, separate ACFs require separate directories for the client and server.

Status Parameter Example

Let's add status parameters to each of the `room` interface operations. We will retain the original operation definitions, without the status parameters, in `room.idl`. The ACF for the interface is shown in Code Sample 3.39.

```
interface room
{
room_description([comm_status,fault_status] call_status);
room_reserve  ([comm_status, fault_status] call_status);
room_cancel   ([comm_status, fault_status] call_status);
room_avail    ([comm_status, fault_status] call_status);
room_events   ([comm_status, fault_status] call_status);
}
```

Code Sample 3.39
`schedule/room.acf`: Defining call status parameters for the `room` interface.

When `IDL` compiles `room.idl` with this `room.acf` in the same directory, it will add the following parameter to the end of each operation signature:

```
/* [out] */ error_status_t *call_status
```

The added parameter appears in the operation prototypes in `room.h` and in the definition of the client and server stubs in `room_cstub.c` and `room_sstub.c`.

Code Sample 3.40 shows a typical remote call using the `call_status` parameter. If a problem is detected during the call, `call_status` is set to an appropriate DCE status code. The `CHECK_CALL` macro inspects the returned call status, and if it does not indicate a successful call, prints the error message corresponding to the DCE status value and returns to the client's `main()` routine. Code Sample 3.41 shows the `print_call_status()` routine (in `sch_util.c`), which uses the `dce_error_inq_text()` call to translate the status value to a text string.

```
#define CHECK_CALL(call_status) \
   if (call_status != error_status_ok) \
   { \
      print_call_status(call_status); \
      return; \
   }

   error_status_t  call_status;
   . . .
   room_description(H, room_name, &room, &status,
                    &call_status);
   CHECK_CALL(call_status);
```

Code Sample 3.40
`schedule/room.c`: Sample remote call using `call_status` parameter.

```
void print_call_status(
   error_status_t call_status)
{
   unsigned char error_text[dce_c_error_string_len];
   int ignored_st;

   dce_error_inq_text(call_status, error_text,
                      &ignored_st);
   printf("%s\n", error_text);
}
```

Code Sample 3.41
`schedule/sch_util.c`: Routine to display a DCE error message

Code Sample 3.42 shows an example of how the operation manager routines in the server have to include and initialize the added `call_status` parameter.

```
void room_description(
     /* [in ] */ handle_t        h,
     /* [in ] */ sch_room_name_t room_name,
     /* [out] */ sch_room_t      *room,
     /* [out] */ sch_status_t    *status,
     /* [out] */ error_status_t *call_status)
{
   *call_status = error_status_ok;
   . . .
}
```

Code Sample 3.42
`schedule/room_server.c`: Addition of the `call_status` parameter

Code Generation

ACFs can be used to control some of the aspects of code generation by **idl**, including selecting which client stubs to generate and whether to use inline or out-of-line marshaling.

Client Stub Routine Generation

A client may not need to call all of the operations in an interface. Take for instance the **room_desc** program discussed in Chapter 2. All it calls is `room_description()`. Consequently, it does not need the client stubs for the other operations in the `room` interface. The **room_desc** program can conserve code space by linking with a client stub object that has been tailored to include just the `room_description()` client stub routine. There are two ACF attributes that can be used for this purpose:

- `no_code`

  Interface or operation attribute. Suppress the generation of the stub routines for the specified operation or for all operations in the interface. If `no_code` is specified for the interface, individual operations can use the `code` attribute to generate the desired stub routines.

- `code`

  Interface or operation attribute. Generate the stub routines for the specified operation or for all operations in the interface. If `code` is specified for the interface, individual operations can use the `no_code` attribute to suppress the undesired stub routines.

The `code` and `nocode` attributes have no effect on server stub generation. A server must always implement all operations in an interface it exports.

Inline and Out-of-line marshaling (pre-DCE 1.1)

Prior to DCE 1.1, **idl** generated inline code for marshaling (and unmarshaling) parameters in the client and server stubs. Indeed, much of the bulk of a pre-

DCE 1.1 stub routine is the inline marshaling code. Using an ACF, you can instead instruct **idl** to generate marshaling routines for some or all of the data types defined in an IDL file. Then parameters of those data types will be marshaled and unmarshaled by calls to the generated routines instead of by inline code. This makes for more compact client and server programs, at the cost of the overhead of making the marshaling procedure calls.

- `out_of_line`

  Interface or typedef attribute. Generate and use marshaling routines. If used for an interface, use marshaling routines for all data types used by the interface attributes. If used with a type, use marshaling routines when that type is used by an operation. If `out_of_line` is specified for an interface, `in_line` can be used with a type to generate inline marshaling for that type. Simple (scalar) data types (`int`, `boolean`, and `char`) are unaffected by the `out_of_line` attribute.

- `in_line`

  Interface or typedef attribute. Use inline marshaling for all types used by the interface or for a selected type. If `in_line` is specified for an interface, it can be overridden by `out_of_line` for a type. `in_line` is the default marshaling strategy prior to DCE 1.1.

With the advent of interpretive marshaling in DCE 1.1, these attributes are no longer relevant and are ignored by the DCE 1.1 IDL compiler.

Binding Handle Options

As mentioned earlier, a binding handle is a pointer to an opaque data structure that records information about a server in use by a client. Setting up a binding handle will be discussed in detail in Chapters 4, 5, and 6. When a client makes a remote call to a server, the binding handle will supply information, such as the server's network address and endpoint, needed by the RPC Runtime to perform the call. Binding handles can also be used by server manager routines to retrieve information about a client, but we won't see a real use for this until Chapter 6.

Typically, the first parameter of an operation is a binding handle that selects the server to execute the operation. There are other options for binding handles that can be specified in an interface's ACF.

- `explicit_handle`

  Interface or operation attribute. Force the first parameter of one or more operations to be an explicit input binding handle. When used as an operation attribute, this alters the signature of the specified operation. When used as an interface attribute, this modifies all operations in the interface. It is the default binding option; if there are no other applicable binding attributes, an operation must have an explicit binding handle as its first parameter.

- `implicit_handle(`*`handle_type handle_name`*`)`

  Interface attribute. Use a variable *`handle_name`* as the binding handle for all operations in the interface. The client sets up the handle variable using the normal DCE calls but does not pass in the binding handle in remote calls. Instead, the client stub routines retrieve the binding from the handle variable. The *`handle_type`* can be `handle_t` for the usual binding handles, or it can be an application-defined custom binding handle type. Custom binding handles will be examined in Chapter 5. Any operation in the interface can include an explicit `handle_t` as its first parameter to override use of the implicit handle for the operation.
- `auto_handle`

  Interface attribute. Use the automatic binding feature for the operations in the interface. With this feature, the operations do not include a handle, and the client stub routines for the operations take care of setting up the binding. Automatic binding will be discussed in greater detail in Chapter 5. Any operation in the interface can include an explicit `handle_t` as its first parameter to override use of the automatic binding for the operation.
- `binding_callout(`*`callout_routine_name`*`)`

  Interface attribute, used with the `auto_handle` attribute. After a client stub routine automatically binds to a server, it will call the named callout routine to perform additional processing for the binding. The use of this attribute will be shown in Chapter 6.

Recall that an interface ACF affects only the interface between the application client or server and its client or server stub routines. Thus it is possible to use an ACF to modify the interface binding characteristics on just the client or the server side. In fact, we will see in Chapter 6 that when security is used and the client uses implicit or automatic handles, the server must use explicit handles. To do this, the client and the server would need different ACFs. But since the different ACFs would have the same name (*`INTERFACE`*`.acf`), they must appear in different directories to be properly processed. The `auto_handle` example in Chapter 5 will demonstrate this.

Data Representation

The data conversion and representation rules used by IDL and RPC were examined earlier in this chapter. You can add your own data manipulation using attributes in the ACF. You might want to do this if you are dealing with a peculiar data type not covered by the usual IDL data representations.

- `represent_as(`*`local_type`*`)`

  Typedef attribute. Map a local data type used by the application into another type to be used for transmission over the network. The full `typedef` is

  ```
  typedef [represent_as(local_type)] net_type;
  ```

  The application must supply some routines that perform the actual mapping. These routines are called by the client and server stubs when they marshal and unmarshal parameters of the local type. They are

  net_type`_from_local()` map local to net type
  net_type`_to_local()` map net to local type
  net_type`_free_inst()` free storage used by net type
  net_type`_free_local()` free storage used by local type

  See Section 18.3.9 of the *OSF DCE 1.1 Application Developer's Guide* for more information on how to use this attribute.

- `transmit_as(`*`trans_type`*`)`

  Typedef attribute. Map a presentation data type to a transmission type. This attribute is very similar to `represent_as`, except that it appears in the IDL file rather than the ACF. The application must supply the following routines called by the client and server stubs.

  ```
  typedef [transmit_as(trans_type)] pres_type;
  ```

  pres_type`_to_xmit()` map pres to transmit type
  pres_type`_from_xmit()` map transmit to pres type
  pres_type`_free_inst()` free storage used by pres type

International Character Code Set Conversion (DCE 1.1)

DCE 1.1 provides extensive facilities for handling international character code sets. DCE takes into consideration the fact that international code sets can use varying sizes to represent characters (e.g., 16 or 32 bits for some Asian character sets).

- `cs_char(`*`local_type`*`)`

  Type attribute. Map a local data type representing the international character set into a type for network transmission. This is similar to the `represent_as` attribute, and is used as follows:

  ```
  typedef [cs_char(local_type)] net_type;
  ```

The application must supply some routines that perform the actual mapping. These routines are called by the client and server stubs when they marshal and unmarshal parameters of the local type. They are

*net_type*_net_size()	compute buffer size needed for local to net type conversion
*net_type*_local_size()	compute buffer size needed for net to local type conversion
*net_type*_to_netcs()	map local to net code set
*net_type*_from_netcs()	map net to local code set

- `cs_rtag, cs_stag, cs_drtag`

  Parameter attributes. When an operation uses an international code set defined by the `cs_char` attribute, it must include parameters tags that describe the code set. The sending tag (`stag`) identifies the code set used for data sent from the client to the server. The desired receiving tag (`drtag`) identifies the code set that the client would like the server to use when returning data. The receiving tag (`rtag`) identifies the code set actually used by the server for returning data.

- `cs_rtag(`*tag_set_routine*`)`

  Interface or operation attribute. Use the named routine to provide the code set tags needed for the operations in an interface or for a particular interface. When this attribute is used, the application does not have to explicitly set the code set tags when an operation is called. This provides transparency for applications using international code sets.

For more information on the use of the international code set facilities, see Chapter 15 of the *OSF DCE 1.1 Application Development Guide*.

Memory Management

There are a couple of ACF attributes used to control the allocation of memory by server stubs.

- `enable_allocate`

  Operation attribute. The data structures used by the `rpc_ss_allocate()` routine (discussed earlier in relation to full pointers) must be initialized prior to the first call to `rpc_ss_allocate()`. Normally this is done automatically by the server stub module when an operation uses full pointers or a type with the `represent_as` attribute. However, an operation manager may need to call `rpc_ss_allocate()` even if it doesn't use these types. In that case, you can force the server stub to initialize the allocation environment by including `enable_allocate` as an attribute of the operation.

- heap

  Type or parameter attribute. Normally, a server stub routine will unmarshal parameter values to storage in the server's stack. With this attribute you can instruct the server stub to allocate storage in the heap for all values of a particular type or for a specific parameter of an operation. You might do this to conserve space on the stack.

IDL Encoding (DCE 1.1)

DCE 1.1 provides a way for an application to use its marshaling and unmarshaling facilities without having to perform a remote call. Data types defined in an IDL file can be marshaled, or *encoded*, into a buffer, and the contents of the buffer can later be unmarshaled, or *decoded*, back into the original data types. This can be used to convert complex data structures linked by pointers into a linear data sequence suitable for storage or for transmission and then to recover the original data structures. Data type conversion is also available when encoding and decoding data. An application using sockets for its data transmission might benefit from the IDL encoding services. The DCE backing store facility (discussed in Chapter 9) also uses the IDL encoding services.

To use the IDL encoding services, you supply encoding and decoding operations defined in an IDL file, use the `encode` and `decode` attributes for the operations in the corresponding ACF. The `IDL` compiler will then generate stub routines that marshal and unmarshal the operation parameters into buffers that are supplied by the application. The stub routines will not make any remote calls; these operations are strictly local and there is no server involved.

DCE provides a set of calls beginning with `idl_es_` to be used with the encoding and decoding of data. These are described in the *OSF DCE 1.1 Application Development Reference*.

Exceptions (DCE 1.1)

Exceptions were discussed in Chapter 2. An exception must be declared and initialized before it can be used. DCE has a set of exceptions that it declares and initializes on the first DCE-related call. You may want to define additional application-specific exceptions, or you may want to override the existing DCE exceptions with your own definitions. You can do this using the `extern_exceptions` interface attribute. The format for this attribute is

```
extern_exceptions(exception_1, exception_2, ...)
```

You are then responsible for declaring and initializing these exceptions in your application.

CHAPTER 4

Basic Client and Server Setup

In this chapter, we will build a complete client and server, using the simplest (and least flexible) methods for the client to find and use (*bind to*) the server. These methods require the client to know the location of the server—that is, the system on which the server is running. In Chapter 5, we will introduce more flexible techniques using CDS.

4.1 Client and Server Modules

The client and server setup will be illustrated using the Room application client and server—the **room** and **room_server** programs. These programs are built from several application modules, linked with the DCE Runtime library (on HP-UX, libdce.sl). The server contains the room_server.c and room_mgr.c modules. The client is represented by the room.c module. Routines common to both the client and server are in sch_util.c.

Server Main

The main() routine of a server is responsible for two sets of tasks: DCE setup and application-specific setup. DCE setup is done by calls to routines in the DCE Runtime library. Application-specific setup may include opening databases and initializing internal data structures.

The main() routine of the room server is in room_server.c. Versions of this module will be discussed in this and future chapters. Application setup and cleanup will be done by the routine room_open() and room_close() in the room_mgr.c module.

Low-level DCE Server Setup

DCE provides a vast number of calls for setting up various server aspects like security and interfaces. Most of these calls are part of RPC and so are prefixed by `rpc_`. Some calls are in other DCE components like security (`sec_`). In general, each of these calls deals with one small feature of DCE setup. The number and complexity of these setup calls depend on the DCE features the server uses. A simple server using only RPC might get by with three or four calls, while a full server using RPC, CDS, security, and Access Control Lists may need dozens of calls. We will look at the low-level DCE setup calls first, for two reasons:

- The low-level calls provide a good tutorial on concepts you will need to know to set up your servers, and
- For DCE products based on DCE 1.0, the low-level calls are the only means available for setting up servers. Until you move to a DCE 1.1 (or later) product, you will have to use these calls.

Integrated DCE Server Setup (DCE 1.1)

Many people have rightfully complained that the large number and complexity of the low-level server setup calls make DCE difficult to use. To remedy this, the DCE 1.1 release provides a small number of high-level calls that integrate the various steps for setting up a server. Moreover, servers built with these calls can be managed by standard DCE tools like the **dcecp** command. Developers using DCE products based on DCE 1.1 (or later versions) will want to use the integrated setup calls. We will examine these calls in Chapter 7.

Server Manager

Typically, the implementation of the operations for an interface (the *managers*) is put in a separate module. This allows all of the application-specific code, including application setup and cleanup, to be collected into this module.

The `room_mgr.c` module holds the implementation of the `room` interface for the room server. This includes definitions for internal data structures, the application setup and cleanup routines `room_open()` and `room_close()`, the operation manager routines, and various support routines. Routines in the manager module will be shown only when needed to illustrate a point. The complete source for `room_server.c` and `room_mgr.c` is included in Appendix B and on the diskette included with this book. A short summary of the manager module is included here.

Application Files and Data Structures

The rooms and their reservations are stored in a flat character file `room_db.dat`. The `room_open()` routine, called when the server starts up, opens this file, reads its contents, and builds an in-memory linked data structure with records for each location, room, and reservation event. The data structure is read and updated by the various room operations. The `room_close()` routine, called when the server terminates, writes the updated contents of the data structure back to `room_db.dat`.

If the room server terminates without having called `room_close()`, the room database file will not be updated with the room reservations and cancellations entered during the server's life. To recover from this possibility, a transaction log file `room_xn.dat` is maintained. This file records each `room_reserve()` and `room_cancel()` operation executed by the server. When the server terminates normally, `room_close()` will erase the transaction log after successfully updating the room database. But if the server crashes, the transaction log will preserve the updates to the database. Then the next time the room server is run, `room_open()` will apply the updates to the room database.

Operation Manager Routines

There is one operation manager routine for each operation defined in `room.idl`. The managers are

- `room_description()`
- `room_reserve()`
- `room_cancel()`
- `room_avail()`
- `room_events()`

Client

The application code for the room client is in the file `room.c`. The `main()` routine consists of DCE client setup calls to establish a binding to the room server and a loop to execute commands. Versions of the client `main()` will be shown as new techniques for binding are introduced.

For each command, there is an execution routine that accepts parameter input and calls the relevant remote procedure. These execution routines will not be shown in the book unless needed to illustrate a point. The full source for `room.c` is available in Appendix B and on the diskette included with this book. The commands and execution routines are

- `d - description()`
- `r - reserve()`
- `c - cancel()`
- `a - avail()`
- `e - events()`

Common Utilities

There are several routines that are used by both the room client and server. These are found in the `sch_util.c` module and the `sch_util.h` include file. The corresponding object `sch_util.o` is linked with both **room** and **room_server**.

Makefile

In Unix, the compilation and linkage of an application is usually controlled by the **make** command and a file (the *makefile*) that specifies the dependencies among application files and how application modules are constructed. The makefile for the room application is shown in Code Sample 4.1. Note that this makefile is for HP-UX; some items like compiler options and file locations may be different for other operating systems. There are three types of tasks that **make** must perform to build this and other DCE applications: IDL compilation, C compilation, and program linkage.

IDL Compilation

An example of an IDL compilation in Code Sample 4.1 is marked **(1)**. This rule states that the interface header and stub object files room.h, room_cstub.o, and room_sstub.o are derived by applying the **idl** command to the interface definition file room.idl. The only IDL flag used is -keep all, which tells **idl** to retain the stub source files room_cstub.c and room_sstub.c. The rule also indicates that the IDL compilation is dependent on sch.h, which in turn is derived from sch.idl.

C Compilation

A typical compilation of a C source is marked **(2)**. This rule states that the room.o object file is derived from the source file room.c by applying the **cc** command. The flags (CFLAGS and INCDIRS) for the compilation are

- -Aa allow ANSI C syntax
- -c generate object file only
- -g including debugging information
- -D_HPUX_SOURCE indicate HP-UX call syntax
- -D_REENTRANT generate reentrant code
- -I. use local header files (e.g. room.h)
- -I/usr/include/reentrant
  use reentrant version of /usr/include files.

The room.c file also has dependencies on the interface header file room.h and sch_util.h, for prototypes for the print routines.

Program Linkage

The rule marked **(3)** in Code Sample 4.1 shows an example of program linkage. The **room** program is derived from the CLIENT_OBJ list of object files using the linking facilities of the **cc** command. The client objects are

- room.o client application code
- room_cstub.o room client stub code
- sch_util.o utility code (for print routines)

The link editor directives -Wl,-Bimmediate,-Bnonfatal specify that library routines from shared libraries should be bound to the program when the program is run, if possible (`immediate`), or when the routine is first called (`nonfatal`). The libraries searched for library routines are the DCE Runtime shared library `/usr/lib/libdce.sl.` (`-ldce`) and Reentrant (thread-safe) C Runtime library (`-lc_r`).

```
IDLFLAGS     = -keep all
CFLAGS       = -Aa -c -g -D_HPUX_SOURCE -D_REENTRANT
INCDIRS      = -I. -I/usr/include/reentrant
LDFLAGS      = -Wl,-Bimmediate,-Bnonfatal
LIBS         = -ldce -lc_r
SERVER_OBJS = room_server.o room_mgr.o room_sstub.o \
              sch_util.o
CLIENT_OBJS = room.o room_cstub.o sch_util.o

all: room room_server

sch.h: sch.idl
        idl $(IDLFLAGS) sch.idl

sch_util.o: sch_util.c sch_util.h sch.h
        cc $(CFLAGS) $(INCDIRS) sch_util.c

room.h room_cstub.o room_sstub.o:room.idl room.acf sch.h
        idl $(IDLFLAGS) room.idl                        (1)

room.o: room.c room.h sch_util.h
        cc $(CFLAGS) $(INCDIRS) room.c                  (2)

room server.o: room server.c room.h
        cc $(CFLAGS) $(INCDIRS) room_server.c

room_mgr.o: room_mgr.c room.h sch_util.h
        cc $(CFLAGS) $(INCDIRS) room_mgr.c

room_server: $(SERVER_OBJS)
        cc $(LDFLAGS) -o room_server $(SERVER_OBJS) \
           $(LIBS)

room: $(CLIENT_OBJS)                                    (3)
        cc $(LDFLAGS) -o room $(CLIENT_OBJS) $(LIBS)
```

Code Sample 4.1
`schedule/Makefile`

4.2 Endpoints and String Bindings

Many of the DCE setup tasks involve establishing bindings between clients and servers. An important component of a binding is the communications pathway (such as a TCP connection) between the client and the server. The server must set up one or more endpoints for the pathways, and the client must discover and use one of those endpoints to establish the pathway. There are a variety of DCE mechanisms to do this. The simplest is the string binding.

Socket Addresses

Let's first review the components of a socket address used with the UDP and TCP protocols, as shown in Figure 4.1. The IP address is a 32-bit field that identifies the system on the network. IP addresses are typically written using the *dot notation* `n1.n2.n3.n4`, where each `ni` is the decimal representation of a byte in the address. Examples of IP addresses are `15.4.24.124` and `15.4.25.126`. (These are real IP addresses on a restricted subnet, so you can't get to them from the Internet.) Each system must have a unique IP address. System vendors are typically assigned ranges of IP addresses by the Network Information Center (NIC), the authority responsible for Internet address administration. Vendors then allocate these addresses to their customers.

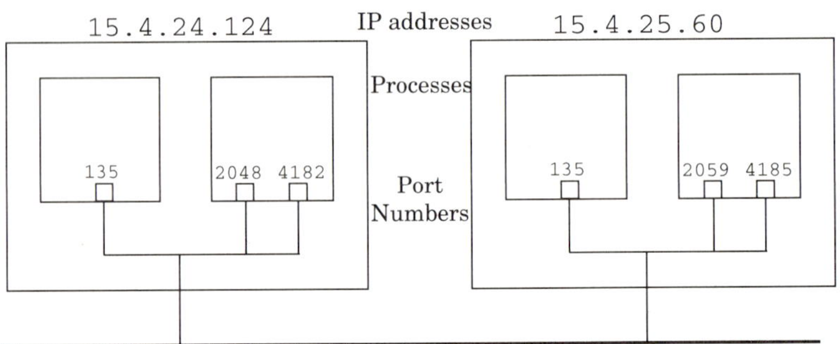

Figure 4.1
Socket Address Components

Since the IP dot notation is not at all mnemonic, systems are usually also assigned alphanumeric *hostnames*, for example, `hpeap827`. Hostnames may be one level for systems at the local site, or may be qualified with one or more organization levels. The fully qualified form of the example hostname is `hpeap827.cup.hp.com`. The higher organization levels (`.hp.com`) are assigned by NIC. Users and programmers prefer to use the hostnames over the IP addresses to designate systems. On Unix systems, hostnames are mapped into IP addresses in the local `/etc/hosts` file or by the Internet domain name service.

In addition to the system IP address, a socket address contains an endpoint which indicates the individual communications endpoint on the system. For UDP and TCP, the endpoint is a 16-bit *port number.* For UDP, the endpoint indicates the socket to which a datagram is sent. For TCP, the endpoint represents one end of a connection. A process may own one or more endpoints.

String Bindings

DCE represents socket addresses in character *string bindings*. The complete format for a string binding is

`object-uuid@protseq:host-addr[endpoint]`

- `object-uuid` specifies an object associated with the binding. It can be omitted if no object is associated with the binding. This component will be discussed in Chapter 8.
- `protseq` is the protocol sequence used for communications between the client and server. For HP-UX DCE, the choices are `ncadg_ip_udp` and `ncacn_ip_tcp`. (For compatibility with NCS applications, `ip` is allowed and is equivalent to `ncadg_ip_udp`.)
- `host-addr` is the address of the host system, either an IP address in dot notation or a hostname.
- `endpoint` is the local endpoint used for communications between the client and server. For UDP and TCP this is the port number. The specification of a string binding also allows protocol-specific options to be included with the endpoint, but no such options are currently defined.

Examples of strings bindings are `ncadg_ip_udp:15.4.24.124[4185]` and `ncacn_ip_tcp:hpeap827[2048]`.

Well-Known Endpoints

Some endpoints are always used for the same purpose by convention. These are called *well-known endpoints* (or sometimes, *well-known addresses*). When a server uses a well-known endpoint, a client will always know to use that endpoint when setting up a binding. Consequently, the client does not need to discover which endpoint the server is using. All the client need know is the host address for the server.

Standard Internet services, such as **ftp** and **telnet**, have well-known endpoints assigned by NIC. For example, **ftp** uses TCP port numbers `20` and `21`. Every **ftpd** server listens on these ports and when you execute **ftp *host-addr***, the **ftp** client knows to connect to port `21` on the indicated host. (DCE itself uses a well-known endpoint, port 135, for its RPC or DCE Daemons, as discussed later in this chapter.) On Unix systems, the local file `/etc/services` lists the well-known endpoints used by standard services.

Use of well-known endpoints for application servers is possible with DCE, but discouraged for the following reasons:

- *Conflicts with other well-known endpoints*

  A chosen endpoint may already be used by another service. You could check the `/etc/services` file to see if the endpoint is already used by an established server. But this will not guard against other private services that might be using the endpoint.

- *Consumption of limited endpoints*

  With TCP and UDP, the number of endpoints is limited by the 16-bit field length. Assigning a unique, well-known endpoint for every DCE server would consume an unacceptable number of endpoints.

- *Privileged range of endpoints*

  On many systems, there is a range of endpoints that are available for use only by privileged programs, that is, programs run under the `root` user. On HP-UX, port numbers `1` through `1023` are so restricted. Your server cannot use a port number within this range unless it is privileged.

Dynamic Endpoints

A program can request that a dynamic endpoint be assigned to it from a pool of available endpoints on the host. The program will then own that endpoint until it terminates. Then the endpoint is returned to the available pool for possible reuse later. Dynamic endpoints make better use of the endpoint range than do well-known endpoints, allowing more programs to own endpoints with less required coordination. However, the actual endpoint used by a program will change every time the program is executed. When a server uses dynamic endpoints, its clients must have a way of discovering which endpoint the server is currently using. The Endpoint Map, discussed in Section 4.5, is DCE's solution to this problem. But for now, we will simply provide the client with a string binding that includes the server's dynamic endpoint.

4.3 Basic Server Setup

In this section, we will begin to examine the DCE calls needed to set up a server to use dynamic endpoints with an interface. Examples of these calls will be taken from the `main()` routine of `room_server.c`.

Checking for DCE Errors

Most of the DCE calls return a `status` parameter to indicate the success or failure of the requested operation. It is important to check the status after each call. The `CHECK_DCE` and `CHECK_DCE_NONFATAL` macros, shown in Code Sample 4.2, are used to do this. If the returned status is not `error_status_ok`, each macro will call `dce_error()` to print out an error message from the application, and an error string that describes the DCE status. `dce_error()`, shown in Code Sample 4.3, obtains the error string using the DCE call `dce_error_inq_text()`.

CHECK_DCE then aborts the program. This may seem to be rather harsh error handling, but a failure of most any of the DCE setup calls will incapacitate the server anyhow. The CHECK_DCE_NONFATAL() macro can be used in cases, such as termination cleanup, where the program should not be aborted on an error.

Since these error handling macros and procedures will be useful for both the client and the server, they reside in the sch_util.h and sch_util.c modules.

```
#define CHECK_DCE(status, errmsg) \
   if (status != error_status_ok) \
     dce_error(status, errmsg, true);

#define CHECK_DCE_NONFATAL(status, errmsg) \
   if (status != error_status_ok) \
     dce_error(status, errmsg, false);
```

Code Sample 4.2
schedule/sch_util.h: CHECK_DCE macros

```
void dce_error(
   unsigned32 status,
   char       *errmsg,
   boolean32  abort)
{
   unsigned char errstr[dce_c_error_string_len];
   int error_status;

   fprintf(stderr, "%s\n", errmsg);
   dce_error_inq_text(status, errstr, &error_status);
   if (error_status == error_status_ok)
   {
      fprintf(stderr, "%s\n", errstr);
   }
   else
   {
      fprintf(stderr,
        "Could not get error text for status 0x%8x\n",
        status);
   }
   if (abort)
   {
      exit(0);
   }
}
```

Code Sample 4.3
schedule/sch_util.c: dce_error()

Setting Up Bindings for Protocol Sequences

The first DCE setup task for the server is to obtain bindings for the protocol sequences (i.e., sockets) on which it will receive remote calls. The server can get bindings for all supported protocol sequences or for a specific protocol sequence.

Using All Supported Protocol Sequences

Usually the server will want to set up bindings for all of the protocol sequences supported by its host. (On HP-UX, two protocols are available: `ncadg_ip_udp` and `ncacn_ip_tcp`.) The call to do this is `rpc_server_use_all_protseqs()`, shown in Code Sample 4.4. After this call, the server will own dynamic endpoints for each of the supported protocol sequences.

The first parameter of `rpc_server_use_all_protseqs()` has an esoteric meaning that you can safely ignore. But if you're curious, it specifies the maximum length for the queue of incoming remote call requests waiting to be processed by the server. The DCE-defined constant `rpc_c_protseq_max_reqs_default` is an implementation default for the maximum number of pending calls. For the `ncacn_ip_tcp` protocol, this becomes the `backlog` parameter for the socket `listen()` call, which determines the maximum number of connect requests that can be queued to a call socket. The default ultimately becomes the constant `SOMAXCONN` defined in `socket.h`. On HP-UX this value is 20. For the `ncadg_ip_udp` protocol, the `max_calls` parameter currently has no meaning.

```
  rpc_server_use_all_protseqs(
     rpc_c_protseq_max_reqs_default, &status);
   CHECK_DCE(status,
     "Cannot get bindings for all protocols");
```

Code Sample 4.4
`schedule/room_server.c main()`: Using all protocol sequences

Using a Specific Protocol Sequence

Occasionally, it might be necessary to restrict the protocol sequences used by a server. There are two ways to do this. For a permanent restriction, the `rpc_server_use_protseq()` call can be used to specify a protocol sequence, as shown in Code Sample 4.5. The first parameter is the string name of the protocol sequence, in this case the `ncadg_ip_udp` protocol. The second parameter is the maximum number of concurrent calls, as described above. This call will yield one dynamic endpoint for the specified protocol.

```
  rpc_server_use_protseq(
      (unsigned_char_p_t) "ncadg_ip_udp",
      rpc_c_protseq_max_reqs_default,
      &status);
   CHECK_DCE(status,
     "Cannot get binding for ncadg_ip_udp");
```

Code Sample 4.5
`schedule/room_server.c main()`: Using a specific protocol sequence

Restricting Protocol Sequences at Runtime

On Unix systems, you can also restrict the protocols at runtime by setting the environment variable RPC_SUPPORTED_PROTSEQ. In the Korn shell (**ksh**), you can use

```
:export RPC_SUPPORTED_PROTSEQS="ncadg_ip_udp"
```

This restricts the supported protocol sequences to ncadg_ip_udp for processes run in this shell. This environment variable can also be used to control what bindings are imported by a client, as discussed in Section 5.3.

Care must be taken when restricting the protocol sequences used by a client and a server to ensure that they still have at least one in common. Otherwise you will experience the connection request rejected or communications failure errors.

Obtaining and Displaying Bindings

Once the bindings for the protocol sequences have been set up, they can be retrieved by calling rpc_server_inq_bindings(). This call returns a vector of the type rpc_binding_vector_t, with a count of the number of bindings and an array binding_h[] of binding handles. The binding vector will be needed in subsequent server setup calls. In Code Sample 4.6, it is used to display the bindings acquired by the server. The call rpc_binding_to_string_binding() converts the binding handles into string bindings that can be printed. Each string binding must be deallocated by a call to rpc_string_free() after it is used. The binding vector returned by rpc_server_inq_bindings() can be deallocated by calling rpc_binding_vector_free().

```
rpc_binding_vector_t *binding_vector;
...

rpc_server_inq_bindings(&binding_vector, &status);
CHECK_DCE(status, "Cannot get server bindings");

printf("Using bindings: \n");
for (i = 0; i < binding_vector->count; i++)
{
   rpc_binding_to_string_binding(
     binding_vector->binding_h[i],
     &string_binding, &status);
   CHECK_DCE(status,
     "Can't convert binding to string");
   printf("   %s\n", string_binding);
   rpc_string_free(&string_binding, &ignored_st);
}
```

Code Sample 4.6
schedule/room_server.c main(): Obtaining and displaying bindings

Output Sample 4.1 shows the bindings displayed by the above code. There are two bindings, one for each of the protocol sequences, `ncadg_ip_udp` and `ncacn_ip_tcp`, supported on HP-UX. The host address is in the IP dot notation: `15.4.25.126`. The endpoints are `1274` and `1506`, for UDP and TCP, respectively. The endpoints will change each time **room_server** is run.

```
Using bindings:

   ncadg_ip_udp:15.4.25.126[1274]
   ncacn_ip_tcp:15.4.25.126[1506]
```

Output Sample 4.1
room_server output: Bindings

Registering an Interface with the RPC Runtime

The RPC Runtime within the server must know which interfaces are exported by the server; that is, which collections of remote procedures the server can execute. The `rpc_server_register_if()` call registers an interface with the RPC Runtime. Code Sample 4.7 shows the call to register the `room` interface with the room server. The input parameters for the call are

- an *interface specification*, which provides the interface UUID and version number, the number of operations within the interface, and other interface information. The interface server stub, generated by the IDL compiler from the interface definition, contains a server interface specification data structure. For version `1.0` of the room interface, this is `room_v1_0_s_ifspec`. It is defined in the interface header file `room.h`, which is included at the beginning of the server.
- a manager type UUID, which identifies the type of objects that can be managed for the interface. Until objects are discussed in Chapter 8, we will use `NULL` to indicated the default manager type.
- a manager entry point vector (EPV), which points to the operation manager routines to be executed for the type of objects specified by the manager type. A value of `NULL` selects a default manager EPV defined in the interface server stub. We will use the default manager EPV until Chapter 8.

```
  rpc_server_register_if(
     room_v1_0_s_ifspec,   /* interface specification */
     NULL,                 /* default manager type    */
     NULL,                 /* default manager EPV     */
     &status);
   CHECK_DCE(status,
  "Cannot register room interface with RPC runtime");
```

Code Sample 4.7
`schedule/room_server.c main()`: Registering an interface with the RPC Runtime

The server's RPC Runtime maintains a table of the interfaces that have been registered by calls to `rpc_server_register_if()`. This table is used to determine which manager routine to call for an incoming remote call request. Figure 4.2 shows an example of the registration table with an entry for the `room` interface and its manager EPV. Different object types are not used with this interface, so the object type UUID is the `nil` UUID. Suppose the server's Runtime receives a call request for the `room_cancel()` operation. The request will contain the `room` interface UUID and version and an operation number. The Runtime will look up the interface UUID and version in the registration table to find the appropriate manager EPV to use. Then it will look up and call the manager entry point corresponding to the operation number—in this case, the `room_cancel()` procedure.

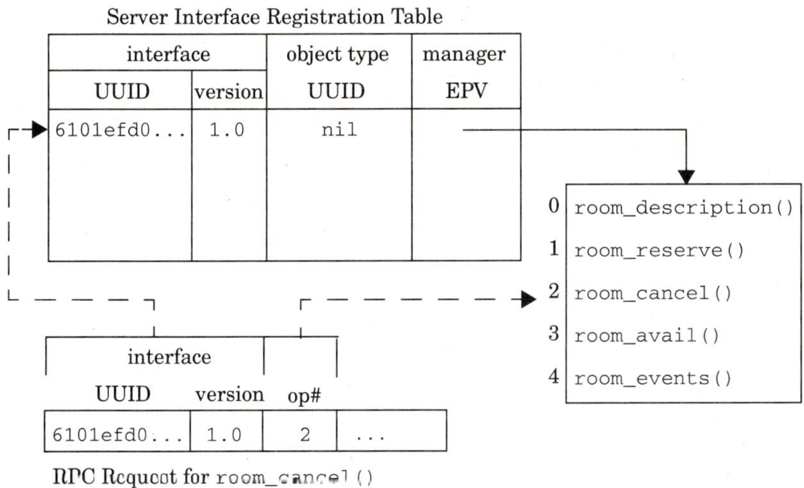

Figure 4.2
Server Interface Registration Table and Lookup

Listening for Remote Calls

After the interface is set up, the server must wait for and execute incoming remote calls for the interface. The `rpc_server_listen()` call, shown in Code Sample 4.8, does this. This call enters the RPC Runtime and creates one or more call threads to execute incoming calls. To avoid any thread-safety problems with multiple call threads, we will set the number of call threads to `1` for now. The server will remain in `rpc_server_listen()` for the remainder of its life, until it is terminated or until an irrecoverable error occurs within the server's RPC Runtime. (In Section 4.8 we will see how a server can be terminated.)

```
printf("\nRoom server listening...\n");
rpc_server_listen(1, &status);
CHECK_DCE_NONFATAL(status,
   "Server stopped listening");
```

Code Sample 4.8
`schedule/room_server.c main()`: Listening for incoming calls, with one call thread

Server Cleanup

When the server terminates, it should clean up data structures that were created for its interface. Code Sample 4.9 shows cleanup calls executed after the call to `rpc_server_listen()` returns. The call to `rpc_server_unregister_if()` removes the interface registration from the server's RPC Runtime. After the registration is removed, the server will reject any incoming calls for that interface. The `rpc_binding_vector_free()` call deallocates storage for the binding vector that was created by the `rpc_server_inq_bindings()`. Note that all of these data structures are within the server process and would have been destroyed anyway when the server terminated. But tidiness in a programmer is always a virtue.

```
rpc_server_listen(...);
printf("Room server shutting down...\n");

rpc_server_unregister_if(room_v1_0_s_ifspec,
   NULL, &status);
CHECK_DCE_NONFATAL(status,
"Cannot unregister room interface with RPC runtime");

rpc_binding_vector_free(&binding_vector, &status);
CHECK_DCE_NONFATAL(status, "Cannot free bind vector");
```

Code Sample 4.9
`schedule/room_server.c main()`: Cleaning up before termination

4.4 Basic Client Setup

In this section we will look at the simplest approach to setting up the **room** client to bind to the **room_server** and to make a remote call. The binding method used here will not suffice for a real client, but it will do until we discuss binding using CDS in Chapter 5.

Using a String Binding

The simplest way for the client to bind to a server is to use a string binding that specifies a protocol sequence, host address, and endpoint used by the server.

The **room_server** displays the string bindings it uses, as shown in Output Sample 4.1. For now, we will require that the user provide a string binding as an argument when running **room**, for example

```
:room ncadg_ip_udp:15.4.25.126[1274]
```

Clearly this is undesirable, because it forces the user to know both the host address and the endpoint of the server. Perhaps the host address could be hard coded in the client, but the endpoint cannot, since it will change each time the server is restarted. Our user will get some relief when Endpoint Mapping is introduced in Section 4.5.

Code Sample 4.10 illustrates the code needed to use the string binding. The `rpc_binding_from_string_binding()` call generates a binding handle `h` from the string binding in `argv[1]`. (`argv[1]` is a Unix/C convention for the first execution argument.) Note that the argument, declared as `char *`, is cast to the type `unsigned_char_p_t` to be compatible in the `rpc_binding_from_string_binding()` call. This casting will be used frequently because DCE almost always requires unsigned character data.

The binding handle `h` points to an opaque data structure set up by the RPC Runtime to hold information about the binding between the client and the server. The binding handle is typically included as the first parameter in remote calls to the server. Here it is declared as a global variable so it can be used in remote calls in other procedures in `room.c`.

```
rpc_binding_handle_t  h;
int main(int argc, char *argv[])
{
  . . .

  if (argc == 2)
  {
     printf("Using string binding %s\n", argv[1]);
     rpc_binding_from_string_binding(
        (unsigned_char_p_t) argv[1], &h, &status);
     CHECK_DCE(status,
     "Cannot convert string binding to handle");
  }
  . . .
}
```

Code Sample 4.10
`schedule/room.c main()`: Using a string binding

Making a Remote Procedure Call

Code Sample 4.11 shows an example of a remote call to the `room_reserve()` operation. Input parameters are

- the binding handle `h`,
- the `room` to be reserved,
- the date and time (`date_time`) for the reservation,
- the identity of the `reserver`, and
- a description (`desc`) of what the room is being reserved for.

Output parameters are

- the `status` of the reservation, set by the server, and
- the `call_status`, added by the `error_status` attribute in `room.acf`, which is set by DCE to an error if the remote call fails.

The macro `CHECK_CALL()` checks the returned call status and if it is not `error_status_ok`, prints the corresponding error message. The `print_sch_status()` call displays the result of the operation. Both `print_call_status()` and `print_sch_status()` are in the `sch_util.c` module.

```
#define CHECK_CALL(call_status) \
   if (call_status != error_status_ok) \
      { print_call_status(call_status); return; }

void reserve()
{
   sch_room_t        room;
   sch_date_time_t   date_time;
   sch_name_t        reserver;
   sch_event_desc_t  desc;
   sch_status_t      status;
   error_status_t    call_status;

      /* Input reservation information... */
   room_reserve(h, room, date_time, reserver, desc,
      &status, &call_status);
   CHECK_CALL(call_status);
   print_sch_status(status);
}
```

Code Sample 4.11
`schedule/room.c`: `reserve()`: Showing a remote call.

When `room_reserve()` is called (assuming that it is the first remote operation performed by the client), the RPC Runtime will use the string binding associated with the binding handle `h` to select the RPC protocol (say, `ncadg_ip_udp`). It will then use the string binding host address (`15.4.25.126`) and endpoint (`1274`) as the destination for its call request packet. The server will execute the operation and return a response packet with the `status` output. `call_status` will be `ok`.

If the server is not executing on the specified host and listening to the specified endpoint, the client will timeout waiting for the response packet. Then the `call_status` returned will be the ever-annoying `communications failure` error. In Section 4.6 we will see how the client can be enhanced to detect if the server is not available before making the remote call.

4.5 Endpoint Mapping

In the example in the last section, we could readily see how inconvenient it would be to require the client (or the client's user) to know the endpoint used by the server. It would be far better for the client not to have to specify the endpoint and to have DCE automatically determine the correct endpoint to be used for remote calls. This feature, called *endpoint mapping*, is indeed provided by DCE.

The Endpoint Map

The *endpoint map* is a data structure that maps interfaces to endpoints for servers exporting the interfaces. Each host system on which DCE has been started has an endpoint map for the servers running on the host.

Endpoint Entry Format

There is one endpoint map entry for each binding registered by a server on the local system. An interface will have one entry for each of its server's endpoints. An entry contains these fields:

- The *object uuid* identifies an object that is associated with the binding. If there is no such object, this field is `nil`. Objects will not be discussed until Chapter 8.
- The *interface uuid and version* identifies the interface associated with the binding. Note that a version number is included, so the endpoint map can contain different bindings for different versions of the same interface.
- The *string bindings* supply protocol sequences and endpoints for the binding. The local system address is also included in all string bindings in the map.
- The *annotation* is a descriptive character string supplied by the server when it registers the binding.

rpcd *and* ***dced***

There is a process on each host that has the responsibility to maintain the host's endpoint map. For the OSF DCE 1.0 to 1.0.3 releases, this process is the RPC Daemon, or **rpcd**. For OSF DCE 1.1 (and later) releases, the new DCE Daemon **dced** maintains the endpoint map.

Each server contacts **rpcd/dced** to register its interfaces and endpoints. Then clients, on both the local and remote systems, can ask **rpcd/dced** to resolve an interface into the set of endpoints used by a server exporting the interface.

The RPC/DCE Daemon itself uses a well-known endpoint: UDP port `135`. Clients send to this port during the endpoint mapping process. The details will be discussed later.

The endpoint map data is stored in a host data file. For HP-UX DCE 1.0 to 1.2, this file is `/opt/dcelocal/var/rpc/rpcdep.dat`. For HP-UX DCE 1.4 or later, it is `/opt/dcelocal/var/dced/Ep.db`. When the RPC/DCE Daemon is restarted, it will read its endpoint map file to restore previous endpoint map entries.

Viewing Endpoint Map Entries

The Endpoint Map can be examined using the RPC Control Program (**rpccp**) or, on DCE 1.1 or later products, the DCE Control Program (**dcecp**).

The **rpccp show mapping** command displays endpoint mappings on the local system. Without further qualification, this command will display all the mappings, which can be quite extensive. (You might want to pipe the command to **more** to view the mappings at your leisure.) You can restrict the display to a set of interfaces (with the **-i** option), or objects (with the **-o** option).

Output Sample 4.2 shows an example of the **rpccp show mapping** command, for the `room` interface as it will be registered by the server in Output Sample 4.1. There are two bindings for dynamic endpoints: one for TCP port number `1506` and one for UDP port number `1274`. There is no object associated with these bindings, so the object uuid is `nil`.

The **rpccp show mapping** command can also be used to display endpoint mappings on other systems. To show the mappings on `hpeap827`, you can use the command

```
:rpccp show mapping ncadg_ip_udp:hpeap827
```

```
:rpccp show mapping -i 6101efd0-89fc-11cd-be27-080009307c01,1.0

mappings:

  <object>          nil
  <interface id>    6101efd0-89fc-11cd-be27-080009307c01,1.0
  <string binding>  ncadg_ip_udp:15.4.25.126[1274]
  <annotation>      Room Server

  <object>          nil
  <interface id>    6101efd0-89fc-11cd-be27-080009307c01,1.0
  <string binding>  ncacn_ip_tcp:15.4.25.126[1506]
  <annotation>      Room Server
```

Output Sample 4.2
rpccp show mapping

The **dcecp** program provided by DCE 1.1 (which is HP-UX DCE 1.4) provides a single command language for managing all DCE components. The general syntax of **dcecp** commands is

```
:dcecp -c object verb [argument] [options]
```

where

- *object* specifies the kind of DCE thing you want to manage,
- *verb* specifies what you want to do to the object,
- *argument* selects one particular object to manage, and
- *options* are addition Unix style options (e.g., **-i**).

The **dcecp** Tool Command Language (TCL) can be used to program scripts for DCE management. TCL will not be discussed further in this book.

Output Sample 4.3 shows the **dcecp** command to display the endpoint map entries for the `room` interface. In this command, the object is **endpoint**, the verb is **show**, there is no argument, and the **-i** option provides the interface and version number. Note that the format of **dcecp** output is a list of attribute/value pairs, each in the format

```
{attribute_name value} or
{attribute_name {value_1 value_2 ...}}
```

```
:dcecp -c endpoint show -i 6101efd0-89fc-11cd-be27-080009307c01,1.0
{{interface {6101efd0-89fc-11cd-be27-080009307c01 1.0}}
 {binding {ncadg_ip_udp 15.4.25.126 1274}}
 {annotation {Room Server}}}

{{interface {6101efd0-89fc-11cd-be27-080009307c01 1.0}}
 {binding {ncacn_ip_tcp 15.4.25.126 1506}}
 {annotation {Room Server}}}
```

Output Sample 4.3
Example of **dcecp endpoint show**

Registering with the Endpoint Map in the Server

To use endpoint mapping, the server setup and cleanup must be enhanced to register and unregister the interface with the local Endpoint Map. No modifications need to be made to the client setup, since the client's RPC Runtime will automatically use endpoint mapping, as described later.

Code Sample 4.12 shows the `rpc_ep_register()` call to register an interface. The input parameters to this call are

- The *server interface* specification, from the interface header and the server stub files, which supplies the interface UUID and version. The interface specification for version `1.0` of the `room` interface is `room_v1_0_s_ifspec`, defined in `room.h`.

- A *binding vector*, which supplies the bindings used by the server. In our server, the binding vector was previously obtained by the `rpc_server_inq_bindings()` call.
- A vector of object UUIDs, which specify what objects the server is managing. A value of `NULL` means no objects. This parameter will be discussed further in Chapter 8.
- A character string *annotation* that describes the server in the Endpoint Map entry.

```
rpc_ep_register(
    room_v1_0_s_ifspec, /* interface specification */
    binding_vector,     /* binding vector          */
    NULL,               /* no object UUID vector   */
    (unsigned_char_p_t) "Room Server", /* annotate */
    &status);
CHECK_DCE(status,
"Cannot register room interface with Endpoint Map");
```

Code Sample 4.12
`schedule/room_server.c main()`: Endpoint registration.

Once an interface has been registered with the Endpoint Map, the resultant entry will persist until it is explicitly removed. The server should remove the entry during its termination cleanup, using the `rpc_ep_unregister()` call. Code Sample 4.13 shows this for the **room_server**. The same input parameters that were used in the registration call are used here, except for the omission of the annotation.

```
rpc_ep_unregister(
    room_v1_0_s_ifspec, /* interface specification */
    binding_vector,     /* binding vector          */
    NULL,               /* no object UUID vector   */
    &status);
CHECK_DCE_NONFATAL(status,
"Cannot unregister room interface with EndpointMap");
```

Code Sample 4.13
`schedule/room_server.c main()`: Endpoint unregistration.

Using a Partial Binding in the Client

Now that we have added endpoint registration to **room_server**, it is no longer necessary to include the endpoint in the string binding argument for the **room** client. Instead, we can use a *partial binding* that includes only the protocol sequence and the host address. DCE will automatically resolve the endpoint, as described next. An example of a partial binding execution argument is

:room ncadg_ip_udp:hpiala3

Endpoint Resolution

If a client makes a remote procedure call using a partially bound handle (one with a server host address but no endpoint) the client's RPC Runtime will try to find an endpoint through the server host's endpoint map. The protocol to do this depends on the protocol sequence of the binding.

ncadg_ip_udp Protocol

When a binding uses the ncadg_ip_udp protocol, RPC uses a technique called *forwarding*, where the client sends its initial request to **rpcd** (or **dced**, for DCE 1.1), and **rpcd/dced** forwards the request to the appropriate server. This is shown in Figure 4.3.

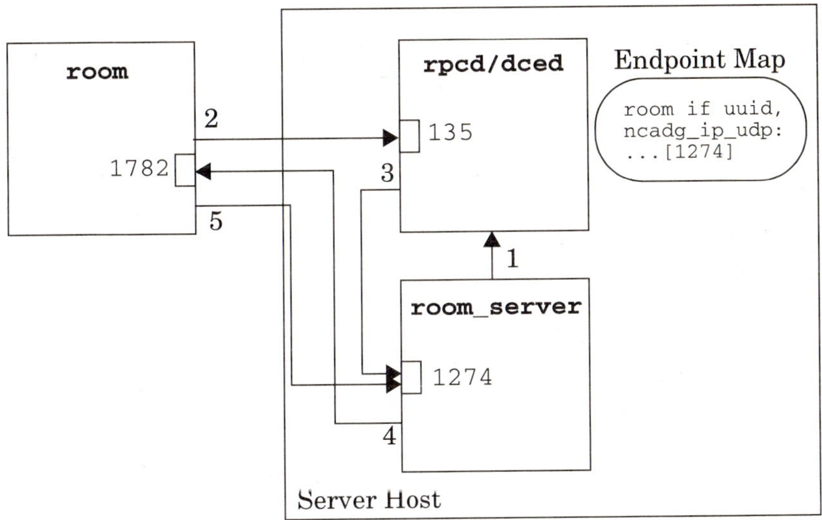

Figure 4.3
Endpoint Resolution with the ncadg_ip_udp protocol

1. **room_server** registers its interface and endpoints (say, UDP port 1274) with the local Endpoint Map.
2. **room** executes a remote call using a partially bound handle to the server host. The client RPC Runtime sends the call request packet to the well-known UDP port (135) on the server host. The call request includes the target interface UUID and version, and the port number for the UDP socket (say, 1782) **room** will use to receive any response.
3. The server host **rpcd/dced** receives the call request and looks up the room interface UUID and version in the endpoint map. If there is an ncadg_ip_udp

binding registered for the interface, **rpcd/dced** forwards the request call packet to the registered endpoint (UDP port `1274`).

4. **room_server** receives the call request packet through its UDP port and executes the remote call. It sends the call response packet back to **room**'s UDP port. The call response packet contain the server's endpoint (UDP port `1274`).
5. **room** receives the call response packet and retains the server's endpoint. The next time **room** makes a call to the server, it will send the request packet directly to the server port `1274`. Consequently, only the first remote call bears the overhead of forwarding.

`ncacn_ip_tcp` Protocol

The forwarding method used for the `ncadg_ip_udp` protocol will not work with the `ncacn_ip_tcp` protocol—the TCP protocol does not provide a way for a process to forward a connection request to another process. The client RPC Runtime must know the server's TCP port number before it can establish the connection. To do this, the client's Runtime makes an idempotent call to the server host **rpcd/dced**, using the `ncadg_ip_udp` protocol. This call retrieves the endpoint to be used in the client's connection request. Figure 4.4 illustrates this process.

1. **room_server** registers its interface and endpoints (say, TCP port `1506`) with the local Endpoint Map.
2. **room** executes a remote call using a partially bound handle to the server host. The client RPC Runtime makes an idempotent call to the well-known UDP port (`135`) on the server host. The call requests that **rpcd/dced** resolve the endpoints for the `room` interface.
3. The server host **rpcd/dced** receives the endpoint resolution call and looks up the `room` interface UUID and version in the endpoint map. **rpcd/dced** then sends a response back to **room** containing the endpoint for the interface, TCP port `1506`.
4. **room** receives the response from **rpcd/dced** with the server's endpoint, TCP port `1506`. It then establishes a connection to that port on the server host to communicate with **room_server**. Subsequent request packets are sent over this connection.

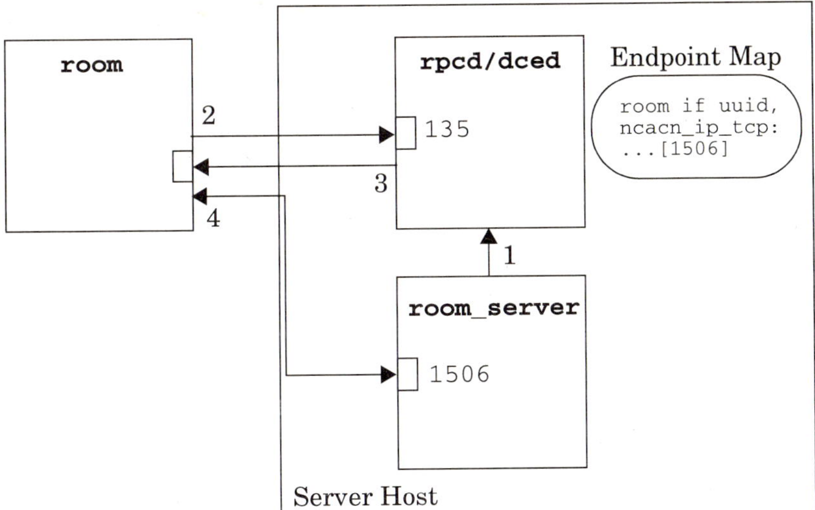

Figure 4.4
Endpoint Resolution with the ncacn_ip_tcp protocol

Let's compare the overhead of endpoint resolution for the ncacn_ip_tcp and ncadg_ip_udp protocols. The dg endpoint mapping requires one (or more) additional packet retransmissions within the server host, between **rpcd/dced** and the server. The cn endpoint mapping requires an additional packet to be sent between the server host **rpcd/dced** and the client. Since external transmissions involve more overhead than internal transmissions, endpoint mapping for cn usually has more overhead than for dg. Recall that the cn protocol already incurs additional overhead for the connection establishment. The overhead for the connection establishment and endpoint mapping occurs only on the first call, so it can be amortized over subsequent calls.

Endpoint Mapping Problems

Here are some possible problems to guard against when using endpoint mapping.

Stale Endpoint Map Entries

If a server that has registered an interface terminates without having unregistered the interface, the registration will still exist in the endpoint map. However, the endpoints in the endpoint map entry will no longer exist. If a client makes a remote call with a partial binding for that interface to the (late) server's host, **rpcd/dced** will attempt to resolve the partial binding with the stale endpoint information. The result will be a `connection request rejected` error for a `ncacn_ip_tcp` binding, or `communications failure` error for a `ncadg_ip_udp` binding (after waiting for the annoying timeout). This undesired behavior can be avoided in two ways:

- Always ensure that `rpc_ep_unregister()` is executed when a server terminates. In Section 4.7, we will see how the server can be terminated correctly.
- Have the client check that the server is actually listening to the endpoint before making the remote call. This will be shown in Section 4.6.

Multiple Servers on the Same Host

There can be only one endpoint map entry for an object, an interface and a protocol sequence. Suppose you want to have two servers for the same interface running on a multiprocessor host system for load balancing over the host's processors. Both servers register the interface and their own bindings with `rpc_ep_register()`. The second server to execute will overwrite the bindings for the first server. This effectively strands the first server; no client can find its bindings. This problem can be solved in two ways:

- Each server can register with separate *server instance objects,* which use a separate object UUID for each instance of the server. This leads to separate endpoint map entries. But it requires that the clients know one of the object UUIDs to bind to a server. Object UUIDs will be discussed in Chapter 8.
- Each server can use `rpc_ep_register_no_replace()`. This call has the same parameters as `rpc_ep_register()`, but it does not overwrite existing endpoint map entries. Instead it adds new endpoint entries. When a client uses a partial binding, the endpoint mapping mechanism will select one of the endpoints for the binding's protocol sequence. It appears that the selection of endpoints is random, so this approach is good for load balancing.

NCS Local Location Broker and ONC Port Mapper

Readers familiar with the Network Computing System (NCS) may recognize that the endpoint map and **rpcd/dced** fulfill the same function for DCE as the *Local Location Broker* (**llbd**) in NCS. This is not surprising, given that NCS is the product from which DCE RPC was derived. In fact, both the DCE **rpcd/dced** and the NCS **llbd** use the same UDP port 135. A side effect of this is that the NCS and DCE products cannot run on the same system. To provide backwards compatibility for NCS-based applications, **rpcd/dced** can accept and respond to NCS local location broker requests. There is a separate file to hold the LLB entries (`/opt/dcelocal/var/rpc/rpcdllb.dat` on HP-UX DCE prior to version 1.4 and `/opt/dcelocal/var/dced/Llb.db` for HP-UX DCE 1.4 and later).

Readers familiar with the Open Network Computing (ONC) product and the Network File System (NFS) from Sun Microsystems may recognize that the ONC *Port Mapper* plays a similar endpoint mapping role for NFS and ONC. But the DCE Endpoint Map and the ONC Port Mapper are not compatible and cannot interoperate.

4.6 Checking for an Active Server

If a client tries to bind to a server that is not currently running, the client may experience a communications error on its first remote call. This may be an inconvenient time to discover that the server is not available. For example, in the **room** client, the user would have already input data for the first operation. Instead, it is desirable to check if a server is active when the binding is established. Code Sample 4.14 shows a function, `is_server_there()`, that returns `true` if a binding points to an active server; otherwise it returns `false`. This function is included in the common module `sch_util.c` in case it is ever needed by other application clients.

```
boolean32 is_server_there(
   rpc_binding_handle_t h,
   rpc_if_handle_t      ifspec)
{
   boolean32  listening;
   unsigned32 status;

   listening = rpc_mgmt_is_server_listening(h, &status);
   if (status == rpc_s_binding_incomplete)
   {
      rpc_ep_resolve_binding(h, ifspec, &status);
      if ((status == ept_s_not_registered) ||
          (status == rpc_s_comm_failure)   ||
          (status == rpc_s_connect_rejected))
      {
        return(false);
      }
      CHECK_DCE(status, "Cannot resolve binding");
      listening =
        rpc_mgmt_is_server_listening(h, &status);
   }

   if ((status == rpc_s_comm_failure) ||
       (status == rpc_s_connect_rejected))
   {
      return(false);
   }
   CHECK_DCE(status,
     "Cannot check if server is listening");
   return (listening);
}
```

Code Sample 4.14
`schedule/sch_util.c: is_server_there()`

The call to rpc_mgmt_is_server_listening() sends a test packet to the server at the socket address associated with the binding. (This is similar to the **ping** command for testing if a host can be reached over an IP network.) If the server is active (that is, if it has called rpc_server_listen()), its RPC Runtime will respond to the test packet and the mgmt call will return true. If the server is not active, the call will return false or a status indicating the type of failure. If the binding is partial, a status of rpc_s_binding_incomplete will be returned. In this case, a call to rpc_ep_resolve_binding() will perform the endpoint mapping appropriate to the binding's protocol. If the endpoint is not registered in the server host's endpoint map (ept_s_not_registered) or the server host's **rpcd/dced** cannot be reached (rpc_s_comm_failure for the dg protocol or rpc_s_connect_ rejected for the cn protocol), then the server is assumed to be inactive or unreachable. If the resolve binding call is successful, the call to rpc_mgmt_is_server_listening() is retried. If a communications failure is detected by either the first or second call, the server is assumed to be unreachable.

Code Sample 4.15 shows the call to is_server_there() in the room client after the binding handle h has been established. Note that after the is_server_there() call, we will have resolved the binding's endpoint, so we can display the full binding.

```
printf("Checking server availability...\n");
if (!is_server_there(h, room_v1_0_c_ifspec))
{
    printf("Server is not responding\n");
    exit(0);
}

rpc_binding_to_string_binding(
  h, &string_binding, &status);
CHECK_DCE(status,
  "Cannot convert binding to string binding");
printf("Using binding %s\n", string_binding);
rpc_string_free(&string_binding, &ignored_st);
```

Code Sample 4.15
schedule/room.c main(): with is_server_there() check

4.7 Stopping a Server

Now that endpoint registration has been added to the server setup, it is imperative that the server correctly clean up after itself. Other server setup (interface registration and protocol setup) was local to the server process and would go away when the server terminated. But the endpoint registration will survive the server unless it is explicitly removed. So now is the time to introduce a technique for properly stopping a server.

We want to be able to send a signal to the server, using either a control-c in the server's window, or a **kill** command with the server's process ID. The server should receive the signal and perform appropriate cleanup. To do this, we will use a separate thread whose sole purpose is to intercept the signal.

Code Sample 4.16 shows the base procedure for the signal catching thread. The signature for `signal_catcher()` is determined by threads, but the `arg` parameter and the return value are not used here. This routine uses the POSIX signal management calls `sigemptyset()`, `sigaddset()`, and `sigwait()` to wait for a `SIGTERM`, `SIGINT`, or `SIGHUP` signal. After the signal occurs, the thread will call the routine `rpc_mgmt_stop_server_listening()`, which will cause the `rpc_server_listen()` call in the server's main thread to complete. Any necessary cleanup can be then be performed.

```
pthread_addr_t signal_catcher(pthread_addr_t arg)
{
    sigset_t mask;
    unsigned32 status;

    sigemptyset(&mask);
    sigaddset(&mask, SIGTERM);
    sigaddset(&mask, SIGINT);
    sigaddset(&mask, SIGHUP);

    rpc_mgmt_stop_server_listening(NULL, &status);
    CHECK_DCE(status, "Cannot stop server listening");
}
```

Code Sample 4.16
`schedule/room_server.c: signal_catcher()`thread

Creating a Thread

Since creation of threads is a common task, we will add a `create_thread()` routine to `sch_util.c`. Code Sample 4.17 shows this routine. It has three input and one output parameters:

- a *thread base routine* that will be executed when the thread is created.
- a *thread name* for display in error messages.
- a *thread id* that is returned by the `pthread_create()`.
- an *argument* that is passed to the thread base routine when it is created. This can be used to pass information to the thread, but it is not used in the `signal_catcher` thread.

```
void create_thread(
   pthread_startroutine_t thread_routine,
   char                   *thread_name,
   pthread_t              *thread_id,
   pthread_addr_t          thread_arg)
{
   unsigned32 status;

   status = pthread_create(thread_id,
     pthread_attr_default, thread_routine, thread_arg);
   if (status != 0)
   {
      fprintf(stderr,
        "Cannot create %s thread\n", thread_name);
      fprintf(stderr, "%s\n", strerror(errno));
      exit(0);
   }
   pthread_yield(); /* Allow thread to run now. */
}
```

Code Sample 4.17
`schedule/sch_util.c: create_thread()`

Code Sample 4.18 shows a `kill_thread()` routine that calls `pthread_cancel()` to kill the specified thread.

```
void kill_thread(
   pthread_t thread_id,
   char      *thread_name)
{
   unsigned32 status;

   status = pthread_cancel(thread_id);
   if (status != 0)
   {
      fprintf(stderr,
        "Cannot kill %s thread\n", thread_name);
      fprintf(stderr, "%s\n", strerror(errno));
   }
}
```

Code Sample 4.18
`schedule/sch_util.c: kill_thread()`

Code Sample 4.19 shows the creation of the signal_catcher thread before the server enters rpc_server_listen(). When the server cleans up, it will kill the signal_catcher thread.

```
create_thread(signal_catcher,"signal catcher",
   &sigcatch_thread, NULL);

rpc_server_listen(...);
...

kill_thread(sigcatch_thread, "signal catcher");
```

Code Sample 4.19
schedule/room_server.c main(): Creating and killing the signal_catcher thread

CHAPTER 5

Client and Server Setup Using CDS

The client and server setup methods presented in the last chapter all suffer from the same problem: They require that the client know the host system on which the server is running. In the examples in Chapter 4, the server host name was input as an argument to the client. If the server location changes, the user must know the new location. This is obviously unacceptable for any real distributed application. We want the client to be able to find the server automatically. DCE provides the Cell Directory Service to solve this problem.

5.1 The Cell Directory

CDS, the Cell Directory Service, provides a general-purpose, distributed directory for information within a DCE cell. Remember that a cell is a collection of systems that are grouped together for administrative, performance, and possibly other reasons. A cell might correspond to a local work group, a campus site, a metropolitan area, a geographic region, or even an entire country, depending on the requirements of the DCE users within the cell. Delineation and configuration of a cell are beyond the scope of this book. See the *OSF DCE Administration Guide* for more information on setting up cells.

DCE RPC uses CDS to store server and object location information, which will be discussed beginning with the RPC Name Space section. CDS can also be used for other purposes through the X/Open Directory Services interface (XDS) and the OSI Object Management interface (XOM). XDS and XOM will not be covered by this book. See the *OSF DCE Application Development Guide* for details on XDS and XOM.

Elements within CDS are *directories* and *objects*. Each of these elements has a name that can include upper- and lowercase letters, digits, and all special characters except those with meaning to CDS (for example, `/` and `*`). Case is significant—for example, `Name` is different from `name`. Names can be any (reasonable) length. In general, you should use descriptive but manageable names.

Directories

CDS contains a hierarchy of directories, much like the Unix file system. Each directory can contain subdirectories or objects. Some directories and objects are predefined by DCE, and some are defined and created by applications and local conventions.

The top-most directory of a cell (the *cell root*) is designated `/.../`*`cell_name`*, or simply `/.:` for the local cell. A sequence of directories, separated by `/`, specifies a directory path, as in Unix. An example of a CDS path is `/.:/subsys/sch/`, where `/.:` is the cell root, `subsys` is a DCE-defined directory, and `sch` is an application-defined subdirectory within `subsys` that will be used for CDS objects associated with the room schedule application. More examples of directories are shown in Figure 5.1.

Objects

CDS objects are leaf entries in directories—that is, an object cannot include another object or directory. An object usually represents something, such as a server, and has *attributes* that contain data about the represented entity. Each attribute has an identifier, the *ISO OID*, and one or more values. The ISO OID is a sequence of integers, like `1.3.22.1.1.1`, that ensures that each type of attribute is uniquely identified. Attributes can be predefined by DCE or defined by an application, using the XDS and XOM interfaces. All of the attributes of interest in this book are predefined.

RPC uses three types of object entries: servers, groups, and profiles. These will be discussed in more detail in Section 5.2. Each of these object types has predefined attributes to hold information relevant to RPC.

Viewing the Cell Directory: **`cdsbrowser`** and **`cdscp`**

The CDS Browser is a useful tool provided with HP-UX DCE for viewing and modifying entries in a cell directory. It provides a Motif graphical user interface with windows for different types of objects in CDS. To browse the cell directory, run **`cdsbrowser`** at your workstation. (Remember to set the `DISPLAY` environment variable used by X-Windows to your workstation display.)

Initially, the Browser will display a window containing the cell root directory, `/.:` and its immediate contents. Figure 5.1 shows the cell directory window. The cell name is `/.../jaja`. The entries marked `D` are directories, such as `/.:/hosts` and `/.:/subsys`. All other entries are objects. Most of the objects are marked with their RPC designations (`S` for servers, `G` for groups, and `P` for profiles). Miscellaneous object designations are O (for an unassigned object) and C (for a CDS clearinghouse, discussed in Section 5.6).

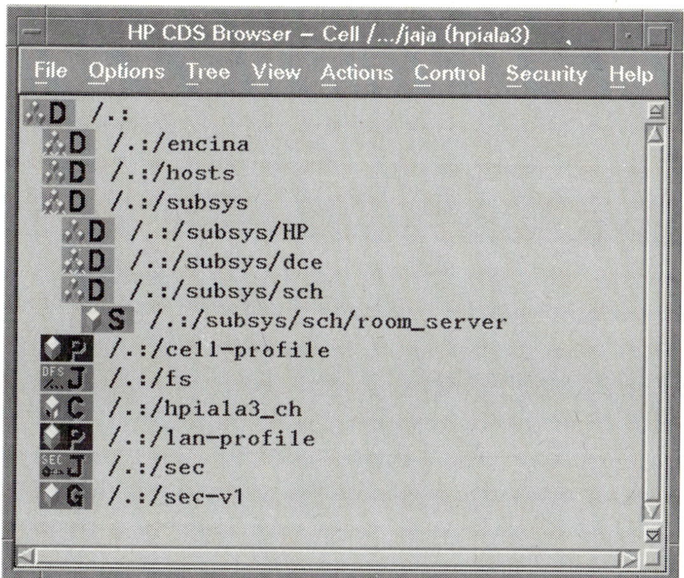

Figure 5.1
cdsbrowser Display: Cell Directories and Objects

The contents of any directory can be displayed (the directory is *expanded*) by double-clicking on the directory name or symbol. In Figure 5.1, the /.:/subsys and /.:/subsys/sch directories have been so expanded. An expanded directory can be *collapsed* again by double-clicking.

If you double-click on an object, you will display another window that shows the object's attributes. Special windows are displayed for RPC objects. Figures 5.2, 5.3, and 5.4 will illustrate these.

The CDS Control Program (**cdscp**) provides a command line interface for viewing and modifying CDS directories and objects. Output Sample 5.1 shows an example of output from a couple of **cdscp** commands. Note that it takes two separate commands to display the top-level directories and objects. In general, **cdscp** is less easy to use than **cdsbrowser**. However, **cdscp** can be used in command scripts, whereas **cdsbrowser** cannot.

The RPC Control program (**rpccp**) that was introduced in Chapter 4 can be used to view and modify CDS objects used by RPC. Examples of this will be shown in Output Samples 5.3, 5.5, and 5.7.

```
:cdscp list directory /.:/*
                         LIST
                    DIRECTORY   /.../jaja
                           AT   1995-07-06-12:40:58
encina
hosts
subsys

:cdscp list object /.:/*
                         LIST
                       OBJECT   /.../jaja
                           AT   1995-07-06-12:41:05
cell-profile
fs
hpiala3_ch
lan-profile
sec
sec-v1
```

Output Sample 5.1
cdscp Display: List Directories and Objects

With HP-UX DCE 1.4 (which corresponds to the OSF DCE 1.1 release), you can also obtain information about entries in CDS using the general DCE control program **dcecp**. Output Sample 5.2 shows the **dcecp** command to list CDS directories and objects. Output Samples 5.4, 5.6, and 5.8 show the commands to display RPC entries for servers, groups, and profiles.

```
:dcecp -c directory list /.:/
/.../jaja/encina /.../jaja/hosts /.../jaja/subsys /
.../jaja/cell-profile /.../jaja/fs /.../jaja/hpiala3_ch
/.../jaja/lan-profile /.../jaja/sec /.../jaja/sec-v1
```

Output Sample 5.2
dcecp Display: List Directories and Objects

5.2 The RPC Name Space

DCE RPC uses the cell directory to hold location information about its servers and objects. This view of the directory is called the *RPC Name Space*. The RPC Name Space is set up to appear independent of the underlying directory service, so in theory something other than CDS could be used with the Name Space. But at the present time the only implementation of the Name Space is on top of CDS.

The RPC Name Space uses three directory object types: *server* entries, *group* entries, and *profiles*. Each of these objects has predefined attributes for relevant information. Servers can create these entries or use existing entries to register their location information. Clients use one or more of these entries to locate a server for an interface. Both clients and servers use the RPC Name Service interface calls, all which have the prefix `rpc_ns_`. Name Space entries can also be created and modified using **cdscp**, **rpccp**, and **dcecp** commands, or the **cdsbrowser** GUI. Creation and modification of Name Space entries is subject to security checks, which will be discussed in Section 5.3.

Server Entry

A server entry provides the location of a server for a particular interface. It is possible to include information for more than one server within one server entry, but for administrative purposes it is best to have one server entry for each server. A server entry contains the following information:

- a list of UUIDs for objects managed by the server
- the interface UUID and version
- a list of string bindings for the protocols used by the server.

The object list in the entry may be empty and in fact will be so in our examples here. Objects will be discussed in Chapter 8.

Note well that the string bindings are partial—that is, they contain the server's host address but not the endpoint used by the server. When a client constructs a binding using a server entry from the RPC Name Space, the binding will also be partial and the endpoint mapping mechanism (discussed in Chapter 4) is used to obtain the server's endpoint.

It may seem odd that the server entry omits the server's endpoint, requiring the additional overhead of endpoint mapping. The intention is to minimize updating of the server entries. When a server is stopped and then restarted (with a different endpoint) on the same node, only the local endpoint map needs to be updated. This cuts down "wear and tear" on CDS (as one DCE source put it). However, if the server removes its own server entry when it terminates (as will be recommended later), the cell directory has to be updated anyway.

Figure 5.2 shows the **cdsbrowser** window for a sample server entry named `room_server`, in the directory `/.:/subsys/sch`. There are no objects listed in the entry. The interface UUID and version specify version `1.0` of the `room` interface. There are two string bindings in the entry, one for the `ncadg_ip_udp` protocol and one for the `ncacn_ip_tcp` protocol. Both of these bindings specify the same server host IP address, `15.4.25.126`. Output Sample 5.3 shows the same server entry displayed using the **rpccp show server** command, and Output Sample 5.4 shows the server entry displayed by **dcecp**.

```
:rpccp show server /.:/subsys/sch/room_server

>>> no matching objects found

binding information:

   <interface id>    6101efd0-89fc-11cd-be27-080009307c01,1.0
   <string binding> ncadg_ip_udp:15.4.25.126[]
   <string binding> ncacn_ip_tcp:15.4.25.126[]
```

Output Sample 5.3
rpccp Display: RPC Server Entry

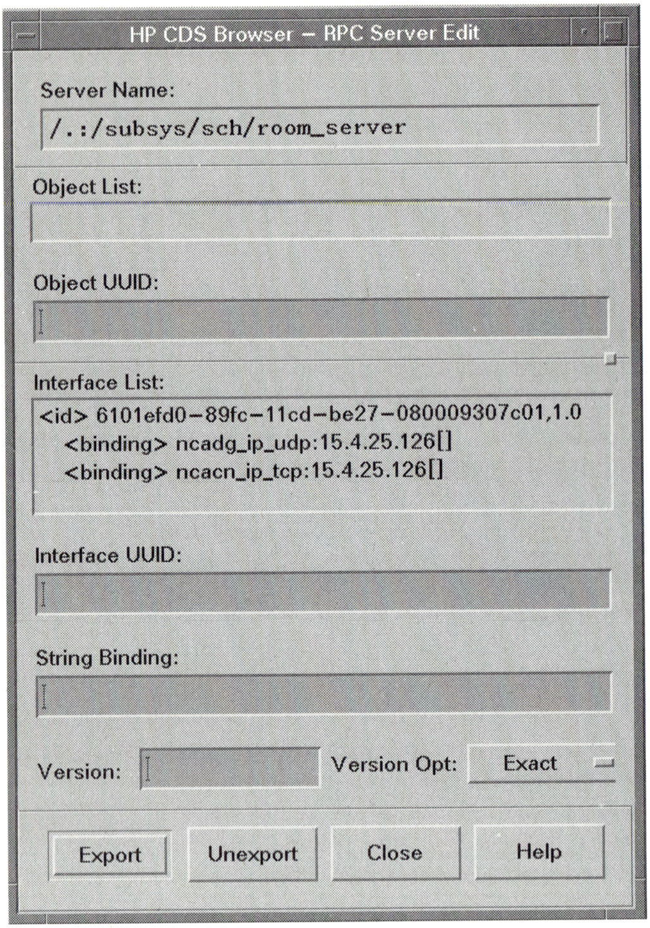

HP CDS Browser – RPC Server Edit

Server Name:

/.:/subsys/sch/room_server

Object List:

Object UUID:

Interface List:

<id> 6101efd0-89fc-11cd-be27-080009307c01,1.0
<binding> ncadg_ip_udp:15.4.25.126[]
<binding> ncacn_ip_tcp:15.4.25.126[]

Interface UUID:

String Binding:

Version: Version Opt: Exact

Export Unexport Close Help

Figure 5.2
cdsbrowser Display: RPC Server Entry for `room` interface.

```
:dcecp -c rpcentry show /.:/subsys/sch/room_server
{6101efd0-89fc-11cd-be27-080009307c01 1.0
  {ncadg_ip_udp 15.4.25.126}
  {ncacn_ip_tcp 15.4.25.126}}
noobjects
```

Output Sample 5.4
dcecp Display: RPC Server Entry

Group Entry

Some applications may have more than one server exporting a particular interface. For these cases it is useful to have a way of grouping Name Space entries for several servers. The RPC group entry provides this. An RPC group entry is a list of RPC Name Space entries. Each group member is represented by its full CDS name. A group can contain server entries or other groups, which allow nesting of groups. A server can dynamically add its server entry to a group through an `rpc_ns_` call, or entries can be statically added to a group through **cdsbrowser**, **rpccp,** or **dcecp**. A client can use a group name in `rpc_ns_` calls to import one or more bindings for servers in the group.

Figure 5.3 shows the **cdsbrowser** window for an RPC group entry used by the `room` client and server. This group has one entry, the server entry shown in Figure 5.2. Output Samples 5.5 and 5.6 show the same group entry displayed by **rpccp** and **dcecp.**

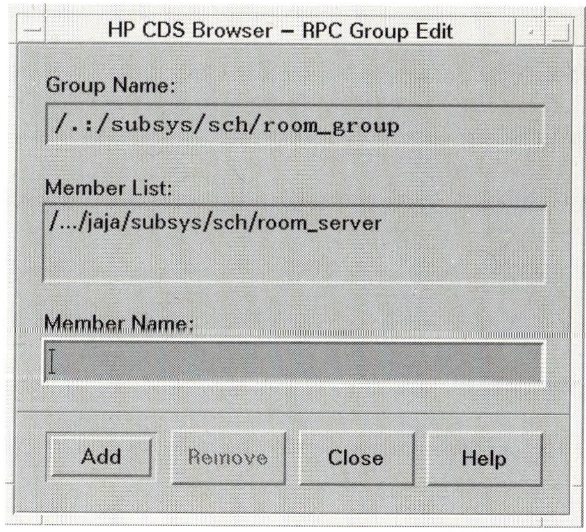

Figure 5.3
cdsbrowser Display: RPC Group Entry for `room_server`

```
:rpccp show group /.:/subsys/sch/room_group

group members:

  /.../jaja/subsys/sch/room_server
```

Output Sample 5.5
rpccp Display: RPC Group Entry

```
:dcecp -c rpcgroup list /.:/subsys/sch/room_group
/.../jaja/subsys/sch/room_server
```

Output Sample 5.6
dcecp Display: RPC Group Entry

Profiles

Profiles provide a way for a user or a group of users to maintain a list of preferred servers for various interfaces. Each element of a profile contains the following information:

- an *interface UUID* and *version number*,
- the name of a *server entry*, *group entry*, or another *profile*,
- an integer *priority* (from `0` to `7`), and
- an *annotation* string.

A server may dynamically add an element to a profile through an `rpc_ns_` call, or an element can be added statically through an **rpccp**, **dcecp**, or **cdsbrowser** command. When a client uses a profile name in `rpc_ns_` calls to import bindings for an interface, RPC will search the profile for elements with matching interface UUIDs and versions and will use the element's server entry, group entry, or profile to construct the bindings. The priority is used to order the bindings found from multiple matching profile members. The annotation provides a description of the purpose of the entry.

Figure 5.4 shows a **cdsbrowser** window with the element list for the predefined profile `/.:/cell-profile`. This is a default profile for all of the users within the local cell. There are a number of elements that are added to this profile during DCE configuration. In addition, the room server can add an element to the cell profile with the `room` interface UUID and its server entry. Clients can use the cell profile to find the room server for their local cell.

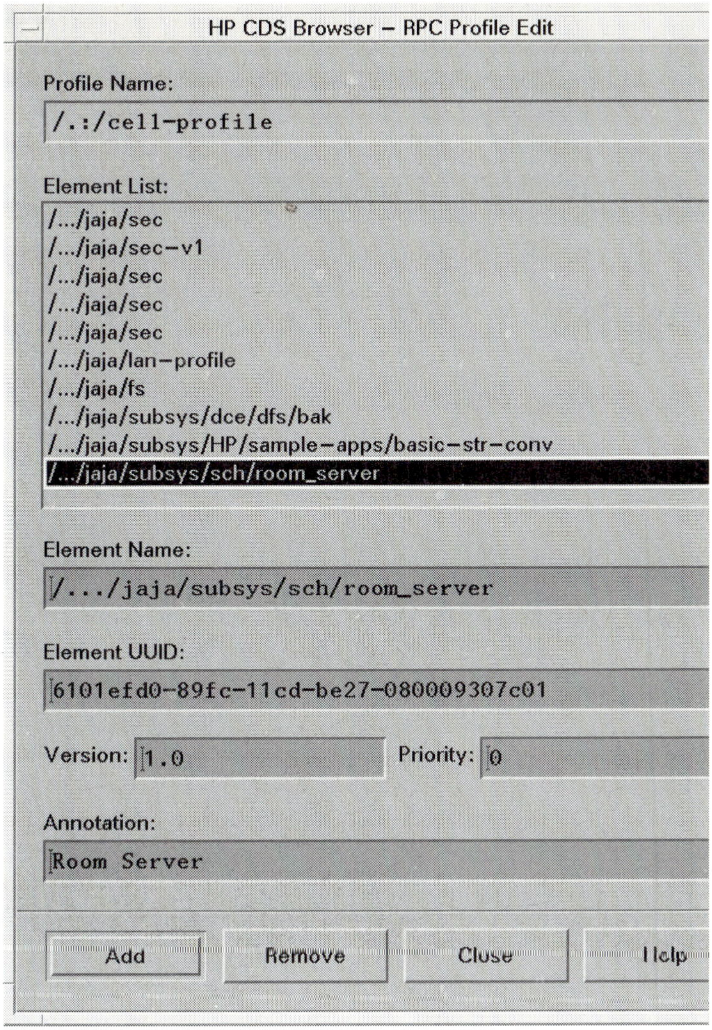

HP CDS Browser – RPC Profile Edit

Profile Name:

/.:/cell-profile

Element List:

/.../jaja/sec
/.../jaja/sec-v1
/.../jaja/sec
/.../jaja/sec
/.../jaja/sec
/.../jaja/lan-profile
/.../jaja/fs
/.../jaja/subsys/dce/dfs/bak
/.../jaja/subsys/HP/sample-apps/basic-str-conv
/.../jaja/subsys/sch/room_server

Element Name:

/.../jaja/subsys/sch/room_server

Element UUID:

6101efd0-89fc-11cd-be27-080009307c01

Version: 1.0 Priority: 0

Annotation:

Room Server

Add Remove Close Help

Figure 5.4
cdsbrowser Display: RPC Profile Entry for `room` interface

Output Samples 5.7 and 5.8 show the room interface member of the cell profile as displayed by **rpccp** and **dcecp**.

```
:rpccp show profile /.:/cell-profile

profile elements:
. . .

  <interface id>    6101efd0-89fc-11cd-be27-080009307c01,1.0
  <member_name>     /.../odss_827/subsys/sch/room_server
  <priority>        0
  <annotation>      Room Server
```

Output Sample 5.7
rpccp Display: RPC Profile Entry

```
:dcecp -c rpcprofile show /.:/cell-profile
...
{{6101efd0-89fc-11cd-be27-080009307c01 1.0}
/.../jaja/subsys/sch/room_server 0 {Room Server}}
```

Output Sample 5.8
dcecp Display: RPC Profile Entry

Default Name Space Entry

RPC allows the user to specify a default Name Space entry using the environment variable RPC_DEFAULT_ENTRY. In **ksh**, you would use the command

```
:export RPC_DEFAULT_ENTRY="/.:/cell-profile"
```

to set the default entry to the cell profile. If a client program omits the Name Space entry in the rpc_ns_ calls to import bindings, its RPC Runtime will use the entry name from RPC_DEFAULT_ENTRY. If this environment variable is not set, the Runtime will return the error name service environment variable not defined.

One use for the default environment variable is to allow you to specify a profile that has been customized to your individual requirements. Suppose that your "local" cell actually spans more than one site, and that each site has its own **room_server**. You want to use the **room_server** for your own site. To accomplish this, you could set up an individual profile that points to the server entry for your local **room_server**. Then you could equate the RPC_DEFAULT_ENTRY variable to your profile. This should be done in your .profile file (if you are using **ksh**) so that the default entry is always set in your shells. Your personal profile could include your preferences for other servers and services as well.

5.3 Server Setup with the RPC Name Space

This section presents the rpc_ns_ calls used by the server to set up and clean up Name Space entries.

Exporting Bindings

The rpc_ns_binding_export() call is used to add the server's interface and binding information to a server entry. This is called *exporting the binding*. This call is made after the `rpc_ep_register()` call and before the `rpc_server_listen()` call. Code Sample 5.1 shows this call for the **`room_server`**. The input parameters for the call are

- the *name space syntax* for the server entry. This allows for different Name Space entry formats in the future. Currently, the default and only supported syntax is CDS.
- a *server entry name* to which the interface and binding will be added. In the example the server entry name is `/.:/subsys/sch/room_server`.
- an *interface specification*, which supplies the interface UUID and version. This is the same interface specification used in Chapter 4 to register the interface with the RPC Runtime and the Endpoint Map. For the `room` interface, this is `room_v1_0_s_ifspec`.
- a *binding vector*, which provides one or more protocol sequence bindings used by the server. This is the same binding vector used in Chapter 4 to register the interface with the Endpoint Map, represented by the `binding_vector` variable and set up by a call to `rpc_server_inq_bindings()`.
- a vector of *object UUIDs*, which specifies what objects the server is managing. A value of **`NULL`** means no objects. This parameter will be discussed further in Chapter 8.

```
   rpc_ns_binding_export(
       rpc_c_ns_syntax_default,
       (unsigned_char_p_t) "/.:/subsys/sch/room_server",
       room_v1_0_s_ifspec,
       binding_vector,
       NULL,              /* no objects */
       &status);
     CHECK_DCE(status, "Cannot export binding");
```

Code Sample 5.1
`schedule/room_server.c main()`: Exporting a binding

Adding a Member to a Group Entry

The `rpc_ns_group_mbr_add()` call can be used to dynamically add a member to a group entry. Code Sample 5.2 illustrates this call. It has four input parameters:

- a *group name syntax* and a *member name syntax*, which allow different Name Space entry name formats. The current default and only supported syntax is CDS.
- a *group entry name*, which selects the RPC group to which the member will be added. In our example, the group name is `/.:/subsys/sch/room_group`.

- a *member entry name*, which will be added to the selected group. This can be a server entry or another group entry. In our example, the member is the server entry `/.:/subsys/sch/room_server`.

```
rpc_ns_group_mbr_add(
   rpc_c_ns_syntax_default,
    (unsigned_char_p_t) "/.:/subsys/sch/room_group",
    rpc_c_ns_syntax_default,
    (unsigned_char_p_t) "/.:/subsys/sch/room_server",
    &status);
 CHECK_DCE(status, "Cannot add member to room_group");
```

Code Sample 5.2
`schedule/room_server.c main()`: Adding a member to a group

Adding an Element to a Profile.

The `rpc_ns_profile_elt_add()` call can be used to add an element to a profile. Code Sample 5.3 shows an example of this call. The input parameters are

- a *profile name syntax* and an *element name syntax*, which allow different Name Space entry name formats. The current default and only supported syntax is CDS.
- a *profile name*, which selects the profile to which the element will be added. The example uses the cell profile, `/.:/cell-profile`.
- an *interface UUID* and *version number*. We will need to extract this from the interface specification, `room_v1_0_s_ifspec`, using the `rpc_if_inq_id()` call.
- an *element name*, which supplies one or more server bindings for the interface. The element may be a server entry, a group entry, or another profile. The example uses a server entry, `/.:/subsys/sch/room_server`.
- an integer *priority*, between 0 (highest) and 7 (lowest), which will be used in ordering elements for the same interface. The priority `0` is used in the example.
- a character string *annotation* that describes the element in displays of the profile. The annotation `"Room Server"` is used in the example.

```
    rpc_if_inq_id(room_v1_0_s_ifspec, &if_id, &status);
    CHECK_DCE(status, "Cannot get room interface UUID");

    rpc_ns_profile_elt_add(
       rpc_c_ns_syntax_default,
       (unsigned_char_p_t) "/.:/cell-profile",
       &if_id,
       rpc_c_ns_syntax_default,
       (unsigned_char_p_t) "/.:/subsys/sch/room_server",
       0,
       (unsigned_char_p_t) "Room Server",
       &status);
    CHECK_DCE(status,
      "Cannot add element to cell-profile");
```

Code Sample 5.3
`schedule/room_server.c main()`: Adding an element to a profile

Removing Exported Bindings

When the server terminates, it can optionally remove its information from the RPC Name Space. It can remove its interface and binding information from its server entry and members from group entries and elements from profiles.

There is some difference of opinion in the DCE community on whether or not a server should remove its Name Space information when it terminates. Those in favor say that the information in the Name Space should be kept current to prevent clients from trying to bind to servers that are no longer running. Those opposed say that frequent modification of the Name Space is not a good use of CDS, especially when the cell directory is replicated. (I personally prefer to have my servers remove their bindings from the Name Space when they terminate.)

The call to remove bindings from a server Name Space entry is `rpc_ns_binding_unexport()`. This action is awkwardly called *unexporting the bindings*. The input parameters to the call are the same as those to the corresponding `rpc_ns_binding_import()`—entry name syntax, server entry name, interface specification, and object vector—with the omission of the binding vector. DCE will remove all of the bindings in the server entry for the interface and objects. Note that an empty RPC server entry reverts to a plain CDS object; its **cdsbrower** symbol changes from an `S` to an `O`. Note also that if two servers are sharing a server entry for the same interface (and the same or no objects), a `rpc_ns_binding_unexport()` from one server will remove the bindings for both servers—one reason not to share server entries between servers.

Code Sample 5.4 shows the rpc_ns_binding_unexport() call for **room_server**. This call is placed after the rpc_server_listen() and before the rpc_ep_unregister().

```
rpc_ns_binding_unexport(
    rpc_c_ns_syntax_default,
    (unsigned_char_p_t) "/.:/subsys/sch/room_server",
    room_v1_0_s_ifspec,
    NULL,
    &status);
  CHECK_DCE_NONFATAL(status,
    "Cannot remove binding from room_server");
```

Code Sample 5.4
schedule/room_server.c main(): Removing an exported binding from a server entry

Removing a Member from a Group Entry

The rpc_ns_group_mbr_remove() call can be used to remove a member from a group. The input parameters for this call are the same as for rpc_ns_group_mbr_add()—the group syntax and name and the member syntax and name. An empty group Name Space entry retains its RPC group attribute; its **cdsbrowser** symbol is still a G. Code Sample 5.5 shows an example of this call for the **room_server**, where the room_server entry is removed from the room_group entry. This call would be made after the rpc_server_listen() and before the rpc_ns_binding_unexport().

```
rpc_ns_group_mbr_remove(
    rpc_c_ns_syntax_default,
    (unsigned_char_p_t) "/.:/subsys/sch/room_group",
    rpc_c_ns_syntax_default,
    (unsigned_char_p_t) "/.:/subsys/sch/room_server",
    &status);
  CHECK_DCE(status,
 "Cannot remove room_server member from room_group");
```

Code Sample 5.5
schedule/room_server.c main(): Removing a member from a group entry

Removing an Element from a Profile

The rpc_ns_profile_elt_remove() call can be used to remove an element from a profile. The input parameters for this call are the same as for rpc_ns_profile_elt_add()—the profile syntax and name, the interface UUID, and the element syntax and name. The priority and the annotation are omitted. An empty profile Name Space entry retains its RPC profile attribute; its **cdsbrowser** symbol is still a P. Code Sample 5.6 shows an example of this call for the **room_server**, where the room_server entry is removed from the cell-profile entry. This call would be made after the rpc_server_listen() and before the rpc_ns_group_mbr_remove() or rpc_ns_binding_unexport().

```
rpc_ns_profile_elt_remove(
    rpc_c_ns_syntax_default,
    (unsigned_char_p_t) "/.:/cell-profile",
    &if_id,
    rpc_c_ns_syntax_default,
    (unsigned_char_p_t) "/.:/subsys/sch/room_server",
    &status);
CHECK_DCE_NONFATAL(status,
   "Cannot remove room_server element from
   cell-profile");
```

Code Sample 5.6
schedule/room_server.c main(): Removing an element from a profile

Security Requirements for Exporting Bindings

General DCE security will not be discussed until Chapter 6. However, a little bit of security is necessary to start using the RPC Name Space. Each Name Space entry is protected against unauthorized access, so the server needs to have the proper permissions to set up its own entries.

DCE Principals

Users in DCE are identified by *principals*. A principal has a name and a password, among other attributes that are not important at the moment. Servers themselves may be identified using principals; in Chapter 6 we will see how this is done. For the time being, though, we will use a user principal for the server's security.

A principal is set up by a DCE cell administrator, someone who has been assigned sufficient authority to do such tasks. If you have not already been assigned a principal, contact your cell administrator. For now, let's assume a user principal, named cwk, has already been assigned to me.

I can establish my principal identity using the **dce_login** command. When I do so, DCE will request the password associated with my principal:

```
:dce_login cwk
Enter Password: <enter password, not displayed>
```

A server can inherit the principal identity of the user who runs it. This is not the recommended way for a server to establish its identity, but it will do until Chapter 6. Assume that I run a server after executing the **dce_login**, so that the server will inherit the identity of my principal, cwk.

Name Space ACLs

Entries in the RPC Name Space are protected using DCE *Access Control Lists (ACLs)*. An ACL is a list of principals and their access rights. ACLs are established by an administrator or other user with sufficient authority to do so. (This authority is itself defined by other ACLs.) ACL concepts and management are quite an involved topic that will be covered in depth in Chapter 9. For now, all we need to know is how to set the ACL for a Name Space entry.

A server needs write access to each Name Space entry it modifies. If a server creates an entry, it needs write access to the CDS directory in which the entry is created. The cell_admin user can set up the appropriate permissions using **acl_edit, cdsbrowser**, or **dcecp**. Output Samples 5.9 and 5.10 show the commands to create the sch directory and the room_server and room_group entries and to assign read (r), write (w), and test (t) permissions for the user principal cwk for the room entries and for the cell profile. (The use of the **-e** option in **acl_edit** will be discussed in Chapter 9.) When the server runs with the cwk principal identity, it can write its binding information to these entries.

```
:dce_login cell_admin cell_admin_password
:cdscp create dir /.:/subsys/sch
:cdscp create obj /.:/subsys/sch/room_server
:cdscp create obj /.:/subsys/sch/room_group
:acl_edit -e /.:/subsys/sch/room_server -m user:cwk:rwt
:acl_edit -e /.:/subsys/sch/room_group -m user:cwk:rwt
:acl_edit -e /.:/cell-profile -m user:cwk:rwt
```

Output Sample 5.9
cdscp and **acl_edit** commands to set up sch directory and cell-profile

```
:dce_login cell_admin cell_admin_password
:dcecp
dcecp> directory create /.:/subsys/sch
dcecp> rpcentry create /.:/subsys/sch/room_server
dcecp> rpcgroup create /.:/subsys/sch/room_group
dcecp> acl modify -e /.:/subsys/sch/room_server -add {user cwk rwt}
dcecp> acl modify -e /.:/subsys/sch/room_group  -add {user cwk rwt}
dcecp> acl modify -e /.:/cell-profile -add {user cwk rwt}
dcecp> quit
```

Output Sample 5.10
dcecp commands to set up sch directory and cell-profile

If a server does not have the proper permissions to access Name Space entries, its rpc_ns_ calls will fail. For example, suppose I forget to execute the **dce_login cwk** prior to running **room_server**. (I tend to do this a lot, which is a good reason to use the server identity establishment techniques presented in Chapter 6.) I will get the error

```
Cannot export binding to /.:/subsys/sch/room_server:
no permission for name service operation (dce / rpc)
```

The security that is required for using the RPC Name Space may seem at this point to be an unnecessary hassle. Bear in mind, however, that without this protection any server could put its bindings into a server entry and fool a client into using it. The Name Space ACLs prevent a "Trojan horse" server from masquerading as another server.

5.4 Client Setup with the RPC Name Space

A client can locate a server for an interface using server, group, or profile Name Space entries. The client can *import bindings* for the server from Name Space entries and use the bindings in remote procedure calls. This section will discuss the `rpc_ns_` calls used by the client to import bindings.

Importing Bindings

A client needs to make three (or more) calls to import bindings for a server. The first call, `rpc_ns_binding_import_begin()`, starts the import activity. Its input parameters are

- a *Name Space entry syntax*, which allows different Name Space entry formats. The current default and only supported syntax is CDS.
- a *Name Space entry name*, which is used to start the search for servers. This can be a server entry, a group entry, or a profile. The search algorithm is explained in more detail in the next section. If the entry name is `NULL`, the value of the `RPC_DEFAULT_ENTRY` environment variable, if it exists, will be used.
- an *interface specification*, which supplies an interface UUID and version number. The Name Space entries will be searched for a server that exports this interface.
- an *object UUID*. The Name Space entries will be searched for a server that manages this object. A value of `NULL` means no object is to be considered. Chapter 8 will discuss this parameter further.

The `rpc_ns_binding_import_begin()` call returns an *import context*, which records the state of the search in the Name Space. Code Sample 5.7 shows this call for the **`room_server`**. It uses the `room_server` Name Space entry.

```
rpc_ns_handle_t    import_context;

rpc_ns_binding_import_begin(
    rpc_c_ns_syntax_default,
    (unsigned_char_p_t) "/.:/subsys/sch/room_server",
    room_v1_0_c_ifspec,
    NULL,                /* no object */
    &import_context,
    &status);
CHECK_DCE(status,"Cannot begin binding import from
    /.:/subsys/sch/room_server");
```

Code Sample 5.7
`schedule/room_server.c main()`: Begin import of bindings

Once the import context has been set up, the server can import one or more bindings using `rpc_ns_binding_import_next()` calls. The input parameter for this call is the import context, and the primary output parameter is a binding handle for a server that exports the desired interface. Each call to `rpc_ns_binding_import_next()` returns another binding from the Name Space entries. In this way, a client can step through the possible bindings for an interface and select a binding for use.

If there are multiple bindings available, they are retrieved in random order. Also, only *compatible* bindings are returned—that is, bindings for protocol sequences that are supported on the client's host. So if a server exports a binding for a protocol that the client cannot use, the client will not even be able to import that binding from the Name Space. Currently, this is a moot point with HP DCE implementations, as they support all—both—of the possible protocol sequences. This might affect an HP-UX client that is importing bindings from a Microsoft NT server. The bindings for NT-only protocol sequences like `ncacn_np` and `ncacn_spx` would not be seen by the HP-UX client.

Code Sample 5.8 shows the `rpc_ns_binding_import_next()` call in the **room** client. This is called only once, to import one binding for the **room_server**. If the **room_server** exports two bindings—one each for the `ncadg_ip_udp` and `ncacn_ip_tcp` protocol—the client will import a binding for one of these protocol sequences. The binding chosen will be random; if **room** is run many times, there should be a 50 percent chance of importing either binding. If **room_server** is not running, the `room_server` entry will be empty and this call will return a status of `rpc_s_no_more_bindings`.

```
rpc_ns_binding_import_next(import_context, &h,
   &status);
if (status == rpc_s_no_more_bindings)
{
   printf("No servers available\n");
   exit(0);
}
CHECK_DCE(status, "Cannot import next binding from
   /.:/subsys/sch/room_server");
```

Code Sample 5.8
`schedule/room_server.c main()`: Import next binding

Finally, after all of the desired bindings have been imported, the client calls `rpc_ns_binding_import_done()` with the import context as an input parameter. This call, shown in Code Sample 5.9, releases any resources used during the search of the Name Space. The import context is no longer valid after this call.

```
rpc_ns_binding_import_done(&import_context, &status);
CHECK_DCE(status,"Cannot complete binding import from
   /.:/subsys/sch/room_server");
```

Code Sample 5.9
`schedule/room_server.c main()`: Complete import of bindings

How the Import of Bindings Works

Figure 5.5 illustrates how the Name Space entries discussed in this section work together to locate a server. Assume the server, group, and profile Name Space entries are set up by the **`room_server`** as shown in Code Samples 5.1, 5.2, and 5.3. The **`room`** client in Code Samples 5.7, 5.8, and 5.9 imports a binding for version `1.0` of the `room` interface, using the `room_server` entry. The client RPC Runtime performs the following steps:

1. Retrieve the bindings from the `/.:/subsys/sch/room_server` server entry for the `room` interface UUID, version `1.0`. Two bindings are found for the `ncadg_ip_udp` and `ncacn_ip_tcp` protocols.
2. Randomly order the two partial string bindings and construct a binding handle for one, say `ncacn_ip_tcp:15.4.25.126[]`.

Later, the client makes a call using the returned binding handle. The RPC Runtime does the following:

3. Resolve the partial `ncacn_ip_tcp` binding using the Endpoint Map on the server's host at IP address `15.4.25.126`. This will insert the server's TCP endpoint `4852` into the binding. Then connect to that endpoint and make the remote call.

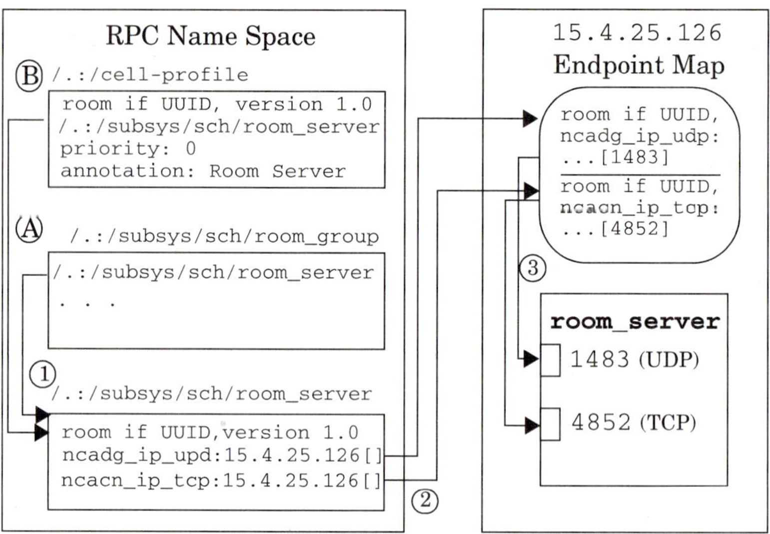

Figure 5.5
Server Location Using Name Space Entries

Now suppose the **room** client uses the `room_group` entry in its call to `rpc_ns_binding_import_begin()`. This adds the initial step:

A. Retrieve the members of the `/.:/subsys/sch/room_group` entry. One member is found: `/.:/subsys/sch/room_server`. Then proceed as above with step 1.

Finally, assume that the **room** client uses `NULL` for the Name Space entry in its `rpc_ns_binding_import_begin()` call, and that the user running **room** has set up an `RPC_DEFAULT_ENTRY` environment variable with the value of `/.:/cell-profile`. This adds the initial step:

B. Retrieve the elements of `/.:/cell-profile` that match the `room` interface UUID, version `1.0`. One such element is found, with the element name `/.:/subsys/sch/room_server`. Then proceed as above with step 1.

Security Requirements for Importing Bindings

The security requirements for importing bindings are much less stringent than for exporting them. All a client needs to import bindings from Name Space entries is to have read access to the entries. The default permissions for Name Space entries usually allow this. ACLs for the `unauthenticated` and `any_other` users typically grant read (`r`) permission to those users who have not executed a **dce_login** and so are unauthenticated, or have logged in using a principal that was not explicitly listed in any other ACLs. This means that any client can normally import bindings for any server.

It is possible to restrict the importation of bindings by limiting the default ACLs on the Name Space entries. You could remove the read permission for the `unauthenticated` and `any_other` users to limit access to only those principals explicitly listed in ACLs. This would prevent clients run by other users from importing bindings from those Name Space entries. For example, if the read permission is removed from the `unauthenticated` user ACL for the `/.:/subsys/sch/room_server` entry, and I run the **room** client without having done a **dce_login**, I get this error:

```
Cannot import next binding from /.:/subsys/sch/room_server:
no permission for name service operation (dce / rpc)
```

However, this would not prevent clients from building their own string bindings for an interface and a known server host location. There are better ways to protect access to servers, which will be discussed in Chapter 9.

5.5 Alternative Client Binding Methods

So far, all remote calls we have seen have used explicit binding handles as their first `in` parameter. There are several alternatives to explicit binding: implicit binding, automatic binding, and custom binding. In each of these, the client does not include a binding handle in each call.

Implicit Binding

With implicit binding, operations do not have a binding handle as their first parameter. Instead, a program variable is designated as the binding handle to be used for each operation in an interface. A new IDL definition for the `room` interface without the binding handle parameters is shown in Code Sample 5.10.

```
[uuid(6101efd0-89fc-11cd-be27-080009307c01),
version(1.0)]
interface room
{
import "sch.idl";

void room_description(
   [in ] sch_room_name_t room_name,
   [out] sch_room_t      *room,
   [out] sch_status_t    *status);

void room_reserve(
   [in ] sch_room_t        room,
```

Code Sample 5.10
`schedule/imp_handle/room.idl`: Interface definition for implicit and automatic binding

```
    [in ] sch_date_time_t  date_time,
    [in ] sch_name_t       reserver,
    [in ] sch_event_desc_t desc,
    [out] sch_status_t    *status);

void room_cancel(
    [in ] sch_room_t      room,
    [in ] sch_date_time_t date_time,
    [in ] sch_name_t      reserver,
    [out] sch_status_t   *status);

void room_avail(
    [in ] sch_date_time_t date_time,
    [in ] long int        n_people,
    [in ] long int        n_pref_locs,
    [in,  size_is(n_pref_locs)]
    sch_loc_name_t  pref_locs[],
    [in ] long int        max_avail_rooms,
    [out] long int       *n_avail_rooms,
    [out, size_is(max_avail_rooms),
    length_is(*n_avail_rooms)] sch_room_t avail_rooms[],
    [out] sch_status_t   *status);

void room_events(
    [in ] sch_room_t            room,
    [in ] sch_short_date_time_t begin_date_time,
    [in ] sch_short_date_time_t end_date_time,
    [out] sch_event_rec_p_t    *room_event_list,
    [out] sch_status_t         *status);
}
```

Code Sample 5.10 (continued)

Implicit binding for the client is specified in an Attribute Configuration File (ACF). Code Sample 5.11 shows the client's ACF for the `room` interface with an `implicit_handle` attribute. This specifies that there will be a variable `h` that will be used as the binding handle for each remote call of the `room` interface.

The client is responsible for setting up the binding handle variables defined by the ACF file. The code in the **room** client to set up the binding handle `h` using the CDS server entry is the same as shown in Code Sample 5.7, 5.8, and 5.9. But the remote calls themselves do not include the binding handles, as shown in Code Sample 5.12.

```
[implicit_handle(handle_t h)] interface room
{
room_description(...);
room_reserve     (...);
room_cancel      (...);
room_avail       (...)
room_events      (...);
 }
```

Code Sample 5.11
`schedule/imp_handle/room.acf`: Specifying implicit binding

```
   room_description(room_name, &room, &status,
      &call_status);
   . . .
   room_reserve(room, date_time, reserver, desc,
      &status, &call_status);
   . . .
```

Code Sample 5.12
`schedule/imp_handle/room.c`: Remote calls using implicit (and automatic) binding

The server of the interface will still use explicit binding handles. This can be accomplished using another ACF for the server. Code Sample 5.13 shows the server's ACF for the `room` interface. The `explicit_handle` attribute forces all of the operation managers to include a binding handle as their first parameter. Then the manager routines in `room_mgr.c` can continue to be used.

```
[explicit_handle] interface room
{
room_description(...);
room_reserve     (...);
room_cancel      (...);
room_avail       (...)
room_events      (...);
 }
```

Code Sample 5.13
`schedule/exp_handle/room.acf`: Specifying explicit binding

Automatic Binding

Automatic binding is similar to implicit binding in that remote calls do not include an explicit binding handle as their first parameter. Consequently, the IDL file in Code Sample 5.10 can be used for automatic binding as well as implicit binding. To use automatic binding, the client ACF specifies the `auto_handle` attribute for the interface, as shown in Code Sample 5.14

```
[auto_handle] interface room
{
room_description(...);
room_reserve    (...);
room_cancel     (...);
room_avail      (...)
room_events     (...);
 }
```

Code Sample 5.14
schedule/auto_handle/room.acf: Specifying automatic binding

Unlike the explicit and implicit binding methods, the client does not need to include any code to set up the binding. Instead, the client server stub routines automatically set up the binding for each remote call. Since the client does not provide any binding information, how does the client server stub module locate a server for the binding? The automatic binding method uses the CDS entry defined by the RPC_DEFAULT_ENTRY environment variable. This variable was previously mentioned as the source of the default when no entry is specified in an rpc_ns_binding_import_begin(). For automatic binding to work, the user must have set RPC_DEFAULT_ENTRY to a CDS entry that can provide, directly or indirectly, a server for the interface used in the remote calls. The default entry can be for a specific server, for a group of servers, or for a profile. One strategy is for each user to set RPC_DEFAULT_ENTRY to a profile that specifies the user's server preferences for interfaces that user might use.

Another feature of automatic binding is rebinding to another server if the original server can no longer be reached. The client stub will detect the failure of a remote call and automatically bind to the next available server as specified by the default entry. For this to work the default entry should be a server group or a profile specifying more than one server for the interface.

The server continues to use explicit binding, even if the client is using automatic binding. The server ACF in Code Sample 5.13 can be used to force the operation managers to include explicit binding handles. The original room_mgr.c managers can then be used for the server.

Custom Binding

The custom binding method lets you use an application-defined parameter, the *custom handle*, in place of the binding handle in client remote calls. The custom handle is declared using a type defined with the handle attribute in an IDL file:

```
typedef [handle] custom_handle_t;
```

The application must provide two routines with a custom handle:

- *custom_handle_t*_bind() — maps the custom handle to a normal binding handle
- *custom_handle_t*_unbind() — releases the binding handle

The client stub routines will call these bind and unbind routines as needed.

Get File Example with Custom Binding

To illustrate custom binding, we will look again at the `get_file` example introduced in Chapter 3. In this application, a source file is transferred from a remote system to a target file on the local system. There are four operations in the `get_file` interface: `get_file_pipe()`, which uses a pipe to transfer the file, and `get_file_begin()`, `get_file_next()`, and `get_file_end()`, which use a context handle in transferring the file.

We will use the combined source file and host name, `file@host`, as the custom handle. The IDL file in Code Sample 5.15 defines `file_host_t` as a character string type with the `handle` attribute. This type designates the custom binding handle, and it is used for the first parameter of the `get_file_pipe()` and the `get_file_begin()` operations. Note that `get_file_begin()` still returns a context handle, which is then used in `get_file_next()` and `get_file_end()`.

```
[uuid(91eea008-c546-11ce-9401-08000948fbd9),
version(2.0)]
interface get_file
{
...
typedef [handle, string, ref] char *file_host_t;
typedef pipe byte file_pipe_t;
typedef [context_handle] void *file_handle_t;

void get_file_pipe(
   [in ] file_host_t    file_host,
   [in ] long int       bufsize,
   [out] file_pipe_t   *file_pipe,
   [out] long int      *file_status);

void get_file_begin(
   [in ] file_host_t    file_host,
   [out] file_handle_t *file_h,
   [out] long int      *file_status);

void get_file_next(
   [in ] file_handle_t  file_h,
   . . .
   [out] long int      *file_status);

void get_file_end(
   [in ] file_handle_t  file_h,
   [out] long int      *file_status);
}
```

Code Sample 5.15

`get_file/custom_handle/get_file.idl`: Specifying custom binding

The bind routine for `file_host_t` is shown in Code Sample 5.16. This routine extracts the server host name from the `file_host` parameter and uses it to construct a string binding and from the string binding, a binding handle. The routine checks that a **get_file_server** is actually running on that system before returning the binding handle.

```
handle_t file_name_t_bind(
    file_name_t file_name)
{
    rpc_binding_handle_t h;
    unsigned_char_p_t     string_binding;
    char                 *host_name;
    unsigned32            status;

    parse_file_name((char *)file_name, NULL, &host_name);

    rpc_string_binding_compose(
        NULL, /* no object UUID */
        (unsigned_char_p_t) "ncacn_ip_tcp",
        (unsigned_char_p_t) host_name,
        NULL, /* no endpoint */
        NULL, /* no options  */
        &string_binding,
        &status);
    CHECK_DCE(status, "Cannot compose string binding");

    rpc_binding_from_string_binding(string_binding, &h,
      &status);
    CHECK_DCE(status, "Cannot convert string binding");

    if (!is_server_there(h, get_file_v1_0_c_ifspec))
    {
        printf("Server at %s is not active\n", host_name);
        exit(0);
    }

    free(host_name);
    return(h);
}
```

Code Sample 5.16
`get_file/custom_handle/get_file.c: file_name_t_bind()`

Code Sample 5.17 shows the unbind routine for `file_name_t`. This routine simply frees the binding handle associated with the custom handle.

```
void file_name_t_unbind(
    file_name_t file_name,
    handle_t    h)
{
    unsigned32 status;

    rpc_binding_free(&h, &status);
    CHECK_DCE(status, "Cannot free binding handle");
}
```

Code Sample 5.17
`get_file/custom_handle/get_file.c: file_name_t_unbind()`

Finally, Code Sample 5.18 shows the remote calls that use the custom binding handle. Here `source_file_host` is a character string of the form `file@host`. The client stub routines for each of these operations will call `file_name_t_bind()` to convert `source_file_host` to a normal binding handle. When each remote call is complete, the client stubs will call `file_name_t_unbind()`.

```
  get_file_pipe((file_name_t) source_file_host,
     bufsize,&file_pipe, &file_status);

  get_file_begin((file_name_t) source_file_host,
     &file_h,&file_status);
```

Code Sample 5.18
`get_file/custom_handle/get_file.c`: Remote calls using custom binding

5.6 CDS Operation

In this section we will look at the components of the Cell Directory Service and how these components work with each other. You do not need to understand the operation of CDS to use the RPC Name Service. However, this knowledge is useful in understanding some of the more subtle aspects of the RPC Name Service.

The Cell Directory Service is itself a sophisticated client-server application that uses DCE facilities. We will look at the server and client sides of CDS. Components on the server and client sides are shown in Figure 5.6.

CDS Server

There are one or more CDS server systems in a DCE cell. Each server system hosts a *clearinghouse* directory database, a *CDS Daemon* process that provides access to the clearinghouse, and a *CDS Advertiser* process that informs the rest of the cell about the existence and location of the clearinghouse.

Clearinghouse

A database of CDS directories and objects is called a *clearinghouse*. (This term was originally used by Xerox for its pioneering distributed naming system in the 1970s.) A clearinghouse consists of disk files on the CDS server host and in-memory data in the CDS Daemon. In the **cdsbrowser** cell directory display, a clearinghouse is represented by the `C` symbol. In Figure 5.1, there is one clearinghouse named `/.:/hpiala3_ch`. Note the inclusion of the CDS server host name `hpiala3` in the clearinghouse name. If you double-click on the clearinghouse, **cdsbrowser** will display a window listing the attributes associated with the clearinghouse. You can also use the command **cdscp show clearinghouse** to display these attributes and a list of the directories contained in the clearinghouse.

On HP-UX systems, clearinghouse disk files are in the `/opt/dcelocal/var/directory/cds` directory. CDS uses a technique called *checkpointing*, borrowed from transaction processing, to synchronize data between the disk files and in-memory storage. Periodically, the CDS Daemon takes a checkpoint when it brings the clearinghouse disk files up to date. In between checkpoints, CDS uses a *transaction log* to keep track of recent changes. If CDS or the system crashes between checkpoints, the clearinghouse can later be recovered to the proper state using the transaction log. Examples of CDS files are

- `cds_files`

  Provides the file directory and prefix for the other files. In this case `/opt/dcelocal/var/directory/cds/jaja#hpiala3_ch`.
- `jaja#hpiala3_ch.checkpoint0000000122`

  Contains the CDS directory structure and object data existing at the last checkpoint.
- `jaja#hpiala3_ch.tlog0000000122`

  Contains the transaction log—the updates since the last checkpoint.
- `jaja#hpiala3_ch.version`

  Keeps track of the version suffix for the checkpoint and tlog files. In this case, `0000000122`. The version is incremented each time CDS is restarted.
- `server_mgmt_acl.dat`

  Holds data related to directory ACLs (Access Control Lists).

CDS Daemon (**cdsd**)

The **cdsd** process controls access to the clearinghouse data. It is a DCE RPC server. As such it exports RPC interfaces that are used by CDS clients to create, read, modify, and update directory entries. The `cds_clerkserver` interface is used by CDS Clerks and the `cprpc_server` interface is used by the CDS and DCE Control Programs (**cdscp** and **dcecp**). The CDS Daemon, like other RPC servers, sets up bindings using one or more protocol sequences, registers its bindings and interfaces with the Endpoint Map on the CDS server host, and listens for incoming RPC requests. However, it does not export the bindings and interfaces to the RPC Name Space. Instead, it uses the CDS Advertiser, as described next.

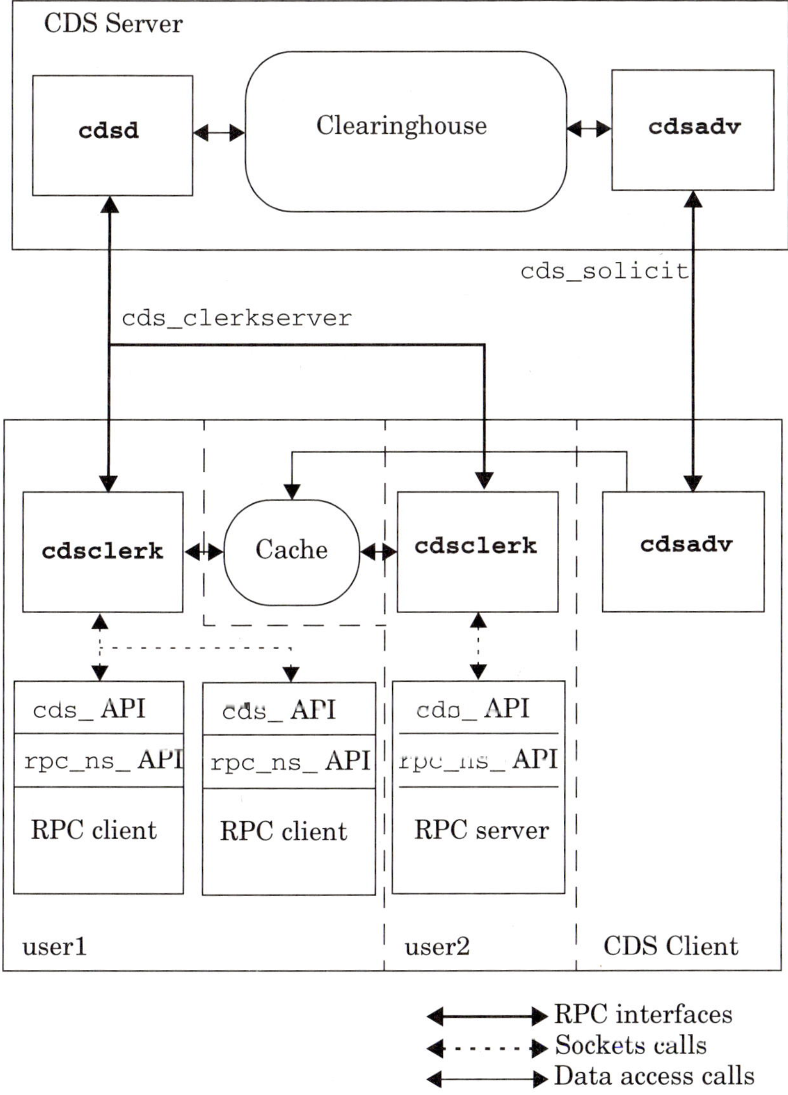

Figure 5.6
CDS Components

When a **cdsd** process starts up, it opens the most recent checkpoint file and reads its contents into memory. It also opens the most recent transaction log and applies its accumulated updates (if any) to the checkpointed clearinghouse data to bring it up to date. Then periodically, **cdsd** will update the next generation of the checkpoint file for the clearinghouse. In between checkpoints, **cdsd** will write updates to the next generation of the transaction log.

Since the clearinghouse data is held in memory in a data structure optimized for searching and updating, access should be fast. But this also means that the memory requirements of **cdsd** are proportional to the size of the clearinghouse. As more directories and objects are added to the clearinghouse, the memory used by **cdsd** will grow. The host system for **cdsd** should have sufficient memory for the anticipated size of the clearinghouse.

CDS Advertiser

The CDS Advertiser process (**cdsadv**) provides the means by which CDS clearinghouses and servers are made known to their clients. There is one **cdsadv** on each CDS server and client system. The CDS Advertiser is both a server and client for the `cds_solicit` interface. When a CDS Daemon starts up and brings its clearinghouse on-line, the CDS Advertiser on its host will broadcast a `cds_Advertise` call, with clearinghouse information and server location, to other **cdsadv** processes. In practice, this broadcast is usually limited to other hosts on the local area network (LAN). The other CDS Advertisers will cache the clearinghouse and server information for subsequent use by CDS clerks.

A CDS Advertiser can also broadcast a `cds_Solicit` call which asks other CDS Advertisers within earshot to respond with their clearinghouse and server information. By using periodic Advertise and Solicit broadcasts, CDS tries to keep all of its components aware of the clearinghouses and servers available in the cell.

Note that since broadcasts are usually limited to the local network, CDS advertisements cannot generally be used to update Advertisers that are not on the same LAN as the Daemon. There is another CDS mechanism that permits an Advertiser to be told explicitly the location of a clearinghouse: the **cdscp set cdscp preferred clearinghouse** command.

Replication and Skulking

Since most DCE applications will depend on the RPC Name Space for server and object location, the underlying Cell Directory Service must be highly available. To achieve this, CDS allows its directories to be *replicated*—that is, CDS can maintain two or more copies of directory data on different systems. A clearinghouse then becomes the collection of directory replicas on a server machine.

There are CDS Daemons running on each system that holds a clearinghouse. Consequently, if one directory replica becomes inaccessible (say, because the server system crashes), CDS clients can use another replica on another system. Note that the CDS Advertiser mechanism described above is responsible for notifying the CDS clients about the replicated CDS Daemons.

Another reason directories might be replicated is to put a CDS Daemon closer to its clients. In a large cell that includes several high-speed LANs interconnected over lower-speed wide-area links, it may be desirable to have a CDS Daemon with the relevant replicated directories on each LAN. Then a CDS client on the LAN can use the local CDS Daemon rather than having to contact another Daemon over a wide-area link. The DCE configuration script, **dce_config**, allows a cell to be partitioned into local subcells for this purpose.

When replicated data is updated, there must be some way to keep the replicas consistent. CDS divides replicas into *master* and *read-only* replicas. There is only one master replica for each directory, which is the initial target for an update. All of the read-only replicas are updated from the master. CDS provides two methods for propagation of updates from the master to the read-only replicas: *immediate propagation* and *skulking*. With immediate propagation, CDS attempts to update all of the read-only replicas when the master replica is updated. With skulking, CDS schedules periodic updates of the read-only replicas from the master. Each CDS directory has an attribute `CDS_Convergence` that controls how updates are propagated. This attribute can have three values:

- **high**—An immediate update is attempted on all replicas. If any replica update fails, the directory is skulked once an hour until all replicas are updated. Otherwise, skulks are scheduled once every 12 hours.
- **medium**—An immediate update is attempted on all replicas. If any replica update fails, the update is attempted in the next scheduled skulk. Skulks are scheduled once ever 12 hours. This is the default convergence setting for the CDS root `/.:/` and is inherited by all subdirectories unless explicitly overridden.
- **low**—No immediate update is attempted. All updates are propagated in the next scheduled skulk. Skulks are scheduled once ever 24 hours.

CDS Client

Any process that reads or updates information in CDS is a *CDS client*. An RPC server that exports bindings and interfaces to the RPC Name Space is a CDS client, as is the RPC client that imports bindings from the Name Space. RPC clients and servers use the `rpc_ns_` calls, which in turn use a CDS client interface to manipulate CDS entries. There may be other CDS clients besides RPC clients and servers. For instance, **cdsbrowser** is a CDS client.

You might think since the CDS Daemon is an RPC server, then the CDS client would be an RPC client that makes remote calls to a Daemon. However, the client architecture of CDS is a bit more baroque. There is an intermediate process, the *CDS*

Clerk (**cdsclerk**), that sits between the CDS client and the CDS Daemon. Also, there is a *CDS Cache* on each client system that is used to cache recently used data.

Cache

When a CDS client on a system first accesses a directory object, the object must be retrieved from the appropriate clearinghouse through its CDS Daemon. This requires a remote call across the network (unless the client and Daemon happen to be on the same system). CDS will cache the retrieved data on the local system. If the same or another CDS client on that system subsequently accesses that object, CDS can use the cached data. This avoids the overhead of another remote call to the Daemon.

On Unix systems, the CDS cache is implemented as a shared memory segment. CDS Clerks can then use the cache through the Unix `shm...()` calls.

The CDS cache has benefits and drawbacks typical of caching schemes. Performance should be improved if there is *locality of reference* among CDS clients on the same system—that is, if the clients tend to use the same directory objects. If there is no locality of reference, the cache will fill with infrequently used data. To keep the cache from growing indefinitely, CDS must discard infrequently used entries. Also, the cached entries might not be up to date. This can be a problem for RPC, which will be addressed in the section on CDS Confidence.

CDS Clerk

The CDS Clerk is the intermediary between a client of CDS and the CDS Daemon. There is one CDS Clerk for each user that is accessing CDS. If the user is running more than one process using CDS, all of those processes will share a CDS Clerk. Moreover, if there are several sessions with the same user ID (e.g., Unix UID), all of those sessions will share the same CDS Clerk. Output Sample 5.11 shows a sample of CDS Clerks on a system, as displayed by the **ps** command. The `-U` flags indicate the users associated with each Clerk: one for `root` and one for `cwk`. The `-u` flags provide the user's UID, and the `-m` flags specify the shared memory segment ID that is used for the CDS Cache.

```
    PID  PARENT COMMAND
... 2076  2070  ... /opt/dcelocal/bin/cdsclerk -U root -u 0 -m 114
... 2297  2070  ... /opt/dcelocal/bin/cdsclerk -U cwk -u 8714 -m 114
```

Output Sample 5.11
CDS Clerk CDS Processes: **ps -ef | grep cdsclerk** output

On Unix systems, CDS clients communicate with their CDS Clerks through *Unix domain sockets*, which is a local interprocess communication mechanism based on the BSD sockets interface. DCE implementations on non-Unix systems either have to emulate this mechanism or replace it with an equivalent native interprocess communication. Note that if a client's Clerk dies or is killed, or if the client-to-Clerk local socket fails, the client will receive the error `Error with socket (dce / cds)`.

CDS Clerks communicate with CDS Daemons using DCE RPC. The locations of the CDS Daemons are obtained through the CDS Advertiser mechanism. CDS Clerks get the Daemon location from the local CDS Cache and create RPC binding handles from the location information.

The CDS client architecture, with the intermediary CDS Clerks, may seem overly complicated. The reason for this appears to be historical. CDS was derived from the DEC Distributed Name Service (DNS) implementation on the Ultrix operating system. Ultrix did not provide shared libraries, so each program needed to include copies of the library code it used. To save on code space, the bulk of the DNS client code was encapsulated in the Clerks, which could be shared among many DNS clients.

Modern operating systems now provide shared libraries, so the original rationale for the CDS Clerk is no longer important. DCE for the Microsoft NT operating system (implemented by Digital) has eliminated the Clerks in favor of direct client-to-Daemon RPCs. Digital may submit this enhancement to OSF for inclusion in a future release of DCE, so other DCE implementations may some day benefit from it.

Cache Confidence

As noted earlier, cached CDS data might become out of date or *stale*. An example of this that can affect RPC applications is when a server deletes its Name Space entries when terminating. If those Name Space entries have been cached on another system, they may be seen by a client of the server. That client will then attempt to connect to the server using the now out of date binding information from the stale entries.

A feature called *cache confidence* can be used to determine whether a CDS client goes to the local cache or to the remote CDS Daemon when getting data from CDS. For work done in **cdscp**, this can be set by the command **cdscp set cdscp confidence =** *value*, where *value* is

- **low**—Get the data from the cache or the most convenient Daemon for any replica.
- **medium**—Bypass the cache and get the data from a Daemon for any replica.
- **high**—Bypass the cache and get the data from the Daemon for the master replica.

Ironically, higher confidence values express lower actual confidence that the cached data will be up to date.

Cache confidence for the RPC Name Space can be set by the `rpc_ns_mgmt_handle_set_exp_age()` call. This sets an expiration age for an Name Space import context. If data in the cache is older than the expiration age, RPC will go to directly to the Daemon to get the data. An expiration age of `0` always causes the cache to be bypassed. Code Sample 5.19 illustrates how this call is used.

```
rpc_ns_binding_import_begin(...,&import_context,...);
CHECK_DCE(...);

rpc_ns_mgmt_handle_set_exp_age(import_context,
   0, &status);
CHECK_DCE(status,
   "Cannot set expiration for import.");

rpc_ns_binding_import_next(import_context, ...);
```

Code Sample 5.19
`schedule/room.c main()`: Setting the import expiration to bypass the CDS cache

5.7 Performance of Binding with CDS

This section examines how choices for the binding method affect the time it takes DCE clients and servers to start up and to shut down. In general, the binding methods that use CDS to locate a server will be significantly slower than binding using a string binding with the server host address. You may notice a delay of a second or more when you start up a server or client that uses CDS. However, this performance penalty is paid up front during startup. The subsequent performance of remote procedure calls is not adversely affected.

Some data are presented here on the start up and shutdown times for clients and servers using various binding methods. The data were obtained by running the **perf_client** and **perf_server** programs that were introduced in Section 2.6 to measure RPC performance. These programs also report the time taken by DCE calls. For this section we will measure the performance of the `rpc_ns_` calls in the client and server. The **perf_client** can measure five binding methods:

- full string binding — no endpoint mapping, no CDS
- partial string binding — use endpoint mapping, no CDS
- `SERVER[_NO_CACHE]` — use server entry in CDS

- GROUP[_NO_CACHE] use group and server entries in CDS
- PROFILE[_NO_CACHE] use profile, group, server entries in CDS

The three CDS methods (SERVER, GROUP, and PROFILE) can each be measured with CDS caching enabled (the default) or disabled (_NO_CACHE) in the client.

The test systems and network configuration used during the measurements were as in Section 2.6: The client was run on an HP9000/730 workstation and the server was run on an HP9000/826 system. There was one CDS Server, running on the 826. The **perf_client** was executed twice for each CDS method to measure the effect of CDS caching.

Table 5.1 and Figure 5.7 compare the DCE calls for server setup and cleanup, with and without CDS. Table 5.2 and Figure 5.8 show the effect of the string and CDS binding methods on the client.

Table 5.1

Performance of Server DCE Calls (millisec)			
DCE Call	No CDS	CDS (1st)	CDS (2nd)
Server Setup			
rpc_server_use_all_protseqs()	211.25	240.63	236.48
rpc_server_register_if()	0.11	0.10	0.10
rpc_ep_register()	144.64	149.04	148.81
rpc_ns_binding_export()		2539.08	675.13
rpc_ns_group_mbr_add()		254.64	255.38
rpc_ns_profile_elt_add()		438.83	456.84
pthread_create() signal catcher	1.43	1.06	1.05
Accumulated Time	357.43	3623.37	1773.78
Server Cleanup			
rpc_ns_profile_elt_remove()		363.41	654.19
rpc_ns_group_mbr_remove()		179.12	180.92
rpc_ns_binding_unexport()		606.29	606.63
rpc_ep_unregister()	47.16	18.66	57.70
rpc_server_unregister_if()	0.11	0.10	0.10
Accumulated Time	47.27	1167.57	1499.55

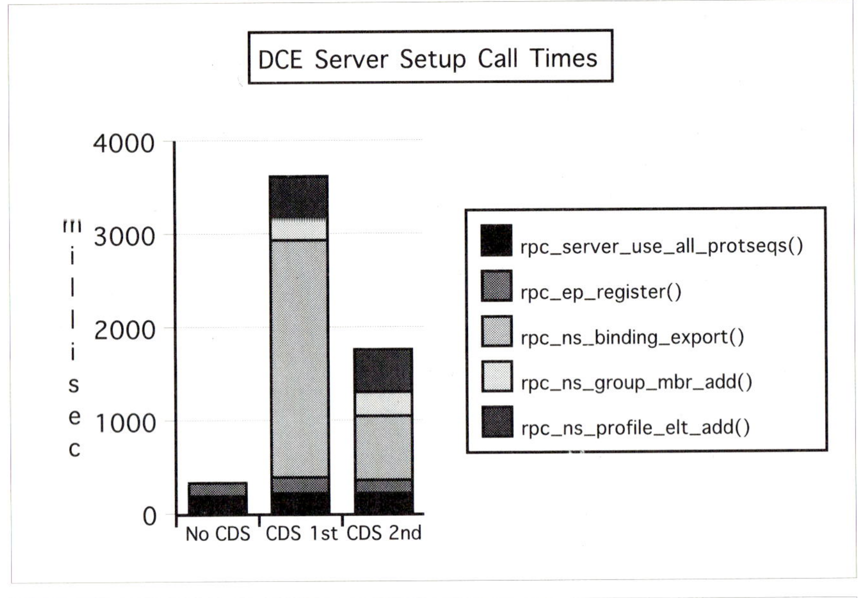

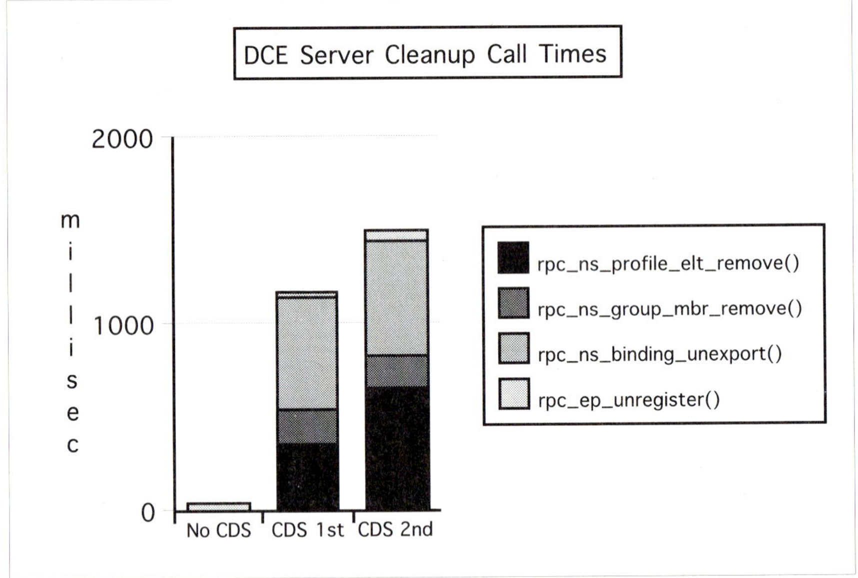

Figure 5.7
Performance of DCE Calls for Server Setup and Cleanup with CDS

Some observations on the server setup and cleanup calls:

- The time to set up the protocol bindings and to register and unregister the interface with the RPC Runtime and with the Endpoint Map are the same whether or not CDS is used.
- The time to export the bindings to the CDS server entry and to add the server to the group and profile dominate the server setup, consuming 80 to 90 percent of the accumulated time. Most of the time is spent in the first CDS call, `rpc_ns_binding_export()`, which has to set up the CDS clerk and cache for the server's user.
- The binding export time drops substantially the second time the server is run, showing the effect of CDS caching on the server entry.

Table 5.2

Performance of Client Binding Methods (millisec)

Binding Method	`string`	`SERVER`		`GROUP`		`PROFILE`	
		1st	2nd	1st	2nd	1st	2nd
`rpc_binding_...()`	207.45	*CDS caching*					
`_import_begin()`		231.46	259.97	254.05	268.43	232.19	240.62
`_import_next()`		335.20	75.07	361.42	127.78	230.82	188.52
`_import_done()`		0.19	0.17	0.23	0.20	0.24	0.23
Accumulated Time	207.45	556.85	335.21	615.70	396.41	463.25	429.38
`rpc_binding_...()`	207.45	*No CDS caching*					
`_import_begin()`		260.67	260.97	235.82	223.80	232.09	238.86
`_import_next()`		301.51	300.79	575.90	588.12	875.07	868.72
`_import_done()`		0.19	0.19	0.23	0.23	0.26	0.25
Accumulated Time	207.45	562.40	561.97	811.97	812.18	1107.45	1107.85

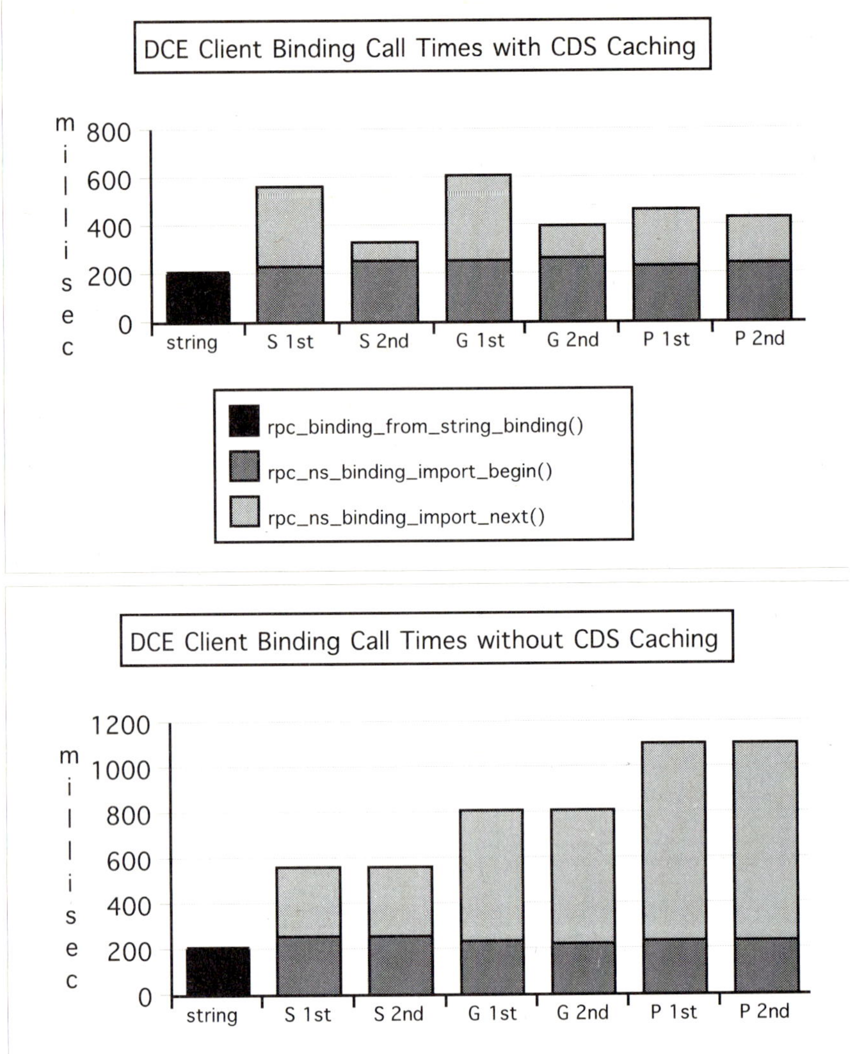

Figure 5.8
Performance of DCE Calls for Client Binding

Comments on the performance of the client binding methods:

- The normal CDS binding methods (using the CDS cache) are from 60 to 300 percent slower than binding using a string binding.
- The import times for the SERVER, GROUP, and PROFILE methods are similar. There is not appreciable additional overhead for using a group or a profile (at least in the normal case using CDS caching).
- When a client is run a second time, the import time normally drops around 40 percent, showing the effect of CDS caching.
- When CDS caching is disabled (by calling rpc_ns_mgmt_handle_set_exp_age()), the import times are the same for the first and second times the client is run. Moreover, the binding times for SERVER, GROUP, and PROFILE methods increase as more entries have to be retrieved from the CDS server.

CHAPTER 6

Security

Security, always an important concern in information systems, becomes even more critical in distributed environments. The very openness and flexibility which make distributed systems attractive and powerful to the good citizens of cyberspace can also be used for unethical and illegal purposes by hackers and computer criminals. Every day brings fresh reports of cyber atrocities in the trade press and even in the popular media. Corporate officers and ordinary citizens rightfully fear attacks on their assets, integrity, and privacy through the Internet.

6.1 Distributed Security Issues and Solutions

DCE provides advanced security features that can be used to protect distributed applications. These features are at the same time powerful and complex to use. This chapter will discuss these facilities and add them to the sample application. But first, let's examine the kinds of security threats a distributed application must face, and the general approaches to defending against these threats. Three major areas of security will be examined:

- *Authentication* proving you are who you say you are.
- *Authorization* determining what you are allowed to do.
- *Data Protection* preventing others from seeing or altering data.

Authentication

Authentication is the process by which a user, program, machine, or other entity establishes and proves its identity to another entity. This is required by the other security areas. For example, an authorization service must know who it is that is attempting to access a resource before it can grant or deny that access. The security of a system or network is only as strong as its authentication. Consequently, authentication is often the weak link subject to attack. This becomes especially true in distributed systems.

User and Password Login

The way a user typically authenticates him- or herself to a computer system is by *logging on* (also known as *signing on* in some circles). During a logon, the user supplies a user ID that is public (or at least not secret) and a password that is known to just the user and the system. The system maintains a table of user IDs and various attributes for each user, including the user's password. On Unix systems, a user ID is typically a short character string derived from the user's name or initials (like `cwk`) and the known user IDs and passwords are found in the file `/etc/passwd`. The passwords in this file are encrypted using a one-way encryption algorithm so they cannot be discovered.

Passwords are subject to attack by interception, guessing, and systematic trial and error. Short, common words are poor choices for passwords. A particularly appalling example would be a password of `root` for the `root` user of a system. To counter this, many password-based authentication systems enforce measures of *password strength*, such as a minimum length, required nonalphabetic characters, and no matches to common words. Also, they may require passwords to be changed periodically. Another check against password attacks is a limit on the number of invalid login attempts by a user. If the limit is exceeded, the user is locked out for some period of time.

Most systems and applications used over networks still use password logins. Common examples in the Unix world are **`telnet`** and **`ftp`**. But user IDs and passwords sent over a network are subject to interception and misuse. Recently there have been many reports of break-ins on the Internet using passwords that were intercepted by so-called sniffer programs. Clearly password authentication alone is insufficient for distributed applications. More sophisticated schemes are needed to thwart increasingly more sophisticated attackers.

Kerberos

In response to the challenge of authentication in a distributed environment, Project Athena at MIT developed the Kerberos service and protocol. Students of Greek mythology will recognize Kerberos (or the Latin version, Cerberus) as the three-headed dog that guarded the gates of Hades.

In Kerberos, users, programs, and machines in the network are *principals* that are assigned networkwide identities. Kerberos maintains a database of principals on a secure system. Associated with this database is the Kerberos *Authentication Server* (AS), to which principals send requests for authentication. The AS is also called the *Key Distribution Center* (KDC), as will be discussed later. Figure 6.1 shows how Kerberos works.

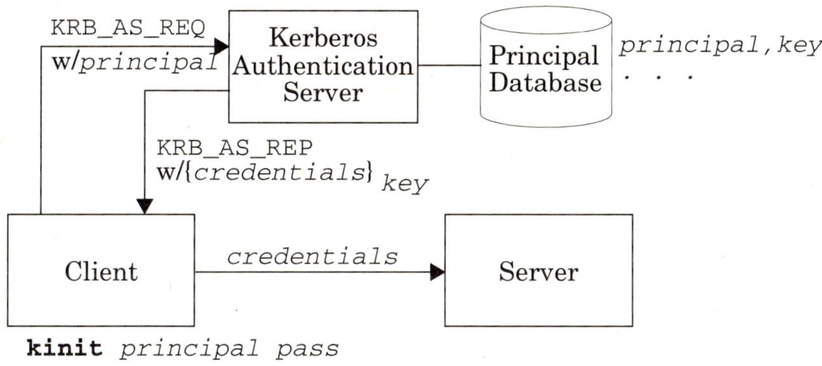

Figure 6.1
Kerberos Authentication

A user establishes his or her principal identity using the **kinit** command. The command requires a principal name and a password, which can be input silently at a prompt. The principal has a key that is derived from this password and is known only to Kerberos. The client sends a *Kerberos Authentication Service Request* (KRB_AS_REQ) to the AS containing the principal's name, but not the password. The AS looks up the principal and its key in its database and returns a *Kerberos Authentication Service Response* (KRB_AS_REP) with information called *credentials*. These credentials are proof that the user has successfully authenticated him- or herself with Kerberos. The credentials are encrypted (see the discussion on DES later) using the principal's key, so the user can decrypt and use the credentials only if he or she supplies the correct password.

Later, a client run by the user can prove to a server that it represents the user by presenting the user's credentials. The actual contents of these credentials are quite complex and will be discussed later in this chapter. Also, many details of the authentication exchange have been omitted.

The DCE Security Service uses Kerberos for authentication. The Security Daemon (**secd**) includes the Kerberos AS and KDC. DCE provides an RPC interface to Kerberos for the Kerberos protocol (the KRB_AS_REQ and KRB_AS_REP messages). DCE 1.1 will also provide the *Generic Security Service Application Programming Interface* (GSS-API), an Internet standard, to allow non-DCE applications to use the DCE Kerberos service.

Advantages of Kerberos are

- *Protection from password disclosure*

  Since a principal's password is not transmitted over the network, it cannot be intercepted by a network snooper. It would take enormously expensive and time-consuming code breaking methods to get the principal's secret key, and hence password, from the encrypted information in the KRB_AS_REP message. (Attempting to get a password this way is called an *off-line attack.*) And, in DCE 1.1, additional levels of encryption have been added (called *preauthentication*) to make off-line attacks even more difficult.

- *Protection from replay*

  An attacker might try to reuse an intercepted Kerberos message to impersonate the user that originally initiated the request—this is called *replay.* Kerberos detects and discards replays. To bound the number of messages it must check, it includes time stamps on each message. Old messages are also rejected.

Possible problems with Kerberos, and DCE's solutions, are

- *Vulnerability of the Authentication Server*

  If the Kerberos Authentication Server or its database are broken into (*compromised*), all principals and their secret keys can be disclosed. The machine containing them must be physically secure; outside access must be strictly limited. Local operating system security must be maximized.

- *Single Point of Failure and Replication*

  If there is only one Kerberos AS, and that AS fails, then no principal on the network can request authentication. The usual solution to this problem is to replicate the Authentication Server and its database on different machines. All of the Kerberos replicas must then be secure. Replication of the DCE Security Service was introduced in the DCE Release 1.0.3.

- *Time Synchronization*

  Since Kerberos time stamps its request and rejects old requests, the time set on the client and Kerberos server machines must agree within certain tolerances. With DCE, time synchronization is provided by the Distributed Time Service (DTS).

- *Password Strength and Maximum Login Attempts*

  Since Kerberos is still dependent on passwords for the initial authentication of principals, password strength should be enforced to ensure passwords are not easily guessed by attackers. Initially there was no password strength enforcement in DCE, but HP has added several such methods to HP DCE 1.4.

Authorization

Authorization is the process by which the operating system or an application decides whether or not to permit an action to be performed on behalf of a user. The user requesting the action must first have authenticated him- or herself so that application can know who is requesting the action.

Example: Unix File System Access Control

The Unix file system provides a familiar example of authorization. Each file has a set of *permissions* that determine who can read, write, or execute the file. These can be displayed using the **ls -l** command; for example

```
:ls -l chap6
-rw-r-----   1 cwk  users    55296 Nov 29 15:59 chap6
```

- Owner (rw-): The owner of the file cwk can read or write the file.
- Group (r--): Any user in the group users can read the file.
- World (---): Anyone else cannot access the file.

When a user opens a file for read, write, or execute access, his or her user ID (uid) and group ID (gid), which were established at login, are compared to the owner and group IDs associated with the target file. The appropriate permissions are used to decide whether or not to allow the user to open the file with the requested access.

Note that it is not possible with this scheme of authorization to give an arbitrary user specific access rights. Any user in the file's group has the same rights, as do all users outside the group. This lack of granularity in authorization is unacceptable for many applications.

Access Control Lists

An access control list (ACL) is a list of users with access permissions. For example, an ACL for the file chap6 might look like

```
user:cwk:rw-
user:abc:r--
group:users:r--
any_other:---
```

This provides the same authorization as the earlier example, with the addition of read permission for the user abc. This user then does not have to be the owner or a member of the users group to read the file.

ACLs provide a finer grain of authorization than do the Unix file permission bits. For this reason, ACLs are frequently required for secure systems. The C2 and higher security classes defined by the U.S. Department of Defense *Trusted Computer System Evaluation Criteria* (the so-called *Orange Book*) require ACLs for authorization. The POSIX standard 1003.6 provides a definition of the format and use of ACLs for open operating systems.

DCE uses ACLs for authorization. An object of interest to a DCE server can have an ACL that specifies the actions that principals are allowed to perform on the object. A DCE application can define arbitrary permissions in addition to the usual read and write permissions. The DCE ACLs are based on the POSIX 1003.6 standard.

The responsibility for managing and enforcing authorization through DCE ACLs rests with the application. When the application server processes a remote call, the server is responsible for retrieving the client's principal identity and searching relevant ACLs for the correct permissions. Prior to DCE 1.1, the server must also implement and export the `rdacl` interface (defined by DCE) to allow its ACLs to be managed through the **`acl_edit`** tool. DCE 1.1 provides an ACL library that does this work for the server. ACLs will be discussed in Chapter 9.

Data Protection

Data protection has two aspects: *integrity* and *privacy.* Integrity ensures that data have not been altered without detection. Electronic funds transfer (EFT) between banks provide an example of an application where data integrity is very important. When one bank transfers funds to another bank, no one else should be able to surreptitiously alter the amount, source, or destination of the transfer.

Privacy ensures that sensitive data is not disclosed. If you are transmitting company secrets (say, data on an upcoming product introduction) over the Internet, you will want to keep that data private.

Both data integrity and privacy are provided by encryption techniques. *Encryption* is a procedure which takes the original data (called the *plaintext*) and scrambles it, using an encryption key, into a form that is incomprehensible (the *ciphertext*). The ciphertext can then be transmitted over a network to its intended recipient. The recipient applies the inverse of the encryption (*decryption*) to the ciphertext using an encryption key to recover the plaintext.

There are two major approaches to encryption which differ in how the encryption and decryption algorithms use the key(s). They are termed *secret* and *public key.* Only secret key is currently used by DCE, so public key will not be discussed here.

Secret Key Encryption: DES

In secret encryption (also called *symmetric key* or *private key* encryption), one key is used for both encryption and decryption. Both the encrypter and the decrypter must have that key. In fact, anyone who has the key can decrypt the ciphertext. Consequently, the key must be a secret that is shared between the encrypter and decrypter. How keys are distributed is a major problem to be solved when using secret key encryption.

The most popular secret key encryption algorithm is the *Data Encryption Standard* (DES), which was developed under the direction of the U.S. National Institute of Standards and Technology in the 1970s. The publicly published DES algorithm uses iterations of a transformation involving alternating transposition and substitution of the data bytes under the control of the key. The key is a sequence of eight bytes (64 bits). One bit in each of the key bytes is used for parity checking, so there are 56 meaningful bits in a DES key. Figure 6.2 illustrates DES.

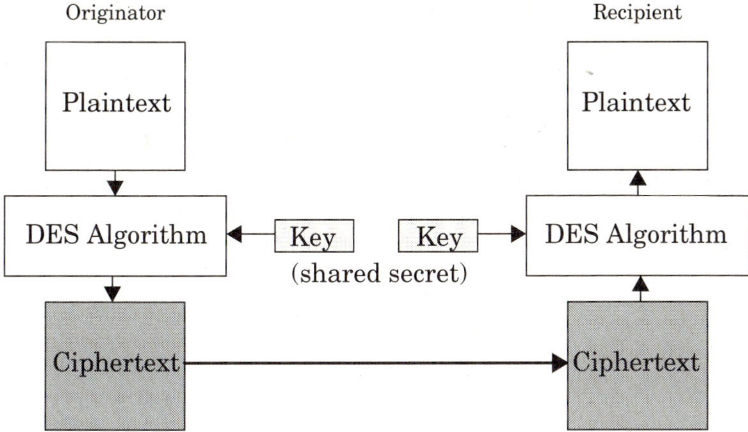

Figure 6.2
Secret Key Encryption with DES

The DES algorithm may be implemented in software or in special-purpose hardware. The overhead of software encryption and decryption is substantial (as we will see in performance results later), so DES encryption hardware may be worthwhile for heavy encryption loads.

DCE uses DES when data privacy is needed. DES is used as the encryption method in the Kerberos authentication protocol, with the initial key derived from the principal's password. The Kerberos Key Distribution Center (KDC) also generates DES keys (called *session keys*) to be used between a client and server for data privacy. Session keys are securely transmitted to the client and the server as part of the Kerberos authentication protocol. This neatly solves the shared secret key problem for DCE.

Session keys also provide considerable immunity to *off-line attacks*, where an attacker attempts to determine (*crack*) an encryption key by cryptoanalysis of plain and cipher texts. Even with massive computing resources, such an attack will take considerable time. By the time the attacker has cracked a session key, it should no longer be in use.

Date Integrity: MD5

In addition to privacy, cryptographic techniques can be used to ensure data integrity—that is, that data in a message has not be altered without detection. To do this, a *cryptographic checksum* is attached to the message. There are two steps in generating this checksum. The first step is to compute a message digest, a short sequence of bytes that acts like a fingerprint for the message. The message digest is generated by a *hash function* applied to the data in the message. To be secure, a hash function must not produce the same digest for two different messages and it must not be feasible to find a message that will produce a given digest. MD5 (for *Message Digest 5*) is a popular hash function which produces a 128-bit digest.

The second step is to encrypt the message digest with DES. The digest is encrypted with the session key known by both the originator and the recipient.

The recipient can verify the integrity of the message by reversing these two steps. The first step is to decrypt the attached message digest, using the DES session key. The second step is to recompute the message digest for the received message, using the same hash function as the originator, and to compare the digest for the received message with the digest for the original data. If the two match, the message has not been altered.

Suppose an attacker intercepted the message, altered it, and resent it to the recipient. Then the message digest for the original message would not match the digest for the received message. The attacker might try to change the attached digest to cover up the message alteration. But then the attacker would need the original DES session key to successfully reencrypt the modified digest.

DCE RPC can provide data integrity using the MD5 hash function and the DES session key generated by Kerberos. If data integrity is selected, a cryptographic checksum is computed and checked for each message between a client and a server. Figure 6.3 illustrates data integrity checking using MD5 and DES.

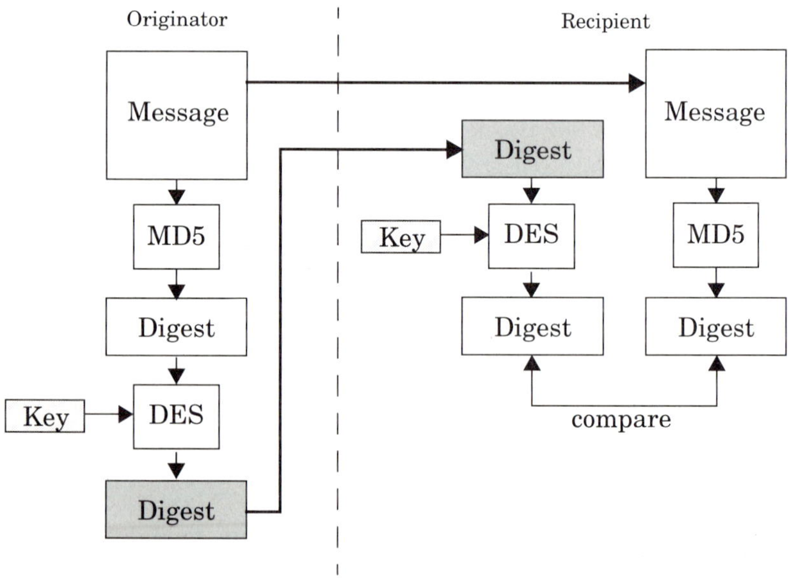

Figure 6.3
Data Integrity Checking with MD5 and DES

Encryption and Export Laws

Encryption is a very powerful tool for ensuring data privacy, both for legitimate and illegitimate purposes. Criminals, terrorists, or hostile foreign powers could use encryption to hide their activities from wiretaps and other types of intelligence gathering. For this reason, the U.S. government restricts the export of products that provide general purpose encryption. In fact, the International Traffic in Arms Regulation (ITAR) classifies encryption products as *munitions*! The US. State Department must grant a license for export of an encryption product, even to friendly countries. Products that use encryption only for authentication are usually allowed to be exported. But products that provide data privacy using DES are still restricted. Some weaker encryption algorithms that use shorter keys can be exported; presumably the US. National Security Agency can break these codes.

Because of these export laws, DCE for export cannot include data privacy. This means that OSF and U. S. vendors have to produce two versions of DCE: a domestic one that provides data privacy and an international one that does not. This is all pretty silly, since there are already many foreign implementations of the publicly available DES algorithm. (For example, an engineer from a German DCE vendor once told me they have their own "German DES.")

6.2 DCE Security Registry

The DCE *Security Registry* is the database used for DCE security. This database contains information about principals and other entities known to the DCE Security Service. It is accessed through the Security Daemon and it can be replicated to ensure that it is available. There is one Security Registry in each DCE cell.

Realms and Cells

In Kerberos, a *realm* is a collection of principals (systems and users) that use a (possible replicated) Kerberos Authentication Server. All of the principals in a realm trust the Kerberos AS for authentication. A realm might coincide with an organization like a department within a company.

DCE maps the Kerberos realm onto the *cell*, which we have already encountered in Chapter 5, in relation to the Cell Directory Service. The cell defines the boundaries for DCE security administration. Security entities, such as user principals, are defined within the context of a cell. All of the principals within the cell trust the cell's Security Daemon (**secd**) for authentication. Figure 6.4 shows a couple of cells, each with their own Security Daemons and Registries.

Intracell Authentication

When a principal wishes to prove its identity to another principal within a cell, it uses *intracell authentication*, which is the Kerberos authentication protocol we have previously discussed. Suppose, in Figure 6.4, a client with principal p1 wishes to authenticate itself to a server with principal p2. The client obtains credentials from the cell's Security Daemon and presents those credentials to the server. Since the server is in the same cell as the client, the server trusts the client's credentials. Another way to look at this is that the client and server each share their secret keys with the same Security Daemon, which is then able to construct credentials that are mutually acceptable.

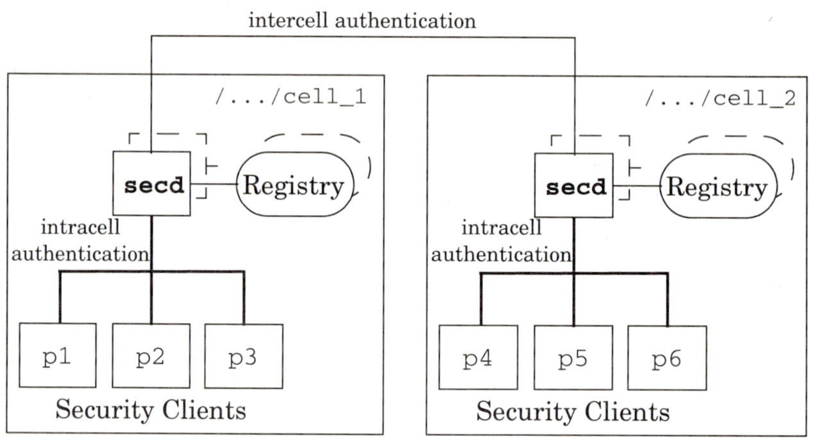

Figure 6.4
DCE Security and Cells

Intercell Authentication

A principal may occasionally need to prove its identity to a principal in another cell. This *intercell authentication* is complicated by the fact that there is no one Security Daemon that knows about both principals. An example from Figure 6.4 is if the client in cell cell_1 with principal p1 wishes to authenticate itself to a server in cell cell_2 with principal p4. The client cannot authenticate itself directly with the Security Daemon in cell_2, because the principal p1 and its secret key are not known in cell_2. To get around this, the client must ask the Security Daemon for its cell to obtain the appropriate credentials from the Security Daemon in the other cell. The two Security Daemons share secret keys to allow them to mutually authenticate themselves.

Fortunately for users and application programmers, intercell authentication is done automatically by the DCE security service when it is needed. The same DCE calls are used for intra- and intercell authentication.

rgy_edit

A user principal with sufficient privileges (for example, cell_admin) can view and alter the contents of Security Registry entries using the **rgy_edit** program. Some examples of **rgy_edit** commands will be shown in the next section. However, full discussion of DCE security administration through **rgy_edit** is beyond the scope of this book. For more information, consult the *OSF DCE Administration Guide* and the *OSF DCE Administration Reference*.

In HP-UX DCE 1.4 (which corresponds to OSF DCE 1.1), registry administration can also be done using the **dcecp** command. Examples of registry management with **dcecp** will also be shown.

Principals, Groups, and Organizations

Most entities defined within a DCE Security Registry are *principals*, *groups*, or *organizations*. These three terms are collectively referred to as *pgo*. Each of these entities is assigned an alphanumeric name for external use and a UUID for internal use.

Principals

Principals are the analog of users in a local operation system like Unix. Following this analogy, the principal name is the equivalent of the Unix user name, and the principal UUID is the equivalent of the Unix UID. However, a principal has the same UUID on every machine, while the same Unix user name may have different UIDs on different systems, which can lead to problems in distributed systems. A user's principal identity is established through a **dce_login** or an integrated login (more on this later.)

Principals in DCE are extended to more than just users. Programs, particularly server programs, can have a principal identity distinct from the user who might have run the program. The program establishes its principal identity through a sequence of DCE calls, which will be discussed in the Server Security Setup section.

Host machines in a DCE cell also have principals assigned to them. A machine's principal identity is set up when DCE is started on the machine, and it can play a role in authentication and other security services. The Client Security Daemon (**sec_clientd**) or DCE Daemon (**dced**) on each machine maintains its identity.

Principals are created, deleted, and viewed using the *principal domain* of **rgy_edit**. Output Sample 6.1 shows examples of some principals. `cwk` is a user (i.e., interactive) principal, `room-server` is a server program principal, and `hosts/hpiala3/self` is a machine principal. Each principal has a Unix UID number (shown on the same line as the principal; these will be discussed shortly), a UUID, whether the name is a primary name (`primary: pr`) or an alias (`primary: al`), and the number of registry objects the principal can create (`unlimited` or `0`).

With DCE 1.1, principals can also be created, deleted, and viewed using **dcecp**. Output Sample 6.2 shows the **dcecp -c principal show** command. In addition to the principal's UUID, this display also includes some information for the principal's account (discussed in a bit).

```
:rgy_edit
Current site is: registry server at /.../jaja/subsys/dce/sec/master
rgy_edit=> domain principal
Domain changed to: principal
rgy_edit=> view cwk -full
cwk                                              8714
  Full name:  Charles Knouse
  Uuid:       0000220a-78ff-21ce-8e00-08000948fbd9
  Primary:  pr   Reserved:   --
  Quota: unlimited
rgy_edit=> view room-server -full
room-server                                     10505
  Uuid:       00002909-bfbc-21ce-9000-08000948fbd9
  Primary:  pr   Reserved:   --
  Quota: unlimited
rgy_edit=> view hosts/hpiala3/self -full
hosts/hpiala3/self                              10100
  Uuid:       00002774-5349-21ce-a800-08000948fbd9
  Primary:  pr   Reserved:   rq
  Quota: 0
```

Output Sample 6.1
rgy_edit output: Viewing principals

```
:dcecp -c principal show cwk     (shows attributes of a principal)
{fullname {Charles Knouse}}
{uid 8714}
{uuid 0000220a-78ff-21ce-8e00-08000948fbd9}
{alias no}
{quota unlimited}
{groups developers}
```

Output Sample 6.2
dcecp output: Viewing principals

Groups and Project Lists

A group in DCE is a collection of one or more principals with something in common—for example, users with the same job title. Groups provide a convenient way to assign ACL permissions to a group of related principals. Output Samples 6.3 and 6.4 show **rgy_edit** and **dcecp** displays for a group named `developers` that contains three principals: `cwk`, `msr`, and `sks`.

Each principal has a *project list* of groups to which it belongs. These groups can be used in access decisions, as discussed in Chapter 9. A principal may have one or more aliases with different project lists. This allows a principal to select, by a **dce_login** with an alias, the list of groups it is currently using. In some cases, it might be necessary to exclude a group from being included in project lists for principals. If the `inprojlist` property of a group is `no`, the group will be excluded from project lists.

```
rgy_edit=> domain group
Domain changed to: group
rgy_edit=> view developers -f -m
rgy_edit=> view developers -f -m
developers                                680
  Uuid:       000002a8-c05e-21ce-9001-08000948fbd9
  Primary:  pr   Reserved:   --
  Project List:1
  3 members
    cwk, msr, sks
```

Output Sample 6.3
rgy_edit output: Viewing a group

```
:dcecp -c group list developers  (lists principals in a group)
/.../jaja/cwk
/.../jaja/msr
/.../jaja/sks
:dcecp -c group show developers  (shows attributes of a group)
{alias no}
{gid 680}
{uuid 000002a8-c05e-21ce-9001-08000948fbd9}
{inprojlist yes}
{fullname {}}
```

Output Sample 6.4
dcecp output: Viewing group information

Organizations

An organization is a group of principals (and their accounts) that can be used to assign default security properties (discussed later). One use for this might be to set up an organization for server principals with security properties appropriate for servers. Output Samples 6.5 and 6.6 show an organization, `eap`, with six principals: `cwk`, `msr`, `sks`, `lms`, `cpk`, and `cjc`.

```
Current site is: registry server at /.../jaja/subsys/dce/sec/master
rgy_edit=> domain org
Domain changed to: org
rgy_edit=> view eap -f -m
eap                                       100
  Uuid:       00000064-c05e-21ce-9002-08000948fbd9
  Primary:  pr   Reserved:   --
  6 members
    cwk, msr, sks, lms, cpk, cjc
```

Output Sample 6.5
rgy_edit output: Viewing an organization

```
:dcecp -c organization list eap       (lists the principals in an org)
/.../jaja/cwk
/.../jaja/msr
/.../jaja/sks
/.../jaja/lms
/.../jaja/cpk
/.../jaja/cjc
:dcecp -c organization show eap       (shows the attributes of an org)
{fullname {}}
{orgid 100}
{uuid 00000064-c05e-21ce-9002-08000948fbd9}
```

Output Sample 6.6
dcecp output: Viewing organization information

Accounts

Each DCE principal has an account that supplies a number of security attributes, including the principal's login password and default group and organization. Many of these attributes control how Kerberos authentication tickets are issued for the principal (more on this later). The DCE account also contains information that can be used to set up a local Unix user for the principal, including a password, a Unix UID, and a login directory and shell. A local Unix user with the principal's attributes can be set up using the **passwd_export** program, which adds the user to the local `/etc/passwd` and `/etc/group` files. Also, DCE principals and the corresponding accounts can be created from `/etc/passwd` and `/etc/group` files by the **passwd_import** program.

Output Samples 6.7 and 6.8 show the account for the principal `cwk`, in the `developers` group and the `eap` organization. The first line of the **rgy_edit** output shows the local Unix user information in the `/etc/passwd` format. The rest of the display shows Kerberos-related attributes for the principal. Note that the account does not have its own UUID.

```
rgy_edit=> domain account
Domain changed to: account
rgy_edit=> view cwk -full
cwk [developers eap]:*:8714:12::/users/cwk::
  created by: /.../jaja/cell_admin  1995/04/17.14:51
  changed by: /.../jaja/cell_admin  1995/04/17.14:52
  password is: valid, was last changed: 1995/04/17.14:51
  Account expiration date: none
  Account MAY be a server principal
  Account MAY be a client principal
  Account is: valid
  Account CAN NOT get post-dated certificates
  Account CAN get forwardable certificates
  Certificates to this service account MAY be issued via TGT
   authentication
  Account CAN get renewable certificates
  Account CAN NOT get proxiable certificates
  Account CAN NOT have duplicate session keys
  Good since date: 1995/04/17.14:51
  Max certificate lifetime: default-policy
  Max renewable lifetime: default-policy
```

Output Sample 6.7
rgy_edit output: Viewing an account

```
:dcecp -c account show cwk
{acctvalid yes}
{client yes}
{created /.../jaja/cell_admin 1995-04-17-14:51:16.000-07:00I-----}
{description {}}
{dupkey no}
{expdate none}
{forwardabletkt yes}
{goodsince 1995-04-17-14:51:00.000-07:00I-----}
{group developers}
{home /users/cwk}
{lastchange /.../jaja/cell_admin 1995-04-17-14:52:37.000-07:00I-----}
{organization eap}
{postdatedtkt no}
{proxiabletkt no}
{pwdvalid yes}
{renewabletkt yes}
{server yes}
{shell {}}
{stdtgtauth yes}
```

Output Sample 6.8
dcecp output: Viewing an account

Policies and Properties

The Security Registry maintains a set of policies and properties that control DCE authentication and authorization. Policies and properties include expiration limits for passwords and credentials, some password composition requirements, and parameters for assignment of local Unix attributes. Some of these policies can have subtle effects for applications that will be discussed later. Output Samples 6.9 through 6.12 show registry policies and properties.

```
rgy_edit=> policy
  Policy:
   Account lifespan:                              forever
   Password min len:                              0
   Password lifespan:                             forever
   Password expiration date:                      none
   Passwords MAY be all spaces, MAY be all alphanumeric
Do you wish to make changes [y/n]? (n) n
```

Output Sample 6.9
rgy_edit output: Viewing registry policies

```
rgy_edit=> properties
   Properties:
    Properties for Registry at:                        /.../odss_827
    Registry is NOT read-only
    Certificates to this server may be generated at any site.
    Encrypted passwords are hidden
    Unix IDs ARE embedded in PGO UUIDs
    Low UID for principal creation:           25807
    Low UID for group creation:               301
    Low UID for org creation:                 100
    Maximum possible UID:                     32767
    Minimum certificate lifetime              5m
    Default certificate lifetime              10h
Do you wish to make changes [y/n]? (n) n
```

Output Sample 6.10
rgy_edit output: Viewing registry properties

```
:dcecp -c registry show
{deftktlife +0-10:00:00.000I-----}
{hidepwd yes}
{maxuid 32767}
{mingid 301}
{minorgid 100}
{mintktlife +0-00:05:00.000I-----}
{minuid 25807}
```

Output Sample 6.11
dcecp output: Viewing registry properties

```
rgy_edit=> authpolicy
   Authorization Policy:
    Max certificate lifetime:                 1d
    Max renewable lifetime:                   4w
```

Output Sample 6.12
rgy_edit output: Viewing authorization policies

6.3 DCE Login

Interactive users establish their identities to DCE in one of two ways: the **dce_login** command or a local system login that has been integrated with DCE.

DCE Login Command

You execute the **dce_login** command to establish your DCE identity from within an existing local session. The command has the syntax

dce_login ***principal_name password*** OR
dce_login ***principal_name***
Enter Password: <***password***>

where *principal_name* and *password* are defined for the user's principal in the Security Registry. To keep the password private, it can be omitted from the command, and the command will request a password.

This command makes a sequence of DCE authentication calls that interact with the Security Daemon to authenticate the user. This will be explained in more detail in the next section. The result of this interaction is a set of credentials that can be used by programs run by the user.

On Unix, the **dce_login** command creates a new shell in which subsequent commands from the user will be executed. The new shell will inherit the environment of the previous shell, except that the new shell will have a new set of DCE credentials. Because of this, it is possible to nest **dce_login**s. When the new shell is exited, the credentials (if any) of the previous shell will become current again. For example

: (original shell 0 with no DCE credentials)
:**dce_login p1 <pass1>**
: (new shell 1 with DCE credentials for p1)
:**dce_login p2 <pass2>**
: (new shell 2 with DCE credentials for p2)
:**exit**
: (back to shell 1 with DCE credentials for p1)
:**exit**
: (back to shell 0 with no DCE credentials)

Displaying DCE Credentials

Once you have logged into DCE, you can display your current credential information with the **klist** command (which was taken from Kerberos). This information includes the names and UUIDs for your cell, the principal you specified in the last **dce_login**, and any groups of which your principal is a member. Also displayed are the expirations for your credentials, your account, and your password. Finally, the ticket cache file and list of tickets you possess are listed. (Kerberos tickets will be examined in more detail in Section 6.8.) Output Sample 6.13 shows an example of a **klist** for principal cwk in the developers group.

```
:klist
DCE Identity Information:
        Warning: Identity information is not certified
        Global Principal: /.../jaja/cwk
        Cell:       7b46b6fc-5349-11ce-a845-08000948fbd9 /.../jaja
        Principal: 0000220a-78ff-21ce-8e00-08000948fbd9 cwk
        Group:      000002a8-c05e-21ce-9001-08000948fbd9 developers
        Local Groups:
                000002a8-c05e-21ce-9001-08000948fbd9 developers
Identity Info Expires: 95/07/17:21:15:00
Account Expires:       never
Passwd Expires:        never

Kerberos Ticket Information:
Ticket cache: /opt/dcelocal/var/security/creds/dcecred_1de8a600
Default principal: cwk_dev@jaja
Server: krbtgt/jaja@jaja
        valid 95/07/17:11:15:00 to 95/07/17:21:15:00
Server: dce-rgy@jaja
        valid 95/07/17:11:15:01 to 95/07/17:21:15:00
Server: dce-ptgt@jaja
        valid 95/07/17:11:15:14 to 95/07/17:13:15:14
Client: dce-ptgt@jaja   Server: krbtgt/jaja@jaja
        valid 95/07/17:11:15:14 to 95/07/17:13:15:14
Client: dce-ptgt@jaja   Server: dce-rgy@jaja
        valid 95/07/17:11:15:17 to 95/07/17:13:15:14
```

Output Sample 6.13
klist output

Frequently, you will be interested only in determining your current principal identity; you don't want the rest of the **klist** output. On Unix, you can filter the **klist** output through **grep** to extract the principal information, as shown in Output Sample 6.14.

```
:klist | grep Princ
        Global Principal: /.../jaja/cwk
        Principal: 0000220a-78ff-21ce-8e00-08000948fbd9 cwk
```

Output Sample 6.14
klist output filtered for principal

Integrated Login

Some DCE vendors provide an option called *integrated login* that allows the equivalent of a **dce_login** to be executed when a user performs a local system login. With integrated login, the DCE principal name and password are the same as the local user name and password. HP-UX, for example, provides versions of **/bin/login** and **vuelogin** to perform integrated DCE login from the `login:` prompt or from the VUE login screen. Once the local login is complete, the user is also logged into DCE and does not need to issue a separate **dce_login** (or enter the password again).

Integrated login is set up when DCE is configured. There are a couple of tools supplied with DCE that can be used to keep the local users and the DCE principals synchronized:

- **passwd_import** creates principals and groups in the DCE Registry that correspond to the existing local Unix users and groups in the files `/etc/passwd` and `/etc/group`.
- **passwd_export** creates local Unix users and groups in the `/etc/passwd` and `/etc/group` files that correspond to the principals and groups in the DCE Registry.

Details on how to use these tools are given in the *DCE Administration Guide*. You should check with your local DCE administrator to see if integration login is in effect on your system.

6.4 Server Security Setup

Now that we have some grounding in the concepts and operation of DCE security, we can look at setting up security for a DCE server. Be forewarned, though, that it takes many calls to do this. The tasks that need to be performed for server security setup are

- Creating a data structure called a *login context* that contains information about the server's principal identity.
- Obtaining a password (actually a key) for the server's principal from a file called the *keytab* file.
- Validating the server's principal identity with the key. (These first three tasks are the equivalent of the **dce_login** command.)
- Creating a thread that will keep the server's identity from expiring by refreshing (revalidating) the identity periodically.
- Registering the server's principal and key information with the DCE Security Runtime.
- Creating another thread that will ensure that the key in the keytab file is kept up to date.

Before we dive into the actual setup routine, we need to look at a couple of items that must be set up prior to the execution of the server: the server's principal and its keytab file.

Server Principal

Like an interactive user of DCE, a server must have a principal identity. The server will establish its identity using this principal during Kerberos authentication. Then clients will specify the server's principal when they set up authenticated remote calls to the server. Also, the server's principal will be used when the server sets up its Name Space entries in CDS. If the server itself makes any authenticated remote calls, its principal will be passed on to the called server.

A server's principal must be created prior to its use by the server. The principal can be set up through **rgy_edit** or **dcecp** by a user with the proper DCE administration privileges (for example, one that has logged onto DCE as cell_admin). Output Samples 6.15 and 6.16 show the commands needed to set up a principal, named room-server, that the **room_server** program will be using. There are actually two things that must be created: the principal itself and an account for the principal. The most important attribute of the principal is its UUID, which is automatically generated by DCE. Most of the other attributes used by the principal are actually associated with its account. The account does not have a distinct name but can be represented by a principal, group, and organization. In the example, the principal is room-server, and the group and organization are both set to none, which is predefined. The initial password for the account is -dce- (an inside joke, known to anyone who has installed DCE). The rest of the many account attributes assume their default values.

```
:rgy_edit
Current site is: registry server at /.../jaja/subsys/dce/sec/master
rgy_edit=> domain principal
Domain changed to: principal
rgy_edit=> add room-server
rgy_edit=> view room-server -f
room-server                                  10505
  Uuid:        00002909-bfbc-21ce-9000-08000948fbd9
  Primary:  pr    Reserved:   --
  Quota: unlimited
rgy_edit=> domain account
Domain changed to: account
rgy_edit=> add room-server -g none -o none -mp <admin_pw> -pw -dce-
rgy_edit=> view room-server -f
room-server [none none]:*:10505:12::/::
  created by: /.../jaja/cell_admin  1995/07/16.15:10
  changed by: /.../jaja/room-server  1995/07/16.15:10
  password is: valid, was last changed: 1995/07/16.15:10
  Account expiration date: none
  Account MAY be a server principal
  Account MAY be a client principal
  Account is: valid
  Account CAN NOT get post-dated certificates
  Account CAN get forwardable certificates
  Certificates to this service account MAY be issued via TGT
   authentication
  Account CAN get renewable certificates
  Account CAN NOT get proxiable certificates
  Account CAN NOT have duplicate session keys
  Good since date: 1995/07/16.15:10
  Max certificate lifetime: default-policy
  Max renewable lifetime: default-policy
```

Output Sample 6.15
rgy_edit output: Setting up the room-server principal and account

```
:dcecp
dcecp> principal create room-server
dcecp> principal show room-server
{fullname {}}
{uid 10505}
{uuid 00002909-bfbc-21ce-9000-08000948fbd9}
{alias no}
{quota unlimited}
{groups none}
dcecp> group add none -member room-server
dcecp> organization add none -member room-server
dcecp> account create room-server1 -group none -organization none \
-mypwd <admin_pw> -password -dce-
dcecp> account show room-server
{acctvalid yes}
{client yes}
{created /.../jaja/cell_admin 1995-07-16-15:10:27.000-07:00I-----}
{description {}}
{dupkey no}
{expdate none}
{forwardabletkt yes}
{goodsince 1995-07-16-15:10:00.000-07:00I-----}
{group none}
{home /}
{lastchange /.../jaja/room-server 1995-07-16-15:10:37.000-07:00I-----}
{organization none}
{postdatedtkt no}
{proxiabletkt no}
{pwdvalid yes}
{renewabletkt yes}
{server yes}
{shell {}}
{stdtgtauth yes}
```

Output Sample 6.16
dcecp commands to set up a server principal and account

Server Principal Name Space ACLs

Since the server's principal will be used to authorize access to its Name Space entries, those entries must include the server principal of their access control lists (ACLs). A DCE administrator or other user with control access to the entries can set up the ACLs with the **acl_edit** or **dcecp** command. Output Samples 6.17 and 6.18 show the commands to set up ACLs on the `room_server`, `room_group`, and `cell-profile` entries to give read, write, and test access to the `room-server` principal.

```
:acl_edit -e /.:/subsys/sch/room_server -m user:room-server:rwt
:acl_edit -e /.:/subsys/sch/room_group -m user:room-server:rwt
:acl_edit -e /.:/cell-profile -m user:room-server:rwt
```

Output Sample 6.17
acl_edit commands to set up Name Space entry permissions for the server principal

```
:dcecp -c acl modify -e /.:/subsys/sch/room_server \
   -add {user room-server1 rwt}
:dcecp -c acl modify -e /.:/subsys/sch/room_group \
   -add {user room-server1 rwt}
:dcecp -c acl modify -e /.:/cell-profile -add {user room-server1 rwt}
```

Output Sample 6.18
dcecp commands to set up Name Space entry permissions for the server principal

Keytab Files

To establish its identity, a principal must provide its name (which is public) and its password (which is a secret shared between the principal and the DCE Security Service). For interactive authentication through **dce_login**, a user can supply the password in the command line or at the `Enter Password:` prompt. But how is the server's principal password to be entered? Some possible solutions are

- Hard code the password in the server. But then the password might be retrieved by inspection of the server program file, and the password cannot be changed easily.
- Have the user who starts the server enter the password. This would be similar to **dce_login**. But it requires any user running the server to know the server's password. It does not work well when a server is started from a script.
- Store the password in a file that the server reads when it establishes its identity. The password can be modified independent of the server program. To maintain the secrecy of the password, it should be encrypted in the file and access to the file should be restricted.

DCE provides the last option with *keytab files*. Each keytab file holds passwordlike keys for one or more servers. Each key can have one or more versions. A server program can retrieve the key for its principal through certain DCE calls. A keytab file is created, and keys set up by **rgy_edit** or **dcecp**. Output Sample 6.19 shows the relevant **rgy_edit** commands. In Output Sample 6.19, the first **ktadd** command creates a keytab file named `room_server_keyfile` (the `-f` option), with the original password `-dce-` (the `-pw` option) for the `room-server` principal (the `-p` option). The second **ktadd** command creates a new, random key for the principal (the `-a` option) and changes the password for `room-server` in the DCE Security Registry to the new key (the `-r` option). The **ktlist** command indicates there are two key versions (the original and the random keys) for the `room-server` principal. The actual keys are not displayed and cannot be obtained from the keytab file except through the key management interface. Note also that once a new random key has been entered into the Security Registry, an interactive user cannot perform a **dce_login** with the principal and the original password. This effectively limits the use of the principal to the server itself. (You may want to hold off randomizing the key until you have debugged the server.)

```
:rgy_edit
rgy_edit=> ktadd -p room-server -pw -dce- -f room_server_keyfile
rgy_edit=> ktadd -p room-server -a -r -f room_server_keyfile
rgy_edit=> ktlist -f room_server_keyfile
/.../jaja/room-server              1
/.../jaja/room-server              2
```

Output Sample 6.19
rgy_edit commands to set up a keytab file

If no keyfile is specified in the **ktadd** or **ktlist** commands, a systemwide keytab file `/krb5/v5srvtab` is used. This file is intended for system services and requires the local system `root` privilege for access. It should not be used for application services.

The **dcecp** commands to set up a keytab file are a bit more complex than **rgy_edit**. Part of the reason is that DCE 1.1 now keeps track of keytab files through each host's **dced** process. Consequently, each keytab has a **dced** object, such as `/.:/hosts/hpiala3/config/keytab/room_server_keyfile`. You can see all of the host's keytab objects using the **dcecp keytab catalog** command. Output Sample 6.20 shows the **dcecp** commands needed to set up the keytab file for the **room_server** server.

```
:dcecp
dcecp> keytab create \            (creates a keytab file)
   /.:/hosts/hpiala3/config/keytab/room_server_keyfile \
   -attr {\
       {storage ./room_server_keyfile} \
       {data {room-server plain 1 -dce-}}}

dcecp> keytab catalog             (lists all keytabs on the host)
...
/.../jaja/hosts/hpiala3/config/keytab/room_server_keyfile

dcecp> keytab add \               (adds a random key version)
   /.../jaja/hosts/hpiala3/config/keytab/room_server_keyfile \
   -member room-server -random -registry

dcecp> keytab show \              (shows keytab contents)
   /.../jaja/hosts/hpiala3/config/keytab/room_server_keyfile
{uuid f7f08d62-aa84-11ce-9ec6-08000948fbd9}
{annotation {}}
{storage ./room_server_keyfile}
{/.../jaja/room-server des 1}
{/.../jaja/room-server des 2}
```

Output Sample 6.20
dcecp commands to set up a keytab file

It is extremely important to restrict local system access to keytab files. Any user with access to a keytab file can start a server that can use the keys in the keytab file. Consequently; access to the keytab should be limited to only the users that are authorized to start the server. Suppose that **room_server** is always started by a user named schadmin. In Unix, the keytab file's permissions should be read and write for schadmin and none for the group and world:

```
:ls -l room_server_keytab
-rw-------    1 schadmin users ... room_server_keytab
```

Establishing the Server's Login Context

The first major task for setting up server security is to establish the server's identity in the form of a login context. A login context is a handle to a data structure that holds information about a principal's identity. Among other things, a login context points to a file in the directory /opt/dcelocal/var/security/creds that holds the DCE Security credentials for the principal. These credentials are set up when the login context is created and validated. There are four calls needed to do this:

- sec_login_setup_identity(), which supplies the principal name, initiates the authentication of the principal identity with the DCE Security Service, and creates the login context data structure.
- sec_login_validate_identity(), which supplies the principal's password or secret key, and completes the authentication of the principal identity. By separating the authentication into two separate calls, DCE minimizes the time the password must be in the server's memory.
- sec_login_certify_identity(), which checks that the authentication was actually performed by the legitimate DCE Security Service. This step is to prevent an attacker from masquerading as the Security Service.
- sec_login_set_context(), which completes the setup of the login context for the principal identity authenticated by the previous calls.

Some of these calls are also used in the **dce_login** program to authenticate the principal for an interactive user. Section 6.8 describes in detail the steps in the authentication process and the messages exchanged between the DCE Security Service and the process requesting the authentication.

The sec_login_validate_identity() call requires the principal's password or key, which can be obtained in any of the three ways discussed in the Keytab File section. We will retrieve the password from the server's keytab file by calling sec_key_mgmt_get_key(). This call will get the latest version of the key, which will be the random key generated by the **rgy_edit -a** or **dcecp -random** commands shown in Output Samples 6.19 and 6.20.

We will need to reuse the validation and certification calls in the identity refresh thread (discussed shortly). So we will put these calls in a routine, validate_identity(), with one input parameter, the login context. Code Sample 6.2 shows the calls to set up the server's identity in main(). These calls occur after the server's bindings are set up and before the rpc_server_register_if(). The server's identity must be established before any rpc_ns_ calls are made that modify Name Space entries. Code Sample 6.1 shows the validate_identity() routine.

```
void validate_identity(
    sec_login_handle_t *login_context)
{
    void                  *key_data;
    sec_login_auth_src_t  authn_source;
    boolean32             reset_password;
    unsigned32            status;

    sec_key_mgmt_get_key(
        rpc_c_authn_dce_secret,
        (unsigned_char_p_t) "room_server_keyfile",
        (unsigned_char_p_t) "room-server",
        0, /* latest key version */
        &key_data,
        (error_status_t *) &status);
    CHECK_DCE(status,
        "Cannot get server key from room_server_keyfile");

    sec_login_validate_identity(
        *login_context,
        (sec_passwd_rec_t *) key_data,
        &reset_password,
        &authn_source,
        &status);
    CHECK_DCE(status,
        "Cannot validate identity for principal");

    sec_key_mgmt_free_key(key_data, &status);
    CHECK_DCE(status, "Cannot free server key.");

    sec_login_certify_identity(*login_context, &status);
    CHECK_DCE(status,
        "Cannot certify identity for principal");
}
```

Code Sample 6.1
schedule/room_server.c: validate_identity()

```
#include <dce/sec_login.h>
#include <dce/keymgmt.h>
. . .

   sec_login_handle_t    login_context;
   . . .
   sec_login_setup_identity(
      (unsigned_char_p_t) "room-server",
      sec_login_no_flags,
      &login_context,
      &status);
   CHECK_DCE(status,
   "Cannot setup identity for room-server principal");

   validate_identity(&login_context);

   sec_login_set_context(login_context, &status);
   CHECK_DCE(status,
     "Cannot set context for room-server principal");
```

Code Sample 6.2
`schedule/room_server.c main()`: Setting server identity

Registering Server Security Information

In addition to setting up an authenticated login context, the server must also register information with its RPC and Security Runtimes using the `rpc_server_register_auth_info()` call. The input parameters to this call are

- the server's *principal* name, which will be used by the Security Runtime to check that incoming service tickets are encoded for this server. The principal used by **room_server** is `room-server`.
- the *authentication service* to be used by clients of the server. This is used to interpret the authentication information from the client. We will specify the DCE Secret Key (e.g., Kerberos) authentication service.
- a *key retrieval function*, which the Security Runtime will call to get the server's key when it is needed during the authentication process. A value of

NULL selects the default method using a keytab file. You could also specify your own function here to provide the server key.

- an *argument* to the key retrieval function. For the default keytab method, this is the name of the keytab file.

Code Sample 6.3 shows the rpc_server_register_auth_info() call in the main() routine of **room_server**. This occurs after the server identity setup code just discussed and before the rpc_server_register_if().

```
rpc_server_register_auth_info(
    (unsigned_char_p_t) "room-server",
    rpc_c_authn_dce_secret,
    NULL, /* use default keytab retrieval method */
    (unsigned_char_p_t) "room_server_keyfile",
    &status);
CHECK_DCE(status,
   "Cannot register server authentication info");
```

Code Sample 6.3
schedule/room_server.c main(): Registering server security information

Refreshing the Server Login Context

The credentials for an authenticated principal will expire after a certain amount of time—the default is eight hours. You will discover this the first time you leave a session in which you have done a **dce_login** and let it sit overnight. The credentials will have expired and when you attempt to use them, say, by running a client that inherits your identity, you will get an error like auth ticket expired. As an interactive user, you can fix the situation by entering another **dce_login** or a **kinit** command. Either of these require you to reenter the password for your principal. The credential timeout is similar to an inactivity timeout for local system logins—it requires you to reenter your password periodically to reconfirm your identity.

Long-lived servers will have the same problem to solve. The credentials of the login context created by sec_login_setup_identity() and sec_login_validate_identity() may eventually expire. When they do, the server will lose its identity and be unable to do certain tasks that require authentication. A common example is cleaning up Name Space entries. If the server's credentials have expired, it cannot remove Name Space entries that it created earlier.

The solution is for the server to *refresh* its login context before it expires. This is the logical equivalent of the interactive user reentering the **dce_login**. To refresh its login context, the server first calls `sec_login_refresh_identity()`. Then it must revalidate the login context via a `sec_login_validate_identity()` call. The second step requires the password again, which must be retrieved from the server's keytab file. This revalidation code is already available in our routine `validate_identity()`.

The server should refresh its login context some amount of time, say 10 minutes, before it expires. The time left before the context expires can be obtained by a call to `sec_login_get_expiration()`. The server can then wait until 10 minutes before expiration time before it performs the refresh and revalidation.

This operation is ideally suited for a thread. The server creates the thread when it sets up the login context. The thread waits for a length of time determined by the expiration time for the login context. Then the thread refreshes the login context and goes back to sleep.

Code Sample 6.4 shows the creation of the `refresh_identity` thread in the server's `main()` routine, using the `create_thread()` routine in `sch_util.c`. This is done after the server's identity is set up.

```
pthread_t refresh_id_thread;
. . .
create_thread(
    refresh_identity,
    "refresh identity",
    &refresh_id_thread,
    (pthread_addr_t) &login_context);
```

Code Sample 6.4
`schedule/room_server.c main()`: Creation of the `refresh_identity` thread

Code Sample 6.5 shows the base routine for the refresh thread. The argument to this routine is a pointer to the server's login context. The loop in the thread determines the wait time by subtracting the expiration time from the current time, calls `pthread_delay_np()` to put the thread to sleep for that length of time, and then refreshes and revalidates the login context. The thread will continue to do this for the life of the server.

```
pthread_addr_t refresh_identity(pthread_addr_t arg)
{
    sec_login_handle_t *login_context =
      (sec_login_handle_t) arg;
    struct timeval      now;
    struct timespec     sleep_time;
    signed32            expiration;
    unsigned32          status;

    while (true)
    {
        sec_login_get_expiration(*login_context,
           &expiration, &status);
        CHECK_DCE(status,"Cannot get context expiration");

        gettimeofday(&now, NULL);
        sleep_time.tv_sec = expiration - now.tv_sec - 600;
        sleep_time.tv_nsec = 0;
        if (sleep_time.tv_sec < 0)
        {
           fprintf(stderr, "Login context expires too soon");
           exit(0);
        }
        pthread_delay_np(&sleep_time);

        sec_login_refresh_identity(*login_context,
           &status);
        CHECK_DCE(status, "Cannot refresh identity");
        validate_identity(login_context),
    }
}
```

Code Sample 6.5
`schedule/room_server.c: refresh_identity()` thread

Managing the Server's Key

The server's key also can expire and must be changed periodically. The lifetime of a key is determined by the policies of the server's principal account or organization or the default cell policy. The default is `forever` (no expiration). The `sec_key_mgmt_manage_key()` call can be used to automatically change a server's key before it expires. This routine waits until the key is about to expire and then generates another random key. Because of this, it must be called from a dedicated

Code Sample 6.6 shows the creation of the key management routine in the server `main()` after the registration of the server security information.

```
pthread_t key_mgmt_thread;
. . .
create_thread(
    key_mgmt,
    "key management",
    &key_mgmt_thread,
    NULL);
```

Code Sample 6.6
`schedule/room_server.c main()`: Creating the key management thread

Code Sample 6.7 shows the base routine for the key management thread. The thread argument is not used here.

```
pthread_addr_t key_mgmt(pthread_addr_t arg)
{
   unsigned32 status;
   sec_key_mgmt_manage_key(
      rpc_c_authn_dce_secret,
      (unsigned_char_p_t) "room_server_keyfile",
      (unsigned_char_p_t) "room-server",
      &status);
   CHECK_DCE(status, "Cannot manage server keys");
}
```

Code Sample 6.7
`schedule/room_server.c: key_mgmt()` thread

Purging a Login Context

When a server terminates, it must destroy any login contexts it has created using `sec_login_purge_context()`. This call purges the credentials file that was created when the login context was authenticated. If not so purged, these credentials files accumulate in the `/opt/dcelocal/var/security/creds` directory. When DCE is restarted, it will purge accumulated `creds` files, which may take minutes if there are large numbers of files. Also, in extreme cases, accumulated `creds` files might fill a disk.

Code Sample 6.8 shows the security cleanup in **`room_server`**, including the release of its login context and the deletion of the security related threads. This is done at the end of the server cleanup, after all of the Name Space entries have been taken care of.

```
    kill_thread(key_mgmt_thread, "key management");
    kill_thread(refresh_id_thread, "refresh identity");

    sec_login_purge_context(&login_context, &status);
    CHECK_DCE_NONFATAL(status,
      "Cannot release login context");
```

Code Sample 6.8
`schedule/room_server.c main()`: Releasing the login context

6.5 Client Security Setup

There are two major things that need to be done in the client for security: establish a login context for the client's principal identity and set up the security in force for each binding the client makes to a server.

Establishing the Client's Login Context

Like the server, the client needs to have a login context that identifies its principal. This is particularly important when a client binds to a server and makes authenticated remote calls, because the client's login context is used in the authentication of the client to the server. There are two ways that the client's login context can be established.

- *Inherit the login context of the user that ran the client.*

  This assumes the user has performed a **dce_login** (or an integrated login) prior to running the client. The **dce_login** obtains credentials for the user's principal and caches them in a `creds` file. The client calls `sec_login_get_current_context()` to create a login context that uses these credentials, or the client can simply specify a default for the login context. The latter will be the method used in the **room** client.
- *Set up a separate login context for the client.*

  The client can call the same sequence of DCE calls found in the **room_server** to create a new login context for its own principal. However, this is not common and will not be illustrated here. A variation of this method is when a server that has set up its own login context itself becomes an authenticated client of another server.

Setting Up Security for Bindings

When a client sets up a binding to a server, it must define the security that it wants to have in force. The client's security must meet minimum levels expected by the server. The client sets up the security for a binding with the `rpc_binding_set` _auth_info() call. This is sometimes called *annotating the binding handle* with security information. The input parameters to rpc_binding_set_auth_info() are

- the *binding handle* for the binding which will be affected by the call. The binding handle was previously obtained from a string binding or by importing it from CDS. In the room client, the binding handle is h.
- the *server's principal name,* needed to request a Kerberos ticket for the server. The **room** client will use room-server for its server principal name.
- the *protection level* that will be used for remote calls. DCE defines a series of protection levels, including authentication, and encryption for data integrity and privacy. These will be discussed in the next section.
- the *authentication service* to be used in authenticating the client to the server. The **room** client uses the DCE Secret Key service (e.g., Kerberos). The client might also specify no authorization (rpc_c_authn_none).
- an *authentication identity* login context that supplies the client's identity. This can be NULL, to specify the default login context. For the **room** client, this is the identity of the client's user, from his or her **dce_login**. The client can also use a login context set up by the sec_login_ calls discussed earlier for the server security setup.
- the *authorization service* to be used by the server in authorizing the client's request. This determines the type of authorization information that is included in the client's request. There are two choices: name authorization (rpc_c_authz_name) and DCE authorization using the Privilege Attribute Certificate (rpc_c_authz_dce). In this chapter we will use name authorization, and in Chapter 9 we will use DCE authorization.

Code Sample 6.9 shows the rpc_binding_set_auth_info() call in the **room** client. This call occurs after the binding is established and before any remote calls are made to **room_server**.

```
rpc_binding_set_auth_info(
    h,
    (unsigned_char_p_t) "room-server",
    rpc_c_protect_level_pkt_integ,
    rpc_c_authn_dce_secret,
    NULL, /* use default login context */
    rpc_c_authz_name,
    &status);
  CHECK_DCE(status,
   "Cannot set up authentication for binding");
```

Code Sample 6.9
schedule/room.c main(): Setting the binding handle's security information

RPC Protection Levels

The protection level parameter in the `rpc_binding_ set_auth_info()` call determines how often the client authenticates itself to the server and whether encryption is used for data integrity or privacy. There are six protection levels defined by DCE, plus a default that is set to one of the six. They are represented by the following defined constants. The meaning of some protection levels is dependent on whether a datagram (`dg`) or a connection (`cn`) RPC protocol is used for the calls. A DCE implementation may upgrade a requested level of protection.

- `rpc_c_protect_level_none`

  No protection. The client is not authenticated to the server, and there are no data integrity checks or encryption for privacy.

- `rpc_c_protect_level_connect`

  The client is authenticated to the server only on its first contact to the server. With a `cn` protocol, this is when the client connects to the server. With a `dg` protocol, this is on the first packet sent from the client to the server. There are no data integrity checks or privacy.

- `rpc_c_protect_level_call`

  The client is authenticated to the server each time it makes a remote call to the server. With a `dg` protocol, the first call request and response packets contain authentication information. There are no data integrity checks nor privacy. For a `cn` protocol, this level is automatically upgraded to `rpc_c_protect_level_pkt`.

- `rpc_c_protect_level_pkt`

  With the `dg` protocol, authentication information is included with each packet exchanged between the client and the server. With a `cn` protocol, the authentication information is included in the messages exchanged between the client and the server. There are no data integrity checks or privacy.

- `rpc_c_protect_level_pkt_integ`

  In addition to authentication information with each packet (for a `dg` protocol) or in the data stream (for a `cn` protocol), this level adds an MD5 encrypted checksum to each packet or message. This checksum is recomputed and decoded by the receiving side. If the data are altered during transmission, the receiving side will be able to detect the alteration and reject the altered data.

- `rpc_c_protect_level_pkt_privacy`

  In addition to the packet level authentication, this level adds DES encryption of the data exchanged in each call. Because of the US. export restrictions on DES discussed earlier, this level may not always be available.

Each of these protection levels provides a higher degree of security, at the cost of additional overhead. The level you choose for your application depends on the requirements of the application, the security of the underlying network, and the amount of overhead you are willing to tolerate for security. If, for instance, your application will always run on a secure in-house network, then a lower protect level like `connect` or `call` may be sufficient. On the other hand, if your application runs over the Internet, where any packet can be seen or altered by an attacker, then you will probably want at least `pkt_integ`. If the data exchanged between the client and the server are sensitive, you should use the `privacy` level to prevent it from being intercepted. The performance impact of each protection level will be examined in Section 6.9.

Setting Up Security with Automatic Binding

Automatic binding was introduced in Chapter 5. With automatic binding, the client stub routines are responsible for setting up the binding to the server, using the CDS entry from the `RPC_DEFAULT_ENTRY` environment variable. A problem arises if security must be set up for the automatic binding: How does the client stub know what security parameters to use? The solution to this problem is the *binding callout routine*, which is supplied by the application and called by the client stub when the binding is set up. The binding callout routine is defined in the Attribute Configuration File (ACF) for the interface. Code Sample 6.10 shows the ACF for the `auto_handle` version of the `room` interface.

```
[auto_handle,binding_callout(room_binding_callout)]
interface room
{
. . .
}
```

Code Sample 6.10
`schedule/auto_handle/room.acf`: Specifying a callout routine for automatic binding

The binding callout routine can set up the necessary security for the binding. Code Sample 6.11 shows the callout routine for the room interface. This routine calls `rpc_binding_set_auth_info()` to set up the server name, authentication and authorization services, protection level, and default login context for the binding.

```
void room_binding_callout(
   rpc_binding_handle_t *h_p,
   rpc_if_handle_t       ifspec,
   error_status_t       *st_p)
{
   unsigned_char_p_t string_binding;
   unsigned32        ignored_st;

   rpc_binding_set_auth_info(
      *h_p,
      (unsigned_char_p_t) "room-server",
      rpc_c_protect_level_pkt_integ,
      rpc_c_authn_dce_secret,
      NULL,
      rpc_c_authz_name,
      st_p);
   CHECK_DCE(*st_p, "Cannot set binding security");
}
```

Code Sample 6.11
`schedule/auto_handle/room.c: room_binding_callout()`

6.6 Manager Security Checks

Now that we have set up security in the server and in the client, what do we do with it? A major purpose of security in a client-server application is to determine if the client is authorized to perform requested operations. This requires that each operation manager within the server retrieve the identity of the client and use it to decide if the client is authorized to execute the operation. There are a couple of ways the authorization decision can be implemented. The primary way, using DCE ACLs, is quite complex and will be the subject of Chapter 9. A simpler alternative, name authorization, will be presented here.

Manager Security Enforcement

Any client that can find a server can make a remote call to the server with or without setting up security. The server is responsible for enforcing that the client meet any protection requirements. To do this, each operation manager in the server must check the security of each incoming call and somehow reject calls that do not conform to the minimum required security. A typical way to reject a nonsecure call is to set a status return to an error indicating a security violation and to immediately return without performing the operation. This will be illustrated in the manager in Code Sample 6.13. (Care must be taken, though, to set certain output parameters, like pointers and arrays, to values that can be properly marshaled during the return to the client. An example is an output pointer that must be set to `NULL` in case of a security violation error.)

We will introduce a new routine, `call_is_secure()`, in the server manager module `room_mgr.c` to check an incoming call for a desired protection level. This type of routine is sometimes called a *reference monitor*. The input parameters to this routine are

- the *binding handle* that is passed into the manager routine from the server stub. The client's security information can be extracted from the binding handle.
- the *expected protection level*, which specifies the minimum protection the client must use to successfully execute the remote call. This is one of the `rpc_c_protect_level_` values.

```
boolean32 call_is_secure(
   rpc_binding_handle_t h,
   unsigned32           expected_prot_level,
   rpc_authz_handle_t   *privs)
{
   char                *cell_name;
   char                 e_server_name[256];
   unsigned_char_p_t    server_name;
   unsigned32           protect_level, authn_service;
   unsigned32           authz_service, status;

   rpc_binding_inq_auth_client(h, privs, &server_name,
      &protect_level, &authn_service, &authz_service,
      &status);
   if (status == rpc_s_binding_has_no_auth)
   {
      return(false);
   }
   CHECK_DCE(status, "Cannot get client security info");

   dce_cf_get_cell_name(&cell_name, &status);
   CHECK_DCE(status, "Cannot get local cell name");
   sprintf(e_server_name, "%s/room-server", cell_name);
   free(cell_name);
```

Code Sample 6.12

`schedule/room_mgr.c: call_is_secure()`

When the name authorization service is used, the output parameter privs of rpc_binding_inq_auth_client() is a pointer to the client's full principal name, in the form /.../cell_name/principal_name. The call_is_secure() routine shown in Code Sample 6.12 returns this priv parameter, so we can check the security of the incoming call and get the client's principal name in one call.

In room_reserve(), shown in Code Sample 6.14, a copy of the client's name is made and saved in the reservation event record as the reserver ID. A copy must be made here because priv points to data associated with the current call, and this data may not persist once the call has completed.

```
void room_reserve(
    /* [in ] */ handle_t          h,
    . . .
    /* [out] */ error_status_t   *call_status)
{
    rpc_authz_handle_t privs;
    . . .
    if (!call_is_secure(h, rpc_c_protect_level_pkt_integ,
                        &privs))
    {
        *status = sch_status_not_secure;
        return;
    }

    r_id_p =malloc(strlen((char *) privs + 1);
    strcpy(r_id_p, (char *) privs);
    /* Save r_id_p in event record. */
    . . .
}
```

Code Sample 6.14
schedule/room_mgr.c: room_reserve() with reserver principal

In room_cancel(), shown in Code Sample 6.15, the client's name pointed to by priv is compared to the reserver ID in the event record for the reservation to be canceled. If the client canceling the reservation is the same as the client who made the reservation, the event record is deallocated (as is the copy of the reserver ID). But if the client attempting the cancel does not match the reserver, the `room_cancel()` operation is aborted with the status `sch_status_not_reserver`.

```
void room_cancel(
    /* [in ] */ handle_t        h,
    . . .
    /* [out] */ sch_status_t    *status)
{
    . . .
    rpc_authz_handle_t privs;

    if (!call_is_secure(h, rpc_c_protect_level_pkt_integ,
                        &privs)
    {
        *status = sch_status_not_secure;
        return;
    }

    if (strcmp(event_p->r_id_p, (char *) privs) == 0)
    {
        /* Delete event record and requestor id. */
    }
    else
    {
        *status = sch_status_not_reserver;
    }
    . . .
}
```

Code Sample 6.15
`room_mgr.c`: `room_reserve()` and `room_cancel()` with reserver principal check

DCE Authorization

If DCE authorization is used instead of name authorization, the `privs` parameter returned by `rpc_binding_inq_auth_client()` is a pointer to a data structure providing the complete credentials for the client, including the client's principal and group membership. DCE authorization is usually used in conjunction with ACLs, to be discussed in Chapter 9.

PAC Type
Authenticated (true/false)
Cell (Realm) UUID
Principal UUID
Primary Group UUID
Number of Local Groups
Local Group 1 UUID
. . .
Local Group m UUID
Number of Foreign Groups
Foreign Group 1 UUID
. . .
Foreign Group n UUID

Figure 6.5
PAC Format (DCE 1.0)

Privilege Attribute Certificate

Prior to DCE 1.1, the credential data structure is the *Privilege Attribute Certificate* (PAC). As illustrated in Figure 6.5, a PAC contains a series of UUIDs that identify the client's cell, principal, and local and foreign groups. Local groups are defined in the client's cell and need only one UUID for identification, while foreign groups are in other cells and require two UUIDS to identify the cell and group. Actually, the entry for each of these elements also contains a pointer for a character string name, but the name field is usually `NULL`.

The PAC data structure is defined as the type `sec_id_pac_t` in `id_base.idl` and `id_base.h` (in `/usr/include/dce`). You can cast the `privs` parameter returned by `rpc_binding_inq_auth_client()` to this type to access the fields within the PAC. The ACL evaluation algorithm discussed in Chapter 9 will make full use of the PAC fields.

Extended PAC (DCE 1.1)

DCE 1.1 has extended the concept of the Privilege Attribute Certificate to include additional security information in the form of *extended registry attributes* (ERAs). These can hold arbitrary data and are defined by ERA schema entries defined using **dcecp**. ERAs will not be discussed in detail here. For more information, see Chapter 28 of the *OSF DCE 1.1 Application Development Guide* and Chapter 32 of the *OSF DCE 1.1 Administration Guide*.

Since the EPAC is more complex than the original PAC format, DCE 1.1 provides an extensive set of calls, the sec_login_cred_ and sec_cred_ calls, for extracting information from EPACs. Some of these calls will be highlighted in Code Sample 6.18 in the next section. Note that the original PAC format can still be retrieved by rpc_binding_inq_auth_client().

6.7 Delegation (DCE 1.1)

In a distributed application, one server may need to make a remote call to another server on behalf of a client. Figure 6.6 shows such a situation, where a client makes RPC 1 to Server 1. When Server 1 executes RPC 1, it makes RPC 2 to Server 2. Then Server 2 makes RPC 3 to Server 3. It may be desirable for Server 2 and Server 3 to know the identity of the originating client as well as the servers involved.

DCE 1.1 provides a facility called *delegation* for this purpose. The client delegates some or all of its authority to a server to allow the server to perform requested tasks. The client is called the *initiator* of the delegation. The server is called a *delegate*. In Figure 6.6, Client is the initiator and Server 1 is a delegate of Client. Server 2 is a delegate of Server 1. The EPACs of the initiator and the delegates are combined to form a *delegation chain*. The delegation chain is attached to the remote calls made between the initiator and the delegates. In Figure 6.6, the delegation chain attached to RPC 3 contains the EPACs for the client principal C, and the server principals S1 and S2.

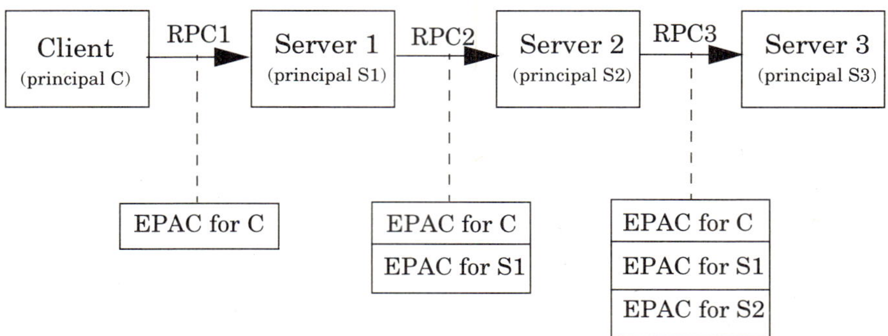

Figure 6.6
Delegation

Becoming an Initiator

Code Sample 6.16 shows how a client enables delegation. First, the client calls sec_login_get_current_context() to obtain a base login context inherited from the user's **dce_login**. From the base login context, the client constructs a new login context with delegation enabled, using the sec_login_become_initiator() call.

When the client calls rpc_binding_set_auth_info() to set up security for the binding handle, it uses the initiator login context. When the client calls the first server using the binding handle, delegation will be enabled, and the server may then pass on the client's credentials to other servers.

Note that the remote call to `delegation_op()` is performed using the client entry pointer vector (EPV) for the `delegation` interface. As we shall see in the next section, the server must use the client EPV, the client stub must be generated with the `-cepv` option, and therefore the client must also use the EPV.

After the client has finished using the initiator login context, it calls `sec_login_purge_context()` to delete it. Note that a new credentials file may be created for the initiator login context, so the purge is necessary to remove the file.

```
sec_login_handle_t   base_login_context;
sec_login_handle_t   initiator_login_context;
. . .
sec_login_get_current_context(&base_login_context,
  &status);
CHECK_DCE(status,
   "Cannot get current login context");

initiator_login_context = sec_login_become_initiator(
   base_login_context,
   sec_id_deleg_type_traced,
   NULL, /* no delegate restrictions */
   NULL, /* no target restrictions   */
   NULL, /* no optional restrictions */
   NULL, /* no required restrictions */
   sec_id_compat_mode_none,
   &status);
CHECK_DCE(status,
   "Cannot set up initiator login context");

rpc_binding_set_auth_info(
   h,
   (unsigned_char_p_t) server_principal,
   rpc_c_protect_level_pkt_integ,
   rpc_c_authn_dce_secret,
   initiator_login_context,
   rpc_c_authz_dce,
   &status);
CHECK_DCE(status,
   "Cannot set up authentication for binding");
. . .
delegation_v1_0_c_epv.delegation_op(h);

sec_login_purge_context(&initiator_login_context,
   &status);
```

Code Sample 6.16
`delegation/delegation_client.c main()`: Enabling delegation

Becoming a Delegate

Code Sample 6.17 shows how a server can add itself to a delegation chain. This sample shows the manager for the delegation_op() operation called by both the delegation client and the intermediate delegation servers. For an intermediate delegation, the next_uuid_binding variable is a string binding to be used to bind to the next server in the chain. The next_principal variable is the principal used by the next server. If these variables are NULL, the server is the last server in the chain and does not become a delegate or call delegation_op().

First, the manager for delegation_op() calls a new DCE 1.1 function, rpc_binding_inq_auth_caller(). This call is very similar in function to the pre-DCE 1.1 rpc_binding_inq_auth_client() function. The difference is that rpc_binding_inq_auth_caller() returns a handle to the caller's credentials that must be used in sec_cred_ calls. This call is used to obtain the full range of information from DCE 1.1 EPACs.

Next, the server calls sec_login_become_delegate() to add itself to the delegation chain. This call is very similar to sec_login_become_initiator(). The base login context is set up by the server main() during its initialization. The creds parameter provides the existing delegation chain from the caller. The result of this call is another login context with a delegation chain including the current server's identity.

Finally, the server calls rpc_binding_set_auth_info() to set up security for the binding handle to the next server. This call uses the delegate login context created by the sec_login_become_delegate(). The binding handle is used in the delegation_op() call to the next server. Note that the client EPV is used. This is necessary to ensure that the client stub for delegation_op(), and not the local manager routine, is called. After the call, the delegate login context is purged.

```
extern unsigned_char_p_t  next_uuid_binding;
extern unsigned_char_p_t  next_principal;
extern sec_login_handle_t base_login_context;

void delegation_op(
   handle_t h)
{
   rpc_authz_cred_handle_t creds;
   rpc_binding_handle_t    next_h;
   sec_login_handle_t      delegate_login_context;
   . . .

   rpc_binding_inq_auth_caller(h, &creds,
     NULL, NULL, NULL, NULL, &status);
   CHECK_DCE(status,
```

Code Sample 6.17
delegation/delegation_mgr.c: delegation_op()

```
      "Cannot get credentials from binding handle");
   . . .

   if ((next_uuid_binding != NULL) &&
       (next_principal != NULL))
   {
      rpc_binding_from_string_binding(
         next_uuid_binding, &next_h, &status);
      CHECK_DCE(status,
         "Cannot convert string binding to binding");

      delegate_login_context= sec_login_become_delegate(
         creds,
         base_login_context,
         sec_id_deleg_type_traced,
         NULL, /* no delegate restrictions */
         NULL, /* no target restrictions   */
         NULL, /* no optional restrictions */
         NULL, /* no required restrictions */
         sec_id_compat_mode_none,
         &status);
      CHECK_DCE(status,
         "Cannot set up delegate login context");

      rpc_binding_set_auth_info(
         next_h,
         next_principal,
         rpc_c_protect_level_pkt_integ,
         rpc_c_authn_dce_secret,
         delegate_login_context,
         rpc_c_authz_dce,
         &status);
      CHECK_DCE(status,
         "Cannot set up authentication for binding");
      . . .
      delegation_v1_0_c_epv.delegation_op(next_h);

      sec_login_purge_context(&delegate_login_context,
         &status);
   }
}
```

Code Sample 6.17 (continued)

Using Delegation Information

Code Sample 6.18 shows how a manager can use the information in the delegation chain for an incoming remote call. As you can see, many DCE calls are needed to retrieve the identities of the initiator and the delegates. The first call is the `rpc_binding_inq_auth_caller()` to obtain a handle to the credentials from the remote call's binding handle.

The credentials are composed of *privilege attributes* (e.g., the EPACs) for the initiator and each delegate in the delegation chain. These privilege attributes are accessed through handles obtained from the credentials handle. The handle to the initiator privilege attribute is provided by `sec_cred_get_initiator()`. The initiator's identity, in the form of a `sec_id_pa_t` structure, is then retrieved from the privilege attribute handle using `sec_cred_get_pa_data()`.

```
void delegation_op(
   handle_t h)
{
   rpc_authz_cred_handle_t creds;
   sec_cred_pa_handle_t     initiator_pa;
   sec_id_pa_t             *initiator_id;
   sec_cred_cursor_t        cred_cursor;
   sec_cred_pa_handle_t     next_delegate_pa;
   sec_id_pa_t             *next_delegate_id;
   . . .

   rpc_binding_inq_auth_caller(h, &creds,
      NULL, NULL, NULL, NULL, &status);
   CHECK_DCE(status,
      "Cannot get credentials from binding handle");

   initiator_pa = sec_cred_get_initiator(creds,
      &status);
   CHECK_DCE(status,
      "Cannot get client privilege attributes");

   initiator_id = sec_cred_get_pa_data(initiator_pa,
      &status);
   CHECK_DCE(status,
      "Cannot get client id from privilege attributes");
```

Code Sample 6.18
`delegation/delegation_mgr.c`: `delegation_op()` printing the delegation chain

```
    printf("Initiator: \n");
    print_id(&initiator_id->principal,
       &initiator_id->realm);

    sec_cred_initialize_cursor(&cred_cursor, &status);
    CHECK_DCE(status,
       "Cannot initialize credentials cursor");
    printf("Delegates: \n");
    do
    {
       next_delegate_pa = sec_cred_get_delegate(
          creds, &cred_cursor, &status);

    if (status != sec_cred_s_no_more_entries)
       {
          CHECK_DCE(status,
          "Cannot get delegate privilage attributes");

          next_delegate_id = sec_cred_get_pa_data(
             next_delegate_pa, &status);
          CHECK_DCE(status,
          "Cannot get delegate id from priv attributes");

          print_id(&next_delegate_id->principal,
             &next_delegate_id->realm);
      }
    }
    while (status != sec_cred_s_no_more_entries);
    . . .
}
```

Code Sample 6.18 (continued)

Access to the delegate privilege attributes is even more complicated; it uses a credentials cursor to step through the list of delegates. The `sec_cred_initialize_cursor()` call initializes the cursor. Each `sec_cred_get_delegate()` call in the `do` loop obtains a handle to the current delegates privilege attribute and advances the cursor to the next delegate's privilege attribute. Each delegate's identity is retrieved from its privilege attribute handle by `sec_cred_get_pa_data()`. When `sec_cred_get_delegate()` has been stepped through all of the delegates, it returns a status of `sec_cred_s_no_more_entries`.

Code Sample 6.19 shows the print_id() routine, which prints the principal name for a sec_id_t identity. Even though the sec_id_t structure has a field for the name, it is usually NULL in an EPAC. So we need to map the principal's UUID (and the realm UUID) to the principal name, using the sec_id_gen_name() call. This call requests that the Security Registry look up the UUIDs and return the principal name. It requires a handle (yet another handle!) to the Registry. Since we want to open the Registry only once, we will do this in the server main(), as shown in Code Sample 6.20. The blank registry name in the sec_rgy_site_open() call indicates the default Registry.

```
extern sec_rgy_handle_t   rgy_h;

void print_id(
   sec_id_t *id,
   sec_id_t *realm)
{
   sec_rgy_name_t pname;
   unsigned32     status;

   sec_id_gen_name(rgy_h, &realm->uuid, &id->uuid,
     NULL, NULL, pname, &status);
   CHECK_DCE(status, "Cannot generate principal name");
   printf("   %s\n", pname);
}
```

Code Sample 6.19
delegation/delegation_mgr.c: print_id()

```
   sec_rgy_site_open((unsigned_char_t *) "", &rgy_h,
     &status);
   CHECK_DCE(status, "Cannot open registry");
```

Code Sample 6.20
delegation/delegation_server.c main() opening the registry

Delegation Restrictions

Once a client has delegated its authority to a server, that server may in turn delegate the client's authority to other servers. The client may not want to delegate its authority to every server in a chain of calls. To prevent this, DCE provides a way for the client, and intermediate servers, to restrict the scope of delegation. The data structure `sec_id_restrictions_set_t` is used to indicate which servers are allowed to become delegates of the client. This data structure is a list of principal and group identities. The `sec_login_become_initiator()` and `sec_login_become_delegate()` calls each have two parameters for delegation restriction:

- the *delegate restrictions*, a list of servers that are allowed to become delegates for this client. In Figure 6.6, server principals S1 and S2 would need to be on the delegate restriction list for the client.
- the *target restrictions*, a list of servers that are allowed to be targets for delegates of this server. In Figure 6.6, server principals S1, S2, and S3 would need to be on the target restriction list for the client.

A value of `NULL` for the restriction parameters means that there are no restrictions imposed on delegation. In addition to these restriction parameters, there are two more parameters available for optional and required application-defined restrictions. The `sec_id_opt_req_t` data structure is used for these; it is a sequence of bytes whose meaning is defined by the application.

Delegation versus Impersonation

There are actually two types of delegation available in DCE. With *traced delegation*, the accumulated EPACs of the servers in the chain are available for use in each server. With *impersonation*, a server completely assumes the identity of the caller for the call, and previous delegation information is not available. The `sec_login_become_initiator()` and `sec_login_become_delegate()` calls have a parameter that selects the type of delegation desired. A server can use `sec_login_become_impersonator()` instead of `_become_delegate()` to impersonate its caller. This call takes the caller's credential handle but does not use a login context from the server.

Caching of Delegate Login Contexts

The creation of a new delegation login context can be a time-consuming operation. In Code Sample 6.17, this operation is performed for each remote call, even if the call has the same chain of initiator and delegates as previous calls. As a performance enhancement, a server can cache the delegate login context it creates. Then the server can reuse a previously created context for subsequent remote calls with the same delegation.

Code Sample 6.21 shows how the delegation_op() manager can be enhanced to cache its delegate login contexts. The cache must have some way of identifying the delegation chain that is associated with a login context. DCE provides sec_cred_get_authz_session_info() for this purpose. This call maps a credential handle from rpc_binding_inq_auth_caller() to a UUID that uniquely identifies the chain of initiator and delegate identities associated with the incoming RPC. This UUID can then be used as the index for a table of cached login contexts. The delegation chain also has an expiration time that is the shortest of the expiration times of each initiator and delegate login contexts. The sec_cred_get_authz_session_info() call returns this expiration time as the number of seconds since the "Unix Epoch"— July 1, 1970. (This is the same time measurement used by the Unix gettimeofday() call.) A login context for the delegation chain cannot be used after its expiration, so if a cached context expires, it needs to be recreated.

There are two functions in delegation_mgr.c for the management of the login context cache:

- lookup_cached_context() searches the cache for a previously created login context that matches the credential UUID. It returns NULL if no matching context is found. If a matching context has expired, it purges the context from the cache and returns NULL.
- cache_context() adds a newly created login context, along with its associated credentials UUID and expiration time, to the context cache. If necessary to make room for the new context, it deletes expired contexts and, if there are no expired contexts, the oldest context.

The implementation of the lookup_cached_context() and cache_cont-ext() functions are not shown here. The full source of the delegation example includes a simple implementation using a linear search of a small array. A more sophisticated implementation might use a hash table. DCE provides a built-in hash function, uuid_hash(), for UUIDs.

How much of a performance improvement does login caching provide? The delegation example, with a client and a chain of four servers run in loopback on an HP9000/847, takes about 5000 milliseconds for each delegation call without caching. With caching, the second and subsequent calls drop to around 100 milliseconds—an 50-fold improvement!

```
void delegation_op(...)
{
  rpc_authz_cred_handle_t creds;
  uuid_t                  creds_uuid;
  sec_timeval_sec_t       expiration;
  . . .
  rpc_binding_inq_auth_caller(h, &creds,
     NULL, NULL, NULL, NULL, &status);
  . . .
  sec_cred_get_authz_session_info(creds, &creds_uuid,
     &expiration, &status);
  CHECK_DCE(status, "Cannot get cred session info");
  delegate_login_context =
     lookup_cached_context(&creds_uuid);

  if (delegate_login_context == NULL) /* not found */
  {
     delegate_login_context =
        sec_login_become_delegate(...);
     . . .
     cache_context(&creds_uuid, delegate_login_context,
        expiration);
  }
  . . .
}
```

Code Sample 6.21
`delegation/delegation_mgr.c: delegation_op()` with context caching

6.8 DCE Authentication Details

This section provides more details on the Kerberos authentication protocol and how DCE uses it. You may skip this section if you don't care to delve into the workings of authentication at this level of detail. But if you want to know what actually happens during a **dce_login** and client-server authentication, read on.

First we will look at the data structures and messages used by the Kerberos service and protocol. These are taken from the defining document for Kerberos, the *Kerberos Version 5 RFC*. (RFC is *Request for Comments*, a term used for Internet documentation.) This discussion covers the basics of Kerberos—many optional features are omitted. Then we will look at how DCE uses and extends Kerberos. This is described in great detail in Chapter 42 of the *OSF DCE Application Development Guide*.

Kerberos Data Structures

There are two important data structures in Kerberos: the ticket and the authenticator. These are used in the messages of the Kerberos protocol and in application messages.

Tickets

Kerberos authentication revolves around the concept of the *ticket*, which is used to prove the identity of a client to a server. When a client wants to authenticate itself to a server, it requests a ticket for the server from Kerberos. The Kerberos Authentication Server (AS) constructs the ticket, including a portion that it encrypts in a secret key known only by the AS and the server. The client then passes the ticket on to the server, which tries to decrypt the encrypted part of the ticket. If the decrypted information is sensible, the server knows that the client obtained the ticket from Kerberos legitimately.

Figure 6.7 shows fields in the ticket, including the fields that are encrypted in the server's key. (Some fields may be omitted or combined.) Each ticket has a version number that can be used to determine the format of the ticket. The ticket includes the realm and principal name for both the target server and for the client that requested the ticket. The client identification is in the encrypted portion, so it cannot be forged by anyone not possessing the server's key. The encrypted part also includes various flags and times that describe how the ticket is to be used and how long it can be used for. The authorization data field provides a place to put application-specific information to be used for authorization. This is used by DCE to hold the Privilege Attribute Certificate (PAC), which will be discussed later.

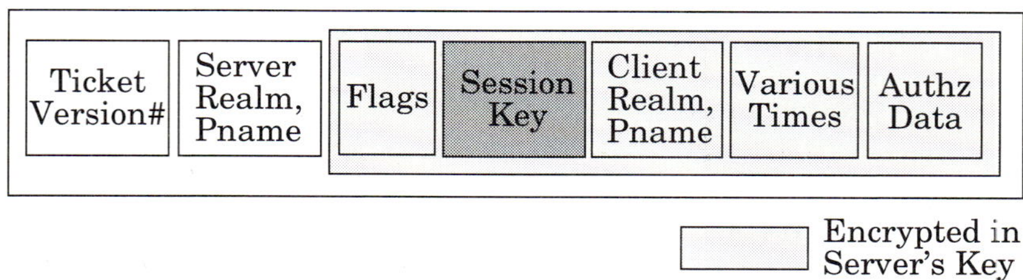

Figure 6.7
Kerberos Ticket Format

An important part of the ticket is the *session key*. This will be used for encryption of data exchanged between the client and the server. Kerberos generates a new session key for each ticket, that is, for each time a client authenticates itself to a server. Using a new encryption key each time a client and a server communicate limits the possibility that the encryption can be broken by an eavesdropping attacker.

The ticket securely conveys the session key from the client to the server. Since the session key is encrypted in the server's secret key, only the server can retrieve it from the ticket. (The client obtains the session key from the KRB_AS_REP or KRB_TGT_REP message, as discussed later.)

Each ticket has a lifetime specified by an *expiration time* within the ticket. Ticket lifetimes are set according to Kerberos policies defined for the realm. (In DCE, the policies are set up for the cell through the ticket lifetime properties in **rgy_edit** or **dcecp**.) Tickets can be reused between a client and server over the lifetime of the ticket, and a user can keep a cache of tickets for reuse.

Authenticators

Kerberos tickets alone are not sufficient to securely authenticate a client to a server. An attacker wanting to impersonate a client could intercept the client's ticket and play it back to the server. The server would not know that the ticket had not been sent by the original client. To prevent this, Kerberos uses an additional piece of data called the *authenticator*, which is encrypted in the session key from the ticket. If the server can sensibly decrypt the authenticator, it proves that the client possesses the session key as well as the ticket. The authenticator format is shown in Figure 6.8. It consists of a version number, the realm and principal names of the client, and a time stamp which is used to detect possible replays. Unlike a ticket, an authenticator can be used only once, so a new authenticator must be generated for each authenticated exchange between the client and the server.

Figure 6.8
Kerberos Authenticator Format

Kerberos Protocol

There are three major request-response message exchanges in the Kerberos protocol: the AS, TGT, and AP exchanges. The first two are between the client and the Kerberos Authentication Service (AS). The third is between the client and the target server. Refer to Figure 6.10 for an overview of these exchanges.

AS (Authentication Service) Exchange

The AS exchange is the initial step in the authentication of a user or client. The KRB_AS_REQ message, sent from the client to the Kerberos AS, requests a special sort of ticket called the Ticket-Granting Ticket (TGT), which will be explained in more detail shortly.

Figure 6.9 shows the format of the KRB_AS_REQ message. Every KRB message begins with a message type and version that identifies the message. The client realm and principal name identify who is making the request (that is, who is asking to be authenticated) and the target server name. For KRB_AS_REQ, the target server is the Ticket-Granting Server (TGS). There are a number of options that specify what kind of ticket is requested (e.g., renewable, postdated, etc.) and various times for requested ticket expiration and renewal. There is space for data to be used for *preauthentication* purposes, which will be examined later. Finally, there is a field called the *nonce*, which is usually a random number generated by the client. The nonce is included in the KRB_AS_REP message to prove that it has not been replayed, and hence it should be unique for each KRB_AS_REQ.

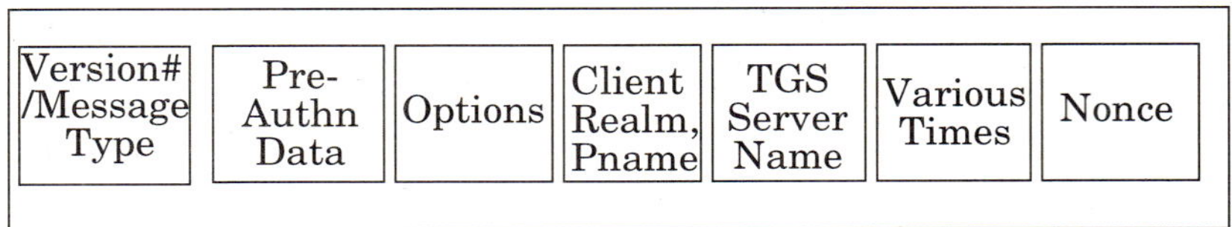

Figure 6.9
KRB_AS_REQ Format

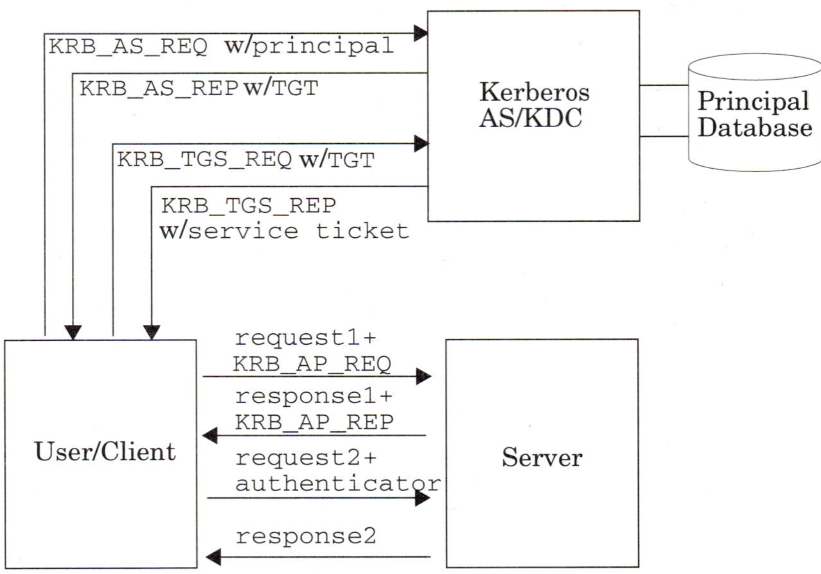

Figure 6.10
Kerberos Authentication Exchanges

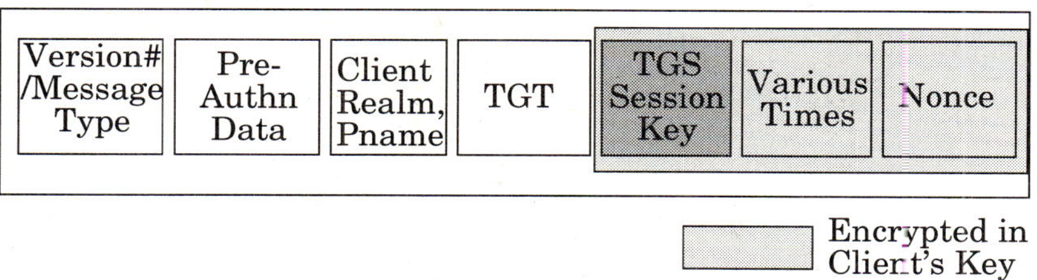

Figure 6.11
KRB_AS_REP Format

Figure 6.11 shows the KRB_AS_REP message that the Kerberos AS sends back to the client in response to the KRB_AS_REQ. This includes a special ticket, the Ticket-Granting Ticket (TGT) for the Ticket-Granting Service. This will be used in the TGT exchange described next. The KRB_AS_REP message also contains data encrypted in a secret key derived from the client's password—the session key generated by the Kerberos KDC and included in the TGT, various times, and the nonce from the client's KRB_AS_REQ. The client must correctly enter his or her password for the security software to decrypt this part of the ticket. Without the correct password, the client cannot retrieve the session key from the KRB_AS_REP, which will be needed in subsequent authentication steps. If the nonce in the KRB_AS_REP is the same value as the nonce in the KRB_AS_REQ, the client can be assured the KRB_AS_REP is not a replay from an attacker masquerading as the Kerberos AS.

TGS (Ticket-Granting Service) Exchange

When a client needs a ticket to authenticate itself to a particular server, it uses the Kerberos Ticket-Granting Service (TGS). To do this, the client must have a Ticket-Granting Ticket (TGT) and a session key that were obtained through the AS Exchange. As we saw above, this required the client (or the user that ran the client) to have supplied the correct password for the client's principal. The client sends a KRB_TGT_REQ message to the Kerberos TGS. The TGS builds a ticket using the secret key of the target server and sends the ticket back to the client in the KRB_TGT_REP message.

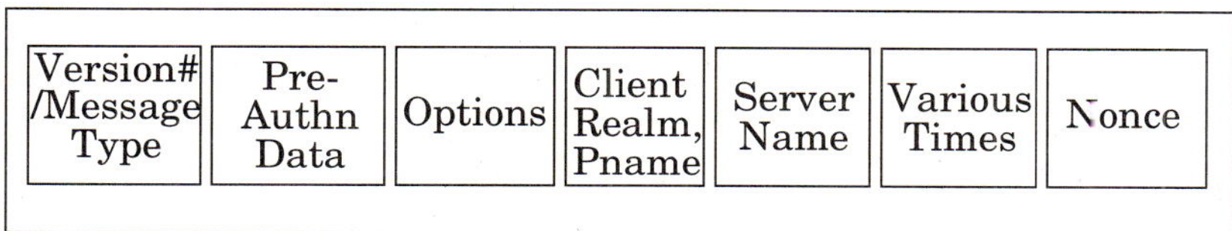

Figure 6.12
KRB_TGS_REQ Format

The formats of the KRB_TGT_REQ and KRG_TGT_REP messages, shown in Figures 6.12 and 6.13, are very similar to those of the KRB_AS_REQ and KRB_AS_REP, respectively. In the KRB_TGT_REQ, the server name is the name of the target server. The ticket returned in the KRB_TGT_REP is encrypted in the target server's secret key and contains a new session key to be used between the client and the server. This service session key is included in the KRB_TGS_REP message, encrypted in the TGS session key the client obtained from the KRB_AS_REP (but only with the correct password!). The client can then decrypt the service session key and use it in the final stage of client-server authentication.

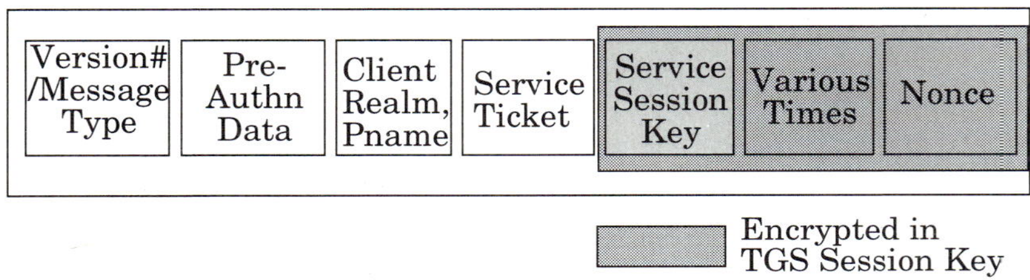

Figure 6.13
KRB_TGS_REP Format

AP (Application) Exchange

Once the client has a ticket and a session key for the target server, it can build the KRB_AP_REQ message, shown in Figure 6.14. This message includes the service ticket and an authenticator that is encrypted with the service session key. The client can know the session key only by successfully completing the AS and TGT exchanges discussed above. The client sends the KRB_AP_REQ directly to the server, either by itself or as a part of the first request from the client to the server. The server receives the KRB_AP_REQ and extracts the service ticket and authenticator. The server decrypts the encrypted part of the ticket with its secret key and so obtains the service session key. With the session key, the server can decrypt the authenticator. The server can compare information from the authenticator and the ticket (like the client principal name) to ensure that the client actually knew the session key. Also, the authenticator provides a current time that must be within a certain limit (usually five minutes) of the current time on the server system. This helps detect replays of the authenticator. If the decrypted authenticator data does not check out, Kerberos will return a Bad Integrity error. This means that the client does not appear to know the correct session key.

The client can request *mutual authentication*, where the server authenticates itself with the client. This is desirable for the client to trust the server. To do this, the KRB_AS_REP message is sent from the server back to the client, either separately or attached to the first application response. This message, shown in Figure 6.15, includes the time stamp from the client's authenticator, encrypted in the service session key. The client can then decrypt and compare the time stamp to what it sent in the KRB_AP_REQ. If the time stamps agree, the client is assured that the server successfully obtained the service session key from the ticket. Only the genuine target server knows the secret key to decrypt the service ticket.

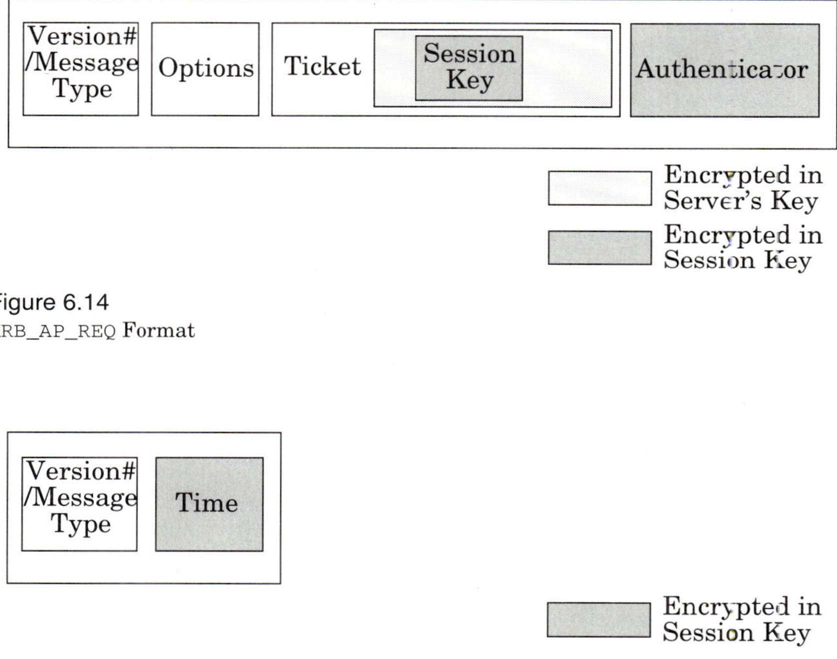

Figure 6.14
KRB_AP_REQ Format

Figure 6.15
KRB_AP_REP Format

Subsequent requests from the client to the server do not need to include an entire KRB_AS_REQ. Only a new authenticator needs to be attached to each message. The server can check each authenticator to ensure that it came from the original, authenticated client and not an impostor. If mutual authentication is in use, the KRB_AP_REQ is attached to each response from the server to the client.

Additional DCE Security Data Structures

DCE extends the Kerberos ticket to include additional DCE-specific information in the form of the PAC and EPAC.

Privilege Attribute Certificate (PAC)

As discussed earlier, the PAC is a DCE data structure that contains the principal and group UUIDs for a client. The standard Kerberos ticket does not include this information, but the ticket format does include an optional field, labeled Authz Data in Figure 6.7, that is available for additional authorization data. DCE puts the PAC for the client principal in the Authz Data field of a service ticket.

A PAC is *certified* (also called *sealed*) by being encrypted with a key that the client does not know. The client cannot then tamper with the PAC—say, to change its principal UUID to another, more privileged principal. When the PAC is initially generated (and stored in the ticket cache), it is encrypted in a secret key known only by the DCE Security Server (see the discussion of the Privilege Service and the PTGT below). In a service ticket, the PAC is encrypted with the server's secret key.

Extended PAC (EPAC)

With DCE 1.1, the PAC data structure has been extended to include additional information such as extended registry attributes (ERAs). The new data structure is called the *Extended PAC* (EPAC). With the addition of an arbitrary number of ERAs that can be of any length, the EPAC may not fit into the maximum size of a Kerberos ticket. Instead, EPACs are stored and transmitted separately from the ticket. To seal the EPAC, a checksum of its contents is placed in the Authz Data field of the ticket. When the EPAC is used, the DCE Security software will recompute its checksum and compare it to the seal to determine if the EPAC has been altered.

DCE Authentication Components

Figure 6.16 shows the DCE Security components involved in authentication. Each of these components will be examined below.

DCE Security Server

The DCE Security Server or Daemon (**secd**) is a server process that holds three DCE Security services: Kerberos, the Privilege Service, and the Registry Service. Each of these services exports an RPC interface used by the DCE Security software. The Security Server (and its Registry Database) may be replicated on different hosts to guarantee availability. Each Security Server must be located on a secure machine.

Kerberos Services

The Kerberos Authentication Service (AS) and Ticket-Granting Service (TGS) are included in the DCE Security Server. These services were examined at length in the last section. They respond to `KRB` requests for Ticket-Granting Tickets (TGTs) and service tickets. DCE provides an RPC interface, `krb5rpc`, that can be used by Security clients to send `KRB` requests and receive `KRB` responses. There is a principal associated with the Kerberos TGS named `krbtgt/`*`cell_name`*, for example, `krbtgt/jaja`.

In DCE 1.1, there is also a non-DCE interface to the DCE Kerberos services through standard GSS-API (Generic Security Service Application Programming Interface) calls. This will allow applications that do not use DCE (for example, applications communicating over BSD sockets) to use the Kerberos services within the DCE Security Server. GSS-API is beyond the scope of this book.

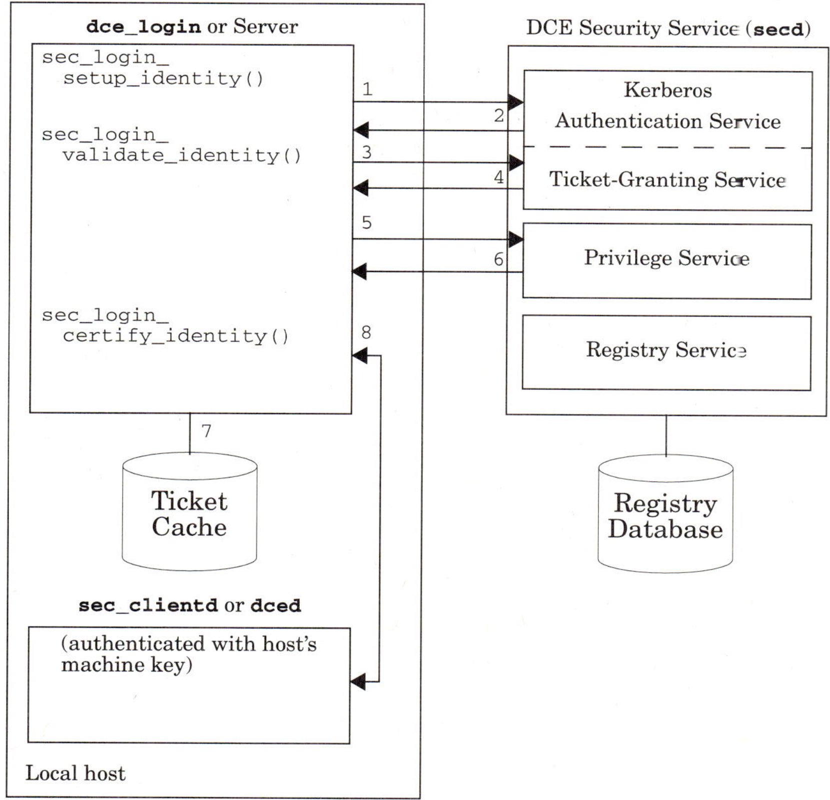

Figure 6.16
DCE Authentication Components and Steps

Privilege Service and the PTGT

The Privilege Service (PS) produces PACs (and EPACs, in DCE 1.1) for client credentials and service tickets. This is a DCE extension, not part of the standard Kerberos services. From the point of view of Kerberos, the Privilege Service is just another service. It uses the principal `dce-ptgt` and exports the `rpriv` RPC interface.

To obtain a PAC, a security client must first obtain a service ticket for the PS from the Kerberos TGS. Then it makes a remote call to the one of the operations in the `rpriv` interface. In response, the PS prepares a special kind of ticket, called the *Privilege Ticket-Granting Ticket* (PTGT). A PTGT acts like a Kerberos TGT, with the addition of the principal's PAC/EPAC. See the discussion on the DCE Authentication Steps for more detail.

Registry Service

The third component of the DCE Security Server is the Registry Service (RS). This service works with the other services in the Security Server to maintain and provide information about principals. The RS exports a large number of RPC interfaces (`rs_acct`, `rs_pgo`, `rs_qry`, etc.) for the access and manipulation of Registry information. (You can see the Endpoint Map entries for these interfaces under the annotation `DCE user registry` when you execute **`rpccp show mapping`**.) The Registry Service uses the principal `dce-rgy`.

Registry Database

The Registry Database contains all of the principal, group, organization (the so-called PGO objects), policy, and other security information associated with a DCE cell. The DCE Security Server maintains an in-memory copy of Registry data that it is using. There are also a set of files that provide stable storage for the Registry. On HP-UX DCE, these files are in the directory `/opt/dcelocal/var/security/rgy_data`. The contents of these files are of course very sensitive. They are protected by encryption and access is restricted to the `root` user alone. The `root` access should then be severely restricted on the Security Server host.

Login Client and the Security Runtime

The login client can be the **`dce_login`** program, another login program such as **`/bin/login`** or **`vuelogin`** that has been enhanced to perform an integrated DCE login, or any application program that sets up its own DCE identity. All login clients call `sec_login_` routines that invoke the Security Runtime library within the login client process. The Security Runtime manages the client side of the DCE authentication, including getting the principal password or key and using it to decrypt sealed Kerberos information. The Security Runtime also manages a cache of tickets for the user, so that tickets—especially the TGT and PTGT—can be reused by other clients run by the user.

Ticket Cache

A ticket cache holds tickets that have been acquired by a user. These tickets can be reused until they expire. In HP-UX DCE, ticket caches are held in files named `/opt/dcelocal/var/security/creds/dcecred_`*XXXXXXXX*, where *XXXXXXXX* is a hexadecimal number. Each user that has executed a **`dce_login`** will have one or more of these files.

The **klist** command displays the contents of a user's ticket cache. Output Sample 6.13 shows such a display. An example of a ticket from that cache is

```
Server: dce-ptgt@jaja
        valid 95/07/17:11:15:14 to 95/07/17:13:15:14
```

This ticket is for the Privilege Server, as indicated by the principal `dce-ptgt`, in the cell `jaja`. The ticket is valid from `11:15:14` on `95/07/17` to `13:15:14` on `95/07/17`, a lifetime of two hours.

Client Security Daemon and the Machine Principal

In DCE, each host machine is assigned a principal of the form `hosts/`*`HOSTNAME`*`/self`, where *`HOSTNAME`* is the name of the machine host set up during DCE configuration. For example, the host `hpiala3` has the machine principal `hosts/hpiala3/self`. A strong (that is, long and random) secret key is generated for each machine principal during that machine's DCE configuration.

When DCE is started on a machine, the DCE Client Security Daemon (**`sec_clientd`**) is started. This process performs a DCE login for the machine principal and its secret key. It uses a special set of DCE calls—`sec_login_setup_first()` and `sec_login_validate_first()`— that retrieve the machine principal and key from DCE configuration files on the machine. Once **`sec_clientd`** has logged on the machine principal, it will maintain a login context for the principal similar to the way the Refresh Identity and Key Management threads do for application servers.

The Client Security Daemon plays roles during the certification of the DCE Security Service (see Step 8 in the DCE Authentication Steps below), and during pre-authentication (added in DCE 1.1).

In DCE 1.1, the Client Security Daemon has been replaced by the Security Certification service of the local DCE Daemon **`dced`**.

DCE Principal Authentication Steps

This section details the steps performed during the authentication of a principal in DCE. This discussion is based on DCE 1.0. There are some differences in authentication for DCE 1.1, particularly in the area of pre-authentication.

Get a Ticket-Granting Ticket

The login client calls `sec_login_setup_identity()`, specifying its principal name. The Security Runtime sends a `KRB_AS_REQ` to the Kerberos Authentication Service (AS) in the DCE Security Server to request a Ticket-Granting Ticket (TGT) for the principal (step 1 in Figure 6.16). Communication to the Kerberos services actually uses remote calls to the `krb5rpc` interface. The `_REQ` messages are input parameters and the `_REP` messages are output parameters.

The AS receives the KRB_AS_REQ, looks up the principal name and secret key in the Registry Database, and prepares a TGT for the principal with a session key (session key 1), encrypted with the TGS secret key. The AS also prepares a KRB_AS_REP containing the TGT and session key 1 encrypted in the principal's secret key and sends it back to the login client (step 2). The login client's Security Runtime retains the KRB_AS_REP and saves the TGT in its ticket cache.

The login client calls sec_login_validate_identity(), specifying its principal's password. The Security Runtime generates the principal's secret key from the password and uses it to retrieve session key 1 from the retained KRB_AS_REP. After the session key is obtained, the local storage for the principal's password and secret key is destroyed. This means that the password is in memory for only a short amount of time, decreasing its susceptibility to being found by an attacker scanning memory. This is also a major reason why the setup and validate calls are separate. The password is not in memory yet while the login client is waiting for the KRB_AS_REP.

Get a Service Ticket for the Privilege Service

Next the Security Runtime generates and sends a KRB_TGT_REQ to the Ticket-Granting Service (TGS) to request a service ticket for the Privilege Service (step 3). The TGS, in the DCE Security Server, receives the KRB_TGT_REQ. It looks up the secret key for the Privilege Service (the dce-ptgt principal) in the Registry and prepares a service ticket encrypted in that secret key. The service ticket contains session key 2. The TGS prepares a KRB_TGT_REP containing the service ticket and session key 2, encrypted in the session key from the AS exchange (session key 1). The TGS sends the KRB_TGT_REP back to the login client (step 4), which saves the PS service ticket in its ticket cache.

Get a Privilege Ticket-Granting Ticket

Next, the login client Security Runtime makes a remote call to the rpriv interface to request a PTGT from the Privilege Service (step 5). This request is in the form of a KRB_TGT_REQ. It also contains an KRB_AP_REQ in the PreAuthn Data field of the KRB_TGT_REQ. The KRB_AP_REQ authenticates the login client to the Privilege Service and includes the PS service ticket and an authenticator. The Privilege Service decrypts the PS service ticket, using its secret key. From the service ticket the PS obtains the identity of the client and session key 2. The Privilege Service then constructs a Privilege Attribute Certification (PAC) for the client, containing the principal and the groups associated with the client identity. The PS also generates yet another session key (session key 3). The PAC and session key 3 are placed in a PTGT, which is encrypted with the Privilege Server's secret key. Finally, the Privilege Service builds a KRB_TGT_REP with the PTGT and with a second copy of the PAC encrypted in session key 3 so that the login client can retrieve the PAC.

This KRB_TGT_REP is sent back to the login client (step 6). The login client Security Runtime caches the PTGT in its ticket cache (step 7).

Certify the Authentication Service

Finally, the login client calls sec_login_certify_identity() to certify that the DCE Security Server which produced the TGT and PTGT is itself authentic. It is possible that what the login client thought was the DCE Security Server was actually an elaborate hoax perpetrated by a sophisticated attacker. This attacker could block access to the real Security Server and substitute a bogus security server which would mimic the Kerberos and Privilege Service protocols. The TGT and PTGT tickets produced by this bogus server would not be valid for client-server authentication.

All that the sec_login_certify_identity() does is to make an authenticated remote call to an interface (rsec_cert) exported by the **sec_clientd** or **dced** process on the local host (step 8). At first it may not be evident how this verifies that the DCE Security Server is authentic. But what this is really doing is testing that the Security Server can build a valid service ticket for the machine principal used by **sec_clientd/dced**. To do this, the Security Server must have the machine principal's secret key, to encrypt the service ticket. If the Security Server is bogus, it will most likely not know that secret key, so the ticket it might produce would be invalid. This would be discovered when **sec_clientd/dced** tried to decrypt the bogus service ticket with the (real) secret key. If the remote call to **sec_clientd/dced** is successful, we are reassured that the DCE Security Server is authentic.

To make the remote call to **sec_clientd/dced**, the login client must first create a binding to the rsec_cert interface exported by **sec_clientd/dced**. To help in this, **sec_clientd/dced** creates a file (/opt/dcelocal/var/security/sec_clientd.binding on HP-UX) that holds string bindings for the interface. The Security Runtime reads these bindings from the file and constructs a binding handle from them. Since the RPC Name Space is not used to create the bindings, the substantial overhead of CDS is avoided. Also, the remote call is within the local host, so there is no network traffic overhead for the certification.

The **dce_login** program does not normally perform the certification step. (You may have already noticed the warning Identity information is not certified in the **klist** display in Output Sample 6.13.) You can force **dce_login** to perform the certification with the **-c** option; however, **dce_login** uses a slightly different certification method which requires that you be a privileged user (e.g., root). Apparently this option is intended only for administrative purposes.

Pre-Authentication (DCE 1.1)

If you thought the DCE principal authentication process just described is already complex beyond the comprehension of mere mortals, hold onto your hats. DCE 1.1 introduces yet another layer of complexity with a feature called *pre-authentication*. This feature solves a couple of possible weaknesses in the original Kerberos protocol:

- The TGT in the `KRB_AS_REP` message is encrypted in a key derived from the principal's password. If the principal is for a person, that person must select and remember the password. Then this password, which despite the best efforts of password strength enforcement, is more susceptible to off-line guessing attacks than a full random secret key.
- An attacker can obtain a TGT for any known principal simply by sending a `KRB_AS_REQ` to Kerberos, since nothing in the `KRB_AS_REQ` needs to be encrypted by any secret key the principal possesses. Then the attacker can subject the TGT to an off-line attack which may (given enough time and computing power) yield the principal's password.

The purpose of pre-authentication is to make such attacks virtually impossible. There are a couple of techniques available for pre-authentication that use the existing PreAuthn Data field in the `KRB` messages. The pre-authentication method used for each principal is determined by the value of its `pre_auth_req` ERA (extended registry attribute).

- `pre_auth_req = NONE`

  No pre-authentication is done, equivalent to DCE 1.0.
- `pre_auth_req = PADATA-ENC-TIMESTAMPS`

  The time stamp pre-authentication method is included in the Kerberos Version 5 Beta 2 implementation. This method puts the current time, encrypted in the principal's secret key, in the PreAuthn Data field of the `KRB_AS_REQ`. When Kerberos receives a `KRB_AS_REQ`, it verifies that the time stamp was encrypted by the principal. This prevents an attacker from asking for a TGT for any principal. However, the TGT is still susceptible to network interception and attack.
- `pre_auth_req = PADATA-ENC-THIRD-PARTY`

  DCE 1.1 provides another pre-authentication method that uses a third party "sponsor" to provide additional encrypted authentication information. This is the local host **dced**, which obtains a Ticket-Granting Ticket (TGT) for the host machine's principal. When a login client begins authentication of its principal, its Security Runtime obtains the machine principal TGT and the session key (session key A) from the TGT. The Security Runtime also creates another session key (session key B). The machine principal TGT and session key B are encrypted by session key A and included in the PreAuthn Data field of the KRB_AS_REQ sent to the Kerberos Authentication Service (AS). The AS obtains session key A from the machine TGT and decrypts session key B using session key A. The AS then uses session key B as well as the client's principal key to encrypt the TGT in the KRB_AS_REP. Finally, the login client uses session key B to retrieve the TGT from the KRB_AS_REP. Even if an attacker intercepted the KRB_AS_REP, he would need to break the strong session key B before attacking the TGT. This greatly increases the effort required to obtain the principal secret key through an off-line attack on an intercepted KRB_AS_REP.

DCE prefers to use third-party pre-authentication because it is the most secure method. See Chapter 30 of the *OSF DCE Administration Guide - Core Components, Version 1.1* for more details.

DCE Client-Server Authentication Steps

This section discusses the steps in the authentication of a client to a server using DCE RPC. Refer to Figure 6.17 for the components and interactions during the client-server authentication.

Get a Service Ticket for the Server

The client calls `rpc_binding_set_auth_info()`, specifying the RPC binding, the target server's principal name, the RPC protection level, the authentication and authorization services, and a login context that provides the client's identity. Typically the login context is inherited from the user who ran the client, and that user has done a **dce_login** (or the equivalent) to establish a principal identity.

The `rpc_binding_set_auth_info()` call adds the security information to the binding data structure and requests a service ticket for the target server. First, the Security Runtime searches the user's ticket cache for a PTGT that represents the login context (step 1 in Figure 6.17). There should be a PTGT for the user from the **dce_login** (unless the login was so long ago that the PTGT has expired).

The client Security Runtime uses the information from the PTGT to construct a KRB_TGT_REQ and sends it to the Ticket-Granting Service in the DCE Security Service (step 2). Using the PTGT information, the TGS prepares a service ticket for the target server. Kerberos generates a new session key (session key 4) for the client and server to use between them. The service ticket includes the session key, and the PAC for the client's principal, encrypted in the server's secret key. The TGS then puts the service ticket and the session key in a KRB_TGT_REP, encrypted in the original session key associated with the PTGT (session key 3) and sends

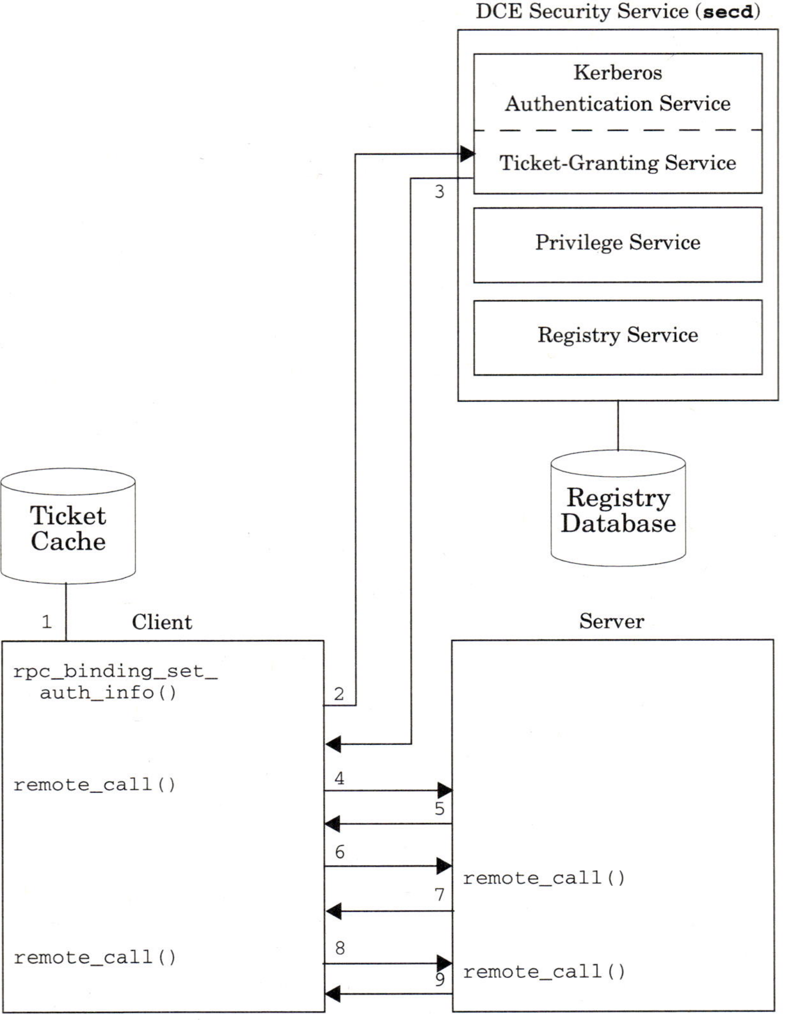

Figure 6.17
DCE Client-Server Authentication Steps

the KRB_TGT_REP back to the client (step 3). The client Security Runtime deposits the service ticket in the ticket cache.

Now that the client has a service ticket, it can authenticate itself to the server. This will be done during the first remote call to the server. In general, the client will construct a KRB_AP_REQ, with the service ticket and an authenticator, and send it to the server. However, like so many of aspects of RPC, this is done differently for the dg and cn protocols.

Let us assume for both protocol cases that the protection level in use is rpc_c_protect_level_pkt_privacy.

Authenticate to the Server: `dg` *Protocol*

When the client makes the first remote call using a datagram (`dg`) protocol, the data in the RPC request packet will be encrypted using session key 4. When the server receives the request packet (step 4), it will note that the data is encrypted, but that it does not (yet) have the session key needed for decryption. The server will make a *callback* to the client, asking "Who Are You?" (sometimes called a *WAY call-back*). This resembles a remote procedure call, but from the server back to the client, and it is handled as a special case with the client's RPC Runtime. The WAY callback challenges the client to authenticate itself. The server generates and sends in the callback a *nonce,* which is a random number, as in the `KRB` messages (step 5). The client encrypts the nonce with the session key and returns the encrypted nonce and a `KRB_AP_REQ` containing the service ticket to the server (step 6). The server can decrypt the service ticket with its own secret key, obtaining session key 4 and the client's PAC. The server also decrypts the nonce from the client and compares it to the original nonce to verify that the client actually knows the session key and did not just replay a ticket from another principal.

Now the server also has the session key and can decrypt the data in the request packet. The server executes the remote procedure with the decrypted data. Then the server builds an RPC response packet, encrypts its data with the session key, and sends it back to the client (step 7). The client's RPC Runtime then decrypts the response packet.

Subsequent calls between the client and server do not require the challenge callback, since both sides know the session key. Each RPC packet is encrypted by its sender and decrypted by its receiver (steps 8 and 9).

Authenticate to the Server: `cn` *Protocol*

With a connection-oriented (`cn`) protocol, there are separate bind and bind_ack packets exchanged after the connection is established but before any RPC requests are sent. The bind packet send from the client (step 4) contains a `KRB_AP_REQ`, with the service ticket and an authenticator. The server decrypts the service ticket with its secret key to obtain session key 4 and the client's PAC. The server also builds a `KRB_AP_REP` and includes it in the bind_ack packet sent back to the client (step 5).

Once the bind exchange is completed, both the client and the server possess the session key and can encrypt and decrypt packets (steps 6 through 9).

6.9 Performance of DCE Security Options

After the discussion in the preceding section on how DCE security actually works, you may well wonder what effect the various DCE security options have on performance. That will be examined in this section, using data from the **`perf_client`** and **`perf_server`** programs that were introduced in Chapter 2. These programs report the time taken by the DCE setup calls and by remote calls that send and receive varying amounts of data.

The test systems and network configuration used during the measurements were as in Section 2.6 and Section 5.7: The client was run on an HP9000/730 workstation and the server was run on an HP9000/826 system. There was one DCE Security Server, running on the 826. To ensure equivalent measurements, a **dce_login** was performed before each **perf_client** test to start with an empty ticket cache. In some tests, **perf_client** was executed a second time to measure the effect of the ticket cache. All times reported are in milliseconds.

Table 6.1 shows the effect of the different RPC protection levels on the client measurements for the `ncacn_ip_tcp` and `ncadg_ip_udp` protocols. Figure 6.18 graphs the call times for the RPC protection levels with `ncacn_ip_tcp`. Table 6.2 and Figure 6.19 illustrate the effect of the ticket caching on the first and subsequent executions of **perf_client** within a **dce_login** session. Table 6.3 shows the performance of **perf_server** startup and cleanup, for initial and subsequent executions. Figure 6.20 plots the server startup times with security.

Table 6.1

Effect of RPC Protection Levels on Remote Calls

Operation	RPC Protection Levels (times in milliseconds)					
	none	connect	call	pkt	integ	privacy
`ncacn_ip_tcp`						
Bind[1]	214.4	945.4	998.8	992.7	943.8	970.0
Initial null	45.5	91.3	94.5	93.2	94.8	95.6
Null	2.1	2.1	2.6	2.8	2.8	2.8
Char in/out (bytes)						
10	2.5	2.6	3.1	3.2	3.5	3.6
100	2.8	2.7	5.6	3.3	4.0	4.7
1000	4.5	4.5	5.4	5.1	10.0	14.1
10000	20.9	21.2	21.3	21.4	48.6	77.3
`ncadg_ip_udp`						
Bind[1]	230.38	973.92	996.2	941.7	937.4	967.4
Initial null	43.1	55.8	55.7	56.4	57.0	56.5
Null	2.5	2.7	2.7	2.7	3.5	3.6
Char in/out (bytes)						
10	2.9	3.2	3.3	3.2	4.0	4.2
100	3.2	3.5	3.3	3.3	4.8	5.1
1000	5.2	5.0	5.2	5.0	10.7	14.7
10000	26.0	26.4	26.4	26.5	60.2	86.3

[1]Bind using:
`rpc_binding_from_string_binding()`
`rpc_binding_set_auth_info()`

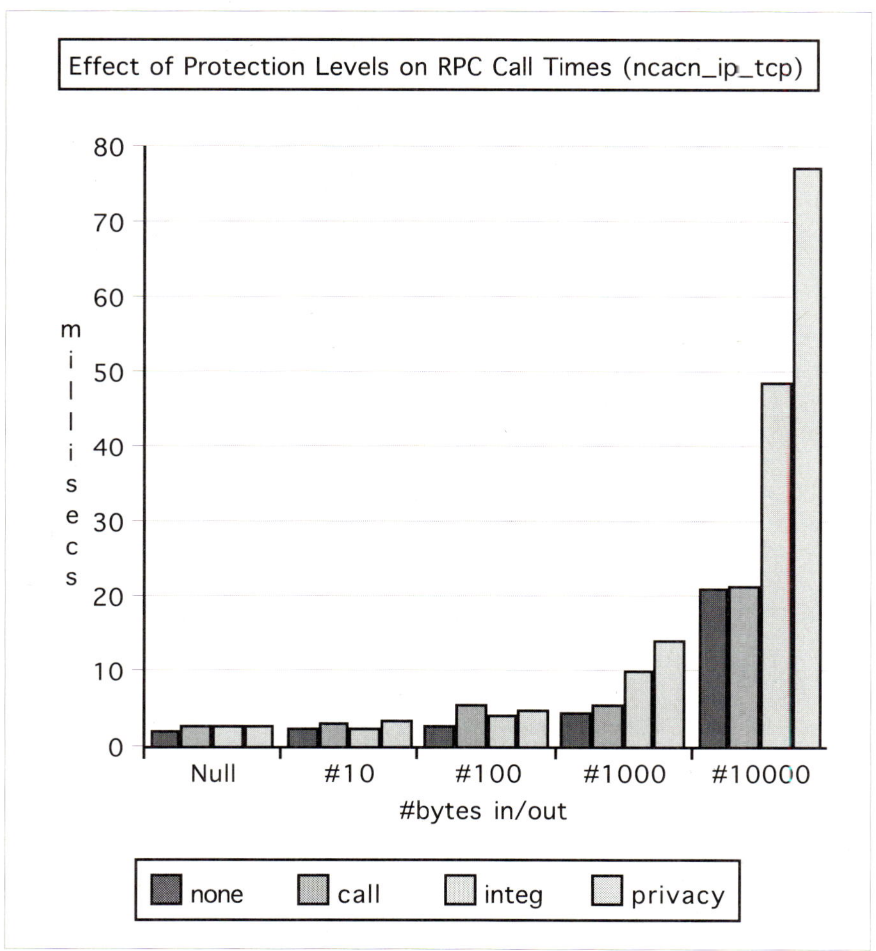

Figure 6.18
Effect of RPC Protection Levels on Remote Calls

Table 6.2

Effect of Security and CDS Caching on DCE Operations						
	RPC Protection Levels					
	none		integ		privacy	
Operation	First	Second	First	Second	First	Second
_import_begin()	222.5	213.6	186.0	195.9	193.0	195.7
_import_next()	2260.8	107.5	1664.7	109.7	1685.9	108.5
_import_done()	0.2	0.2	0.2	0.2	0.2	0.2
_set_auth_info(	0.7	0.6	410.0	23.5	414.9	24.0
Accumulated time	2484.2	321.9	2260.9	329.3	2294.0	328.4

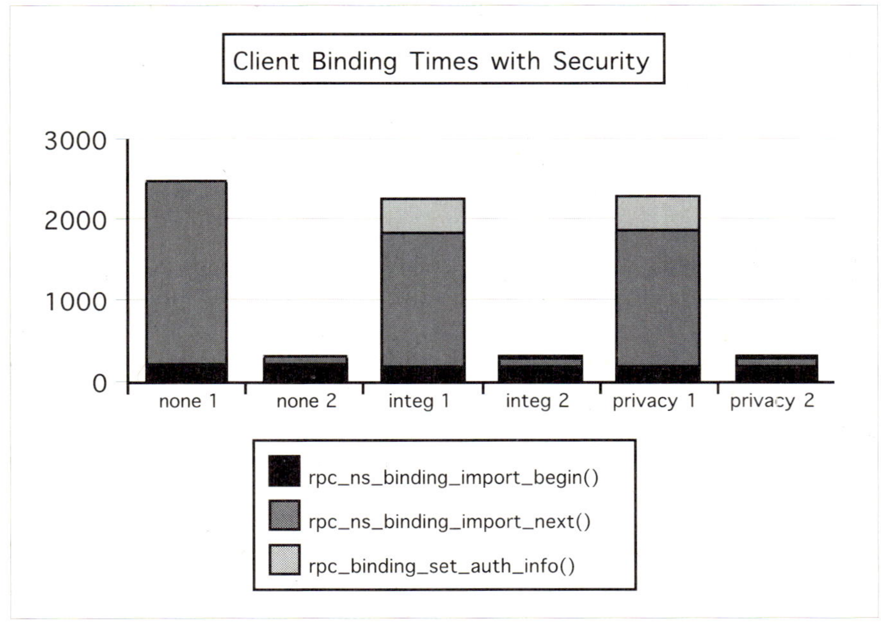

Figure 6.19
Initial and Subsequent Client Binding Times with Security

Table 6.3

Effect of Security on Server Operations				
	No Security		Security	
Operation	First	Second	First	Second
Server Setup				
rpc_server_use_all_protseqs()	240.6	236.5	248.9	238.8
sec_login_setup_identity()			779.0	769.4
sec_key_mgmt_get_key()			19.9	19.7
sec_login_validate_identity()			404.1	414.9
sec_login_certify_identity()			761.8	780.3
sec_login_set_context()			281.8	280.8
sec_login_get_expiration()			0.1	0.1
pthread_create() refresh_id			1.4	1.3
pthread_create() key_mgmt			40.2	41.1
rpc_server_register_if()	0.1	0.1	0.1	0.1
rpc_ep_register()	149.0	148.8	273.4	272.1
rpc_ns_binding_export()	2539.1	675.1	3048.2	3019.3
rpc_ns_group_mbr_add()	254.6	255.4	269.7	270.3
rpc_ns_profile_elt_add()	438.8	456.8	551.7	524.8
pthread_create() signal_catch	1.0	1.0	0.9	0.9
Accumulated Time	3623.3	1773.8	6681.3	6634.1
Server Cleanup				
rpc_ns_profile_elt_remove()	363.4	654.2	418.9	389.8
rpc_ns_group_mgr_remove()	179.1	180.9	192.5	189.7
rpc_ns_binding_unexport()	606.3	606.6	633.2	634.6
rpc_ep_unregister()	18.7	57.7	62.2	62.0
rpc_server_unregister_if()	0.1	0.1	0.1	0.1
pthread_cancel() refresh_id			0.1	0.1
pthread_cancel() key_mgmt			0.1	0.1
sec_login_release_context()			0.1	0.1
Accumulated Time	1167.6	1499.5	1307.3	1275.8

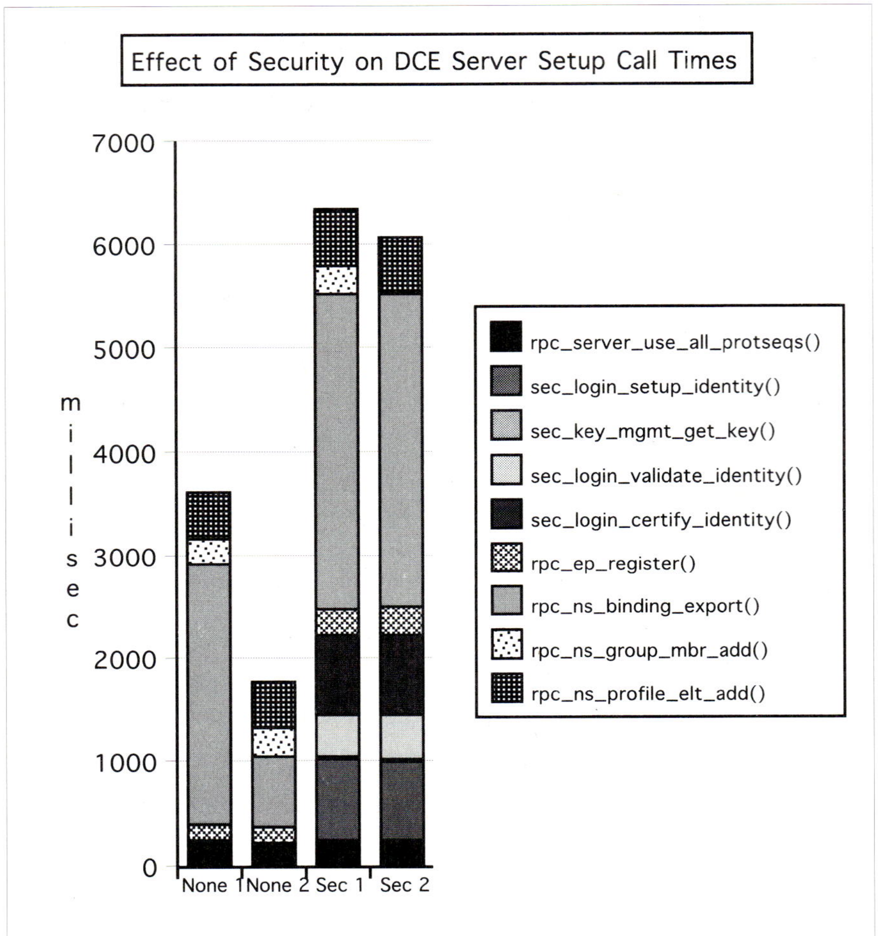

Figure 6.20
Effect of Security on Server Setup Calls

Observations on the security performance data:

- The first remote call is two times slower with any protection level for the `ncacn_ip_tcp` protocol, due to the added overhead of the authentication information in the bind exchange. For the `ncadg_ip_udp` protocol the first call is about 25 percent slower.

- Remote calls with the protection levels from `none` to `pkt` show little performance degradation, regardless of the amount of data exchanged. There is no data-related security processing at these levels, and the length of the additional authentication data is small.
- The `pkt_integ` protection level increases remote call times by a factor of two, because of the checksum computation over the call data. This would decrease remote call throughput up to a half.
- The `privacy` protection level increases remote call times by a factor of three, due to the cost of software data encryption. Throughput declines to a third of the unencrypted rate.
- Table 6.2 shows that the client setup time for the second execution of the client using security and CDS is much faster than the first, by a factor of up to 8. Much of this improvement comes from CDS caching. The time for the `rpc_binding_set_auth_info()` call drops from around 400 milliseconds to 25, due to caching of service tickets.
- Table 6.3 shows that security has a large impact on the startup of the server. The setup time for the server doubles, from three to six seconds, with the addition of the `sec_login` calls for authentication. Note also that the setup time for the server does not decrease on subsequent executions. The server obtains a new set of tickets each time it runs. Even the `rpc_ns_binding_export()` time, which decreases dramatically without security, stays the same. Security has little effect on the server cleanup time.

CHAPTER 7

Server Management in DCE 1.1

In the previous chapters, we have seen how a server can be set up using the low-level DCE calls that have been available since the original release of DCE. There are a number of shortcomings with these calls, including

- Many low-level DCE calls are required to set up the server. Frequently these calls require duplicate parameters. For example, the interface specification occurs in the `rpc_server_register_if()`, `rpc_ep_register()`, `rpc_ns_binding_export()`, and `rpc_if_inq_id()` calls. Coding all of the necessary low-level calls is quite tedious, even if you have an example from which you can cut and paste.
- Parameters like the server's principal name, keytab file, and CDS entry names are usually hard-coded in the server source. If they need to be changed, the server must be recompiled.
- Management of the server's execution is outside of the scope of DCE. A server must be started by hand or by a script and stopped by sending it a signal of some sort.

DCE 1.1 provides some server management facilities that integrate various low-level functions and server configuration using the **dcecp** command. This chapter examines these facilities.

7.1 Server Configuration with dcecp

Server configuration information can be set up using the `server` and `keytab` objects of the **dcecp** command. This information is stored in a database managed by the local **dced** process and can be retrieved by the server when it starts up. Each configured server has a configuration record with the name

/.:/hosts/*HOST_NAME*/config/srvrconf/*SERVER_NAME*

where *HOST_NAME* is the name of the local host on which the server will execute, and *SERVER_NAME* is a name that identifies the server. Code Sample 7.1 shows the **dcecp** command to create the configuration record for the **room_server**.

```
HOST=`hostname`

dcecp -c server create /.:/hosts/$HOST/config/srvrconf/room_server \
 -program rcom_server \
 -entryname /.:/subsys/sch/room_server \
 -services { \
   {ifname {Room Server}} \
   {annotation {Room Server}} \
   {interface  {6101efd0-89fc-11cd-be27-080009307c01 1.0}} \
 } \
 -principals room-server \
 -keytabs {06f2e522-bbaf-11ce-8f56-08000948fbd9} \
 -starton explicit \
 -directory {$PWD}
```

Code Sample 7.1
schedule/integ_mgmt/server_config.ksh: Create the server's configuration record

Let's look at each component of this command.

- -program room_server

  Provides the name of the program file to be run when the server is executed. This program file is in the directory supplied by the directory attribute.

- -entryname /.:/subsys/sch/room_server

  Provides a CDS entry name to be used for exporting the server's interfaces to the RPC Name Space.

- -services

  Specifies the interfaces (services) that the server will export. One or more interfaces can be listed. Each interface has a name, an annotation used by the Endpoint Map, and a UUID and version number.

- -principals room-server

  Specifies one or more principals that the server will use when it establishes its identity. We will use one principal here.

- -keytabs {06f2e522-bbaf-11ce-8f56-08000948fbd9}

  Indicates one or more keytab files that will be used by the server when it establishes its identity. Each keytab file is identified by a UUID that is assigned when the corresponding keytab object is created. Code Sample 7.2 shows the keytab object that is used by the **room_server**.

- `-starton explicit`

  Lists the ways in which the server can be started. The choices will be detailed in Section 7.3.

- `-directory {$PWD}`

  Specifies the directory from which the server is to be executed.

Creation of server configuration records is protected by ACLs on the server configuration object `/.:/hosts/`*HOST_NAME*`/config/srvrconf`. You must have `i` permission on this object to successfully create a configuration record. With the default ACLs, only the host principal `/.:/hosts/`*HOST_NAME*`/self` has this permission. When you log in as the host's `root` user, you automatically get the host principal identity. Consequently, only `root` (or users explicitly granted permission by `root`) can configure, start, and stop servers. Not even `cell_admin` has these privileges by default.

The keytab file used by the server requires additional configuration. Code Sample 7.2 shows the **`dcecp keytab create`** command to set up the keytab file for the **`room_server`**.

```
dcecp -c keytab create /.:/hosts/$HOST/config/keytab/room_server \
 -attr { \
    {uuid 06f2e522-bbaf-11ce-8f56-08000948fbd9} \
    {storage $PWD/room_server_keyfile} \
    {data room-server plain 1 -dce-} \
 }
```

Code Sample 7.2
`schedule/integ_mgmt/server_config.ksh`: Create the server's keytab file

The attributes of the keytab file are

- `uuid 06f2e522-bbaf-11ce-8f56-08000948fbd9`

  The UUID that identifies the keytab file in server configuration records, such as the one defined in Code Sample 7.1.

- `storage $PWD/room_server_keyfile.`

  The path for the keytab file.

- `data room-server plain 1 -dce-`

  The server's principal and an initial (version `1`) key (`-dce-`) in plain text. This key will be automatically encrypted using DES.

7.2 Integrated Server Setup

DCE 1.1 provides a small set of calls that can use the server configuration information stored in **`dced`** to set up a server. These few high-level calls replace most of the many low-level calls we have used for server setup. These integrated server management calls will be used in a new **`room_server`** `main()` module.

Setting Up Security

Code Sample 7.3 shows the high-level call to set up the server's security. Using information from the server's configuration record, it will

- Get the server's key from its keytab file.
- Set up and validate the server's identity, using its key.
- Set the current login context to the server's identity.
- Register the server's security information with the RPC Runtime.
- Create a key management thread.

```
dce_server_sec_begin(
    dce_server_c_login | dce_server_c_manage_key,
    &status);
CHECK_DCE(status, "Cannot start server security");
```

Code Sample 7.3
`schedule/integ_mgmt/room_server.c main()`: Setting up server security

When the server terminates, it calls `dce_server_sec_done()` to clean up its security, as shown in Code Sample 7.4. This releases the login context created by `dce_server_sec_start()`.

```
dce_server_sec_done(&status);
CHECK_DCE(status, "Cannot stop server security");
```

Code Sample 7.4
`schedule/integ_mgmt/room_server.c main()`: Cleaning up server security

Registering the Server

There are two high-level calls needed to perform the bulk of the server set up work, using the server's configuration information. First, the `dce_server_inq_server()` call obtains the server's configuration record from **dced**. Then, the `dce_server_register()` call performs various registration using the server record. These tasks include

- Register the interfaces with the server's RPC Runtime.
- Set up the protocol sequence bindings to be used by the server.
- Register the interfaces and bindings with the local Endpoint Map.
- Export the interfaces and bindings to the server's CDS entry.

The data types used with these calls are defined in dced_base.idl and dced_base.h, in /usr/include/dce. In addition to the server record, the dce_register_server() call requires an array of interface records, one for each interface it will export. Each interface record includes the interface specification, a manager entry point vector, and a list of manager types. You may recognize these items as the input parameters to the rpc_server_register_if() call, which is embedded in dce_server_register(). The entry point vector can be set to NULL to use the default managers, and the list of manager types can be set to NULL to use the default type. These parameters will be discussed in more detail in Chapter 8. The dce_server_register() call returns a handle to the server that will be passed into the dce_server_unregister() call. Code Sample 7.5 shows the dce_server_register() call for the **room_server**.

```
server_t *server_rec;
dce_server_register_data_t if_recs[1];
dce_server_handle_t        server_h;
. . .

dce_server_inq_server(&server_rec, &status);
CHECK_DCE(status, "Cannot get server information");

if_recs[0].ifhandle   = room_v1_0_s_ifspec;
if_recs[0].epv        = NULL;
if_recs[0].num_types = 0;
if_recs[0].types      = NULL;

dce_server_register(
    dce_server_c_ns_export,
    server_rec,
    if_recs,
    &server_h,
    &status);
CHECK_DCE(status, "Cannot register server");
```

Code Sample 7.5
schedule/integ_mgmt/room_server.c main(): Registering the server

When a server terminates, it calls `dce_server_unregister()` to clean up the registrations made by `dce_server_register()`. Code Sample 7.6 shows this call. It does the following:

- Unregisters the server. This does the following:
- Removes the interfaces and bindings from the server's CDS entry.
- Removes the interfaces and bindings from the local Endpoint Map.
- Unregisters the interface with the server's RPC Runtime.

```
dce_server_unregister(&server_h, &status);
CHECK_DCE_NONFATAL(status, "Cannot unregister");
```

Code Sample 7.6
`schedule/integ_mgmt/room_server.c main()`: Unregistering the server

What Is *Not* Done by Integrated Server Setup

The integrated server management calls go a long way to easing the setup of a DCE server. However, there are still some things that these calls do not do. We will still have to use the low-level DCE calls to accomplish several tasks.

Refreshing the Server's Identity

Conspicuously absent from the lists of tasks performed by the `dce_server_sec_begin()` call is creation of a refresh identity thread. This appears to be a major oversight in the design of this call, which must be remedied by reintroducing all the code for the refresh identity thread from Chapter 6. The original `refresh_identity()` base routine, shown in Code Sample 6.5, can be used here without modification. The `refresh_identity()` routine uses the `validate_identity()` routine in Code Sample 6.1. Some minor changes must be made to `validate_identity()` to allow it to be used here. The original routine used hard-coded principal and keytab file names. Here we will need to get those items from the server's configuration record. The principal name is a field in the server record; actually, the field is a list of principal names from which we will select the first. (Note that this requires that the server record be a global variable, so it can be set in `main()` and accessed from `validate_identity()`.) The keytab file name is more of a problem. The server record has a field for a list of keytab files, but it includes only the keytab object UUIDs, and there are no calls to convert a keytab UUID to a keytab file name. Fortunately, there is an undocumented environment variable, `DCED_KEYTAB_FILE`, that is set up to pass the keytab file name to the server when it is created. Code Sample 7.7 shows the revised `validate_identity()` routine.

```
void validate_identity(
   sec_login_handle_t *login_context)
{
   unsigned_char_p_t    keyfile;
   void                *key_data;
   sec_login_auth_src_t authn_source;
   boolean32            reset_password;
   unsigned32           status;

   keyfile =
     (unsigned_char_p_t) getenv("DCED_KEYTAB_FILE");

   sec_key_mgmt_get_key(
      rpc_c_authn_dce_secret,
      keyfile,
      (unsigned_char_p_t)server_rec->prin_names.list[0],
      0,
      &key_data,
      (error_status_t *) &status);
   CHECK_DCE(status, "Cannot get server key");

   sec_login_validate_identity(
      *login_context,
      (sec_passwd_rec_t *) key_data,
      &reset_password,
      &authn_source,
      &status);
   CHECK_DCE(status, "Cannot validate identity");

   sec_key_mgmt_free_key(key_data, &status);
   CHECK_DCE(status, "Cannot free server key.");

   sec_login_certify_identity(*login_context, &status);
   CHECK_DCE(status,
     "Cannot certify identity for server principal");
}
```

Code Sample 7.7
schedule/integ_mgmt/room_server.c: validate_identity()

```
dce_server_sec_begin(...);
. . .
sec_login_get_current_context(&login_context,
   &status);
CHECK_DCE(status, "Cannot get login context");

sec_login_certify_identity(login_context, &status);
CHECK_DCE(status, "Cannot certify identity");

dce_server_inq_server(...);
. . .

create_thread(
    refresh_identity,
    "refresh identity",
    &refresh_id_thread,
    (pthread_addr_t) &login_context);
```

Code Sample 7.8
`schedule/integ_mgmt/room_server.c main()`: Creating the refresh identity thread

Code Sample 7.8 shows the additions needed to the **`room_server`** `main()` to create the refresh identity thread. First, we need to call `sec_login_get_current_context()` to retrieve the login context created by `dce_server_sec_begin()`. This login context will be passed to the refresh identity thread. The `dce_server_sec_begin()` call does not certify the login context, which happens to be required to get the login's expiration in `refresh_identity()`. So we need to add a call to `sec_login_certify_identity()`. Finally, we will create the refresh identity thread after the `dce_server_inq_server()` call, which gets the configuration information including the server's principal.

Setting Up Group and Profile Entries

The server configuration record includes only a server entry name, and `dce_server_register()` exports only the interfaces and bindings to that server entry name. If we also want our server to add members to a group or elements to a profile, we need to use the low-level `rpc_ns_` calls discussed in Chapter 5. Code Sample 7.9 shows these calls, modified to use the server entry name from the server configuration record.

```
    rpc_ns_group_mbr_add(
        rpc_c_ns_syntax_default,
        (unsigned_char_p_t) "/.:/subsys/sch/room_group",
        rpc_c_ns_syntax_default,
        (unsigned_char_p_t) server_rec->entryname,
        &status);
    CHECK_DCE(status, "Cannot add member to group.");

    rpc_if_inq_id(room_v1_0_s_ifspec, &if_id, &status);
    CHECK_DCE(status, "Cannot get room interface UUID");

    rpc_ns_profile_elt_add(
        rpc_c_ns_syntax_default,
        (unsigned_char_p_t) "/.:/cell-profile",
        &if_id,
        rpc_c_ns_syntax_default,
        (unsigned_char_p_t) server_rec->entryname,
        0,
        (unsigned_char_p_t) "Room Server",
        &status);
    CHECK_DCE(status, "Cannot add element to profile");
```

Code Sample 7.9
`schedule/integ_mgmt/room_server.c main()`: Adding to a group and a profile

Catching Signals

The integrated server management calls make no provision for catching signals. A signal catcher thread can be added to the server using the `signal_catcher()` base routine from Code Sample 4.16 and the `create_thread()` call shown in Code Sample 4.19.

The use of signals for terminating the server becomes less important with the DCE 1.1 server management facilities. As we shall see in the next section, the usual way to stop a server will be to send it an RPC stop request, not a signal. However, it is still valuable to catch signals to recover from a possible **kill**.

7.3 Server Execution Management

Once a server is configured using the **dcecp server create** command, it can be executed under control of the local **dced** process. There are **dcecp** commands for starting and stopping the server, as well as determining if the server is executing properly. These commands can be issued from any system in the network, so that application servers can be centrally controlled.

Starting the Server

The -starton option of the **dcecp server create** command specifies one or more ways in which a server can be started. These are

- auto

  The server will be started automatically upon the reception of its first RPC request. Because of endpoint mapping, this request will first be sent to **dced**, which will start the server and forward the request on to the new server.

- boot

  The server will be started at system startup after the local **dced** has been started.

- explicit

  The server can be started by a **dcecp** command, of the form

  **dcecp -c server start **

  /.:/hosts/*HOST_NAME*/config/srvrconf/*SERVER_NAME*

  You must have i permission for the server configuration object /.:/hosts/*HOST_NAME*/config/srvrconf to start the server. As noted earlier, this means that you must be the host root user.

- failure

  The server will be restarted if it fails, that is, if **dced** detects that the server exited with a nonsuccessful completion code.

Server Execution Environment

In each of the startup cases listed above, the server process is created as a background process by **dced**. This differs in the following ways from executing the server within a terminal window:

- No stdout or stderr

  When a server is run in a window or a terminal screen, its output (the stdout and stderr files) appears in the window or screen. When a server is started by **dced** in the background, its stdout and stderr output is lost. In this case, the server can open a disk file and direct its output to that file. Then you can **tail** the output file when the server is started to follow its execution. The **room_server** modules have been modified to write their output to a file named room_server.out.

  A more comprehensive (and more complicated) approach to this problem is to use the DCE 1.1 serviceability calls. These allow you to redirect messages from the server to log files. Chapter 4 of the *OSF DCE 1.1 Application Programming Guide* discusses the serviceability interface.

- Execution as `root`

  Unless otherwise specified, a server started by **dced** will run under the local `root` identity. This allows the server access to most local files and other objects. It also allows the server to cause a lot of damage if it happens to run amok. The **dcecp server create** command provides the `-uid` and `-gid` options to specify an alternative user and group identity with which a server is started. Note that this allows the server to be started with a user identity without having to supply the user's password.

- **dced** execution record

  When a server is started, an execution record is created for the server, of the form

  `/.:/hosts/`*HOST_NAME*`/config/srvrexec/`*SERVER_NAME*

  This record combines the information from the server's `srvrconf` record, with data about the executing server process, such as its bindings. Output Sample 7.1 shows the execution record for an instance of the **room_server**, executing on the host `hpialb2`.

  Note: The display on Output Sample 7.1 was produced on a beta version of HP-UX DCE 1.4. When I tried this on the release version, the `bindings` attribute is empty. This has consequences for the **dcecp server stop** command, as we will soon see.

```
dcecp> server show /.../boosha/hosts/hpialb2/config/srvrexec/room_server
{uuid 7719ff8c-c543-11ce-be9d-080009421b3c}
{program room_server}
{arguments {}}
{prerequisites {}}
{keytabs 06f2e522-bbaf-11ce-8f56-08000948fbd9}
{entryname /.:/subsys/sch/room_server}
{services
 {{ifname {Room Server}}
  {annotation {Room Server}}
  {interface {6101efd0-89fc-11cd-be27-080009307c01 1.0}}
  {bindings
   {ncadg_ip_udp 15.4.24.89 3420}
   {ncacn_ip_tcp 15.4.24.89 1129}}
  {objects {}}
  {flags {}}
  {entryname {}}}}
{principals /.../boosha/room-server}
{starton explicit}
{uid 0}
{gid 0}
{dir /users/cwk/book/examples/schedule}
```

Output Sample 7.1
dcecp output: Displaying a server execution record.

Stopping the Server

A server started by **dced** can be stopped by a **dcecp server stop** command. The syntax of this command is

```
dcecp -c server stop \
   /.:/hosts/HOST_NAME/config/srvrexec/SERVER_NAME \
   [-method method]
```

There are four methods available for stopping a server.

- `rpc`

  dced executes `rpc_server_stop_listening()` with the server as its target. This sends a special request to the server which causes its `rpc_server_listen()` to complete. The server must provide the proper authorization for this management function, as discussed later. `rpc` is the default method for **dcecp server stop**.

  Note: This option relies on the `bindings` attribute in the `srvrexec` record for the server. As noted above, this attribute appears to be empty on the release version of HP-UX DCE 1.4. Consequently, a **server stop -method rpc** fails with a `no bindings` error.

- `soft`

  dced sends the server a soft kill signal, for example, a `SIGTERM`. If the server has a signal catcher thread, it will catch the soft kill and gracefully terminate the server.

- `hard`

  dced sends the server a hard kill signal, for example, a `SIGKILL`. Hard kills cannot be caught by the server; consequently the server will be terminated without being given a chance to clean up.

- `error`

  dced sends a state-preserving signal, such as SIGABRT. This causes the server to abort, leaving a core file recording its state at the time of the abort.

To stop a server, you must have `s` permission on the server's execution record `/.:/hosts/`*HOST_NAME*`/config/srvrexec/`*SERVER_ NAME*. By default, only the local `root` user has this privilege.

Authorizing Management Functions

For the `rpc` server stop method to work, the server must authorize the necessary management request. This is done with an application-supplied management authorization function. Whenever a management request is received by the server, it will call the management authorization function to determine if the caller is allowed to perform the function.

Code Sample 7.10 shows the `rpc_mgmt_set_authorization()` call to set up a management authorization function named `mgmt_authz_fn()`.

```
rpc_mgmt_set_authorization_fn(mgmt_authz_fn,&status);
CHECK_DCE(status, "Cannot set mgmt authz function");
```

Code Sample 7.10
`schedule/integ_mgmt/room_server.c main()`: Setting an authorization function

Code Sample 7.11 shows the `mgmt_authz_fn()` function itself. Its parameters are determined by DCE and include the caller's binding handle and the requested management operation. The authorization function can use these parameters to decide if it will allow the operation to proceed. This implementation is tailored to allow the `rpc_c_mgmt_stop_server_listen` only from the host principal, which is the identity of the host `root` user. The **dced** process also uses the host principal identity when it executes a **dcecp server stop** command.

First, `mgmt_authz_fn()` constructs the host principal name `/.../`*CELL_NAME*`/hosts/`*HOST_NAME*`/self`, getting the cell name from `dce_cf_get_cell_name()` and the host name from `gethostname()`. Then it calls `rpc_binding_inq_auth_client()` to get the client's privileges and the authorization service used by the client. This function can handle either name or DCE authorization. For name authorization, `privs` is the client's principal name, which can be compared directly to the host principal name. For DCE authorization, `privs` is a pointer to the client's PAC, which contains the client's cell (realm) and principal UUIDs. We have to use the Security Registry to convert the host principal to its cell and principal UUIDs before we can check them against the client's PAC information.

The `mgmt_authz_fn()` function might also be implemented checking an ACL that grants permission to stop the server. This is more flexible, but requires additional ACL setup, as detailed in Chapter 9.

```
boolean32 mgmt_authz_fn(
   rpc_binding_handle_t client_binding,
   unsigned32            req_mgmt_op,
   unsigned32           *st)
{
   sec_rgy_handle_t   rgy_h;
   rpc_authz_handle_t privs;
   char               host_name[256];
   char              *cell_name;
   char              *host_pname;
   uuid_t             cell_uuid;
   uuid_t             host_puuid;
   unsigned32         authz_service;
   unsigned32         status, ignored_st;
   boolean32          authorized;

#  define PAC ((sec_id_pac_t *) privs)
#  define UUID_EQ(uuid1, uuid2) \
     uuid_equal(&(uuid1), &(uuid2), &ignored_st)

   *st = rpc_s_ok;
   if (req_mgmt_op == rpc_c_mgmt_stop_server_listen)
   {
      if (gethostname(host_name, sizeof(host_name))==-1)
      {
         perror("Cannot get hostname: ");
         exit(1);
      }
      dce_cf_get_cell_name(&cell_name, &status);
      CHECK_DCE(status, "Cannot get local cell name");
      host_pname = malloc(strlen(cell_name) +
                          strlen(host_name) +
                          strlen("hosts//self") + 1);
      sprintf(host_pname, "%s/hosts/%s/self",
        cell_name, host_name);
      free(cell_name);
```

Code Sample 7.11
schedule/integ_mgmt/room_server_im: mgmt_auth_fn()

```
      rpc_binding_inq_auth_client(client_binding,
         &privs, NULL, NULL, NULL, &authz_service,
         &status);

      switch (authz_service)
      {
         case rpc_c_authz_name:
            authorized =
               (strcmp((char *)privs, host_pname)==0);
            break;

         case rpc_c_authz_dce:
            sec_rgy_site_open((unsigned_char_t *) "",
               &rgy_h, &status);
            CHECK_DCE(status,
               "Cannot open Security Registry");
            sec_id_parse_name(rgy_h, host_pname, NULL,
               &cell_uuid, NULL, &host_puuid, &status);
            CHECK_DCE(status,
               "Cannot convert host principal to UUID");
            sec_rgy_site_close(rgy_h, &status);
            CHECK_DCE(status, "Cannot close Registry");

            authorized =
            (PAC->authenticated &&
            UUID_EQ(PAC->realm.uuid, cell_uuid) &&
            UUID_EQ(PAC->principal.uuid, host_puuid));
            break;
      }
      free(host_pname);
   }
   else /* all other management operations */
   {
      authorized = true;
   }
   return(authorized);
}
```

Code Sample 7.11 (continued)

CHAPTER 8

Objects and Managers

To illustrate the concepts in DCE object management, let's revisit the Room Schedule sample application. In the preceding chapters, this application consisted of one server and one or more clients. Now let's add a couple of additional requirements for this application:

- There can be more than one server, with each server maintaining the reservations for rooms in one or more locations. The room database can be thought of as *partitioned* by location. Each location is still managed by only one server, so the database is *not replicated*. There will be only one server executing on any host.
- Room reservations for some locations have been and will continue to be managed by an existing *legacy* application that does not use DCE. Our room scheduling application will interface with the legacy scheduler to provide a uniform interface for all room locations.

These new requirements can be met using objects and managers. Each location can be designated as an *object* to be *managed* by a room server. The second requirement means that a room server needs to provide two implementations of the `room` interface: one to work directly with our room database and one to interface with the legacy application and convert the `room` operations into commands for the legacy scheduler. These two implementations can be *managers* for the `room` interface, and the DCE object management facilities can be used to route requests to the right implementation.

Figure 8.1 illustrates how the revised Room Schedule application will work. In the case shown, there are seven location objects managed by two room servers. Reservations for rooms in locations 44L, 44M, and 44U are managed by Room Server 1 directly using the native room manager implementation. Reservations for rooms in locations 43L and 43U are managed by Room Server 2, also using the native room manager implementation. Finally, room reservations for locations 01L and 01U are handled by the legacy room scheduler. Room Server 1 interfaces with the legacy room scheduler, using the legacy manager implementation, to make reservations for rooms in locations 01L and 01U.

The Room Client makes remote calls for the operations in the `room` interface to Room Server 1 and 2. The Room Client is unaware of the existence of the legacy scheduler. To reserve a room in locations 01L and 01U, the client calls Room Server 1. Room Server 1 then takes care of converting the reservation into an appropriate command to the legacy scheduler.

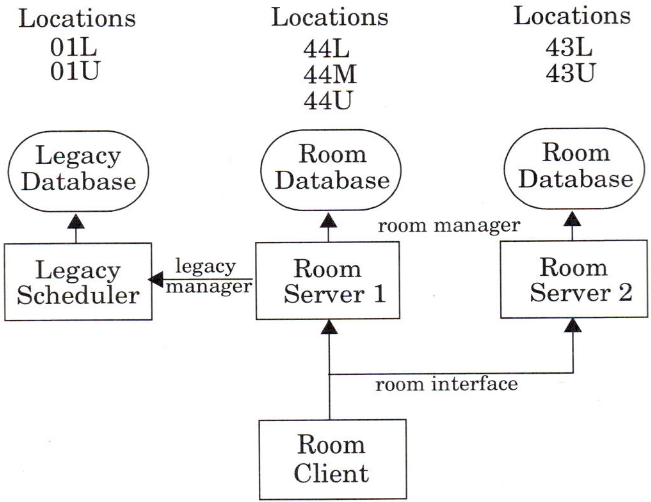

Figure 8.1
The Room Schedule application with multiple servers and a legacy interface

8.1 Server Object Setup

This section details the setup calls needed in **room_server** to provide the location objects and their managers and to allow multiple servers to be active.

Security Modifications

There are no security modifications needed for the location objects. The same security setup code discussed in Chapter 6 can be used for the new server. However, each server needs a unique principal and keytab file.

Server Principal

The original server principal was `room-server`. Now, each server will use the principal `room-server.`*HOST_NAME*, where *HOST_NAME* is the name of the host on which the server will execute. All of the server principals will be members of a security group room-server-group. This group will be used by the client to verify that a target server is legitimate.

Server Keytab File

The original keytab file was room_keyfile. Each server will now use room_keyfile.HOST_NAME. A distinct principal and keytab file allows each server to manage its keys independently.

Code Sample 8.1 shows a script to create the room server group. This script is executed once for the entire cell. Code Sample 8.2 shows a script to create a room server principal and keytab file. This is executed once for each server on the server's host. Both of these scripts must be executed by a user (like cell_admin) with sufficient DCE administrative privileges. The rgy_create_host.ksh also requires the administrator's password to create the server's account.

```
echo "Creating room-server-group"
echo "
domain group
add room-server-group
quit" | rgy_edit
```

Code Sample 8.1
schedule/obj/rgy_create.ksh: Create the room group

```
ADMIN_PW=$1
if [[ -z $ADMIN_PW ]]
then
   echo "Expected your administrator's password in arg 1"
   exit
fi
S_HOST=`hostname`
echo \
 "Creating room-server.$S_HOST and room_keyfile.$S_HOST"
echo "
domain principal
add room-server.$S_HOST
domain account
add room-server.$S_HOST -g room-server-group -o none \
  -mp $ADMIN_PW -pw -dce-
ktadd -p room-server.$S_HOST -pw -dce- \
  -f room_keyfile.$S_HOST
ktadd -p room-server.$S_HOST -a -r \
  -f room_keyfile.$S_HOST
quit" | rgy_edit
```

Code Sample 8.2
schedule/obj/rgy_create_host.ksh: Create a server principal and keytab file

Registering Object Types and Managers

Each object managed by a server will have an object type, and the object types will determine the manager implementation used for the object. Objects and object types are identified using UUIDs.

Object Types

The **room_server** defines two object types, one for locations managed by the room server itself (the native locations) and one for locations managed by the legacy schedule application. Each location record in the room database will include a UUID for the location and an indication of the object type. These will be stored in the in-memory data structure built when the **room_server** reads its room database. (This means that legacy locations must have records in the room database to indicate their object types.) Code Sample 8.3 shows the hard-coded UUID strings used for each object type.

```
uuid_t native_obj_type_uuid =
  {0x2a6e0418, 0xbfbb, 0x11ce, 0xb7, 0x7b, 0x08, 0x00,
   0x09, 0x48, 0xfb, 0xd9};
uuid_t legacy_obj_type_uuid =
  {0x76f05606, 0xbfbb, 0x11ce, 0xa6, 0x8d, 0x08, 0x00,
   0x09, 0x48, 0xfb, 0xd9};
```

Code Sample 8.3
`schedule/obj/room_server.c main()`: Object type UUIDs

Manager Entry Point Vectors

A manager can be thought of as a set of routines that implement the operations of an interface. Each manager has an entry point vector (EPV) that lists its implementation routines. The EPVs use a type defined in the interface header file generated by the IDL compiler from the interface definition. For version `1.0` of the `room` interface, this type is `room_v1_0_epv_t`. Code Samples 8.4 and 8.5 show the definition of the EPVs for the room and the legacy implementations.

```
room_v1_0_epv_t native_mgr_epv =
{
    room_description,
    room_reserve,
    room_cancel,
    room_avail,
    room_events,
};
```

Code Sample 8.4
`schedule/obj/room_mgr.c`: Native room manager EPV

```
room_v1_0_epv_t legacy_mgr_epv =
{
    legacy_description,
    legacy_reserve,
    legacy_cancel,
    legacy_avail,
    legacy_events,
};
```

Code Sample 8.5
`schedule/obj/legacy_mgr.c`: Legacy room manager EPV

Registration

The server must register each object type with the manager that will be used for objects of that type. The `rpc_server_register_if()` call includes input parameters for the object type UUID and the manager EPV. Previously, these parameters were `NULL`, indicating a default object type and manager. There is an `rpc_server_register_if()` call for *each* object type/manager pair that the server supports. Code Sample 8.6 shows two such calls for the room and legacy object types and managers.

```
    rpc_server_register_if(
        room_v1_0_s_ifspec,
        &native_obj_type_uuid,
        (rpc_mgr_epv_t) &room_mgr_epv,
        &status);
    CHECK_DCE(status,
        "Cannot register room manager with RPC runtime");

    rpc_server_register_if(
        room_v1_0_s_ifspec,
        &legacy_obj_type_uuid,
        (rpc_mgr_epv_t) &legacy_mgr_epv,
        &status);
    CHECK_DCE(status,
        "Cannot register legacy manager with RPC runtime");
```

Code Sample 8.6
`schedule/obj/room_server.c main()`: Registering object types and managers

Registering Objects

Each object that the server manages must be registered along with its object type. The `rpc_object_set_type()` call is used for this. It takes the object UUID and its associated object type UUID as input and enters them into a table maintained by the server's RPC Runtime.

In the **room_server**, the location object UUIDs (and their object types) are part of the room database and are read into the in-memory data structure by the `room_open()` function in `room_mgr.c`. This data structure is not visible in `room_server.c`, so we need an interface between the two modules to obtain the information we need to register the location objects. For this purpose, `room_mgr.c` provides two functions, `room_loc_begin()` and `room_loc_next()`. As you have probably guessed from their names, these functions use a cursor of sorts to step through the location records.

- `room_loc_begin()` initializes the cursor `loc_p` to point to the first location record.
- `room_loc_next()` returns information from the location record pointed to by `loc_p` and advances `loc_p` to the next record.

Code Sample 8.7 shows how the location objects are registered. Each location record provides the location name, its object UUID, and its object manager (type) UUID. The manager UUIDs must be either the room manager or the legacy manager UUID. This code fragment also counts the number of location objects, which will be useful later when an object UUID vector is allocated.

```
n_loc_obj = 0;
room_loc_begin(&loc_p);
while (loc_p != NULL)
{
    room_loc_next(&loc_p, &loc_name, &loc_obj_uuid_p,
        &loc_otype, &loc_admin);

    if (strcmp (loc_otype, "native") == 0)
    {
        loc_obj_type_uuid_p = &native_obj_type_uuid;
    }
    else if (strcmp(loc_otype, "legacy") == 0)
```

Code Sample 8.7
`schedule/obj/room_server.c main()`: Registering objects

```
        {
            loc_obj_type_uuid_p = &legacy_obj_type_uuid;
        }
        . . .
        rpc_object_set_type(loc_obj_uuid_p,
            loc_obj_type_uuid_p, &status);
        CHECK_DCE(status, "Cannot set object type");

        n_loc_obj++;
    }
```

Code Sample 8.7 (continued)

How the Object and Type UUIDs Are Used by RPC

Figure 8.2 illustrates how the server interface and object registration tables are used by the server's RPC Runtime when it processes an incoming remote call request. (In this discussion I will abbreviate the always cumbersome UUIDs. You will still get the idea.)

1. The server receives a request to execute the `room_cancel()` operation for a room in the `44L` location. The request packet contains the following:
   - the object UUID for the 44L location (`21689b0e...`)
   - the `room` interface UUID (`6101efd0...`) and version (`1.0`)
   - the operation number (`2`) for the `room_cancel()` operation
2. The RPC Runtime looks up the request's object UUID in the object registration table to obtain the object type UUID (`2a6e0418...`) associated with the 44L location.
3. The Runtime looks up the request's interface UUID and version, and the object type UUID, in the server interface registration table to obtain a pointer to the room manager entry point vector to be used for this call.
4. The Runtime looks up operation `2` in the room manager entry point vector and invokes the `room_cancel()` manager routine to execute the operation.

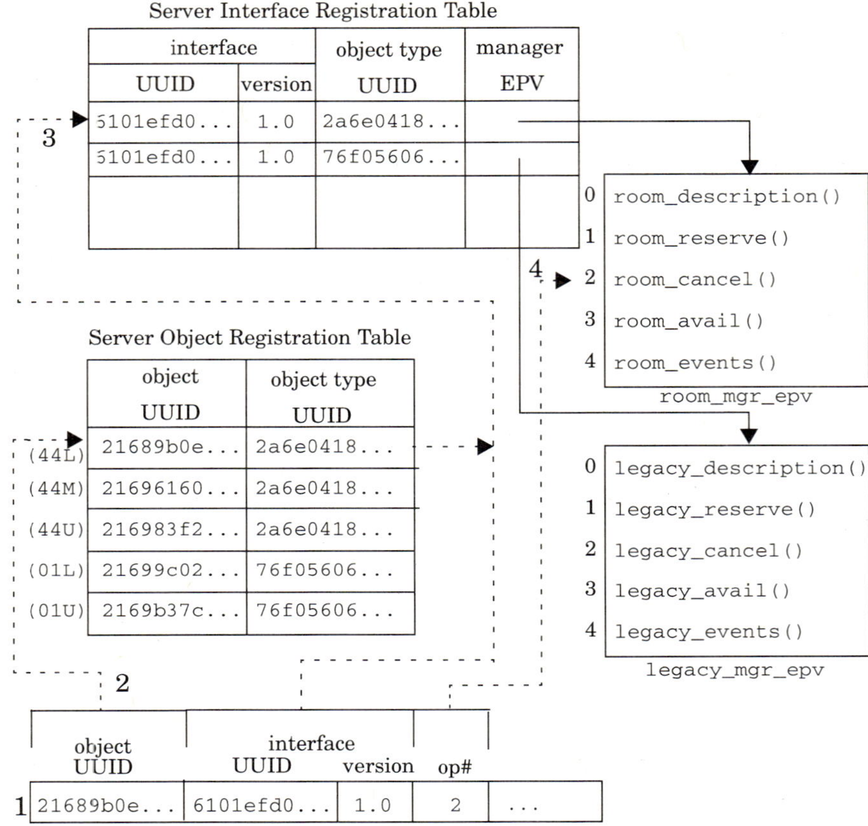

Figure 8.2
Server Interface and Object Registrations Table and Lookup

Registering Objects with the Endpoint Map and CDS

Objects managed by a server must also be registered with the interface and the server's bindings in the local host Endpoint Map and in one or more RPC Name Space entries in CDS.

Object Vector

Both the registration with the Endpoint Map and with the RPC Name Space will require a vector of object UUIDs, one UUID for each object managed by the server. The allocation and initialization of the UUID vector is up to the application. Code Sample 8.8 shows the code to do this for the **room_server**. It uses the `room_loc_begin()` and `room_loc_next()` routines to get the object UUIDs. It also uses the count of objects computed in Code Sample 8.7.

```
uuid_vector_t          *loc_obj_vector;
. . .
loc_obj_vector = (uuid_vector_t *)
  malloc(sizeof(uuid_vector_t) +
     n_loc_obj * sizeof(uuid_p_t));
loc_obj_vector->count = n_loc_obj;
i = 0;
room_loc_begin(&loc_p);
while (loc_p != NULL)
{
   room_loc_next(&loc_p, &loc_name, &loc_obj_uuid_p,
     &loc_otype, &loc_admin);
   loc_obj_vector->uuid[i] = loc_obj_uuid;
   i++;
}
```

Code Sample 8.8
`schedule/obj/room_server.c main()`: Constructing the object UUID vector

Registering with the Endpoint Map

The `rpc_ep_register()` call has an input parameter for an object UUID vector. In previous use of this call, that parameter was `NULL` to indicate no objects were to be registered. Now we will use the object vector constructed in Code Sample 8.8. Code Sample 8.9 shows the registration of the objects with the Endpoint Map.

```
rpc_ep_register(
    room_v1_0_s_ifspec,
    binding_vector,
    loc_obj_vector,
    (unsigned_char_p_t) "Room Server",
    &status);
CHECK_DCE(status,
  "Cannot register with Endpoint Map");
```

Code Sample 8.9
`schedule/obj/room_server.c main()`: Registering objects with the Endpoint Map

The `rpc_ep_register()` call results in one Endpoint Map entry for each object in the object vector and each binding in the binding vector. If there are five objects in the object vector and two bindings in the binding vector, there will be ten entries added to the Endpoint Map. Each entry will have the same annotation—in this case, `Room Server`. Output Samples 8.1 and 8.2 show some of the entries for **`room_server`**.

```
:rpccp show mapping -i 6101efd0-89fc-11cd-be27-080009307c01,1.0

mappings:

  <object>           21689b0e-c6bd-11ce-b35f-08000948fbd9
  <interface id>     6101efd0-89fc-11cd-be27-080009307c01,1.0
  <string binding>   ncadg_ip_udp:15.4.25.126[2657]
  <annotation>       Room Server

  <object>           21696160-c6bd-11ce-b35f-08000948fbd9
  <interface id>     6101efd0-89fc-11cd-be27-080009307c01,1.0
  <string binding>   ncadg_ip_udp:15.4.25.126[2657]
  <annotation>       Room Server
   . . .
  <object>           21689b0e-c6bd-11ce-b35f-08000948fbd9
  <interface id>     6101efd0-89fc-11cd-be27-080009307c01,1.0
  <string binding>   ncacn_ip_tcp:15.4.25.126[1916]
  <annotation>       Room Server

  <object>           21696160-c6bd-11ce-b35f-08000948fbd9
  <interface id>     6101efd0-89fc-11cd-be27-080009307c01,1.0
  <string binding>   ncacn_ip_tcp:15.4.25.126[1916]
  <annotation>       Room Server
```

Output Sample 8.1
rpccp output: Viewing Endpoint Map entries for objects

```
:dcecp -c endpoint show -interface \
   6101efd0-89fc-11cd-be27-080009307c01,1.0

{{object 21689b0e-c6bd-11ce-b35f-08000948fbd9}
 {interface {6101efd0-89fc-11cd-be27-080009307c01 1.0}}
 {binding {ncadg_ip_udp 15.4.25.126 2657}}
 {annotation {Room Server}}}

{{object 21696160-c6bd-11ce-b35f-08000948fbd9}
 {interface {6101efd0-89fc-11cd-be27-080009307c01 1.0}}
 {binding {ncadg_ip_udp 15.4.25.126 2657}}
 {annotation {Room Server}}}
. . .
{{object 21689b0e-c6bd-11ce-b35f-08000948fbd9}
 {interface {6101efd0-89fc-11cd-be27-080009307c01 1.0}}
 {binding {ncacn_ip_tcp 15.4.25.126 1916}}
 {annotation {Room Server}}}

{{object 21696160-c6bd-11ce-b35f-08000948fbd9}
 {interface {6101efd0-89fc-11cd-be27-080009307c01 1.0}}
 {binding {ncacn_ip_tcp 15.4.25.126 1916}}
 {annotation {Room Server}}}
```

Output Sample 8.2
dcecp output: Viewing Endpoint Map entries for objects

The object UUIDs are used in the resolution of endpoints for partially bound RPC requests. When **rpcd** or **dced** receives a dg RPC request to be forwarded or a resolution request for a cn RPC request, it will look up the request's object UUID and interface UUID and version in the Endpoint Map to find the endpoint to be used.

Two servers using different object UUIDs for the same interface can execute concurrently on the same host. Each server will have its own entries in the host's Endpoint Map, distinguished by object UUID and with different endpoints.

Exporting Objects to the NS Server Entry

Like rpc_ep_register(), the rpc_ns_binding_export() call has an input parameter for an object UUID vector. In previous use of this call, that parameter was NULL to indicate no objects were to be registered with the Name Space server entry. Now we will use the object vector constructed in Code Sample 8.8. Code Sample 8.10 shows the export of the objects managed by the server to a Name Space entry of the form /.:/subsys/sch/room_server.*HOSTNAME*, where *HOSTNAME* is the name of the server's host.

```
ns_server_entry  = make_name(
   "/.:/subsys/sch/room_server.", hostname);
. . .
rpc_ns_binding_export(
    rpc_c_ns_syntax_default,
    ns_server_entry,
    room_v1_0_s_ifspec,
    binding_vector,
    loc_obj_vector,
    &status);
CHECK_DCE(status,
   "Cannot export binding to room server entry");
```

Code Sample 8.10
schedule/obj/room_server.c main(): Exporting objects to the server entry in CDS

Output Samples 8.3 and 8.4 show the results of the rpc_ns_binding_export() for a **room_server** running on the host hpiala3 that manages five location objects. Output Samples 8.5 and 8.6 show the results for a second server on the host hpialb2 that manages two location objects

```
:rpccp show entry /.:/subsys/sch/room_server.hpiala3

objects:

  21689b0e-c6bd-11ce-b35f-08000948fbd9
  21696160-c6bd-11ce-b35f-08000948fbd9
  216983f2-c6bd-11ce-b35f-08000948fbd9
  21699c02-c6bd-11ce-b35f-08000948fbd9
  2169b37c-c6bd-11ce-b35f-08000948fbd9

binding information:

  <interface id>   6101efd0-89fc-11cd-be27-080009307c01,1.0
  <string binding> ncadg_ip_udp:15.4.25.126[]
  <string binding> ncacn_ip_tcp:15.4.25.126[]
```

Output Sample 8.3
rpccp output: Viewing the room server entry for host hpiala3

```
:dcecp -c rpcentry show /.:/subsys/sch/room_server.hpiala3
{6101efd0-89fc-11cd-be27-080009307c01 1.0
 {ncadg_ip_udp 15.4.25.126}
 {ncacn_ip_tcp 15.4.25.126}}
{21689b0e-c6bd-11ce-b35f-08000948fbd9
  21696160-c6bd-11ce-b35f-08000948fbd9
  216983f2-c6bd-11ce-b35f-08000948fbd9
  21699c02-c6bd-11ce-b35f-08000948fbd9
  2169b37c-c6bd-11ce-b35f-08000948fbd9}
```

Output Sample 8.4
dcecp output: Viewing the room server entry for host hpiala3

```
:rpccp show entry /.:/subsys/sch/room_server.hpialb2

objects:

  c8f5db8c-c6d3-11ce-b79f-080009421b3c
  c8f6be44-c6d3-11ce-b79f-080009421b3c

binding information:

  <interface id>   6101efd0-89fc-11cd-be27-080009307c01,1.0
  <string binding> ncadg_ip_udp:15.4.24.89[]
  <string binding> ncacn_ip_tcp:15.4.24.89[]
```

Output Sample 8.5
rpccp output: Viewing the room server entry for host hpialb2

```
:dcecp -c rpcentry show /.:/subsys/sch/room_server.hpialb2
{6101efd0-89fc-11cd-be27-080009307c01 1.0
 {ncadg_ip_udp 15.4.24.89}
 {ncacn_ip_tcp 15.4.24.89}}
{c8f5db8c-c6d3-11ce-b79f-080009421b3c
  c8f6be44-c6d3-11ce-b79f-080009421b3c}
```

Output Sample 8.6
dcecp output: viewing the room server entry for host hpialb2

Adding the NS Server Entry to an NS Group Entry

The **room_server** has already added its server entry name to the Name Space group /.:/subsys/sch/room_group. Previously there was only one server entry in the group at a time. Now, there can be more than one server running at a time, so the group may contain more than one server entry name. Output Samples 8.7 and 8.8 show the group with servers running on hosts hpiala3 and hpialb2.

```
:rpccp show group /.:/subsys/sch/room_group

group members:

  /.../jaja/subsys/sch/room_server.hpiala3
  /.../jaja/subsys/sch/room_server.hpialb2
```

Output Sample 8.7
rpccp output: Viewing the room group entry

```
:dcecp -c rpcgroup list /.:/subsys/sch/room_group
/.../jaja/subsys/sch/room_server.hpiala3
/.../jaja/subsys/sch/room_server.hpialb2
```

Output Sample 8.8
dcecp output: Viewing the room group entry

Adding the NS Server Entry to an NS Profile Entry

The **room_server** also adds its server entry to the cell profile entry, /.:/cell-profile. Now, with more than one server executing, there can be more than one profile element for the room interface in the cell profile. Output Samples 8.9 and 8.10 show elements for the servers on hpiala3 and hpialb2. Since each element is at the same priority, a client using the cell profile has an equal probability of binding to either server.

```
:rpccp show profile /.:/cell-profile

profile elements:
. . .

  <interface id>    6101efd0-89fc-11cd-be27-080009307c01,1.0
  <member_name>     /.../jaja/subsys/sch/room_server.hpiala3
  <priority>        0
  <annotation>      Room Server

  <interface id>    6101efd0-89fc-11cd-be27-080009307c01,1.0
  <member_name>     /.../jaja/subsys/sch/room_server.hpialb2
  <priority>        0
  <annotation>      Room Server
```

Output Sample 8.9
rpccp output: Viewing the room elements in the cell profile.

```
:dcecp -c rpcprofile show /.:/cell-profile

{{6101efd0-89fc-11cd-be27-080009307c01 1.0} /.../jaja/subsys/sch/room_
server.hpiala3 0 {Room Server}}
{{6101efd0-89fc-11cd-be27-080009307c01 1.0} /.../jaja/subsys/sch/room_
server.hpialb2 0 {Room Server}}
```

Output Sample 8.10
rcpcp output: Viewing the room elements in the cell profile.

Exporting Objects to Location Entries in the Name Space

As we will soon see, the **room** client will need to be able to find the correct server for a location object, given a location name like 44L. The client does not know the UUID for the location object, so it cannot search the room_server.*HOST_NAME* entries to find the right server. To solve this problem, the **room_server** will also set up a Name Space server entry for each location object. These entries have the form /.:/subsys/sch/room/*LOCATION*, where *LOCATION* is the location name. An example is /.:/subsys/sch/room/44L.

Code Sample 8.11 shows how the location entry is set up. Again, we use the room_loc_begin() and room_loc_next() routines to retrieve the location information from the in-memory room database. For each location, we set up an object UUID vector with only the one location object UUID. (Note that because uuid_vector_t is defined with an array of one UUID, we can declare one_loc_obj_vector directly and we don't have to dynamically allocate it.) Then we call rpc_ns_binding_export() with the location entry name, the object vector, room interface specification, and the server's binding vector.

Output Samples 8.11 and 8.12 show the location object entry for the 44L location. It indicates that the server for this location is at the IP address 15.4.25.126. Comparing this to the server entries displayed in Output Samples 8.3 and 8.4, we see that this is the server on host hpiala3.

```
:dcecp -c rpcentry show /.:/subsys/sch/room/44L
{6101efd0-89fc-11cd-be27-080009307c01 1.0
 {ncadg_ip_udp 15.4.25.126}
 {ncacn_ip_tcp 15.4.25.126}}
{21689b0e-c6bd-11ce-b35f-08000948fbd9}
```

Output Sample 8.11
dcecp output: Viewing a location object NS entry.

```
    room_loc_begin(&loc_p);
    while (loc_p != NULL)
    {
       unsigned_char_p_t loc_ns_server_entry;
       uuid_vector_t     one_loc_obj_vector;

       room_loc_next(&loc_p, &loc_name, &loc_obj_uuid_p,
         &loc_otype, &loc_admin);
       one_loc_obj_vector.count    = 1;
       one_loc_obj_vector.uuid[0] = loc_obj_uuid;
       loc_ns_server_entry =make_name(
         "/.:/subsys/sch/room/", (char *)loc_name);

       rpc_ns_binding_export(
          rpc_c_ns_syntax_default,
          loc_ns_server_entry,
          room_v1_0_s_ifspec,
          binding_vector,
          &one_loc_obj_vector,
          &status);
       CHECK_DCE(status,
         "Cannot export binding to location entry");
       free(loc_ns_server_entry);
    }
```

Code Sample 8.11
`schedule/obj/room_server.c main()`: Exporting objects to location entries in CDS

```
:rpccp show entry /.:/subsys/sch/room/44L

objects:

  21689b0e-c6bd-11ce-b35f-08000948fbd9

binding information:

  <interface id>   6101efd0-89fc-11cd-be27-080009307c01,1.0
  <string binding> ncadg_ip_udp:15.4.25.126[]
  <string binding> ncacn_ip_tcp:15.4.25.126[]
```

Output Sample 8.12
rpccp output: Viewing a location object NS entry.

Creating CDS Entries and Their ACLs

There are two scripts used to create the various CDS entries used by the `obj` version of the room application. The first script, shown in Code Sample 8.13, creates the directories and the room group and is executed once for the entire cell. The second script, shown in Code Sample 8.14, is executed on each server host system. It creates the `room_server` entry for the host and the location entries for the locations managed on this host. It also sets up ACLs on the various CDS entries to allow the principal used by the server on the host to write to the CDS entries.

```
cdscp create dir /.:/subsys/sch
cdscp create obj /.:/subsys/sch/room_group
cdscp create dir /.:/subsys/sch/room
```

Code Sample 8.12
`schedule/obj/cds_create.ksh`: Create the `room_group` and sch and `room` directories

```
S_HOST=`hostname`
cdscp create obj /.:/subsys/sch/room_server.$S_HOST
for LOC in "$@"
do
   cdscp create obj /.:/subsys/sch/room/$LOC
done
acl_edit -e /.:/subsys/sch/room_server.$S_HOST \
  -m user:room-server.$S_HOST:rwt
acl_edit -e /.:/subsys/sch/room_group \
  -m user:room-server.$S_HOST:rwt
acl_edit -e /.:/subsys/sch/room \
  -m user:room-server.$S_HOST:rwt
for LOC in "$@"
do
   acl_edit -e /.:/subsys/sch/room/$LOC \
     -m user:room-server.$S_HOST:rwt
done
acl_edit -e /.:/cell-profile \
  -m user:room-server.$S_HOST:rwt
```

Code Sample 8.13
`schedule/obj/cds_create_host.ksh`: Create the `room_server` and location entries

Server Cleanup with Objects

Cleanup of the server's NS entries and Endpoint Map entries and unregistration of the server's interfaces are affected by objects. In general, if an object UUID or an object UUID vector was used when the entry was set up, it must be included when the entry is cleaned up. Code Sample 8.15 shows the cleanup code in the `obj` version of **`room_server`**.

It is possible to remove one or more objects from a Name Space entry or the Endpoint Map while leaving the remaining objects in place. The object vectors used in the `rpc_ns_binding_unexport()` or `rpc_ep_unregister()` would include only the object UUIDs to be removed.

```
    rpc_ns_binding_unexport(
       rpc_c_ns_syntax_default,
       (unsigned_char_p_t) ns_server_entry,
       room_v1_0_s_ifspec,
       loc_obj_vector,
       &status);
    CHECK_DCE_NONFATAL(status,
      "Cannot unexport binding from server entry");

    room_loc_begin(&loc_p);
    while (loc_p != NULL)
    {
       unsigned_char_p_t loc_ns_server_entry;
       uuid_vector_t     one_loc_obj_vector;

       room_loc_next(&loc_p, &loc_name, &loc_obj_uuid_p,
         &loc_otype, &loc_admin);
       one_loc_obj_vector.count    = 1;
       one_loc_obj_vector.uuid[0] = loc_obj_uuid;
       loc_ns_server_entry = make_name(
         "/.:/subsys/sch/room/", (char *)loc_name);
```

Code Sample 8.14
`schedule/obj/room_server.c main()`: Object cleanup

```
    rpc_ns_binding_unexport(
        rpc_c_ns_syntax_default,
        (unsigned_char_p_t) loc_ns_server_entry,
        room_v1_0_s_ifspec,
        &one_loc_obj_vector,
        &status);
     CHECK_DCE_NONFATAL(status,
       "Cannot unexport binding from location entry");
     free(loc_ns_server_entry);
  }

  rpc_ep_unregister(
     room_v1_0_s_ifspec,
     binding_vector,
     loc_obj_vector,
     &status);
  CHECK_DCE_NONFATAL(status,
    "Cannot unregister with Endpoint Map");

  rpc_server_unregister_if(room_v1_0_s_ifspec,
    &room_mgr_uuid, &status);
  CHECK_DCE_NONFATAL(status,
    "Cannot unregister room manager");

  rpc_server_unregister_if(room_v1_0_s_ifspec,
    &legacy_mgr_uuid, &status);
  CHECK_DCE(status,
    "Cannot unregister legacy manager");
```

Code Sample 8.14 (continued)

8.2 Client Object Use

The **room** client can now be modified to use three ways to bind to a server:

- Use a room location name and the corresponding location entry in the Name Space.
- Use a default server specified by the `RPC_DEFAULT_ENTRY` environment variable, or the cell profile.
- Use the server entries listed in the room server group entry.

Binding to a Server

Since the **room** client now has more than one way to bind to a server, it will be useful to have a general routine for binding to a server. The `bind_to_server()`

procedure, shown in Code Sample 8.16, will return a binding handle for a server indicated by an RPC Name Space entry. The `rpc_ns_binding_import_begin()` call includes an input parameter for an object UUID. When an object UUID is specified, `rpc_ns_binding_import_next()` will return a binding handle that indicates that object. Only NS server entries that include that object will be imported.

However, as mentioned earlier, the **room** client does not know the UUIDs for location objects. So we will continue to specify `NULL` for the object UUID in the `rpc_ns_binding_import_begin()`. Then we will get a binding handle with a default object. The default object will depend on the type of NS entry used in the binding.

Recall that the `rpc_ns_mgmt_handle_set_exp_age()` call will cause CDS to bypass its local cache to get the most up-to-date version of the NS entry information. If the bindings in the NS entry change, this ensures that the **room** client will get the correct bindings, at a cost to performance for multiple accesses to the same entry.

The `CHECK_DCE_RETURN` macro checks the status returned by a DCE call and displays an error message if the call was not successful. But unlike the `CHECK_DCE` macro, `CHECK_DCE_RETURN` will return instead of aborting the program. This allows the **room** client to use active **room_servers** if even other **room_servers** are not available.

```
#define CHECK_DCE_RETURN(status, msg) \
   CHECK_DCE_NONFATAL(status, msg); \
   if (status != error_status_ok) \
   { \
      return(NULL); \
   }

rpc_binding_handle_t bind_to_server(
   unsigned_char_p_t ns_entry_name)
{
   rpc_binding_handle_t      h;
   rpc_ns_handle_t           import_context;
   . . .
   unsigned32                status, ignored_st;

   rpc_ns_binding_import_begin(
      rpc_c_ns_syntax_default,
      ns_entry_name,
      room_v1_0_c_ifspec,
      NULL,                 /* default object */
      &import_context,
      &status);
```

Code Sample 8.15

`schedule/obj/room.c: bind_to_server()` importing a binding from a CDS entry

```
    CHECK_DCE_RETURN(status,
      "Cannot begin binding import");

    rpc_ns_mgmt_handle_set_exp_age(import_context, 0,
      &status);
    CHECK_DCE_RETURN(status,
      "Cannot set expiration for import.");

    rpc_ns_binding_import_next(import_context, &h, &status);
    if (status == rpc_s_no_more_bindings)
    {
       printf("Server is not available\n");
       return(NULL);
    }
    CHECK_DCE_RETURN(status,
      "Cannot import next binding");

    rpc_ns_binding_import_done(&import_context, &status);
    CHECK_DCE_RETURN(status,
      "Cannot complete binding import");

    if (!is_server_there(h, room_v1_0_c_ifspec))
    {
       printf("Server is not responding\n");
       return(NULL);
    }
    . . .
    return(h);
}
```

Code Sample 8.15 (continued)

Setting Up Security for the Binding

The binding handle returned by `bind_to_server()` must have the authentication and protection level expected by the **room_server**. The binding security is set by the `rpc_binding_set_auth_info()` call, as described in Section 6.5. In the case where there was only one **room_server**, the server principal name in this call was hard-coded to be `/.:/room-server`. Now that there is more than one server, and each server has its own principal name, we can no longer use a fixed server principal name in the `rpc_binding_set_auth_info()` call. Instead, we can find out what principal the target server is using by calling `rpc_mgmt_inq_server_princ_name()` as shown in Code Sample 8.17.

Now there is another problem to solve. When the client used a hard-coded principal name which we created and controlled, we could be assured that when the **room** client mutually authenticated with its server, it was indeed the legitimate **room_server**. Now, the **room** client cannot know a priori by the principal used by a target server whether that server is legitimate. The room client can inspect the server's principal to confirm that it is in the form `room_server.`*HOST_NAME*. But it cannot know whether the principal was created for this application or whether it was created and used by an impostor.

The solution to this problem is to use a security group to verify the legitimacy of the target server. Each legitimate **room_server** principal will be a member of `room-server-group`. This group is created and controlled by us, so an impostor cannot add another principal to the group. The **room** client can then check if the target server's principal is a member of `room-server-group`, using `sec_rgy_pgo_is_member()`. Unfortunately, it takes a page of code to make this call. First, we must extract the cell name and principal name from the full server principal by calling `sec_id_parse_name()`. Then we have to bind to the DCE Security Registry server in the server principal's cell. The `sec_rgy_site_bind()` call takes as input the cell name and RPC authentication information to be used in setting up the binding. Finally, we can call `sec_rgy_pgo_is_member()`, which will return `true` if the server principal is in the `room-server-group`.

```
rpc_binding_handle_t bind_to_server(
   unsigned_char_p_t ns_entry_name)
{
   rpc_binding_handle_t       h;
   . . .
   unsigned_char_p_t          server_principal;
   sec_rgy_name_t             cell_name;
   sec_rgy_name_t             principal_name;
   sec_rgy_name_t             group_name;
   sec_rgy_handle_t           rgy_h;
   sec_rgy_bind_auth_info_t auth_info;
   unsigned32                 status, ignored_st;
   . . .
   /* Set up binding h. */

   rpc_mgmt_inq_server_princ_name(
      h,
      rpc_c_authn_dce_secret,
```

Code Sample 8.16
`schedule/obj/room.c: bind_to_server()` setting security for the binding

```
        &server_principal,
        &status);
    CHECK_DCE_RETURN(status, "Cannot get server principal");
    sec_id_parse_name(
        sec_rgy_default_handle,
        server_principal,
        cell_name,
        NULL,
        principal_name,
        NULL,
        &status);
    CHECK_DCE_RETURN(status, "Cannot parse principal name");

    auth_info.info_type = sec_rgy_bind_auth_dce;
    auth_info.tagged_union.dce_info.authn_level =
      rpc_c_protect_level_pkt_integ;
    auth_info.tagged_union.dce_info.authn_svc   =
      rpc_c_authn_dce_secret;
    auth_info.tagged_union.dce_info.authz_svc   =
      rpc_c_authz_dce;
    auth_info.tagged_union.dce_info.identity    = NULL;

    sec_rgy_site_bind(
        (unsigned_char_t *) cell_name,
        &auth_info,
        &rgy_h,
        &status);
    CHECK_DCE_RETURN(status, "Cannot bind to registry");

    strcpy((char *) group_name, "room-server-group");
    if (!sec_rgy_pgo_is_member(
            rgy_h,
            sec_rgy_domain_group,
```

Code Sample 8.16 (continued)

```
            group_name,
            principal_name,
            &status))
    {
       printf("Server is not a member of the group\n");
       return(NULL);
    }
    sec_rgy_site_close(rgy_h, &status);
    CHECK_DCE(status, "Cannot close security registry");
    rpc_binding_set_auth_info(
       h,
       server_principal,
       rpc_c_protect_level_pkt_integ,
       rpc_c_authn_dce_secret,
       NULL,
       rpc_c_authz_name,
       &status);
    CHECK_DCE_RETURN(status,
      "Cannot set up authentication for binding");

    rpc_string_free(&server_principal, &ignored_st);
    return(h);
}
```

Code Sample 8.16 (continued)

Binding to a Location Object

The first kind of binding we will examine is binding by location. Most of the room commands require the room's location as input. The `bind_to_server_by_location()` routine, in Code Sample 8.19, returns a binding handle for the location object UUID and the **room_server** than manages that location. This routine constructs the location NS server entry `/.:/subsys/sch/room/`*LOCATION* and calls `bind_to_server()` with this entry to obtain the binding.

Location Cache

A user may execute several **room** commands for the same location, say, to check on room availability, to reserve a room, and to confirm the reservation. The **room** client should not reconstruct the binding for the same location for each command. Consequently, we will add a cache of locations that have been visited by the client and the binding handles that have been created for those locations. This cache will be a singly linked list of records, one for each location.

- `find_binding_by_location()` searches the linked list for a record that matches a specified location name. This routine is shown in Code Sample 8.18.
- `bind_to_server_by_location()` adds a new location and binding handle to the location cache. This routine is shown in Code Sample 8.19.
- The `GET_BINDING` macro calls `find_binding_by_location()` to find a binding in the location cache. If it isn't found, it calls `bind_to_server_by_location()` to create a new binding. This macro is shown in Code Sample 8.19.

```
typedef struct LOC_REC_T {
    struct LOC_REC_T *next;
    sch_loc_name_t       loc_name;
    rpc_binding_handle_t h;
} loc_rec_t;

loc_rec_t *location_list = NULL;

rpc_binding_handle_t find_binding_by_location(
    sch_loc_name_t loc_name)
{
    loc_rec_t *loc_p;

    for (loc_p = location_list; loc_p != NULL;
        loc_p = loc_p->next)
    {
        if (strcmp(loc_p->loc_name, loc_name) == 0)
        {
            return(loc_p->h);
        }
    }
    return(NULL);
}
```

Code Sample 8.17
`schedule/obj/room.c`: The location cache and `find_binding_by_location()`

```
rpc_binding_handle_t bind_to_server_by_location(...)
{
    rpc_binding_handle_t h;
    unsigned_char_p_t    loc_ns_server_name;
    loc_rec_t *loc_p;

    loc_ns_server_entry = make_name(
         "/.:/subsys/sch/room/", (char *)loc_name);

    h = bind_to_server((unsigned_char_p_t) ns_entry_name);
    free(ns_entry_name);

    if (h != NULL)
    {
       loc_p = (loc_rec_t *) malloc(sizeof(loc_rec_t));
       CHECK_MALLOC(loc_p);
       strcpy(loc_p->loc_name, loc_name);
       loc_p->h = h;
       loc_p->next    = location_list;
       location_list = loc_p;
    }

    return(h);
}

#define GET_BINDING(loc_name, h) \
    (h) = find_binding_by_location(loc_name); \
    if ((h) == NULL) \
    { \
       (h) = bind_to_server_by_location(loc_name); \
    } \
    if ((h) == NULL) \
    { \
       printf("Cannot bind to server\n"); \
       return; \
    }
```

Code Sample 8.18
`schedule/obj/room.c: bind_to_server_by_location()` and `GET_BINDING`

Use of Binding by Location

Code Sample 8.20 illustrates the use of binding by location in the execution of the r (reserve) command. The user enters a room location and the GET_BINDING macro returns a binding handle for the location. This might be a new binding or a previously cached binding. The binding handle is then used in the remote call room_reserve().

```
void reserve()
{
   rpc_binding_handle_t h;
   sch_room_t          room;
   . . .
   GET("Room location? ", room.loc);
   . . .
   GET_BINDING(room.loc, h);
   room_reserve(h, room, date_time, reserver, desc,
     &status, &call_status);
   . . .
}
```

Code Sample 8.19
schedule/obj/room.c: reserve() using binding by location

Binding to the Default Server

The room client will still bind to a server (the default server) when it is started, as shown in Code Sample 8.21. It uses either the value of the RPC_DEFAULT_ENTRY environment variable, or the cell profile.

```
rpc_binding_handle_t default_h;
. . .
ns_entry_name = getenv("RPC_DEFAULT_ENTRY");
if (ns_entry_name == NULL)
{
    ns_entry_name = (unsigned_char_p_t) "/.:/cell-profile";
}
default_h = bind_to_server(ns_entry_name);
```

Code Sample 8.20
schedule/obj/room.c main(): Binding to the default server

Using the Default Server

The d (description) command of the **room** client requires just the room name, not its location. (A principal use of this command is to discover a room's location.) So the client cannot use binding by location for this command. Instead, the client will initially try the default binding in the room_description() remote call, as shown in Code Sample 8.22. The theory is that a user will usually be interested in rooms in locations that are managed by the default server designated for the user.

```
room_description(default_h, room_name, &room,
   &sch_status, &call_status);
CHECK_CALL(call_status);
```

Code Sample 8.21
schedule/obj/room.c: description() using the default server binding

Binding Using the Group Entry

If the room in a description command is not in a location managed by the default server, the **room** client must search other **room_servers**. The NS entry room_server_group provides a list of the server entries that can be searched for the room. We will use a trio of DCE calls to obtain the members of the group:

- rpc_ns_group_mbr_inq_begin()
- rpc_ns_group_mbr_inq_next()
- rpc_ns_group_mbr_inq_done()

These use the now-familiar context cursor technique for retrieving items from a collection of data. The context is the same type as used for importing bindings, and rpc_ns_mgmt_handle_set_exp_age() can be used with the context to ensure that the most up-to-date data is retrieved from the group entry. Each server entry member is used to create a binding handle and each binding is used in a room_description() remote call, until the room is found or all of the members have been tried. The **room** client does not cache these bindings. Also, no attempt is made to determine which server is the default server, so the default server is tried a second time. Code Sample 8.23 shows the use of the group entry.

```
void description()
{
   . . .
   rpc_ns_handle_t      mbr_inq_context;
   unsigned_char_p_t    ns_entry_name;
   rpc_binding_handle_t h;
   unsigned32           status;
   sch_status_t         sch_status;
   error_status_t       call_status;
   . . .
   room_description(default_h, ...);
   if (sch_status == sch_status_room_not_found)
   {
      rpc_ns_group_mbr_inq_begin(
         rpc_c_ns_syntax_default,
         (unsigned_char_p_t) "/.:/subsys/sch/room_group",
         rpc_c_ns_syntax_default,
         &mbr_inq_context,
         &status);
      CHECK_DCE(status,
        "Cannot begin getting group members");

      rpc_ns_mgmt_handle_set_exp_age(mbr_inq_context, 0,
        &status);
      CHECK_DCE(status, "Cannot set expiration for import.");

      while (sch_status == sch_status_room_not_found)
      {
         rpc_ns_group_mbr_inq_next(mbr_inq_context,
           &ns_entry_name, &status);
         if (status == rpc_s_no_more_members)
         {
            break;
         }
         CHECK_DCE(status, "Cannot get next group member");
```

Code Sample 8.22

`schedule/obj/room.c: description()` binding using the group entry

```
            h = bind_to_server(ns_entry_name);
            room_description(h, room_name, &room, &sch_status,
              &call_status);
            CHECK_CALL(call_status);
        }

        rpc_ns_group_mbr_inq_done(&mbr_inq_context, &status);
        CHECK_DCE(status, "Cannot end getting group member");

        rpc_binding_free(&h, &status);
        CHECK_DCE(status, "Cannot free server binding");
    }
    . . .
}
```

Code Sample 8.22 (continued)

You may be wondering why we did not use the `rpc_ns_binding_ import()`, `_next()`, and `_done()` calls with the NS group entry. If we had done that, we may have gotten more than one binding for each server (say, for the `ncadg_ip_udp` and `ncacn_ip_tcp` protocol sequences). Then we would have had to either redundantly query the servers using more than one binding or add additional logic to determine when a binding was redundant and shouldn't be used.

CHAPTER 9

Access Control

Chapter 6 on security devoted many pages to how a client authenticates itself to a server. In this chapter, we will see how the server uses the client's identity to decide what operations can be performed on behalf of the client. This subject of *authorization* or *access control* was touched upon in Section 6.1. DCE provides Access Control Lists (ACLs) for the purpose of access control. Prior to DCE 1.1, much of the work of managing and using ACLs was left as an exercise for the application developer. DCE 1.1 introduces an ACL library that hides most of the ACL management from the application. We will use this ACL library here. But first, let's take a look at the purpose of access control and how it is implemented using DCE ACLs.

9.1 Access Control Policies

Each system or application component has policies for controlling access to objects within that component. Users of Unix (and other modern operating systems) are well aware of the access control policies enforced by the file system. Objects in the file system—files, directories, and devices—are protected by *permissions* that specify who can do what to the object. For example, a file with the permissions `666 (rw-rw-rw)` can be read and written by any user, while a file with permissions `600 (rw-------)` can be read and written only by the user that owns the file. The security of the file system is determined by the local system login authentication and the file access control.

We will look at two examples of access control policies using the DCE: the Cell Directory Service, and our `room` sample application.

CDS Access Control

Each CDS object has an ACL which determines who can read, modify, or delete the object. We have already seen some of these ACLs in Chapter 5. Each ACL entry specifies the access rights for a DCE principal (or group of principals). The access rights are expressed by standard permissions such as read (`r`), write (`w`), control (`c`), and test (`t`).

CDS access control affects how clients and servers use the RPC Name Space. The principal used by a server must have write access to the server, group, and profile entries it uses to export its bindings. A client principal must have read access to one of those entries to import the binding from the Name Space. The CDS access control, along with DCE principal authentication, prevents unauthorized servers from exporting their bindings into other servers' entries, and clients from importing bindings for servers they are not authorized to use.

The CDS makes use of the container and object ACL types, which will be discussed in more detail in Section 9.3. Each CDS directory is a container, and when an object is created in a directory, it will inherit an initial ACL from its container directory. This feature automatically conveys protection onto newly created CDS objects.

CDS access control is implemented by the CDS Server. This means that the CDS Server incorporates the code necessary to manage and evaluate its ACLs. Also, the CDS Database provides permanent storage for these ACLs. (As of DCE 1.1, CDS uses the ACL library for these tasks.)

Room Application Access Control

Our `room` application provides an opportunity to see what an application must do to use the DCE ACL facility. We would like to control who can reserve and cancel reservations for rooms. There are three permissions needed:

- `Inquire` request information about a room and its reservations,
- `Reserve` make a reservation for a room, and
- `Cancel` cancel a reservation (without being the reserver).

We might want to give `Inquire` permission to everyone on the site, while restricting `Reserve` permission for a room to members of a particular group on the site. Only certain administrative personnel would have `Cancel` permission, with the power to override the reservations of others. Finally, we will want to prevent anyone from outside of the site (for example, hackers roaming the Internet) from being able to use the `room` service at all. The room access control should be flexible enough to allow modification of the permissions for individuals and groups as the needs and policies of the site change.

We will use ACLs to provide access control for the `room` service. Each room will have an ACL that will indicate who can inquire about, reserve, and cancel reservations for the room. To do this, the **room_server** will use the ACL library routines discussed in this chapter.

9.2 DCL ACL Entries

Each entry in a DCE ACL specifies the access rights for one or more principals, depending on the type of the entry. The general format of an ACL entry (for the **acl_edit** tool) is

type[:*key*]:*permissions*

where

type	specifies the type of the ACL entry,
key	identifies the principal or group for which the entry applies (some ACL types omit the key), and
permissions	provides the set of permissions allowed the principal(s) for which the entry applies.

In **dcecp**, the : are replaced by spaces: *type* [*key*] *permissions*.

There are internal and external forms of an ACL entry. The internal form uses UUIDs for principal, group, and cell identification, and a bit mask for the permissions set. The internal form is used for ACL storage and evaluation. The external form uses character strings for the type, principal, group, and cell names and permissions. The external form is suitable for use in commands and displays.

ACL Entry Types

There are a total of 20 types of ACLs defined by the DCE. These can be grouped into five categories based on their usage and format.

Object Owner Entries

Objects protected by ACLs may have *owners* or *effective users* defined for them. Each subsystem or application is responsible for defining who the owner is for each object, and that information is stored with the objects, separate from the object ACLs. For example, the owner of a file is the user that created the file. Object owner ACLs do not contain keys, since the user information is implied by the object type.

- user_obj:*permissions*

  The user_obj entry defines the permissions for a principal who owns or is otherwise associated with the object. There is only one user_obj entry allowed for an object.

- group_obj:*permissions*

  The group_obj entry defines the permissions for a group that owns or is otherwise associated with the object. There is only one group_obj entry allowed for an object.

Local Cell Entries

An object may have one or more ACL entries that specify the permissions for particular principals and groups within the local cell. These entries include a principal or group name, except for the `other_obj` entry.

- `user:`*`principal_name`*`:`*`permissions`*

  The `user` entry specifies the permissions granted for a particular user principal. These entries can be used to grant access for users that are not covered by other ACL entries, or to override the permissions granted by other entries.

- `group:`*`group_name`*`:`*`permissions`*

  The `group` entry specifies the permissions for a group of principals. It is often more economical to grant permissions to groups than to individual principals. Also, group permissions may be easier to manage. For the `room` application, a group might represent all of the users in a particular location or organization, and reservation privileges can be assigned based on location or organization.

- `other_obj:`*`permissions`*

  The `other_obj` entry provides default permissions for all principals within the local cell that are not otherwise covered by a `user_obj`, `group_obj`, `user`, or `group` entry. There can be only one `other_obj` entry in an ACL. The `room` application might use an `other_obj` entry to establish a minimum set of permissions for all users within the local cell.

Foreign Cell Entries

An application server might receive requests from clients in cells other than the local cell—from *foreign cells*. Since a principal or group name is unique only with a cell, foreign cell principals and groups must be qualified by their cell names. An application may put a different degree of trust in a foreign cell than in the local cell, which can affect the level of permissions granted to users in foreign cells.

- `foreign_user:`*`cell_name/principal_name`*`:`*`permissions`*

  The `foreign_user` entry grants permissions to a principal in the indicated cell.

- `foreign_group:`*`cell_name/group_name`*`:`*`permissions`*

  The `foreign_group` entry grants permissions to a group of principals in the indicated cell.

- `foreign_other:`*`cell_name`*`:`*`permissions`*

  The `foreign_group` entry grants permissions for any principals in the indicated cell not otherwise covered by `foreign_user` or `foreign_group` entries.

- `any_other:`*`permissions`*

  The `any_other` entry defines the permissions for all foreign users not covered by other `foreign_user`, `foreign_group`, or `foreign_other` entries. There can be only one any_other entry in an ACL. It establishes a minimum level of access for any authenticated user in any cell.

Delegate Entries (DCE 1.1)

DCE 1.1 introduces the delegation facility, which was described in Section 6.7. With this feature, a client can delegate its authority to a server acting on its behalf. The server can then use the client's identity to gain authorization for remote calls it makes to other servers during the execution of the client's request. You may want to give a server acting as a delegate for a client a different set of permissions than you would give to the original client. DCE 1.1 adds a set of delegate ACL types for this purpose that apply when the caller seeking authorization is a delegate. These follow the pattern of the existing nondelegate ACL types:

- user_obj_delegate:*permissions*
- group_obj_delegate:*permissions*
- other_obj:*permissions*
- user_delegate:*principal_name*:*permissions*
- group_delegate:*group_name*:*permissions*
- foreign_user_delegate:*cell/principal_name*:*permissions*
- foreign_group_delegate:*cell/group_name*:*permissions*
- foreign_other_delegate:*cell_name*:*permissions*
- any_other_delegate:*permissions*

Mask Entries

In addition to the various ACL entry types, there are two ACL mask entries that can filter the permissions supplied by the other ACL entries. The mask entries do not include keys. There can be at most one of each type of mask in an ACL.

- mask_obj:*permissions*

  The mask_obj mask filters the permissions set from all ACL entries except the user_obj and other_obj entries. The permissions from these entries are logically ANDed with the mask permissions to determine the effective permissions. One situation where the mask_obj mask might be used is to temporarily limit the permissions defined by the entry ACL entries. The absence of the mask_obj mask does not limit the granted permissions.

- unauthenticated:*permissions*

  The unauthenticated mask filters the permissions granted to any user that does not have an authenticated identity—a client, perhaps, that has not done a **dce_login** and is allowed to make a call without security. Any permissions granted the user are logically ANDed with this mask to determine the effective permissions. The unauthenticated mask can be used to set a maximum limit on the permissions granted to unauthenticated users. If there is no unauthenticated mask, no permissions will be granted to unauthenticated users.

Permissions

Every ACL entry includes a set of permissions that define what access rights are granted by the ACL entry. Each permission indicates a discreet access right which is either granted or denied. Internally, a permission set is represented by a bitset of 32 bits, with each permission occupying a bit. This normally limits an ACL to 32 permissions, although there is a technique called *chaining* that allows more permissions. Externally, a permission set is represented by a string of characters, each character indicating a granted permission. Each application is free to interpret a permission set as it sees fit. Some applications will use a standard set of permissions, while others might invent new permissions as needed.

Standard Permissions

There is a set of seven standard permissions that are used by DCE services (like CDS) and are available for use by applications. The first three permissions (`rwx`) should be familiar from the Unix file system. The other permissions provide additional control over an object not available through the standard Unix permissions. Each permission is represented by a character (sometimes called a *permission token*), a one-word description, and a bitmask that sets the permission in a bitset of the type `sec_acl_permset_t`. Each bitmask has a constant definition named `sec_acl_perm_X`, where *X* is the permission description (e.g., `sec_acl_perm_read = 0x00000001`). This type and the constants are defined in `/usr/include/dce/aclbase.idl` (and `aclbase.h`).

Table 9.1

Standard DCE Permissions

Permission		Bitmask	Grants right to ...
`r`	read	`0x000000001`	read data from object.
`w`	write	`0x000000002`	write data to object.
`x`	execute	`0x000000004`	execute object (e.g. a program).
`c`	control	`0x000000008`	control object access (e.g. modify ACL).
`i`	insert	`0x000000010`	create new objects.
`d`	delete	`0x000000020`	delete objects.
`t`	test	`0x000000040`	test object access (ACL).

You are free to use the standard permissions for your applications. But you should try to use these permissions in ways that are consistent with their usual meaning—for example, the `r` permission should be related to reading data from an object like a file or a database entry.

Application-Defined Permissions

You can define new permissions for an application if the standard permissions do not cover all of the needed access rights. Each application-defined permission will have a token character string, a string description, and a bitmask. You may choose these to fit the needs of the application, but they should not conflict with the standard permissions. For example, don't assign r to a new permission that means something other than read. The bitmask for a new permission should not be in the range used by the standard permissions. In aclbase.idl, there is a sequence of constants sec_acl_perm_unused_*XXXXXXXX*, where *XXXXXXXX* is the hexadecimal bitmask, that can be used for new permissions.

ACL Examples

This section provides a couple of examples of ACLs, one for CDS that uses the standard permissions and one for the room application that uses custom permissions.

CDS Object ACL

Output Sample 9.1 shows the DCE 1.1 ACL entries for the CDS object /.:/subsys/sch/room_server.hpiala3, which is an RPC Name Space server entry for the room server.

```
unauthenticated:r--t---
user:cell_admin:rwdtc--
user:room-server.hpiala3:rw-t---
group:subsys/dce/cds-admin:rwdtc--
group:subsys/dce/cds-server:rwdtc--
any_other:r--t---
```

Output Sample 9.1
ACL for CDS Object /.:/subsys/sch/room_server.hpeap827

The permissions used are

- r read the bindings from the server entry.
- w change the bindings in the server entry.
- d delete the server entry.
- t test access to the server entry.
- c change the server entry ACL (grant access to the entry).
- i create new directory entries.
- a administer directory replication.

Most of these entries were inherited from the object's parent directory. The user entry for cell_admin grants the cell_admin principal all of the access rights except i and a. The groups subsys/dce/cds-admin and subsys/dce/cds-server are established during DCE configuration to represent the CDS administration and server components. The group entries grant any principal in these groups all of the access rights except i and a. The user entry for room-server.hpiala3 grants the read, write, and test permissions to the principal used by the **room_server** on the hpiala3 host, so that the **room_server** can write its bindings to the server entry. The any_other entry allows any other principal to read from and test access to the server entry, so that any client can obtain the room server's bindings. The unauthenticated mask (along with the any_other entry) allows any unauthenticated user to read and test the server entry.

Room Application ACL

The room application will have an ACL for each room that can be reserved through the **room_server**. The room ACLs will use the following custom permissions. To keep from conflicting with the standard permissions r, c, and i, the room permissions will use uppercase tokens.

- R reserve a room for an event.
- C cancel a room reservation (made by someone else).
- I inquire about a room and its reservations.
- t test access to the room through its ACL.
- c change the room's ACL (grant access to the room).

```
user:cell_admin:RCIct
user:cwk:RCI-t
group:mktg:--I--
any_other:R-I-t
```

Output Sample 9.2
ACL for the Landmark room (/.:/subsys/sch/room/44M/Landmark)

Output Sample 9.2 shows a sample ACL for the Landmark room. Two of these ACL entries are set up as defaults by the **room_server**. Each location has a designated administrator; for the Landmark room's location (**44M**) this is cell_admin. The user entry for cell_admin grants all of the available permissions, including the ability to set up ACL entries for other users. The any_other entry grants the R, I, and t permissions to all authenticated users, unless overridden by other ACL entries. This gives all authenticated users the right to reserve or inquire about the room and to check its ACL.

The other two ACL entries have been added by the location administrator cell_admin. The user entry for cwk grants all of the permissions except c, so cwk can cancel other people's reservations but cannot change the room's ACL. The group entry for mktg grants only the I permission to any user that is a member of that group. This allows those users to inquire about the room but prevents them from reserving it. (Apparently they abused their room reservation privileges in the past.)

9.3 Object Access Control

Each ACL refers to an object of interest to DCE or an application. An object's ACL determines the access rights for users of that object. In the room application, for example, each room known to the application has an ACL that determines who can use the room. The DCE ACL facilities provide a way to name the ACL for an object and rules for how the ACLs can be inherited.

Object ACL Naming

The ACL for an object has a name of the form

server_path/component_name

where

server_path	is the CDS path name for an RPC Name Space entry that points to the object's server, and
component_name	selects the object within the server. This name must be simple; it can't contain slashes.

It is the responsibility of the object's server to map the component name to the right object and ACL. How the server does this is not defined by DCE.

For the room application, the ACL for a room is named /.:/subsys/sch/room/*location_name*/*room_name*. The ACL for the Landmark Room, for example, is /.:/subsys/sch/room/44M/Landmark. (For simplicity here, we will assume that all room names are single words, with no imbedded spaces.)

ACL Inheritance

DCE defines two classes of objects in relation to ACLs. *Container objects* can contain other objects, while *simple objects* do not contain other objects. CDS directories are container objects, while other CDS entries are simple. When an object is created, it can inherit one or more base ACLs from its container object. There are three types of ACLs used in this inheritance. Figure 9.1 shows the inheritance relationships among the ACLs for containers and simple objects.

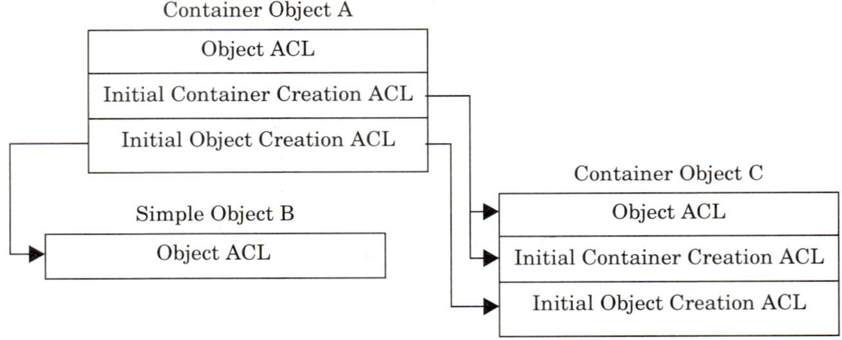

Figure 9.1
Inheritance of ACLs from Container Objects

Object ACL

Every container and simple object has an object ACL, which controls access to the object itself. The rooms in the `room` application are simple objects, so they have only object ACLs.

Initial Object Creation ACL

Each container object has an initial object creation ACL. When a simple object B is created within a container A, B inherits A's initial object creation ACL as its object ACL. When another container C is created within container A, C inherits A's initial object creation ACL as its initial object creation ACL.

Initial Container Creation ACL

Each container object also has an initial container creation ACL. When a container C is created within a container A, C inherits A's initial container creation ACL as both its object ACL and its initial container creation ACL.

ACL Storage

It is the responsibility of the application to provide storage for the ACLs used by application objects. The application will need in-memory copies for some or all of the object ACLs to use for authorization of incoming requests. In addition, ACLs need to be stored in some permanent storage, usually on disk, so they continue to exist after the application server has terminated.

ACL Storage in a DCE Backing Store.

DCE 1.1 provides a general facility for storing information with *backing stores*. A backing store is a collection of data items, indexed by either a name (character string) or by a UUID. DCE uses an efficient retrieval method, either hashing or B-trees, for data in a backing store. Associated with a backing store is a disk file that provides stable storage for the data items. A server opens a backing store and reads and writes data items to the store. The ACL library introduced in DCE 1.1 assumes that the application's ACLs are held in a backing store indexed by UUID.

Consequently, each ACL must be assigned a UUID. Section 9.4 will discuss the calls necessary for setting up a backing store for ACLs.

Backing stores can also be used for storing application object data. There is a standard header available for objects that includes fields for the object's ACL UUID, and if the object is a container, the UUIDs for its initial object and initial container ACLs as well.

The **room_server** could store its location, room, and reservation data in one or more backing stores. However, at this point, we will continue with the original design using an ASCII database file and a linked data structure in memory for the `room` application data. The file and data structure will be enhanced to include the ACL UUIDs for each room.

Roll Your Own ACL Storage

Prior to DCE 1.1, an application had to provide its own storage and retrieval method for its ACLs. A pre-DCE 1.1 version of the **room_server** could attach the ACLs to the room records in the server's linked data structure. It could also convert the ACLs to character strings and include the ACL strings in the room database. This would require substantial additional code in the `room_open()` and `room_close()` routines.

9.4 ACL Setup

This section describes the DCE 1.1 ACL library calls used by an application server to set up its ACLs. (The ACL library is included in `libdce.sl` on HP-UX DCE.) This includes creating a backing store to hold the ACLs, defining the permissions for the ACL, registering the ACL manager, setting up default ACL entries, and defining a name-to-ACL UUID resolver function to be used by the ACL library.

Creating an ACL Database

Code Sample 9.1 shows the code in the `main()` procedure of `room_server.c` that creates a new room ACL database or opens an existing database. First, this calls `access()` with the backing store file name `room_acl_db` to determine if the database already exists. Then this calls `dce_db_open()` to either create or open the backing store. The parameters to this call are

- the *filename* used for the backing store stable storage.
- the *backend type*, which specifies the data storage and retrieval mechanism used by the backing store. Choices are `bsd4.4-hash` (a hash table) `bsd4.4-btree` (a B-tree), or `NULL`, which defaults to the hash mechanism.
- *flags* that control how the backing store is used. Values include

`db_c_index_by_name`	use character strings as the index
`db_c_index_by_uuid`	use UUIDs as the index
`db_c_std_header`	use standard headers for items
`db_c_acl_uuid_header`	use ACL headers for items
`db_c_readonly`	open backing store for read only
`db_c_create`	create the backing store

- a *conversion function* that converts a data item from the data type used by the application to a format that can be written to the backing store. The original data item may be a linked data structure; the backing store format is a linear sequence of bytes. This conversion is also called *serializing* the data. The conversion function is defined using IDL encoding (Chapter 3). The ACL library provides a function `dce_rdacl_convert()` for serializing ACLs.

```
#include <unistd.h>
#include <dce/dce.h>
#include <dce/dbif.h>
. . .
int main(...)
{
  . . .
  dce_db_handle_t        acl_db_h;
  unsigned32             db_create_flag;
  . . .
  if ((access("room_acl_db", R_OK) == -1) &&
      (errno == ENOENT))
  {
     db_create_flag = db_c_create;
  }
  else
  {
     db_create_flag = 0;
  }

  dce_db_open(
      "room_acl_db",
      NULL,  /* default backend_type - a hash table */
      db_c_index_by_uuid | db_create_flag,
      (dce_db_convert_func_t) dce_rdacl_convert,
      &acl_db_h,
      &status);
  CHECK_DCE(status, "Cannot open ACL database");
  . . .
  rpc_server_listen(...);
  . . .
  dce_db_close(&acl_db_h, &status);
  CHECK_DCE(status, "Cannot close ACL database");
  . . .
}
```

Code Sample 9.1
`schedule/obj/room_server.c main()`: Creation of the ACL database

Defining ACL Permissions

The application must define the permissions used by its ACLs. There is a DCE data type, sec_acl_printstring_t, that is used to define one permission. It includes

- a character string *token* (usually one character) that is used to represent the permission in ACL permission strings,
- a character string *description* that describes the permission, and
- a *permissions set*, a bitmask that sets one (or possibly more) bits in a 32-bit value that represents permissions in ACL entries and in ACL library calls.

The set of permissions to be used with an ACL is defined by an array of sec_acl_printstring_t constants. Code Sample 9.2 shows the definition of the R, C, I, c, and t permissions in the **room_server**.

```
#include <dce/aclif.h>
#include <dce/secidmap.h>
. . .

static sec_acl_printstring_t
  room_acl_perms_printstrings[] =
{
/* token  description                    permset          */
   {"R",  "Reserve a room",        sch_acl_perm_reserve },
   {"C",  "Cancel any reservation",sch_acl_perm_cancel },
   {"I",  "Inquire about a room",  sch_acl_perm_inq     },
   {"c",  "control a room ACL",    sch_acl_perm_control  },
   {"t",  "test access for a room ACL",sch_acl_perm_test}
};
#define N_ROOM_ACL_PERMS 5

static sec_acl_printstring_t room_acl_help_printstring =
   {"room_acl", "Room ACL Manager", 0};
```

Code Sample 9.2
schedule/obj/room_server.c: Definition of room ACL permissions

Code Sample 9.2 also defines some descriptive help information for the ACL in a printstring named room_acl_help_printstring. This information can be obtained with **acl_edit** or **dcecp**.

The actual bitset values of each permission are defined along with other application constants in sch.idl as shown in Code Sample 9.3. These values are defined using the sec_acl_perm_ constants defined in /usr/include/dce/acl-base.idl. The c and t permissions use the standard values for the control and test permissions. The I, R, and C permissions use unused permissions available for assignment to application-specific permissions.

```
interface sch
{

import "dce/aclbase.idl";
. . .
const sec_acl_permset_t sch_acl_perm_inq     =
  sec_acl_perm_unused_00000080;
const sec_acl_permset_t sch_acl_perm_reserve =
  sec_acl_perm_unused_00000100;
const sec_acl_permset_t sch_acl_perm_cancel  =
  sec_acl_perm_unused_00000200;
const sec_acl_permset_t sch_acl_perm_control =
  sec_acl_perm_control;
const sec_acl_permset_t sch_acl_perm_test    =
  sec_acl_perm_test;
}
```

Code Sample 9.3.
`schedule/obj/sch.idl`: Assigning room ACL permissions.

Registering an ACL Manager

All of the ACLs for a particular type of object are managed by an *ACL manager*, which encompasses the ACL backing store, the definition of the ACL's permissions, and a method of mapping objects to their ACLs. The ACL manager is set up, after the ACL backing store is open, by calling `dce_acl_register_object_type()`, as shown in Code Sample 9.4. The input parameters for this call are

- The backing store *database handle*, returned by `dce_db_open()`. The ACL library will retain this handle with the ACL manager so it can retrieve ACLs from the backing store as needed. The ACL database handle in the example is `acl_db_h`.
- The *manager type UUID* which identifies the ACL manager. This can be used to distinguish between different kinds of ACLs for the same object. The ACL manager UUID in the example is the hard-coded value of `room_acl_mgr_uuid`. ACL managers should have fixed UUIDs.
- The *number of permissions* defined by the ACL manager. (Actually, this is the number of items in the `printstring` array parameter next.) The room ACL uses five permissions.
- An *array of printstrings* that defines the permission tokens, description, and bitmask values for each of the ACLs permissions. The `room_acl_perms_printstrings` array defined in Code Sample 9.2 defines the `I`, `R`, `C`, `c`, and `t` permissions.
- A *help printstring* that provides a name (in the token field) and description for the ACL manager. The `permset` field is not used. In the example,

`room_acl_perms_printstrings` provides a name `room_acl` and a description "`Room ACL Manager`".

- Permission bitmask values for the *control* and *test permissions* defined for the ACL. These are needed by the ACL library when it services requests to test or modify ACLs for this manager.
- A *resolver function* (and its *argument*) to map an object identifier (either a character string name or a UUID) to the UUID for the ACL associated with the object. This function will be discussed shortly.
- *flags* that provide further information. Values include

`db_acl_c_orphans_ok`	ok to remove all `c` permissions
`db_acl_c_has_owner`	ACL has a `user_obj` entry.
`db_acl_has_groups`	ACL has a `group_obj` entry

No flags are set up for the room ACL manager.

```
uuid_t room_acl_mgr_uuid    =
   {0x4e203958, 0x47ac, 0x11ce, 0x8f, 0x8c, 0x08, 0x00,
   0x09, 0x30, 0x7c, 0x01};
. . .
int main(...)
{
  . . .
  dce_db_open(...);
  . . .
  dce_acl_register_object_type(
      acl_db_h,
      &room_acl_mgr_uuid,
      N_ROOM_ACL_PERMS,
      room_acl_perms_printstrings,
      &room_acl_help_printstring,
      sch_acl_perm_control,
      sch_acl_perm_test,
      room_acl_resolve,     /* resolver function         */
      NULL,                 /* no argument for resolver */
      0,                    /* no flags                  */
      &status);
  CHECK_DCE(status, "Cannot set up room ACL manager");

  if (db_create_flag == db_c_create)
  {
      room_acl_setup(acl_db_h);
  }
```

Code Sample 9.4
`schedule/obj/room_server.c main()`: Set up of the room ACL manager

Setting Up Default ACL Entries

When the ACL database is first created, it will be devoid of ACLs for any objects and users. The application must set up default ACL entries that allow at least a minimum level of access to application objects. Each default object ACL should include at least one entry granting the control permission to someone. This allows someone to set up additional ACL entries for the object. If you do not set up a default ACL entry with the c permission, the ACL is an *orphan* and can never be changed.

The **room_server** will set up ACLs for each room it manages. Each of these ACLs will have two default entries:

- user:*loc_admin_user*:RCIct

  This grants all permissions to a user defined as the administrator for the room's location in the room database. The administrator can reserve rooms, cancel any reservation, inquire about rooms, and grant access to the room with additional ACL entries. Note that this entry could also have been implemented as a user_obj entry, with the location administrator as the object owner.

- any_other:RIt

  This allows any other authenticated user to inquire about and to reserve rooms.

Code Sample 9.5 shows the room_acl_setup() function, which is called after the ACL backing store is created and the ACL manager is registered. This function is in the room_mgr.c module, where it has access to the location and room data structure built from the room database. The input to room_acl_setup() is the ACL database handle from dce_db_open().

Before setting up the default ACLs, room_acl_setup() calls rpc_sm_enable_allocate() to set up the memory management environment used by the dce_db_ calls. This is done automatically by RPC for operation managers; a server needs to call rpc_sm_enable_allocate() only when it accesses a backing store outside of its manager routines. Be forewarned, though, that failure to include this easily overlooked call results in unpredictable fatal errors in the server (as I found out to my own frustration).

Each location administration user is stored in the location records as a principal name. To create an ACL entry for the administration user, room_acl_setup() must convert the principal names to their UUIDs by calling sec_id_parse_name(). This requires a handle to the Security Registry, obtained by the sec_rgy_site_open() call.

The two for loops in room_acl_setup() step through the locations and the rooms for each location. Within the inner for loop is the code to create the room's ACL and its default entries. First, it initializes the ACL with the room ACL manager

UUID and no entries in `dce_acl_obj_init()`. Then, it adds the default entry for the location administration user with `dce_acl_obj_add_user_entry()` and the default entry for all other users with `dce_acl_obj_add_obj_entry()`. For some reason unknown to me, `dce_acl_obj_add_obj_entry()` does not accept an ACL entry type of `sec_acl_e_type_other_obj`. So instead we must use `sec_acl_e_type_any_other` to set up an `any_other` entry. This seems to have the same effect as an `other_obj` entry.

When the room ACL has been given its default entries, it is written to the backing store by `dce_db_store_by_uuid()`, using the ACL UUID from the room record. This call invokes the conversion function defined for the backing store. For the ACL database, this is the built-in function `dce_rdacl_convert()` provided in the ACL library. This function converts the ACL to a sequence of bytes that can be written to the backing store. After it is written to the backing store, the in-memory copy of the ACL is deallocated by `dce_acl_obj_free_entries()`.

```
#include <dce/id_base.h>
#include <dce/rgybase.h>
#include <dce/dce_cf.h>
#include <dce/dce.h>
#include <dce/dbif.h>
#include <dce/aclif.h>
. . .
extern uuid_t               room_acl_mgr_uuid;
. . .
void room_acl_setup(
   dce_db_handle_t acl_db_h)
{
   loc_rec_t          *loc_p;
   room_rec_t         *room_p;
   sec_rgy_handle_t    rgy_h;
   uuid_t              loc_admin_uuid;
   dce_db_header_t     std_header;
   sec_acl_t           acl;
   unsigned32          status;
#  define NORMAL_ROOM_PERMS \
      sch_acl_perm_inq | sch_acl_perm_reserve | \
      sch_acl_perm_test
```

Code Sample 9.5
`schedule/obj/room_mgr.c: room_acl_setup()`

```
#   define ADMIN_ROOM_PERMS \
        NORMAL_ROOM_PERMS | sch_acl_perm_cancel | \
        sch_acl_perm_control

    rpc_sm_enable_allocate(&status);
    CHECK_DCE(status, "Cannot enable allocation");

    sec_rgy_site_open((unsigned_char_t *) "", &rgy_h,
        &status);
    CHECK_DCE(status, "Cannot open Security Registry");

    for (loc_p = loc_list; loc_p != NULL;
          loc_p = loc_p->next)
    {
        sec_id_parse_name(rgy_h, loc_p->loc_admin, NULL, NULL,
          NULL, &loc_admin_uuid, &status);
        CHECK_DCE(status,
          "Cannot convert admin principal to UUID");

        for (room_p = loc_p->room_list; room_p != NULL;
              room_p = room_p->next)
        {
            dce_acl_obj_init(&room_acl_mgr_uuid, &acl,
              &status);
            CHECK_DCE(status,
              "Cannot initialize location ACL");

            dce_acl_obj_add_user_entry(
                &acl,
                ADMIN_ROOM_PERMS,
                &loc_admin_uuid,
                &status);
            CHECK_DCE(status,
              "Cannot add admin ACL permissions");
            dce_acl_obj_add_obj_entry(
                &acl,
                sec_acl_e_type_other_obj_deleg,
                NORMAL_ROOM_PERMS,
                &status);
            CHECK_DCE(status,
              "Cannot add normal ACL permissions");
            dce_db_store_by_uuid(
                acl_db_h,
```

Code Sample 9.5 (continued)

```
                &(room_p->acl_uuid),
                &acl,
                &status);
            CHECK_DCE(status,
              "Cannot store room ACL in ACL database");

            dce_acl_obj_free_entries(&acl, &status);
            CHECK_DCE(status, "Cannot free ACL entries");
        }
    }

    sec_rgy_site_close(rgy_h, &status);
    CHECK_DCE(status, "Cannot close Registry");
}
```

Code Sample 9.5 (continued)

Resolving ACL Components

The ACL library needs some way of mapping objects to their ACLs which is dependent on how the application names and stores its objects and ACLs. To do this, the application server provides a resolver function that it registers with the ACL manager. The ACL library calls the resolver function when it needs to map an object name or UUID to an ACL. We will see how this is used later in the discussion of the `rdacl` interface implementation in the ACL library. The resolver function used with the room ACL manager is `room_acl_resolve()`, shown in Code Sample 9.6

The calling sequence of each resolver function is defined by DCE in the `dce_acl_resolver_func_t` type. The input parameters for a resolver function are

- a *binding handle* for the caller of an `rdacl` operation. An object UUID can be extracted from this binding handle to be used in the resolution. For `room_acl_resolve()`, this will be the UUID of the location object.
- a character string *component name* that further discriminates the object to be resolved. For `room_acl_resolve()`, this will be the room name.
- An *ACL type* that selects the type of ACL requested: the object ACL, the initial default object ACL, or initial default container ACL. For `room_acl_resolve()`, this should always be `sec_acl_type_object`.
- An *ACL manager type UUID*, which can be used to select the specific ACL if the object has more than one ACL manager. For `room_acl_resolve()`, this should always match the UUID in `room_acl_mgr_uuid`.
- A boolean flag *writing*, which is not used in DCE 1.1.
- An *argument* of any type that is specific to the resolver function. It is set in the `dce_acl_register_object_type()` call. For objects which are themselves stored in backing stores, this might be the object's backing store handle.

The main output parameter for a resolver function is the UUID of the ACL for the object selected by the handle object and component name and for the specified ACL type and manager. The ACL library can then use the ACL UUID to fetch the actual ACL from the ACL database.

Code Sample 9.6 shows the implementation of the `room_acl_resolve()` function. This function finds the location corresponding to the object UUID in the binding handle, and the room within that location that matches the component name. The room's ACL UUID is returned from its room record.

```
void room_acl_resolve(
   handle_t                   h,
   sec_acl_component_name_t component_name,
   sec_acl_type_t             sec_acl_type,
   uuid_t                     *mgr_type,
   boolean32                  writing,
   void                       *resolver_arg,
   uuid_t                     *acl_uuid,
   error_status_t             *status)
{
   loc_rec_t    *loc_p;
   room_rec_t   *room_p;
   uuid_t        loc_obj_uuid;
   unsigned32    ignored_st;

   *status = error_status_ok;

   if (!uuid_equal(mgr_type, &room_acl_mgr_uuid,
      &ignored_st))
   {
      uuid_create_nil(acl_uuid, &ignored_st);
      *status = sec_acl_unknown_manager_type;
      return;
   }

   if (sec_acl_type != sec_acl_type_object)
   {
      uuid_create_nil(acl_uuid, &ignored_st);
      *status = sec_acl_invalid_acl_type;
      return;
   }
```

Code Sample 9.6
`schedule/obj/room_mgr.c: room_acl_resolve()`

```
    rpc_binding_inq_object(h, &loc_obj_uuid, status);
    CHECK_DCE_NONFATAL(*status,
      "Cannot get location object for resolution");
    if (*status != error_status_ok)
    {
        return;
    }

    for (loc_p = loc_list; loc_p != NULL;
         loc_p = loc_p->next)
    {
        if (uuid_equal(&loc_p->loc_obj_uuid,
                       &loc_obj_uuid, &ignored_st))
        {
            for (room_p = loc_p->room_list; room_p != NULL;
                 room_p = room_p->next)
            {
                if (ROOM_NAME_EQ(room_p->room.name,
                                 component_name))
                {
                    memcpy(acl_uuid, &room_p->acl_uuid,
                           sizeof(uuid_t));
                    return;
                }
            }
            break; /* room not found in location */
        }
    }

    uuid_create_nil(acl_uuid, &ignored_st);
    *status    = sec_acl_object_not_found;
}
```

Code Sample 9.6 (continued)

Built-In Resolver Functions

The ACL library provides two built-in resolver functions to be used when the object itself is stored in a backing store with a standard header of the type `dce_db_dataheader_t`. The standard header includes UUID fields for the object, initial object creation, and initial container creation ACLs. The built-in resolver functions retrieve the header for the object and return the appropriate ACL UUID. The resolver argument for these functions is a handle for the opened object backing store. The resolver functions are

- `dce_acl_resolve_by_uuid()`

  This function extracts the object UUID from the binding handle parameter, retrieves the object header from the object backing store using the UUID, and returns the specified ACL from the object header. It ignores the component name parameter.

- `dce_acl_resolve_by_name()`

  This function uses the component name to locate the object in its backing store, retrieves the object header, and returns the specified ACL from the object header. It ignores the binding handle parameter.

For an example of how these resolver functions are used, and how the backing store can be used for the storage of object data, see the generic sample application in Appendix A of the *OSF DCE 1.1 Application Guide - Introduction and Style Guide*.

9.5 ACL Evaluation

Now that we have a way to set up ACLs, we can finally use them for their intended purpose: to determine if a client making a remote procedure call is authorized to perform the requested operation. To determine this, the ACL for the object being accessed is evaluated against the credentials of the client. The result of the evaluation will be a set of permissions that are granted to the client, which are used to determine if the client is authorized to perform the operation on the object.

ACL Evaluation Algorithm

DCE defines an algorithm for the evaluation of an ACL and a client's credentials, based on the types of entries present in the ACL. The client's credentials may consist of a single privilege attribute (PAC or EPAC) or a delegation chain with two or more EPACs for the initiator client and one or more delegate servers. The overall algorithm is

- If the credentials have a delegation chain,

  Evaluate the initiator EPAC in the client's credentials.

  If access is denied, then stop; otherwise continue.

  For each delegate EPAC in the credentials,

    Evaluate the delegate EPAC.

    If access is denied, then stop; otherwise continue.

- Otherwise (includes DCE prior to DCE 1.1),

  Evaluate the client's EPAC (or PAC) as an initiator.

Evaluation of one EPAC

Here is the algorithm for evaluating one PAC or EPAC, which may be for an initiator or a delegate. (Prior to DCE 1.1, `_delegate` entries do not exist and so are not used in the ACL evaluation.) The ACL entries are evaluated in this order:

- `user_obj:`*`permissions`*

  Check if there is a `user_obj` entry. If there is, check if there is a user object owner associated with the object. If there is, and the EPAC is for an initiator, check if the EPAC principal is the user object owner. If there is a match, the `user_obj` entry permissions are granted. If there is a `user_obj` entry, but no user object owner, no permissions are granted.

- `user_obj_delegate:`*`permissions`*

  Similar to the `user_obj` check, except that the permissions are granted if the EPAC is for a delegate as well as an initiator.

- `user:`*`principal_name`*`:`*`permissions`*

  If the EPAC is an initiator from the local cell, check if there is a `user` entry that matches the EPAC's principal. If there is, the matching entry permissions are granted, masked by any `mask_obj` entry permissions.

- `user_delegate:`*`principal_name`*`:`*`permissions`*

  Similar to the `user` check, except that the permissions are granted if the EPAC is for a delegate as well as an initiator.

- `foreign_user:`*`cell_name/principal_name`*`:`*`permissions`*

  If the EPAC is an initiator and is from a foreign cell, check if there is a `foreign_user` entry that matches the client's cell and principal. If there is, the matching entry permissions are granted, masked by any `mask_obj` entry permissions.

- `foreign_user_delegate:`*`cell/principal_name`*`:`*`permissions`*

  Similar to the `foreign_user` check, except that the permissions are granted if the EPAC is for a delegate as well as an initiator.

- `group_obj:`*`permissions`*
- `group_obj_delegate:`*`permissions`*
- `group:`*`group_name`*`:`*`permissions`*
- `group_delegate:`*`group_name`*`:`*`permissions`*
- `foreign_group:`*`cell_name/group_name`*`:`*`permissions`*
- `foreign_group_delegate:`*`cell/group_name`*`:`*`permissions`*

If there are no matching user entries, permissions are accumulated from *all* group entries (for an initiator EPAC) or *all delegate* group entries (for a delegate EPAC) that match *any* of the groups listed in the EPAC. This includes the group owner associated with the object and the `group_obj` or `group_obj_delegate` entry, if they exist. (Unlike the `user_obj` entry, access is not denied if there is a `group_obj` entry but no group owner for the object.) If the EPAC is from the local cell, all `group` and `group_delegate` entries are checked. If the EPAC is from a foreign cell, all `foreign_group` and `foreign_group_delegate` entries are checked. If any matching group entries are found, the permissions granted are the logical OR of the permissions of all matching groups, masked by any `mask_obj` entry permissions.

- `other_obj:`*`permissions`*

  If no matching user or group entries are found, if the EPAC is an initiator from the local cell, and if there is an `other_obj` entry, the permissions from the `other_obj` entry are granted.

- `other_obj_delegate:`*`permissions`*

  Similar to the `other_obj` check, except that the permissions are granted if the EPAC is for a delegate as well as an initiator.

- `foreign_other:`*`cell_name`*`:`*`permissions`*

  If no matching user or group entries are found, if the EPAC is an initiator from a foreign cell, and if there is a `foreign_other` entry that matches the EPAC's cell, the permissions from the `foreign_other` entry are granted, masked by any `mask_obj` entry permissions.

- `foreign_other_delegate:`*`cell_name`*`:`*`permissions`*

  Similar to the `foreign_other` check, except that the permissions are granted if the EPAC is for a delegate as well as an initiator.

- `any_other:`*`permissions`*

  If no other matching entries are found, and there is an `any_other` entry, the permissions from the `any_other` entry are granted, masked by any `mask_obj` entry permissions. If there are no matching entries at all, no permissions are granted.

- `any_other_delegate:`*`permissions`*

  Similar to the `any_other` check, except that the permissions are granted if the EPAC is for a delegate as well as an initiator.

- `unauthenticated:`*`permissions`*

  If the EPAC is unauthenticated, then any of the permissions granted by the above rules are masked by the `unauthenticated` permissions. If the client is unauthenticated and there is no `unauthenticated` entry, no permissions are granted.

Client Authorization

The ACL library function `dce_acl_is_client_authorized()` performs the evaluation of a client's credentials and an object's ACL. An operation manager in a server can call this function to determine if the client is authorized to perform requested operation on the object. The input parameters for this call are

- the *binding handle* representing the caller.
- the *ACL manager type UUID*, used to distinguish between different ACLs for the object.
- the *ACL UUID* identifying the target object's ACL.
- the *object owner UUID* and the *group owner UUID* for the object, if they exist.
- the *desired permissions* needed to perform the requested operation.

`dce_acl_is_client_authorized()` retrieves the ACL entries from the ACL database using the ACL UUID and retrieves the client's PAC from the binding handle. Then it applies the ACL evaluation algorithm to determine the granted permissions, and if the granted permissions include the desired permissions, it sets the output parameter `authorized` to `true`. Otherwise it sets `authorized` to `false`.

Code Sample 9.7 shows the `client_is_authorized()` function, which is called by the operation managers in `room_mgr.c`. This function is a wrapper for `dce_acl_is_client_authorized()` that returns the authorization decision for a client's binding handle and a room's ACL.

Code Sample 9.8 illustrates the use of `client_is_authorized()` in the `room_reserve()` operation manager. This manager finds the record for the room indicated by the `room` input parameter and calls `client_is_authorized()` with the client's binding handle, the ACL UUID from the room record, and a requirement that the client have the Reserve permission. If the authorization fails, the manager will return a status of `sch_status_not_authorized`. Note that the caller's security is checked prior to the authorization check, so an unauthorized client will get the error `sch_status_not_secure`, even if there is an `unauthorized` ACL entry for the room.

```
boolean32 client_is_authorized(
   rpc_binding_handle_t h,
   uuid_t               *acl_uuid,
   sec_acl_permset_t    required_perms)
{
   boolean32  authorized;
   unsigned32 status;

   dce_acl_is_client_authorized(
      h,
      &room_acl_mgr_uuid,
      acl_uuid,
      NULL,      /* no object owner */
      NULL,      /* no object group */
      required_perms,
      &authorized,
      &status);
   CHECK_DCE_NONFATAL(status,
     "Cannot check client authorization");
   if (status != error_status_ok)
   {
      return(false);
   }
   else
   {
      return(authorized);
   }
}
```

Code Sample 9.7
`schedule/obj/room_mgr.c`: `client_is_authorized()`

```
void room_reserve(
   /* [in ] */ handle_t         h,
   /* [in ] */ sch_room_t       room,
   . . .
   /* [out] */ sch_status_t    *status,
   . . .)
```

Code Sample 9.8
`schedule/obj/room_mgr.c`: `room_reserve()` with client authorization

```
{
    room_rec_t          *room_p;
    . . .

    if (!call_is_secure(h, . . .))
    {
        *status = sch_status_not_secure;
        return;
    }
    . . .
    find_room(room, &room_p, status);
    . . .

    if (!client_is_authorized(h, &room_p->acl_uuid,
                               sch_acl_perm_reserve))
    {
        *status = sch_status_not_authorized;
        return;
    }
    . . .
}
```

Code Sample 9.8 (continued)

Examples of ACL Evaluation

Following are some examples of ACL evaluation. These examples use the ACL shown in Table 9.2.

Table 9.2 Sample ACL Entries

i	entry_type	id	realm	permissions
	default_realm	jaja		
1	user	cell_admin		RCIct
2	user	cwk		RCI-t
3	group	mktg		--I--
4	foreign_group	execs	ba.hp.com	RCI-t
4	any_other			R-I-t

PAC with Matching User

Table 9.3 Sample PAC for Matching User

Field	Value
authenticated	true
realm	jaja
principal	cwk
group	developers
num_groups	2
group[0]	developers
group[1]	gsy
num_foreign_groups	0

Table 9.3 shows a PAC for a user cwk and memberships in the developers and gsy groups. The first matching entry is the user entry for cwk. This yields the permissions RCI-t. This client can perform all of the room operations but cannot alter room ACLs.

PAC with a Local Cell User

Table 9.4 Sample PAC with Matching Groups

Field	Value
authenticated	true
realm	jaja
principal	jill
group	finance
num_groups	2
group[0]	finance
group[1]	gsy
num_foreign_groups	0

Table 9.4 shows a PAC for a principal abc, with membership in the finance and gsy groups. There is no matching user entry for jill, and no matching group entries for finance or gsy, so the any_other entry applies. This gives the user the R-I-t permissions, allowing her to reserve and inquire about rooms but not to cancel other people's reservations.

PAC with a Matching Group

Table 9.5 Sample PAC with Matching Groups

Field	Value
authenticated	true
realm	jaja
principal	jack
group	mktg
num_groups	2
group[0]	mktg
group[1]	gsy
num_foreign_groups	0

Table 9.5 shows a PAC for a principal jack, with membership in the mktg and gsy groups. There is no matching user entry for jack, so the group entries are used. There is a match for the mktg groups, so the granted permissions are --I--. Even though this client is authenticated, he is restricted to only inquiring about rooms by virtue of his membership in mktg.

PAC for matching foreign group

Table 9.6 Sample PAC with Matching Foreign User

Field	Value
authenticated	true
realm	pa.hp.com
principal	lew
group	execs
num_groups	1
group[0]	execs
num_foreign_groups	0

Table 9.6 shows a PAC for a foreign user. The realm is pa hp.com and the principal is lew. The PAC is not in the ACL's default realm of jaja. The foreign_group ACL entry matches the PAC's realm and a group, so that provides the granted permissions RCI-t. This grants lew the right to arbitrarily cancel room reservations.

Unauthenticated PAC

Table 9.7 Sample PAC with unauthenticated user

Field	Value
authenticated	false
realm	pa.hp.com
principal	bill
group	none
num_groups	1
group[0]	none
num_foreign_groups	0

Finally, Table 9.7 shows a PAC for a user outside of the local cell that is not authenticated. The foreign principal `bill` and group `none` do not match any `foreign_user` or `foreign_group` entries, so the `any_other` entry applies. But since there is no `unauthenticated` mask, no permissions are granted.

9.6 ACL Editing and the `rdacl` Interface

DCE provides programs, **acl_edit** and (in DCE 1.1) **dcecp**, that can be used to set up and modify entries for any ACL. We have already used **acl_edit** in Chapter 5 to set up the necessary permissions to use CDS entries. Now we will see how **acl_edit** and **dcecp** can be used to control the ACLs for any object, including the rooms in our `room` application.

acl_edit

The syntax for the **acl_edit** command is

:**acl_edit [-e]** *server_path/component* [-*command*]

where

server_path	is an RPC Name Space entry name identifying the server maintaining the ACL,
component	identifies the object within the server, and
command	is an optional ACL editing command to execute. If the command is omitted, **acl_edit** accepts ACL editing commands from `stdin`.

In some cases, the *component* may be omitted. Then *server_path* can be ambiguous. It could mean an ACL for a CDS entry or an ACL maintained by the server indicated by *server_path*. To clarify this case, the **-e** option can be used to indicate that the *server_path* refers to a CDS entry of that name.

Some ACL editing commands are

- **m** ***acl_entry*** modify/add the entry in the component's ACL
- **d** ***acl_entry*** delete the entry from the component's ACL
- **l** list the entries for the component's ACL
- **p** print the permissions for the component's ACL
- **t** ***permissions*** test if the user is granted the indicated permissions by the component's ACL

Examples of **acl_edit** commands for the room application are shown in Output Sample 9.3. The first **l** command lists the default ACL entries for the Landmark room. The commands **m user:cwk:RCIt** and **m group:mktg:I** add entries for the user cwk and the group mktg. These modifications are shown by the second **l** command.

```
:acl_edit  /.:/subsys/sch/room/44M/Landmark
sec_acl_edit> l

# SEC_ACL for /.:/subsys/sch/room/44M/Landmark:
# Default cell = /.../jaja
user:cell_admin:RCIct
any_other:R-I-t
sec_acl_edit> m user:cwk:RCIt
sec_acl_edit> m group:mktg:I
sec_acl_edit> l
# SEC_ACL for /.:/subsys/sch/room/44M/Landmark:
# Default cell = /.../jaja
user:cell_admin:RCIct
user:cwk:RCI-t
group:mktg:--I--
any_other:R-I-t
sec_acl_edit> e
```

Output Sample 9.3
acl_edit: Viewing and modifying an ACL for an object

dcecp

The syntax for the **dcecp** subcommands for ACLs is

```
:dcecp
dcecp>acl verb server_path/component [options]
```

where

verb	designates the action on the ACL
server_path	is an RPC Name Space entry name identifying the server maintaining the ACL, and
component	identifies the object within the server.

The ACL verbs include

- **check** — check your permissions granted by the ACL
- **delete** — delete the ACL
- **modify** — add or modify an ACL entry
- **permissions** — get the permissions defined for the ACL
- **replace** — replace the ACL with another ACL
- **show** — display the ACL entries

Output Sample 9.4 illustrates how **dcecp** can be used to display and modify an ACL. The first **show** displays the default ACL entries for the Landmark room. The **modify** commands add ACL entries for the user cwk and the group mktg. The second **show** displays the effect of these modifications.

```
:dcecp
dcecp> acl show /.:/subsys/sch/room/44M/Landmark
{user cell_admin RCIct}
{any_other R-I-t}
dcecp> acl modify /.:/subsys/sch/room/44M/Landmark \
   -add {user cwk RCIt}
dcecp> acl modify /.:/subsys/sch/room/44M/Landmark \
   -add {group mktg I}
dcecp> acl show /.:/subsys/sch/room/44M/Landmark
{user cell_admin RCIct}
{user cwk RCI-t}
{group mktg --I--}
{any_other R-I-t}
dcecp> quit
```

Output Sample 9.4
dcecp: Viewing and modifying an ACL for an object

The rdacl Interface

To perform their functions, the **acl_edit** and **dcecp** programs make remote procedure calls to the server that manages the target ACL. These remote calls are defined by DCE in the rdacl interface. Any server that manages ACLs must then implement and export the rdacl interface. Figure 9.2 illustrates this for the room application. The **room_server** exports both the room interface (defined by the application) and the rdacl interface (defined by DCE). The room client uses the room interface, while **acl_edit** uses the rdacl interface.

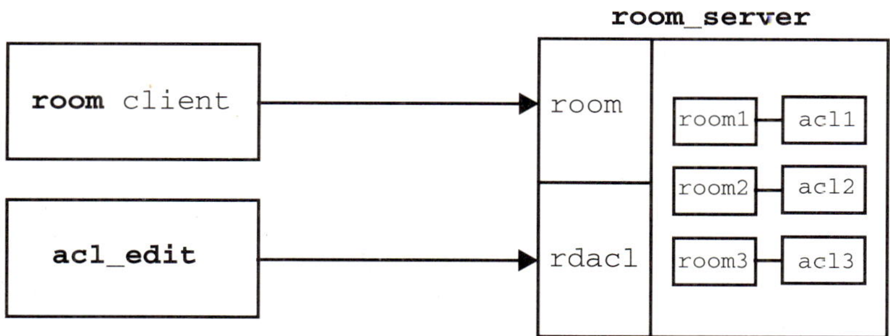

Figure 9.2
Rdacl Interface in the room server.

The rdacl interface is defined by the IDL file rdaclif.idl in the directory /usr/include/dce. This IDL file is compiled by the IDL compiler just like any other IDL file, producing the header file rdaclif.h, the client stub object file rdaclif_cstub.o (which is linked into **acl_edit**), and the server stub object rdaclif_sstub.o (which is linked into the room server). The operations in the rdacl interface are

- rdacl_lookup()
  Returns the ACL for a component.
- rdacl_replace()
  Replaces the ACL for a component.
- rdacl_get_access()
  Returns the access rights for the client from the component's ACL.
- rdacl_test_access()
  Checks if the client has permissions in the component's ACL
- rdacl_test_access_on_behalf()
  Checks if another user has permissions in the component's ACL.
- rdacl_get_manager_types()
  Returns the types of ACLs associated with the component.
- rdacl_get_manager_types_semantics()
  Returns the types of ACLs and their POSIX semantics.
- rdacl_get_printstring()
  Returns the permissions and help printstrings for an ACL manager.
- rdacl_get_referral()
  Gets a referral to another server that can update the component's ACL (used only with replicated servers).

The ACL library introduced in DCE 1.1 provides an implementation of the `rdacl` interface that is tied into the ACL database registered in the `dce_acl_register_object_type()` call that sets up the ACL manager. The ACL library (part of `libdce.sl` on HP-UX DCE) includes the server stub `rdaclif_stub.o`, so you do not have to explicitly link your application server with this object file.

Prior to DCE 1.1, the implementation of the `rdacl` interface was left as an extensive exercise for the reader. If you used ACLs in your server, you had to provide your own managers for each of the `rdacl` operations, along with your own implementation of the ACL evaluation algorithm provided by `dce_acl_is_client_authorized()` in DCE 1.1. You also had to IDL-compile `rdaclif.idl` and link the `rdaclif_stub.o` object into your application.

Setting up the `rdacl` Interface

Even with the ACL library, you have to set up the `rdacl` interface using the same steps as you used setting up your application interface. These are shown in Code Sample 9.9. They are

- Register the `rdacl` interface with the server's RPC Runtime, using the `dce_acl_v1_0_epv` manager entry point vector that is built into the ACL library. The `rdacl` interface must be registered with each object type used by the server.
- Register the `rdacl` interface, the server's objects and the server's bindings with the local Endpoint Map.
- Export the `rdacl` interface, the server's bindings, and relevant objects to the appropriate RPC Name Space entries in CDS. The **`room_server`** will export this interface to each room location server entry, `/.:/subsys/sch/room/`*LOCATION*.

```
rpc_server_register_if(
   rdaclif_v1_0_s_ifspec,
   &native_obj_type_uuid,
   (rpc_mgr_epv_t) &dce_acl_v1_0_epv,
   &status);
CHECK_DCE(status,
  "Cannot register rdaclif interface with RPC");
rpc_server_register_if(
   rdaclif_v1_0_s_ifspec,
   &legacy_obj_type_uuid,
   (rpc_mgr_epv_t) &dce_acl_v1_0_epv,
   &status);
```

Code Sample 9.9
`schedule/obj/room_server.c main()`: Setting up the `rdacl` interface

```
CHECK_DCE(status,
   "Cannot register rdaclif interface with RPC");
. . .

rpc_ep_register(
    rdaclif_v1_0_s_ifspec,
    binding_vector,
    loc_obj_vector,
    (unsigned_char_p_t) "Room ACL Manager",
    &status);
CHECK_DCE(status,
"Cannot register rdaclif interface with Endpoint");
. . .

room_loc_begin(&loc_p);
while (loc_p != NULL)
{
   . . .
   rpc_ns_binding_export(
       rpc_c_ns_syntax_default,
       loc_ns_server_entry,
       rdaclif_v1_0_s_ifspec,
       binding_vector,
       &one_loc_obj_vector,
       &status);
   CHECK_DCE(status,
      "Cannot export binding to rdaclif entry");
   . . .
 }
```

Code Sample 9.9 (continued)

Like the application interface, the `rdacl` interface must be cleaned up when the server terminates. The steps for this, shown in Code Sample 9.10, are

- Remove the `rdacl` interface and server bindings from the server entries. In the **room_server**, these are the room location entries. Note, however, that we do not include the location object in the `rpc_ns_binding_unexport()` for the `rdacl` interface. We do not want to remove the object before the second `rpc_ns_binding_unexport()` for the `room` interface.
- Remove the `rdacl` interface entries from the local Endpoint Map.
- Remove the `rdacl` interface registration from the server's RPC Runtime.

```
room_loc_begin(&loc_p);
while (loc_p != NULL)
{
   . . .
   rpc_ns_binding_unexport(
      rpc_c_ns_syntax_default,
      loc_ns_server_entry,
      rdaclif_v1_0_s_ifspec,
      NULL,
      &status);
   CHECK_DCE(status,
     "Cannot unexport binding from rdaclif entry");

   rpc_ns_binding_unexport(
      . . .
      room_v1_0_s_ifspec,
      &one_loc_obj_vector,    /* Remove object now. */
      &status);
   . . .
}
. . .
rpc_ep_unregister(
   rdaclif_v1_0_s_ifspec,
   binding_vector,
   loc_obj_vector,
   &status);
CHECK_DCE_NONFATAL(status,
  "Cannot unregister rdaclif interface w/Endpoint ");
. . .

rpc_server_unregister_if(
   rdaclif_v1_0_s_ifspec,
   &native_obj_type_uuid,
   &status);
CHECK_DCE(status,
   "Cannot unregister rdaclif interfacewith RPC");

rpc_server_unregister_if(
   rdaclif_v1_0_s_ifspec,
   &legacy_obj_type_uuid,
   &status);
CHECK_DCE(status,
   "Cannot unregister rdaclif interface with RPC");
```

Code Sample 9.10
`schedule/obj/room_server.c main()`: Cleaning up the `rdacl` interface

The sec_acl Interface

DCE provides a set of calls, prefixed by sec_acl_, that encapsulate the remote calls to the rdacl interface for a client like acl_edit. These calls correspond closely to the underlying rdacl operations. They include

- sec_acl_bind()

  Binds to the server indicated by the *server_path* part of the ACL name.
- sec_acl_lookup()

  Returns the ACL for a component.
- sec_acl_replace()

  Replaces the ACL for a component.
- sec_acl_get_access()

  Returns the access rights for the client from the component's ACL.
- sec_acl_test_access()

  Checks if the client has permissions in the component's ACL.
- sec_acl_test_access_on_behalf()

  Checks if another user has permissions in the component's ACL.
- sec_acl_get_manager_types()

  Returns the types of ACLs associated with the component.
- sec_acl_get_manager_types_semantics()

  Returns the types of ACLs and their POSIX semantics.
- sec_acl_get_printstring()

  Returns the permissions and help printstrings for an ACL manager.

How acl_edit Works

Let's look at how **acl_edit** uses the sec_acl interface when it edits an ACL. Assume the commands shown in Output Sample 9.3 are executed.

1. **acl_edit** calls sec_acl_bind() with the entry name /.:/subsys/sch/room/44M/Landmark.
   - sec_acl_bind() looks for a server entry in CDS for the entire entry name /.:/subsys/sch/room/44M/Landmark, which is not found.
   - Then sec_acl_bind() looks for a server entry for the *server_path* part of the entry, /.:/subsys/sch/room/44M, and finds the room location object entry.
   - sec_acl_bind() sets up an RPC binding to the **room_server**, using the server entry /.:/subsys/sch/room/44M, and returns a sec_acl handle for the binding. This binding includes the object UUID for location 44M.

2. **acl_edit** calls sec_rgy_cell_bind() to open the Security Registry and gets the local cell name.

3. **acl_edit** calls sec_acl_get_mgr_types_semantics() to get the UUID of the ACL manager defined for the object indicated by the component name Landmark. It uses the binding handle obtained in step 1.

   - sec_acl_mgr_get_types_semantics() makes a remote call to rdacl_get_mgr_types_semantics() in the **room_server**.
   - The **room_server** executes the manager for the rdacl_get_ mgr_types_ semantics() operation in the ACL library.
   - The ACL library calls the resolver function for each registered ACL manager to resolve the component name Landmark. The room ACL manager is the only registered ACL manager in the **room_server** and its resolver function is room_acl_resolve().
   - room_acl_resolve() locates the location record that matches the object UUID in the binding handle, then finds the room record that matches the component name Landmark. room_acl_resolve() returns the ACL UUID from the room record.
   - The ACL library retrieves the ACL database record corresponding to the room ACL UUID and verifies that the ACL uses the registered ACL manager. The ACL library then returns the ACL manager UUID.

4. **acl_edit** calls sec_acl_get_printstring() to obtain the permission information for the object's ACL manager.

   - sec_acl_get_printstring() makes a remote call to rdacl_get_printstring() in the **room_server**.
   - The **room_server** executes the manager for the rdacl_get_printstring() operation, in the ACL library.
   - The ACL library retrieves and returns the printstring information registered with the ACL manager,

5. acl_edit calls sec_acl_lookup() to retrieve the current ACL for the object.

   - sec_acl_lookup() makes a remote call to rdacl_lookup() in the **room_server**.
   - The **room_server** executes the manager for the rdacl_lookup() operation in the ACL library.
   - The ACL library calls the resolver function for the location object and the component name Landmark. room_acl_resolve() returns the UUID for the ACL.
   - The ACL library retrieves the ACL from the ACL database, using the ACL

UUID. This ACL is cached locally for display and modification by **acl_edit** commands.

6. The user issues an **l** (list) command. **acl_edit** displays the cached ACL, converting principal and group UUIDs to their names using the Security Registry, and converting permission bitmasks to their tokens using the ACL manager printstring information.
7. The user issues some **m** (modify) commands: **m user:cwk:RCIt** and **m group:mktg:I**. **acl_edit** converts the principal and group names in the commands to UUIDs using the Security Registry and the permission strings into bitmasks using the printstring information. **acl_edit** updates its cached copy of the ACL but does not (yet) send the update to the **room_server**.
8. The user issues another **l** command, and **acl_edit** displays the updated ACL in its cache.
9. The user enters **e** (exit). At this point, **acl_edit** calls `sec_acl_replace()` to update the permanent copy of the ACL for the `Landmark` room.
   - `sec_acl_replace()` makes a remote call to `rdacl_replace()` in the **room_server**.
   - The **room_server** executes the manager for the `rdacl_replace()` operation in the ACL library.
   - The ACL library calls the resolver function for the location object and the component name `Landmark`. `room_acl_resolve()` returns the UUID for the ACL.
   - The ACL library calls `dce_acl_is_client_authorized()` with the ACL UUID and the defined control permission for the ACL manager to check that the client user has the right to modify the ACL.
   - `dce_acl_is_client_authorized()` gets the client's credentials from the binding handle, fetches the ACL from the ACL database, and evaluates the ACL against the client's credentials. If the client is not authorized to control the ACL, the `rdacl_replace()` operation will return with `sec_acl_invalid_permission`.

     Note that **acl_edit** always calls `sec_acl_replace()` on exit, even if the ACL was not modified. Consequently, if you lack the control permission in the ACL, you will get the `permission not valid for this acl` error when exiting **acl_edit**, even if you made no attempt to modify the ACL.
   - If the authorization check succeeded, the ACL library stores the new copy in the ACL database.

CHAPTER 10

Threads

In the client and server examples up to this point, we have always used only one thread executing application code. Each server had only one call thread, created by calling `rpc_server_listen()` with an argument of `1`. This limits the server to executing only one remote call at a time. This may not be acceptable for a server with many concurrent clients. DCE allows a server to execute more than one remote call at a time using multiple call threads. But if multiple call threads are used, the operation managers within the server will have to take precautions to ensure the execution of a remote call in one call thread does not interfere with concurrent execution of another remote call in another call thread.

Also, it is sometimes desirable for a server or a client to create additional threads to handle various tasks. We have already used threads for a few DCE tasks in the server: catching signals, refreshing the server's login context, and managing the server's key. In this chapter we will see some examples of threads used for application tasks and the facilities available for coordinating application threads.

10.1 Concurrency Control

Consider the following two fragments of operation managers for the `room` interface. Code Sample 10.1 shows a section of the `room_events()` manager that scans the linked list of reservation event records attached to a room record. Code Sample 10.2 shows a section of the `room_cancel()` manager that unlinks and deallocates the event record for a canceled reservation

```
void room_events(...)
{
   . . .
   for (event_p = room_p->event_list;
         ((event_p != NULL) && (event_p->end < begin));
         event_p = event_p->next)
   {
   }
   . . .
}
```

Code Sample 10.1
`schedule/room_mgr.c`: `room_events()` scanning the event list for a room

```
void cancel(...)
{
   . . .
   UNLINK(event_p, room_p->event_list);
   free(event_p);
   . . .
}

void room_cancel(...)
{
   . . .
   cancel(...);
   . . .
}
```

Code Sample 10.2
`schedule/room_mgr.c`: `room_cancel()` unlinking and deallocating an event record

Now consider what might happen when one client calls `room_events()` for room A, and a second client concurrently calls `room_cancel()` for a reservation in the same room. The server assigns the execution of the `room_events()` operation to call thread 1 and the `room_cancel()` operation to call thread 2. Call thread 1 executes first and starts scanning the event list for room A until it gets to event 2. Then the DCE Threads subsystem switches execution to call thread 2, which unlinks and deallocates the record for event 2. Then execution switches back to call thread 1, which tries to reference a field in the event 2 record. But the event 2 record was deallocated by the other call thread, so the reference is invalid. This situation is shown in Figure 10.1.

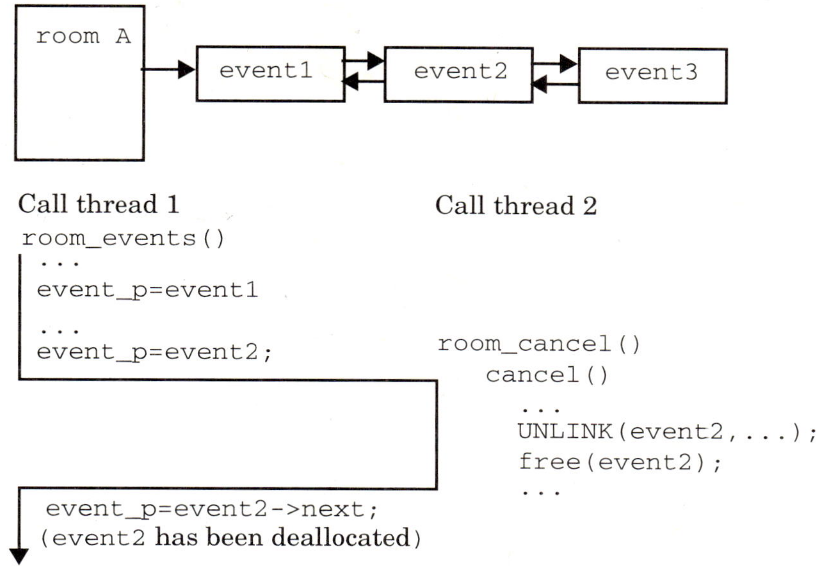

Figure 10.1
Concurrent call execution without data protection

Data Protection with Mutexes

What is needed to solve the problem described above is a way to keep two threads from both concurrently executing sections of code that can interfere with one another. These are sometimes called *critical sections*; it is critical that section A be executed completely before section B is allowed to execute, otherwise data corruption might result. Another way to describe this is that if a thread is executing section A, then any other thread must be excluded from executing section B until section A is completed.

DCE Threads provides the *mutex* (for mutual exclusion) facility for protecting critical sections. A mutex is a data structure that can be locked and unlocked. If thread 2 attempts to lock a mutex that is already locked by thread 1, thread 2 will be blocked until thread 1 unlocks the thread. By locking a mutex around critical sections, threads can be assured that they can execute their critical sections without interference from other threads.

The problem cited above can be solved by associating a mutex with the room record. Whenever a thread uses the room's event list, it must lock the room's mutex. Call thread 1 executes the `room_events()` operation, which locks the room mutex and begins scanning the event list. DCE Threads then switches to call thread 2 for the `room_cancel()` operation. The `room_cancel()` also attempts to lock the room mutex, but since call thread 1 holds the mutex lock, call thread 2 will be blocked. This gives call thread 1 the chance to complete scanning the event list and finish execution of `room_events()`. At the end of the routine thread 1 unlocks the room mutex. This allows call thread 2 to run again, with the room mutex locked. Call thread 2 then completes the execution of the `room_cancel()` operation. Using the room mutex, the `room_events()` and `room_cancel()` operations are able to exclude each other from interfering with the execution of their critical sections. Figure 10.2 illustrates the use of the room mutex to protect the room's event list.

Mutex Setup

A mutex is declared as a variable or a data structure field of the type `pthread_mutex_t`, which is defined in the header file `/usr/include/pthread.h`. (Note well that `pthread.h` is *not* in `/usr/include/dce` like every other DCE header file.) Code Sample 10.3 shows a mutex added to the room record definition.

```
typedef struct ROOM_REC_T {
   . . .
   pthread_mutex_t     mutex;
   event_rec_t        *event_list;
   . . .
} room_rec_t;
```

Code Sample 10.3
`schedule/room_mgr.c`: `room_rec_t` with mute

A mutex must be initialized before use by a call to the DCE routine `pthread_mutex_init()`. This call, like the other calls provided by DCE Threads, is actually defined by the POSIX 1003.4 specification, *Threads Extensions for Portable Operating Systems*. Consequently, it looks a bit different from other DCE calls. In particular, it does not return status in an output parameter. Instead it follows the error reporting used by many Unix calls: It returns `0` for success and `-1` for failure and sets the global variable `errno` to a pthread error number. The error can then be displayed using the `perror()` call.

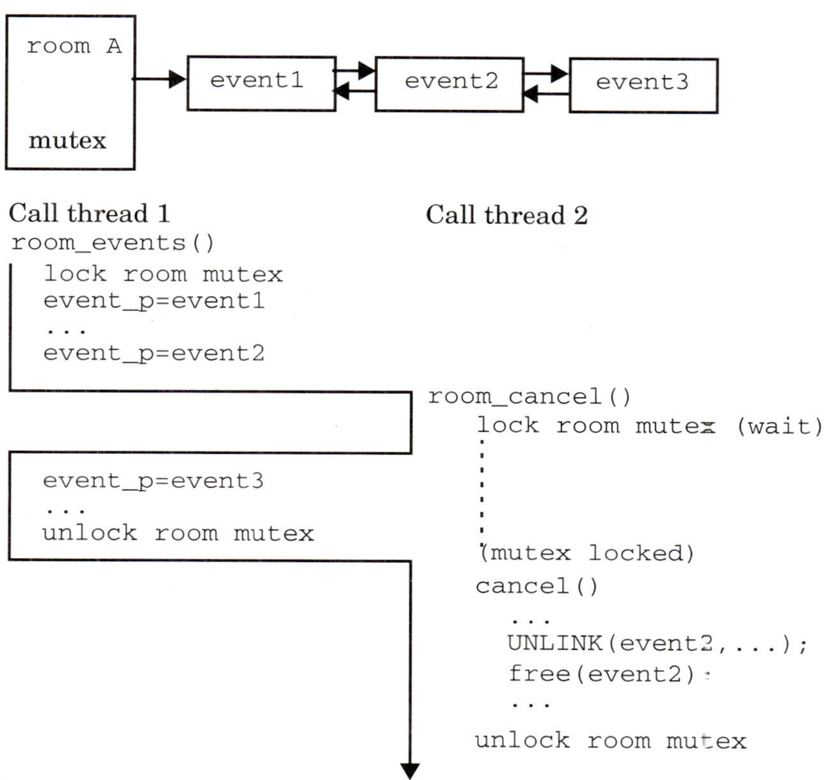

Figure 10.2
Concurrent call execution with data protection

The `pthread_mutex_init()` call takes two input parameters: a pointer to the mutex to initialize and an attribute that indicates the type of mutex. We will always use `pthread_mutexattr_default` to initialize a simple mutex.

Code Sample 10.4 shows the initialization of the room record mutex in the `room_open()` routine. This is done when the room record is allocated. There will be one mutex for each room record.

```
void room_open()
{
  . . .
     case '+':
        MALLOC(new_room_p, room_rec_t);
        . . .
        if (pthread_mutex_init(&(new_room_p->mutex),
                       pthread_mutexattr_default) != 0)
        {
            printf(...);
            perror("Error: ");
            exit(1);
        }
        . . .
}
```

Code Sample 10.4
schedule/room_mgr.c: room_open() room record setup with mutex initialization

Mutex Locking and Unlocking

Mutex locking and unlocking are done through the pthread calls pthread_mutex_lock() and pthread_mutex_unlock(). Like the other pthread calls, these return 0 for success and -1 for failure and set errno to an error number. Each of these routines takes one input parameter, a pointer to the mutex to be locked or unlocked.

Since mutex locking and unlocking will be done in a number of places, it is useful to have macros that include the pthread call and the error checking. Code Sample 10.5 shows these macros for the room mutex.

```
#define LOCK_ROOM_MUTEX(room_p) \
   if (pthread_mutex_lock(&(room_p->mutex)) != 0) \
   { \
      printf(...); \
      perror("Error: "); \
   }


#define UNLOCK_ROOM_MUTEX(room_p) \
   if (pthread_mutex_unlock(&(room_p->mutex)) != 0) \
   { \
      printf(...); \
      perror("Error: "); \
   }
```

Code Sample 10.5
room_mgr.c: LOCK_ROOM_MUTEX and UNLOCK_ROOM_MUTEX macros

The room record mutex needs to be locked in each operation manager that uses the room's event list. Code Samples 10.6 and 10.7 show this for the `room_events()` and `room_cancel()` operations. When these macros are added, these operations will exhibit the behavior shown earlier in Figure 10.2.

```
void room_events(...)
{
    . . .
    LOCK_ROOM_MUTEX(room_p);

    for (event_p = room_p->event_list;
         ((event_p != NULL) && (event_p->end < begin));
         event_p = event_p->next)
    . . .
    UNLOCK_ROOM_MUTEX(room_p);
    *status = sch_status_ok;
}
```

Code Sample 10.6
`schedule/room_mgr.c`: `room_events()` with mutex locking

```
void room_cancel(...)
{
    . . .
    LOCK_ROOM_MUTEX(room_p);

    cancel(...);
    . . .
    UNLOCK_ROOM_MUTEX(room_p);
}
```

Code Sample 10.7
`schedule/room_mgr.c`: `room_cancel()` with mutex locking

Problems with Mutexes

While mutexes are essential for the correct operation of multithreaded applications, they also introduce a new range of problems that you must take care to avoid. Improper mutex locking is a sure way to hang a server. Here are some things to look out for.

Leaving a Mutex Locked

One of the most common problems is forgetting to unlock a mutex after the critical section protected by the mutex is complete. Then the next time a thread attempts to lock the mutex, it will block forever. If the blocked thread is a server call thread, the client that made the call will appear to be hung. When you lock a mutex in a routine, make sure that the mutex is unlocked at all exits from the routine, including error exits.

Relocking a Mutex in the Same Thread

When a thread tries to lock a simple mutex (one that was created with the `pthread_mutexattr_default` attribute) that it has already locked, the thread will hang. An example is: Routine A locks mutex M and calls routine B, which also tries to lock mutex M. One way to avoid this is to keep the locking of a mutex at the same level of routine calls.

Deadlock between Two or More Mutexes

Deadlock is a classic problem that is studied in every Operation System 101 course. With threads and mutexes, deadlock can happen when thread 1 locks mutex A, thread 2 locks mutex B, then thread 1 tries to lock mutex B and thread 2 tries to lock mutex A. This is shown in Figure 10.3. Deadlock can be even more insidious, with an arbitrary number of threads and mutexes involved in very obscure ways. A solution to deadlock is to require all threads to lock all mutexes in the same order. With this rule, thread 1 would lock mutex A, thread 2 would try to lock mutex A and be blocked. Thread 1 would lock mutex B, do its work, and unlock mutexes B and A. Then thread 2 would unblock and lock mutexes A and B. This is shown in Figure 10.4.

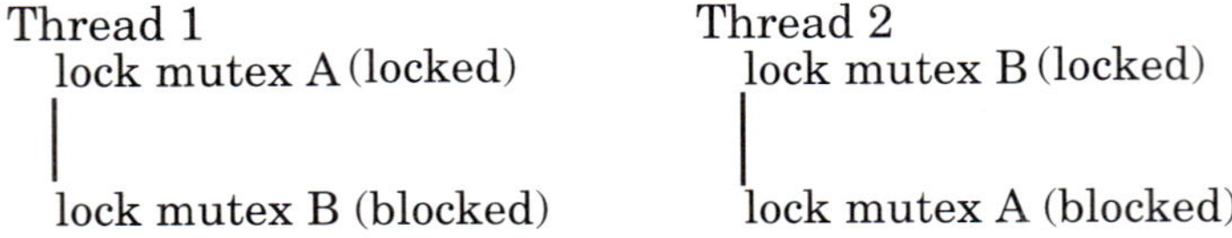

Figure 10.3
Deadlock with threads and mutexes

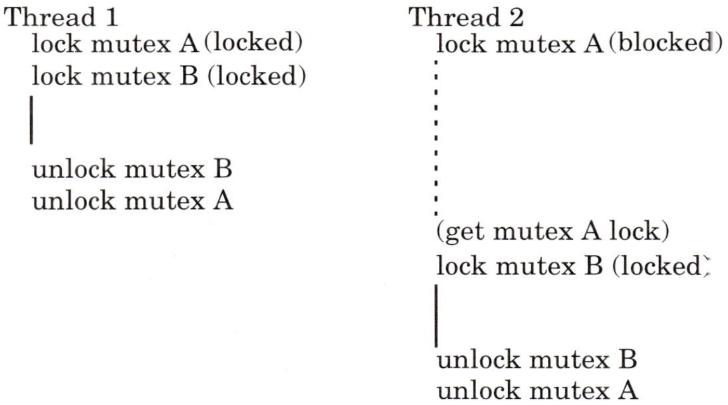

Figure 10.4
Deadlock prevention by enforcement of mutex locking order

Thread-Safe Libraries

As long as we are discussing problems introduced by multithreading, we should look at the libraries used by an application. These libraries may employ their own global variables and other things that could be at risk when multiple threads execute routines in a library. The term *thread-safe* means that the library takes its own precautions to prevent problems in a threaded application. An example of a thread-safe library in HP-UX is the re-entrant C library, `libc_r.sl`, with which we have been linking our DCE clients and servers. HP has designed this library so that C library calls like `sprintf()` and `strtok()` can be called by more than one thread concurrently. The DCE Runtime library, `libdce.sl`, is itself thread-safe. The DCE components within the Runtime library use mutexes for protection of global data. The RPC Runtime library alone uses dozens of mutexes.

Many libraries and subsystems that might be used by a client or server are not thread-safe. Database libraries, for example, are often not thread-safe. You can still call routines in a non-thread-safe library, but you need to provide your own mutex protection to serialize entry into the library. This might look like

```
MUTEX_LOCK(library_mutex);
library_call(...);
MUTEX_UNLOCK(library_mutex);
```

As threaded programming (and DCE) becomes more prevalent, vendors will likely enhance their product libraries to be thread-safe.

10.2 Application Threads

In addition to the main and call threads, an application client or server may create other threads for various purposes. One example is to schedule a periodic task within the application. We have already seen this with the Refresh Identity and Key Management threads in Chapter 6. Now we will look at an example with the room application server itself.

Creating a Thread

Let's first review the creation of a thread, as encapsulated in the `create_thread()` function shown again in Code Sample 10.8. This function calls `pthread_create()` with these input parameters:

- a *thread attribute* data structure which can specify thread creation parameters like the thread stack size, scheduling class, and scheduling priority. The attribute structure is created by `pthread_attr_create()` and its various parameters set by calls like `pthread_attr_setsched()`. However, we will use the default thread creation parameters specified by the constant `pthread_attr_default`.
- the *thread base routine* that will be executed when the thread is created. This routine must conform to the signature

  `pthread_addr_t` *`thread_routine`*`(pthread_addr_t` *`arg`*`)`

  where *`arg`* is a single parameter for both input and output to the base routine.
- the *thread argument*, the value to be passed to the *`arg`* parameter of the base routine. This is a pointer to a data area (usually a structure) that includes any input values to the routine and space for any output from the routine.

The `pthread_create()` call returns in an output parameter a *thread id* of type `pthread_t`, which can be used to identify the created thread in other pthread calls. Like the other pthread calls, `pthread_create()` returns `0` if the thread was successfully created. If the creation failed, it returns `-1` and sets `errno` to an appropriate error number.

After a thread is created, it will be scheduled for execution by the DCE Threads software. Normally, the created thread will not be executed until the current thread reaches a blocking point. But we will usually want our threads to start immediately. The `pthread_yield()` call causes the current thread to block and any waiting threads to execute. This allows the created thread to run immediately until it blocks. Then control will pass back to the original thread.

Terminating a Thread

A thread can be terminated in one of two ways: It can terminate itself by exiting its base routine (or by calling `pthread_exit()`), or it can be killed by another thread calling `pthread_cancel()`. Code Sample 10.9 shows the `kill_thread()` routine, which kills a thread indicated by a thread ID. The `pthread_cancel()` call causes a `pthread_cancel_e` exception to be raised in the target thread.

```
create_thread(
   pthread_startroutine_t thread_routine,
   char                   *thread_name,
   pthread_t              *thread_id,
   pthread_addr_t          thread_arg)
{
   unsigned32 status;

   status = pthread_create(
              thread_id,
              pthread_attr_default,
              thread_routine,
              thread_arg);
   if (status != 0)
   {
      fprintf(out_fd, "Cannot create %s thread\n",
        thread_name);
      fprintf(out_fd, "%s\n", strerror(errno));
      exit(0);
   }
   pthread_yield();
}
```

Code Sample 10.8
`schedule/sch_util.c: create_thread()`

Without special programming, the cancellation will terminate the thread. The thread cancel can be caught with a `TRY CATCH` block and handled in a way to prevent the thread from being terminated. This can in fact be used as an interthread signaling mechanism, which is done extensively in DCE RPC. However, the condition variable mechanism discussed in Section 10.3 is a better signaling method for application programming.

Normally, thread cancellations take effect when the target thread reaches certain *cancellation points*, for example, a blocking pthreads call. This is called *synchronous* or *general cancelability.* A thread can prevent itself from begin canceled in a critical region by calling `pthread_setcancel(CANCEL_OFF)`. A thread can also open itself to being canceled at any point (*asynchronous cancelability*) by calling `pthread_setasynccancel(CANCEL_ON)`. This is not usually advisable, due to the potential for problems with randomly terminating application code.

```
void kill_thread(
   pthread_t thread_id,
   char      *thread_name)
{
   unsigned32 status;

   status = pthread_cancel(thread_id);
   if (status != 0)
   {
      fprintf(out_fd, "Cannot kill %s thread\n",
        thread_name);
      fprintf(out_fd, "%s\n", strerror(errno));
   }
}
```

Code Sample 10.9
`schedule/sch_util.c`: `create_thread()` and `kill_thread()`

An Application Thread Example: The Scrubber Thread

The **`room_server`** needs some way of removing old reservations from its data structures. Otherwise its database will fill up with data that is no longer relevant, consuming memory and slowing access time. What is needed is something that periodically removes reservation events that are older than the current time. This can be done using a "scrubber" thread that cleans out the data structure. Code Sample 10.10 shows the base routine for the scrubber thread. It gets the current time (in the Unix Epoch format) and scans the location list, the rooms in each location, and the events for each room for reservations that are older than the current time. It unlinks and deallocates each old event. Note that it locks the room mutex while it is scrubbing the room's event list. This prevents any other thread from accessing the event list while it is being modified. After the routine completes scrubbing the entire data structure, it will go to sleep for an hour. Consequently, this thread will scrub the room reservations every hour.

```
pthread_addr_t room_event_scrubber(pthread_addr_t arg)
{
   struct timeval    now;
   struct timespec   sleep_time;
   loc_rec_t        *loc_p;
   room_rec_t       *room_p;
   event_rec_t      *event_p;

   while (true)
   {
      gettimeofday(&now, NULL);

      for (loc_p = loc_list; loc_p != NULL;
           loc_p = loc_p->next)
      {
         for (room_p = loc_p->room_list; room_p != NULL;
              room_p = room_p->next)
         {
            LOCK_ROOM_MUTEX(room_p);
            for (event_p = room_p->event_list;
                 (event_p != NULL) &&
                 (event_p->end < now.tv_sec);
                 event_p = event_p->next)
            {
               UNLINK(event_p, room_p->event_list);
               free(event_p);
            }
            UNLOCK_ROOM_MUTEX(room_p);
         }
      }
      sleep_time.tv_sec  = 60*60; /* 1 hour from now */
      sleep_time.tv_nsec = 0;
      pthread_delay_np(&sleep_time);
   }
}
```

Code Sample 10.10
`schedule/room_mgr.c: room_event_scrubber()`

The scrubber thread is created after the room database is opened and read into memory in the `room_open()` procedure. This means that any old reservations will immediately be scrubbed from the database. The scrubber thread will be killed before the room database is written back to its disk file, in `room_close()`. This is shown in Code Sample 10.11.

```
pthread_t scrubber_thread;

void room_open()
{
  . . .
  create_thread(
      room_event_scrubber,
      "room_event_scrubber",
      &scrubber_thread,
      NULL);
}

void room_close()
{
  . . .
  kill_thread(scrubber_thread, "room_event_scrubber");
  . . .
}
```

Code Sample 10.11
`schedule/room_mgr.c`: Creating and killing the scrubber thread

10.3 Worker Threads and Thread Coordination

Sometimes it is useful to create a number of threads to perform tasks in parallel. By overlapping the tasks you may be able to do the tasks quicker than if they were executed serially. The threads created for the tasks are sometimes called *worker threads*. After completing their tasks, the worker threads are usually terminated.

The **`room`** client presents an opportunity to illustrate the use of worker threads. Consider the **`d`** (description) command that retrieves the description of a room. The input to this command is the name of the room without its location. (Indeed, you may be using this command to find the location for a room.) With the multiple server version of the **room_server** discussed in Chapter 8, the client may need to send the `room_description()` operation to each of the servers registered in the `room_group`. In Chapter 8, this was done serially; the client `description()` routine bound to each server and executed the remote call until it found the room or it ran out of servers. Now we will modify the client to create worker threads to do this task. Each worker thread will bind to one server and make the `room_description()` remote call. The worker threads will do this in parallel. When one thread finds the room, it will signal the client main thread with the result. The client main thread will then kill the other worker threads. If all of the worker threads fail to find the room, the client main thread must be notified. Figure 10.5 illustrates the serial and parallel approaches.

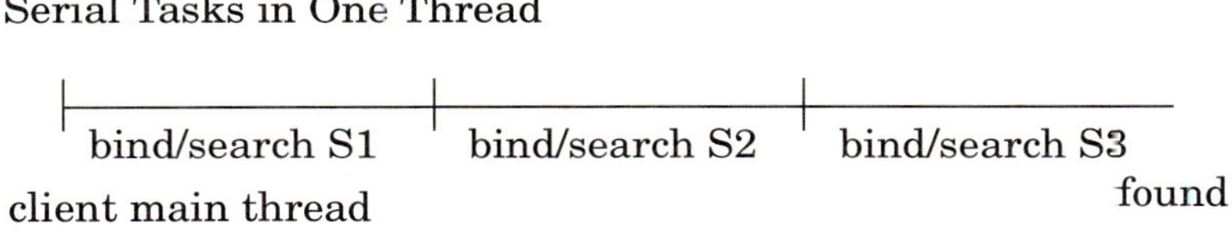

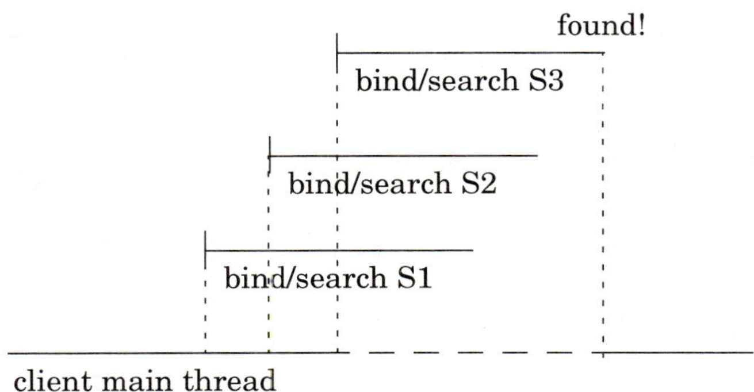

Figure 10.5
Serial Tasks within a Thread versus Parallel Worker Threads

Synchronization with Condition Variables

The worker threads must have some way to signal the client main thread when they have completed their tasks. The client main thread must then wait while the worker threads do their work. DCE provides *condition variables* for this kind of synchronization. A condition variable is a data structure that can be waited on and signaled. Each condition variable is associated with some condition that must become true before a waiting thread can continue.

In the **room** client example, the waiting thread is the client main thread, and the condition is: "Either a worker thread has successfully found the room, or all threads have tried and failed to find the room." The condition is represented by one or more global variables that are set by the threads in question. The **room** client uses the boolean variable `desc_all_done_or_found` to represent the condition; it will be initialized to `false` and set to `true` when either a thread finds the room, or all threads have tried and failed. Also associated with this condition will be a count of the threads still trying: `n_active_desc_threads`. The condition variable itself is `desc_cond`. These variables are declared in Code Sample 10.12.

A mutex is always associated with a condition variable. This mutex must be locked when the waiting thread waits on the condition variable, and it must be locked while any thread changes the underlying condition. In the **room** client, the `desc_mutex` variable is associated with the `desc_cond` variable. `desc_mutex` must be locked when a thread modifies `desc_all_done_or_found` or `n_active_desc_threads`.

```
pthread_mutex_t   desc_mutex;
pthread_cond_t    desc_cond;
int               n_desc_threads;
int               n_active_desc_threads;
boolean32         desc_all_done_or_found;
```

Code Sample 10.12
`schedule/obj/thread/room.c`: Condition variable and mutex

A condition variable is initialized by calling `pthread_cond_init()`. There is a condition variable attribute defined, but we will always use the default `pthread_condattr_default`. A thread waits on a condition variable by calling `pthread_cond_wait()`, which takes as input both the condition variable and its associated mutex. Another thread can signal the waiting thread by calling `pthread_cond_signal()`. Like all of the pthread calls, these calls return `0` for success and `-1` for failure, and set `errno`. Code Sample 10.13 shows macros that encapsulate the condition variable (and mutex) calls and the related error checking.

```
#define MUTEX_INIT(mutex) \
   if (pthread_mutex_init(&mutex,
         pthread_mutexattr_default) != 0) \
      perror("Cannot initialize mutex:");

#define MUTEX_LOCK(mutex) \
   if (pthread_mutex_lock(&mutex) != 0) \
      perror("Cannot lock mutex:");

#define MUTEX_UNLOCK(mutex) \
   if (pthread_mutex_unlock(&mutex) != 0) \
      perror("Cannot unlock mutex:");

#define COND_INIT(cond) \
   if (pthread_cond_init(&cond,
         pthread_condattr_default) != 0) \
      perror("Cannot initialize conv variable:");

#define COND_WAIT(cond, mutex) \
   if (pthread_cond_wait(&cond, &mutex) != 0) \
      perror("Cannot wait on cond variable:");

#define COND_SIGNAL(cond) \
   if (pthread_cond_signal(&cond) != 0) \
      perror("Cannot signal cond variable:");

#define DETACH(thread_id) \
   if (pthread_detach(&thread_id) != 0) \
      perror("Cannot detach thread:");
```

Code Sample 10.13
`schedule/obj/thread/room.c`: pthread macros

The Worker Thread and Its Argument

The base routine for the room client worker thread is try_one_desc(), which is shown in Code Sample 10.15. The argument passed to the base routine is a pointer to the desc_arg_t structure, shown in Code Sample 10.14. This structure contains both the input and output parameters needed by try_one_desc(). The input includes the name of the server entry to which to bind and the name of the room to find. The output includes the room record (if the room is found), the status of the search, and the status of the remote room_description() call. The structure also includes a boolean field done that is set by the thread if it has completed its remote call.

```
typedef struct {
   unsigned_char_p_t ns_entry_name;/* in */
   sch_room_name_t   room_name;     /* in */
   sch_room_t        room;          /* out */
   sch_status_t      sch_status;    /* out */
   error_status_t    call_status;   /* out */
   boolean32         done;          /* out */
} desc_arg_t;
```

Code Sample 10.14
schedule/obj/thread/room.c: Thread argument

The try_one_desc() function first calls bind_to_server() with the server Name Space entry from the thread argument. Then it makes the room_description() remote call to the server, using the input and output parameters in the thread argument.

Once the remote call is completed, it sets the done field in the thread argument to true and determines if the client main thread should be signaled. First, try_one_desc() locks the desc_mutex. Next, it decrements n_active_desc_threads. Finally, if all of the threads are done (n_active_desc_threads == 0) or if it has found the target room (desc_arg_p->sch_status == sch_status_ok), the worker thread signals the condition variable to wake the waiting client thread. Before exiting, it unlocks the desc_mutex.

```
pthread_addr_t try_one_desc(pthread_addr_t arg)
{
   desc_arg_t            *desc_arg_p = (desc_arg_t *) arg;
   rpc_binding_handle_t h;
   unsigned32             status, ignored_st;

   h = bind_to_server(desc_arg_p->ns_entry_name);
   if (h != NULL)
   {
      room_description(
         h,
         desc_arg_p->room_name,
         &desc_arg_p->room,
         &desc_arg_p->sch_status,
         &desc_arg_p->call_status);

      rpc_binding_free(&h, &status);
      CHECK_DCE(status, "Cannot free server binding");
   }
   rpc_string_free(&desc_arg_p->ns_entry_name,
     &ignored_st);
   desc_arg_p->done = true;

   MUTEX_LOCK(desc_mutex);
   n_active_desc_threads--;
   if ((desc_arg_p->sch_status == sch_status_ok) ||
       (n_active_desc_threads == 0))
   {
      desc_all_done_or_found = true;
      COND_SIGNAL(desc_cond);
   }
   MUTEX_UNLOCK(desc_mutex);
}
```

Code Sample 10.15
schedule/obj/thread/room.c: try_one_desc()

Creating and Waiting for the Worker Threads

The `description()` routine, executed in the **room** client main thread, creates the worker threads, waits for their signal, and if necessary kills them. The code to do this will be presented in three chunks, starting with Code Sample 10.16.

```
void description()
{
   . . .
   pthread_t              desc_thread[MAX_DESC_THREADS];
   desc_arg_t             desc_arg   [MAX_DESC_THREADS];

   /* Try the default server */
   if (sch_status == sch_status_room_not_found)
   {
      rpc_ns_group_mbr_inq_begin(...);
      . . .
      n_desc_threads = 0;
      while (n_desc_threads < MAX_DESC_THREADS)
      {
         rpc_ns_group_mbr_inq_next(
            mbr_inq_context,
            &desc_arg[n_desc_threads].ns_entry_name,
            &status);
        if (status == rpc_s_no_more_members)
         {
            break;
         }
        . . .
        strcpy(desc_arg[n_desc_threads].room_name,
           room_name);
         desc_arg[n_desc_threads].done = false;
         n_desc_threads++;
      }
      rpc_ns_group_mbr_inq_done(...);
      . . .
   }
```

Code Sample 10.16
`schedule/obj/thread/room.c: description()`

Code Sample 10.16 shows how the thread arguments, in the `desc_arg` array, are initialized. The server entries are retrieved from the `room_group`, using `rpc_ns_group_mbr_inq_begin()` and a loop calling `rpc_ns_group_mbr_inq_next()`. Each pass of the loop gets the next server entry and sets up the next thread argument in desc_arg. In addition to setting a pointer to the server entry, this copies the room name into the thread argument and initializes its done flag to false.

Code Sample 10.17 shows the next segment of description(), which creates each worker thread using the thread arguments in the desc_arg array. Once all the threads are created, it will wait for a signal from a worker thread on the desc_cond variable.

```
void description()
{
      . . .
      n_active_desc_threads  = n_desc_threads;
      desc_all_done_or_found = false;
      for (i = 0; i < n_desc_threads; i++)
      {
         create_thread(
            try_one_desc,
            "try_one_desc",
            &desc_thread[i],
            (pthread_addr_t) &desc_arg[i]);
      }

      if (n_desc_threads > 0)
      {
         MUTEX_LOCK(desc_mutex);
         while (!desc_all_done_or_found)
         {
            COND_WAIT(desc_cond, desc_mutex);
         }
         MUTEX_UNLOCK(desc_mutex);
      }
     . . .
}
```

Code Sample 10.17
schedule/obj/thread/room.c: description()

Before calling pthread_cond_wait(), the client main thread must lock the mutex associated with the condition variable. Within pthread_cond_wait(), this mutex will be unlocked to allow other threads to lock it. The pthread_cond_wait() call will block until it receives a signal from another thread. Then it will relock the mutex and return. Consequently, the waiting thread must unlock the mutex after its pthread_cond_wait() call.

The while loop around the pthread_cond_wait() call is there to take care of a peculiar feature of condition variables: that the condition variable might be spuriously signaled before the condition is true. So it is recommended that the waiting thread test the condition to make sure that it has actually been satisfied. A signaling thread will set `desc_all_done_or_found` to `true` before signaling the condition variable.

The final chunk of the `description()` routine is shown in Code Sample 10.18. This piece is reached after the condition variable has been signaled. Then either one worker thread found the room, or all worker threads have completed without success. To find out which condition occurred, `description()` will look at the output fields of the thread arguments in the `desc_arg` array. If it finds one with a successful completion status, it will keep the room information from the thread's successful `room_description()` call.

If a worker thread has completed, it will still have allocated resources. The `pthread_detach()` call marks those resource for allocation. `description()` calls the `DETACH` macro for each completed worker thread.

Finally, if a thread has not completed at this point, `description()` will kill the thread. (Some other thread must have been successful in finding the room.) Note that when a thread is canceled, its resources are automatically released and `pthread_detach()` is not called.

```
void description()
{
        . . .
        for (i = 0; i < n_desc_threads; i++)
        {
            if (desc_arg[i].done)
            {
                if ((desc_arg[i].sch_status == sch_status_ok)
                  && (desc_arg[i].call_status == rpc_s_ok))
                {
                    memcpy(&room, &desc_arg[i].room,
                      sizeof(sch_room_t));
                    sch_status = desc_arg[i].sch_status;
                }
                DETACH(desc_thread[i]);
            }
            else
            {
                kill_thread(desc_thread[i],"try_one_thread");
            }
        }
    }

   /* Display room record. */
}
```

Code Sample 10.18
`schedule/obj/thread/room.c: description()`

Joining with a Thread

Another facility for synchronizing threads is *joining*. Say thread A creates a worker thread B. You want thread A to block until thread B completes its task. Thread A can call `pthread_join()` with thread B's ID. It will block in `pthread_join()` until thread B completes. This call also has an output parameter for a status value returned from the thread. This status value is set in `pthread_exit()`.

10.4 Thread Considerations for Libraries

If you are writing a library that will be used in a threaded process, there are some additional things you may need to include to ensure that your library functions properly. If the library uses global variables or static variables ("own" variables as discussed in Chapter 2), you will have to use mutexes to control concurrent use of the variables. If you are creating threads, you may need to use condition variables as well.

Once Initialization

Suppose you have a function in your library named `mylib_init()`, which is responsible for initializing everything your library needs in the process. This may include initializing mutexes and condition variables, as well as initializing data structures that aren't related to threads. Suppose now that two threads within the process both execute `mylib_init()` concurrently. There is the danger that the second initialization call will interfere with the first. You can think of the initialization code as a critical section that must be completed without interference. You might then think of using a mutex to protect the critical section. But then, how is this mutex to be initialized? It cannot be initialized in `mylib_init()`, because that is the call it is protecting.

To solve this dilemma, DCE provides a facility to ensure that an initialization routine is executed once and only once. The actual initialization code is put into a second routine, say `mylib_init_once()`. This routine is then executed using the `pthread_once()` call, which also includes a data structure called a *once block*. The once block serves as a temporary mutex to prevent any other thread from executing a routine through `pthread_once()` using the same once block. Code Sample 10.19 shows an example of once initialization.

Thread-Specific Data

A library may need to retain data between its calls. A typical example of this is an initial open call that sets up some data that is later used by other calls in the library. In a nonthreaded process, this requirement can be satisfied by a global variable within the library, as shown by Code Sample 10.20.

```
pthread_once_t mylib_once_block = pthread_once_init;

void mylib_init_once()
{
  /* the real initialization code */
}

void mylib_init()
{
  pthread_once(&mylib_once_block, mylib_init_once);
}
```

Code Sample 10.19
Library initialization with `pthread_once()`

```
mylib_data_t *mylib_data;

void mylib_open(...)
{
  mylib_data = (mylib_data_t *)
     malloc(sizeof(mylib_data_t));
  /* initialize mylib_data */
  . . .
}

void mylib_op(...)
{
  /* use mylib_data */
  . . .
}
```

Code Sample 10.20
Library global data

Now, consider what would happen if two threads within the same process executed these calls. Thread 1 executes `mylib_open()`, which allocates `mylib_data` for thread 1's data. Then thread 2 executes `mylib_open()`, which allocates another `mylib_data` for thread 2's data, replacing thread 1's data. Then thread 1 executes `mylib_op()`. Instead of using thread 1's data, this call uses thread 2's data.

To solve this problem, DCE provides *thread-specific data*. Instead of one global variable, the library can allocate a variable specific to each thread. The thread-specific data is identified by a key, assigned by a call to `pthread_keycreate()`. This call also sets up a *destructor* function that will be called when a thread terminates to deallocate its thread-specific data.

The data key should be assigned only once for all of the threads in the process. Consequently, the `pthread_keycreate()` call should be executed under the control of a `pthread_once()` call. Code Sample 10.21 shows this for our library example. (In this example, I have omitted the error checking for the pthread calls.) Thread 1 calls `mylib_open()`, which calls `pthread_once()`, which calls `mylib_init_once()`, which calls `pthread_keycreate()` to assign a value to `mylib_key`. Then thread 2 calls `mylib_open()`, which calls `pthread_once()`, but `mylib_once_block` indicates that the once routine has already been called, so `pthread_keycreate()` is not called again.

Once the thread-specific data key has been established, the data for a thread can be set using `pthread_setspecific()` and retrieved using `pthread_getspecific()`. `mylib_open()` allocates a `mylib_data_t` structure, initializes it, and calls `pthread_setspecific()` to set the `mylib_key` data for the thread. Then `mylib_op()` calls `pthread_getspecific()` to retrieve the threads value for the `mylib_key`.

Suppose thread 1 calls `mylib_open()`, which allocates a data area 1 and sets the `mylib_key` value for thread 1 to point to data area 1. Then thread 2 calls `mylib_open()`, which allocates a data area 2 and sets the `mylib_key` value for thread 2 to point to data area 2. When thread 1 calls `mylib_op()`, it will retrieve the value for data area 1. When thread 2 calls `mylib_op()`, it will retrieve the value for data area 2. In this way, library data can be kept separate among concurrent threads.

```
pthread_once_t mylib_once_block = pthread_once_init;
pthread_key_t mylib_key;

void mylib_destructor(pthread_addr_t key)
{
   free(key);
}

void mylib_init_once()
{
  pthread_keycreate(&mylib_key,&mylib_destructor);
}

void mylib_open(...)
{
  mylib_data_t *mylib_data;

  pthread_once(&mylib_once_block, mylib_init_once);

  mylib_data = (mylib_data_t *)
     malloc(sizeof(mylib_data_t));
  /* initialize mylib_data */

  pthread_setspecific(mylib_key, mylib_data);
  . . .
}

void mylib_op(...)
{
  mylib_data_t *mylib_data;

  pthread_setspecific(mylib_key, &mylib_data);
  /* use mylib_data */
  . . .
}
```

Code Sample 10.21
Library thread-specific data

10.5 CMA Threads Implementation

Most DCE implementations, including HP-UX DCE, use the CMA (Concert Multithread Architecture) threads package that originated with Digital. CMA provides *user-space threads*, implemented within the processes of the underlying operating system.

Thread Stacks in the Process Address Space

Each thread has a stack to contain the local variables and execution markers for the procedures called within the thread. CMA allocates the thread stacks out of a big chunk of the process heap. Since all thread stacks are in the same address space, an errant thread can damage other thread's stacks (as well as process global data).

Thread Scheduling Using Virtual Alarms

Threads within a process are scheduled and dispatched by CMA. When a running thread comes to a blocking point like a `read()` or a `pthread_cond_wait()`, CMA will dispatch the next waiting thread. A computation-intensive thread (or just a thread in an infinite loop) may not come to a blocking point for a long time, if ever. To keep such a thread from monopolizing the process, CMA uses *virtual alarm* signals to periodically interrupt the running thread. If the thread has used up its assigned quantum of time, CMA will dispatch another waiting thread.

Because of thread scheduling, the trapping of virtual alarms should be disabled when debugging a DCE client or server, as will be recommended in Appendix A. Also, application code should not use the virtual alarm signal. If the application needs to perform periodic tasks, it should use a thread as discussed earlier in this chapter.

Wrappers and the Null Thread for Blocking Operations

If a thread makes a call that could block, such as a `read()` for a file or a `recv()` on a socket, that call must not be allowed to block the entire process. To prevent this, CMA uses *wrappers* for blocking functions. Each blocking function is replaced by a CMA wrapper function by definitions in the header file `cma_ux.h` in `/usr/include/dce`. This header is included by `pthread.h`. For example, `read()` is replaced by `cma_read()`. The wrapper functions are responsible for setting up the operation so that it blocks the thread but not the entire process.

CMA uses a special thread, called the *null thread*, to handle blocking calls. Normally, the null thread is not visible to the application. The null thread waits on events on behalf of other threads in the process. When a thread calls a wrapper for a blocking operation on a file or a socket, the wrapper adds the file or socket descriptor to a set of descriptors used by the null thread. The wrapper then calls `pthread_cond_wait()` to wait on a condition variable especially set up for blocking that thread.

Meanwhile, when all other threads have blocked or otherwise yielded, the null thread calls `select()` with its descriptor set to wait for any incoming events. This `select()` will block the entire process. When an event, like a file descriptor becoming readable, completes the `select()`, the null thread will determine which thread is waiting for the event and will call `pthread_cond_signal()` on that thread's condition variable. The blocked thread will resume execution and perform the original operation to completion. Figure 10.6 illustrates the interaction between a blocked application thread and the null thread.

The wrapper function and null thread strategy for managing blocking works only if the blocking code is compiled with the wrapper function definitions. If a blocking call is in an existing library that has not been modified for DCE, the call will still block the entire process.

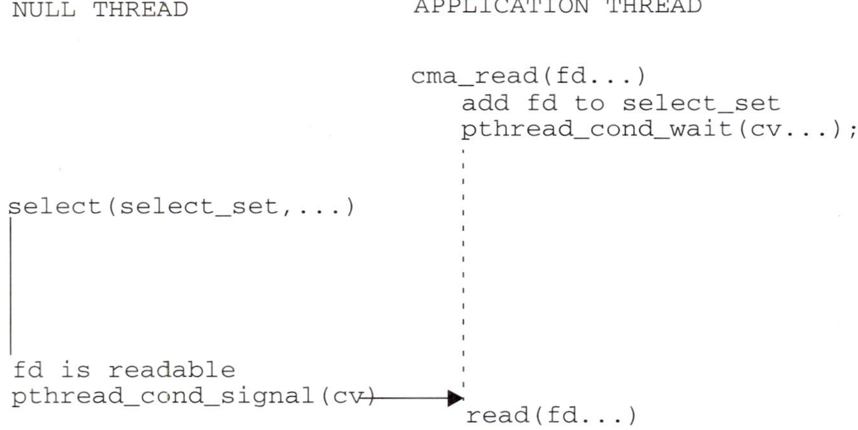

Figure 10.6
The CMA Null Thread and Blocking Operations

Thread Timer

Some thread calls will block for a specified amount of time. The `pthread_delay_np()` call blocks for a given length of time. The `pthread_cond_timedwait()` call waits on a condition variable until a specified timeout occurs. To handle these sorts of calls, CMA maintains a list of timer events. When the CMA scheduler runs in the process, say, when a process blocks or when a virtual alarm pops, it will look at the timer list to see if the next event should be initiated. When all of the threads in the process are blocked, the null thread will be waiting in `select()` for unblocking events. The null thread must wake up when a timer event pops. To do this, it uses the timeout parameter of `select()`, set to the time for the next timer event. If no unblocking event occurs, the `select()` will return when its timeout occurs. The null thread will then set up the timer event for execution.

APPENDIX A

Hints for Debugging DCE Applications

This appendix provides some hints on how to debug a DCE client-server application on HP-UX DCE.

- Use loopback on one test system.

  An application client and server can be run on the same test system using loopback. This localizes your testing effort and decreases the test system requirements, at least for the initial testing of an application.

- Use separate windows for each client and server.

  Preferably, you can debug your application from a workstation or a PC that provides multiple windows logged onto the test system. Run the server in one window and the client in another, with output from each to their respective windows. If necessary, more than one client or server can be run using multiple windows.

- Use a connection-oriented RPC protocol.

  If you are going to be setting breakpoints in the server, you do not want the client timing out while it is waiting for a datagram response from the server. This can be avoided by issuing this command before running the client:

  ```
  :export RPC_SUPPORTED_PROTSEQS=ncacn_ip_tcp
  ```

- Set breakpoints at operation manager entry points.

  A good way to debug a server is to set breakpoints in the manager routines for its operations. Then you can run the client and step through the execution of the remote calls as necessary.

- In **xdb**, turn off signal interrupts.

  If you are using the **xdb** debugger, you should disable certain signal interrupts, with the commands

`z 20 sr`	virtual alarm
`z 12 sr`	bad argument to system call

  DCE threads use the virtual alarm for its thread scheduling, so if you do not disable the virtual alarm trap, it will continually go off while you are debugging a client or server. (I don't know why the bad argument to system call needs to be disabled—perhaps just DCE folklore.)

  You can set up an `.xdbrc` file in your `$HOME` directory to include these commands, so they will always be executed when you use **xdb**.

- Use **dde** for thread awareness.

  The **xdb** debugger does not support threads well. The **dde** debugger has been enhanced to support threads, with the ability to display thread stacks.

Room Schedule Example

This appendix contains listings of the source modules for the object version of the Room Schedule sample application found in the `schedule/obj` directory of the accompanying diskette. The files listed are

• `sch.idl`	defines types and constants
• `room.idl`	defines the `room` interface
• `room.acf`	adds error status to `room` operations
• `room.c`	source for the **room** client
• `room_server.c`	source for the **room_server** `main()`.
• `room_mgr.c`	source for the native `room` managers
• `legacy_mgr.c`	source for the legacy `room` managers
• `sch_util.c`	source for common routines
• `sch_util.h`	header for common routines and defines
• `rgy_create.ksh`	script to create cell security group
• `rgy_create_host.ksh`	script to create host security principal
• `rgy_delete.ksh`	script to delete cell security group
• `rgy_delete_host.ksh`	script to delete host security principal
• `cds_create.ksh`	script to create cell CDS entries
• `cds_create_host.ksh`	script to create host CDS entries
• `cds_delete.ksh`	script to delete cell CDS entries
• `cds_delete_host.ksh`	script to delete host CDS entries
• `Makefile`	Makefile to build the application
• `room_db.dat1`	sample room database for server 1
• `room_db.dat2`	sample room database for server 2

B.1 schedule/obj/sch.idl

```
/*
 * sch.idl
 *
 * Defines data types and constants used by the room schedule application.
 */

interface sch
{

import "dce/aclbase.idl";

/*
 * sch_date_time_t
 *     Represents a time interval on a date, with format yy-mm-dd hh:mm-hh:mm.
 *     The times (hh:mm) are in 24-hour time. An example 94-07-18 13:00-14:00
 *     represents 1:00 pm to 2:00 pm on July 18, 1994.  Local time is assumed.
 */

typedef [string] char sch_date_time_t[22];

/*
 * sch_short_date_time_t
 *     Represents a time on a date, with format yy-mm-dd hh:mm.  The time
 *     (hh:mm) is in 24-hour time. An example 94-07-18 13:00 represents 1:00 pm
 *     on July 18, 1994.  Local time is assumed.
 */

typedef [string] char sch_short_date_time_t[15];

/*
 * sch_event_desc_t
 *     Describes an event for which a room reservation is made.
 */

typedef [string] char sch_event_desc_t[20];

/*
 * sch_loc_name_t
 *     Names a location, such as a building or site, that contains rooms.
 */

typedef [string] char sch_loc_name_t[10];

/*
 * sch_name_t
 *     Names a person making a reservation.
 */

typedef [string] char sch_name_t[20];

/*
 * sch_room_desc_t
 *     Provides additional description of a room, such as pillar location or
 *     special facilities.
 */
```

```
typedef [string] char sch_room_desc_t[30];

/*
 * sch_room_name_t
 *    Names a room.  The room name is assumed to be unique within a location.
 */

typedef [string] char sch_room_name_t[20];

/*
 * sch_status_t
 *    Indicates the status of a room interface RPC call.  Valid values are
 *    defined below as sch_status_...
 */

typedef long int sch_status_t;

/*
 * sch_room_t
 *    Provides information for a room: location, name, maximum capacity,
 *    and additional description.
 */

typedef struct {
   sch_loc_name_t   loc;
   sch_room_name_t  name;
   long int         max_people;
   sch_room_desc_t  desc;
} sch_room_t;

/*
 * sch_event_t
 *    Provides information about an event for which a room is reserved:
 *    the date and time, who made the reservation, and what the room was
 *    reserved for.
 */

typedef struct {
   sch_date_time_t  date_time;
   sch_name_t       reserver;
   sch_event_desc_t desc;
} sch_event_t;

/*
 * sch_event_rec_t, sch_event_rec_p_t
 *    Used to build doubly linked lists of events.
 */

typedef struct SCH_EVENT_REC_T {
   [ptr] struct SCH_EVENT_REC_T *prev;
   [ptr] struct SCH_EVENT_REC_T *next;
   sch_event_t  event;
} sch_event_rec_t;

typedef [ptr] sch_event_rec_t *sch_event_rec_p_t;

/*
 * Valid values for sch_status_t.
```

```
 */

const sch_status_t sch_status_ok              = 0;
const sch_status_t sch_status_loc_not_found   = 1;
const sch_status_t sch_status_room_not_found  = 2;
const sch_status_t sch_status_room_unavail    = 3;
const sch_status_t sch_status_bad_date_time   = 4;
const sch_status_t sch_status_event_not_found= 5;
const sch_status_t sch_status_not_reserver    = 6;
const sch_status_t sch_status_not_secure      = 7;
const sch_status_t sch_status_not_authorized  = 8;

const sch_status_t sch_status_unimplemented   = -1;

/*
 * ACL permission bits
 *    inquire - caller can view data about a room and its reservations
 *    reserve - caller can make a room reservation
 *    cancel  - caller can cancel any reservation for a room (without
 *              being the original reserver).
 *    control - caller can modify a room ACL.
 */

const sec_acl_permset_t sch_acl_perm_inq     = sec_acl_perm_unused_00000080;
const sec_acl_permset_t sch_acl_perm_reserve = sec_acl_perm_unused_00000100;
const sec_acl_permset_t sch_acl_perm_cancel  = sec_acl_perm_unused_00000200;
const sec_acl_permset_t sch_acl_perm_control = sec_acl_perm_control;
const sec_acl_permset_t sch_acl_perm_test    = sec_acl_perm_test;

}
```

B.2 schedule/obj/room.idl

```
/*
 * room.idl
 *
 * Defines the room reservation interface.
 */

[uuid(6101efd0-89fc-11cd-be27-080009307c01), version(1.0)]
interface room
{

import "sch.idl";

/*
 * room_description()
 *    Returns the information for a room.  The room location is not
 *    required for this call; all locations will be searched for the room.
 */

void room_description(
   [in ] handle_t        h,
   [in ] sch_room_name_t room_name,
   [out] sch_room_t      *room,
   [out] sch_status_t    *status);

/*
 * room_reserve()
 *    Reserves a room for an event at a date and time and for a reserver.
 *    The room location and name must be set in room.
 */

void room_reserve(
   [in ] handle_t          h,
   [in ] sch_room_t        room,
   [in ] sch_date_time_t   date_time,
   [in ] sch_name_t        reserver,
   [in ] sch_event_desc_t desc,
   [out] sch_status_t     *status);

/*
 * room_cancel()
 *    Cancels a room reservation at a date and time and for the original
 *    reserver.  The room location and name must be set in room.
 */

void room_cancel(
   [in ] handle_t        h,
   [in ] sch_room_t      room,
   [in ] sch_date_time_t date_time,
   [in ] sch_name_t      reserver,
   [out] sch_status_t   *status);



/*
 * room_avail()
```

```
 *    Returns an array of rooms that are available at a date and time, and
 *    can hold a certain number of people.  The returned rooms are ordered
 *    by one or more preferred locations.
 */

void room_avail(
   [in ] handle_t        h,
   [in ] sch_date_time_t date_time,
   [in ] long int        n_people,
   [in ] long int        n_pref_locs,
   [in,  size_is(n_pref_locs)]
          sch_loc_name_t  pref_locs[],
   [in ] long int        max_avail_rooms,
   [out] long int       *n_avail_rooms,
   [out, size_is(max_avail_rooms), length_is(*n_avail_rooms)]
          sch_room_t      avail_rooms[],
   [out] sch_status_t   *status);

/*
 * room_events()
 *    Returns a linked list of events for which a room is reserved between
 *    begin and end dates and times.  The room location and name must be set
 *    in room.
 */

void room_events(
   [in ] handle_t               h,
   [in ] sch_room_t             room,
   [in ] sch_short_date_time_t begin_date_time,
   [in ] sch_short_date_time_t end_date_time,
   [out] sch_event_rec_p_t     *room_event_list,
   [out] sch_status_t          *status);
}
```

B.3 schedule/obj/room.acf

```
/*
 * room.acf
 *
 * Defines local attributes to the room reservation interface:
 *    - Adds a call_status parameter to each operation.
 */

interface room
{
room_description([comm_status, fault_status] call_status);
room_reserve    ([comm_status, fault_status] call_status);
room_cancel     ([comm_status, fault_status] call_status);
room_avail      ([comm_status, fault_status] call_status);
room_events     ([comm_status, fault_status] call_status);
}
```

B.4 schedule/obj/room.c

```
/*
 * room.c
 *
 * The client for the room schedule application. This provides a (rudimentary)
 * interactive interface to make room reservations through the room server.
 * A real production system would replace this client with a nicer graphical
 * user interface.
 *
 * Commands are:
 *     d - display the description for a room
 *     r - make a room reservation
 *     c - cancel a room reservation
 *     e - display the reservation events for a room during a given period
 *     a - display rooms that are available (not reserved) during a given
 *         period, ordered by preferred location.
 *
 * The room client can import a server binding from several CDS entries:
 *
 *     - Default server; used first for room description
 *       - RPC_DEFAULT_ENTRY environment variable, if defined
 *       - cell-profile, otherwise
 *     - All servers in /.:/subsys/sch/room_group, used for room description
 *       if room not found in default server
 *     - Server for a particular location: /.:/subsys/sch/room/LOCATION, used
 *       for all operations that specify a location
 */

#include <stdio.h>
#include <malloc.h>
#include <dce/dce_error.h>
#include <dce/binding.h>
#include <dce/pgo.h>
#include "room.h"
#include "sch_util.h"

/*
 * GET macro
 *    Prints a prompt and inputs a string.
 *
 * CHECK_CALL macro
 *    Checks if the call_status returned by a remote call is an error, and
 *    if so prints an error message and returns.
 */

#define GET(prompt, target) \
   printf(prompt); \
   gets((char *) target)

#define CHECK_CALL(call_status) \
   if (call_status != error_status_ok) \
   { \
      print_call_status(call_status); \
      return; \
   }

#define CHECK_CALL_RETURN_NULL(call_status) \
   if (call_status != error_status_ok) \
```

```
    { \
       print_call_status(call_status); \
       return(NULL); \
    }

#define CHECK_MALLOC(p) \
    if ((p) == NULL) \
    { \
       printf("Out of memory\n"); \
       exit(1); \
    }

/*
 * Forward procedure declarations.
 */

void description(), reserve(), cancel(), avail(), events(), help();

/*
 * Location cache
 *    A linked list of locations and server binding handles that have
 *    already been used by the client.
 */
typedef struct LOC_REC_T {
    struct LOC_REC_T *next;
    sch_loc_name_t       loc_name;
    rpc_binding_handle_t h;
} loc_rec_t;

loc_rec_t *location_list = NULL;

/*
 * find_binding_by_location()
 *    Returns a cached binding for the location; if no cached binding is
 *    found, returns NULL.
 */
rpc_binding_handle_t find_binding_by_location(
    sch_loc_name_t loc_name)
{
    loc_rec_t *loc_p;

    for (loc_p = location_list; loc_p != NULL; loc_p = loc_p->next)
    {
       if (strcmp(loc_p->loc_name, loc_name) == 0)
       {
          return(loc_p->h);
       }
    }
    return(NULL);
}

/*
 * CHECK_DCE_RETURN macro
 *    Variant of CHECK_DCE macro that returns NULL instead of aborting
 *    the program on a DCE error.
 */
#define CHECK_DCE_RETURN(status, msg) \
    CHECK_DCE_NONFATAL(status, msg); \
```

```
    if (status != error_status_ok) \
    { \
       return(NULL); \
    }

/*
 * bind_to_server()
 *    Binds to the server indicated by the NS entry name.
 *       - Imports a binding from CDS
 *       - Checks that the server at that binding is active.
 *       - Gets the server's principal and verifies that it is a room server.
 *       - Sets up security for the binding.
 */
rpc_binding_handle_t bind_to_server(
   unsigned_char_p_t ns_entry_name)
{
   rpc_binding_handle_t      h;
   rpc_ns_handle_t           import_context;
   unsigned_char_p_t         server_principal;
   sec_rgy_name_t            cell_name;
   sec_rgy_name_t            principal_name;
   sec_rgy_name_t            group_name;
   sec_rgy_handle_t          rgy_h;
   sec_rgy_bind_auth_info_t auth_info;
   unsigned32                status, ignored_st;

      /*
       * Import a binding from the NS entry, bypassing any local CDS cache
       * to make sure we get the latest bindings.
       */
   printf("Binding to server at %s\n", ns_entry_name);
   rpc_ns_binding_import_begin(
      rpc_c_ns_syntax_default,
      ns_entry_name,
      room_v1_0_c_ifspec,
      NULL,              /* default object */
      &import_context,
      &status);
   CHECK_DCE_RETURN(status, "Cannot begin binding import");

   rpc_ns_mgmt_handle_set_exp_age(import_context, 0, &status);
   CHECK_DCE_RETURN(status, "Cannot set expiration for import.");

   rpc_ns_binding_import_next(import_context, &h, &status);

   if (status == rpc_s_no_more_bindings)
   {
      printf("Server is not available\n");
      return(NULL);
   }
   CHECK_DCE_RETURN(status, "Cannot import next binding");

   rpc_ns_binding_import_done(&import_context, &status);
   CHECK_DCE_RETURN(status, "Cannot complete binding import");

      /*
       * Have a binding to the room server. Check if the server is indeed
       * responding before proceeding.
```

```
     */
  if (!is_server_there(h, room_v1_0_c_ifspec))
  {
     printf("Server is not responding\n");
     return(NULL);
  }

     /*
      * Get the server's principal name from the server. We will need to
      * verify that this principal is a legitimate room server, that is, it
      * is in the room-server-group.
      */
  rpc_mgmt_inq_server_princ_name(
     h,
     rpc_c_authn_dce_secret,
     &server_principal,
     &status);
  CHECK_DCE_RETURN(status, "Cannot get server's principal");

     /*
      * The server principal is /.../cell_name/principal_name. We will
      * need the cell_name to bind to the appropriate Security Registry
      * and the principal_name to check the group membership.
      */
  sec_id_parse_name(
     sec_rgy_default_handle,
     server_principal,
     cell_name,
     NULL,
     principal_name,
     NULL,
     &status);
  CHECK_DCE_RETURN(status, "Cannot parse principal name");

     /*
      * Bind to the cell's Security Registry. This requires some
      * RPC authentication parameters.
      */
  auth_info.info_type                           = sec_rgy_bind_auth_dce;
  auth_info.tagged_union.dce_info.authn_level = rpc_c_protect_level_pkt_integ;
  auth_info.tagged_union.dce_info.authn_svc     = rpc_c_authn_dce_secret;
  auth_info.tagged_union.dce_info.authz_svc     = rpc_c_authz_dce;
  auth_info.tagged_union.dce_info.identity      = NULL;

  sec_rgy_site_bind(
     (unsigned_char_t *) cell_name,
     &auth_info,
     &rgy_h,
     &status);
  CHECK_DCE_RETURN(status, "Cannot bind to registry");

     /*
      * Finally, check if the server principal is in the room-server-group.
      */
  strcpy((char *) group_name, "room-server-group");
  if (!sec_rgy_pgo_is_member(
        rgy_h,
        sec_rgy_domain_group,
```

```
            group_name,
            principal_name,
            &status))
    {
        printf("Server principal is not a member of the room server group\n");
        return(NULL);
    }

    sec_rgy_site_close(rgy_h, &status);
    CHECK_DCE(status, "Cannot close security registry");

        /*
         * Set up security for the binding, including the target server
         * principal, the RPC protection level, and the authentication and
         * authorization services. Use the default login context, established
         * by the user's dce_login.
         */
    rpc_binding_set_auth_info(
        h,
        server_principal,
        rpc_c_protect_level_pkt_integ,
        rpc_c_authn_dce_secret,
        NULL,
        rpc_c_authz_dce,
        &status);
    CHECK_DCE_RETURN(status, "Cannot set up authentication for binding");

    rpc_string_free(&server_principal, &ignored_st);

    return(h);
}

/*
 * bind_to_server_by_location()
 *    Binds to the server for a location, using the CDS entry /.:/subsys/sch/
 *    room/LOCATION. If successful, adds the location and binding to the
 *    location cache.
 */
rpc_binding_handle_t bind_to_server_by_location(
    sch_loc_name_t loc_name)
{
#   define ROOM_NS_PREFIX "/.:/subsys/sch/room/"
    rpc_binding_handle_t h;
    unsigned_char_p_t    ns_entry_name;
    loc_rec_t           *loc_p;

    ns_entry_name = (unsigned_char_p_t)
        malloc(strlen(ROOM_NS_PREFIX) + strlen(loc_name) + 1);
    CHECK_MALLOC(ns_entry_name);
    sprintf((char *) ns_entry_name, "%s%s", ROOM_NS_PREFIX, loc_name);

    h = bind_to_server((unsigned_char_p_t) ns_entry_name);
    free(ns_entry_name);

    if (h != NULL)
    {
        loc_p = (loc_rec_t *) malloc(sizeof(loc_rec_t));
        CHECK_MALLOC(loc_p);
```

```
        strcpy(loc_p->loc_name, loc_name);
        loc_p->h = h;

        loc_p->next    = location_list;
        location_list = loc_p;
    }

    return(h);
}

/*
 * GET_BINDING macro
 *     Gets a binding for a location, either using a previously cached binding
 *     or by constructing a new binding.
 */
#define GET_BINDING(loc_name, h) \
    (h) = find_binding_by_location(loc_name); \
    if ((h) == NULL) \
    { \
        (h) = bind_to_server_by_location(loc_name); \
    } \
    if ((h) == NULL) \
    { \
        printf("Cannot bind to server\n"); \
        return; \
    }

/*
 * Binding handle for the default server.
 */
rpc_binding_handle_t default_h;

int main(int argc, char *argv[])
{
    unsigned_char_p_t string_binding;
    unsigned_char_p_t ns_entry_name;
    char              command[10];
    idl_boolean       done;
    loc_rec_t        *loc_p;
    unsigned32        status;
    unsigned32        ignored_st;
    sch_status_t      sch_status;
    error_status_t    call_status;

    /*
     * Bind to the default server.
     */
    ns_entry_name = (unsigned_char_p_t) getenv("RPC_DEFAULT_ENTRY");
    if (ns_entry_name == NULL)
    {
        ns_entry_name = (unsigned_char_p_t) "/.:/cell-profile";
    }

    default_h = bind_to_server(ns_entry_name);

    done = false;
    while (!done)
```

```
    {
       /*
        * Get and execute a command. Each of these routines makes a remote
        * call to the room server to perform the requested operation.
        */
       GET("\nCommand? ", command);
       switch (command[0])
       {
          case 'd': description();  break;
          case 'r': reserve();      break;
          case 'c': cancel();       break;
          case 'a': avail();        break;
          case 'e': events();       break;
          case 'q': done = true;    break;
          case 'h':
          case '?': help();         break;
          default:
              printf("Unknown command\n");
              help();
              break;
       }
    }

       /*
        * Done executing commands. Free the default server and cached
        * location bindings.
        */
    if (default_h != NULL)
    {
       rpc_binding_free(&default_h, &status);
       CHECK_DCE(status, "Cannot free default binding");
    }

    for (loc_p = location_list; loc_p != NULL; loc_p = loc_p->next)
    {
       if (loc_p->h != NULL)
       {
          rpc_binding_free(&loc_p->h, &status);
          CHECK_DCE(status, "Cannot free location binding");
       }
    }
}

void help()
{
   printf("\nCommands:\n");
   printf("   d - print the description of a room\n");
   printf("   r - reserve a room for a date and time\n");
   printf("   c - cancel a room reservation\n");
   printf("   a - list available rooms in preferred locations for");
   printf(" date and time\n");
   printf("   e - list events for which a room is reserved, between start");
   printf(" and end dates and times.\n");
   printf("   q - quit\n");
   printf("   h - quit\n");
   printf("   ? - help\n\n");
}
```

```
void description()
{
   sch_room_name_t       room_name;
   sch_room_t            room;
   rpc_ns_handle_t       mbr_inq_context;
   unsigned_char_p_t     ns_entry_name;
   rpc_binding_handle_t h;
   boolean32             using_server;
   unsigned32            status;
   sch_status_t          sch_status;
   error_status_t        call_status;

   GET("Room name? ", room_name);

      /*
       * First try to find the room in the default server, if it exists.
       */
   if (default_h != NULL)
   {
      room_description(default_h, room_name, &room, &sch_status, &call_status);
      CHECK_CALL(call_status);
   }
   else
   {
      sch_status = sch_status_room_not_found;
   }

   if (sch_status == sch_status_room_not_found)
   {
         /*
          * The room was not in the default server. Try every server in
          * the room group.
          */
      rpc_ns_group_mbr_inq_begin(
         rpc_c_ns_syntax_default,
         (unsigned_char_p_t) "/.:/subsys/sch/room_group",
         rpc_c_ns_syntax_default,
         &mbr_inq_context,
         &status);
      CHECK_DCE(status, "Cannot begin getting group members");

      rpc_ns_mgmt_handle_set_exp_age(mbr_inq_context, 0, &status);
      CHECK_DCE(status, "Cannot set expiration for import.");

      while (sch_status == sch_status_room_not_found)
      {
         rpc_ns_group_mbr_inq_next(mbr_inq_context, &ns_entry_name, &status);
         if (status == rpc_s_no_more_members)
         {
            break;
         }
         CHECK_DCE(status, "Cannot get next group member");

         h = bind_to_server(ns_entry_name);
         if (h != NULL)
         {
            room_description(h, room_name, &room, &sch_status, &call_status);
            CHECK_CALL(call_status);
```

```
            rpc_binding_free(&h, &status);
            CHECK_DCE(status, "Cannot free server binding");
          }
        rpc_string_free(&ns_entry_name, &ignored_st);
      }

      rpc_ns_group_mbr_inq_done(&mbr_inq_context, &status);
      CHECK_DCE(status, "Cannot end getting group member");
   }

   if (sch_status == sch_status_ok)
   {
      printf("Room location      : %s\n", room.loc);
      printf("Room name          : %s\n", room.name);
      printf("Room description   : %s\n", room.desc);
      printf("Maximum occupancy : %i\n", room.max_people);
   }
   else
   {
      print_sch_status(sch_status);
   }
}

void reserve()
{
   rpc_binding_handle_t h;
   sch_room_t        room;
   sch_date_time_t  date_time;
   sch_name_t        reserver;
   sch_event_desc_t desc;
   sch_status_t      status;
   error_status_t    call_status;

   GET("Room location? ", room.loc);
   GET_BINDING(room.loc, h);

   GET("Room name     ? ", room.name);
   GET("Date, time (yy-mm-dd hh:mm-hh:mm) ? ", date_time);
   GET("Reserved by  ? ", reserver);
   GET("Event        ? ", desc);

   room_reserve(h, room, date_time, reserver, desc, &status, &call_status);
   CHECK_CALL(call_status);
   print_sch_status(status);
}

void cancel()
{
   rpc_binding_handle_t h;
   sch_room_t       room;
   sch_date_time_t date_time;
   sch_name_t       reserver;
   sch_event_t      event;
   sch_status_t     status;
   error_status_t  call_status;

   GET("Room location? ", room.loc);
```

```
   GET_BINDING(room.loc, h);

   GET("Room name    ? ", room.name);
   GET("Date, time (yy-mm-dd hh:mm-hh:mm) ? ", date_time);
   GET("Reserved by  ? ", reserver);

   room_cancel(h, room, date_time, reserver, &status, &call_status);
   CHECK_CALL(call_status);
   print_sch_status(status);
}

void avail()
{
   rpc_binding_handle_t h;
   sch_date_time_t date_time;
   char            n_people_str[4];
   idl_long_int    n_people;
   idl_long_int    n_perf_locs;
#  define          MAX_PERF_LOCS   10
   sch_loc_name_t  perf_loc[MAX_PERF_LOCS];
   sch_loc_name_t  one_perf_loc[1];
#  define          MAX_AVAIL_ROOMS 20
   sch_room_t      avail_room[MAX_AVAIL_ROOMS];
   idl_long_int    n_avail_rooms;
   idl_long_int    n_all_avail_rooms;
   sch_status_t    status;
   error_status_t  call_status;
   idl_long_int    i, j;

   GET("Date, time (yy-mm-dd hh:mm-hh:mm) ? ", date_time);
   GET("Number of people    ? ", n_people_str);
   n_people = atoi(n_people_str);
   printf("Preferred locations ? (max of %i; terminate with <return>)\n",
           MAX_PERF_LOCS);
   n_perf_locs = 0;
   for (i = 0; i < MAX_PERF_LOCS; i++)
   {
      printf("Location %i        ? ", i+1);
      gets((char *) perf_loc[i]);
      if (strcmp(perf_loc[i], "") == 0)
      {
         break;
      }
      n_perf_locs++;
   }

   printf("\nLocation   Name                    #  Description\n");
   printf("---------- -------------------- --- -------------------------\n");

   n_all_avail_rooms = 0;
   for (i = 0; i < n_perf_locs; i++)
   {
      strcpy(&one_perf_loc[0], &perf_loc[i]);
      h = find_binding_by_location(perf_loc[i]);
      if (h == NULL)
      {
         h = bind_to_server_by_location(perf_loc[i]);
      }
```

```
      if (h == NULL)
      {
         continue;
      }
      room_avail(h, date_time, n_people, 1, one_perf_loc, MAX_AVAIL_ROOMS,
         &n_avail_rooms, avail_room, &status, &call_status);
      CHECK_CALL(call_status);

      if (status == sch_status_ok)
      {
         for (j = 0; j < n_avail_rooms; j++)
         {
            printf("%-10s %-20s %3i %-30s\n",
                   avail_room[j].loc, avail_room[j].name,
                   avail_room[j].max_people, avail_room[j].desc);
         }
         n_all_avail_rooms += n_avail_rooms;
      }
      else
      {
         print_sch_status(status);
      }
   }
   if (n_all_avail_rooms == 0)
   {
      printf("No rooms available\n");
   }
}

void events()
{
   rpc_binding_handle_t h;
   sch_room_t             room;
   sch_short_date_time_t begin_date_time;
   sch_short_date_time_t end_date_time;
   sch_event_rec_p_t      ev_list;
   sch_status_t           status;
   error_status_t         call_status;
   sch_event_rec_p_t      ev_p;
   sch_event_rec_p_t      next_ev_p;

   GET("Room location? ", room.loc);
   GET_BINDING(room.loc, h);

   GET("Room name     ? ", room.name);
   GET("Begin date, time (yy-mm-dd hh:mm) ? ", begin_date_time);
   GET("End   date, time (yy-mm-dd hh:mm) ? ", end_date_time);

   room_events(h, room, begin_date_time, end_date_time, &ev_list, &status,
       &call_status);

   CHECK_CALL(call_status);
   if (status == sch_status_ok)
   {
      if (ev_list != NULL)
      {
         printf("\nDate     Time        Event                    Reserver\n");
         printf("-------- ----------- -------------------- --------------------\n");
```

```
        for (ev_p = ev_list; ev_p != NULL; ev_p = next_ev_p)
        {
            printf("%-20s %-20s %-20s\n",
                   ev_p->event.date_time,
                   ev_p->event.desc,
                   ev_p->event.reserver);
                   next_ev_p = ev_p->next;
            free(ev_p);
        }
    }
    else
    {
       printf("No events in specified period.\n");
    }
  }
  else
  {
     print_sch_status(status);
  }
}
```

B.5 schedule/obj/room_server.c

```
/*
 * room_server.c
 *
 * Mainline of the room schedule application server. Sets up the server's
 * security, protocols, interface, and an ACL manager and enters the RPC
 * Runtime to execute remote calls. When interrupted by a signal, cleans up
 * the ACL manager, the interface, the protocols, and security and quits.
 *
 * All of the application-dependent code is in room_mgr.c, including the
 * application setup and cleanup, the managers for the room interface
 * operation, and application ACL callout routines.
 */

#include <stdio.h>
#include <time.h>
#include <pthread.h>
#include <signal.h>
#include <unistd.h>
#include <dce/sec_login.h>
#include <dce/keymgmt.h>
#include <dce/aclif.h>
#include <dce/dce.h>
#include <dce/dbif.h>
#include <dce/secidmap.h>

#include "room.h"
#include "sch_util.h"
#include "room_mgr.h"

FILE *out_fd = stdout;

extern room_v1_0_epv_t native_mgr_epv;    /* defined in room_mgr.c */
extern room_v1_0_epv_t legacy_mgr_epv;  /* defined in legacy_mgr.c */

unsigned_char_p_t server_principal;
unsigned_char_p_t server_keyfile;

uuid_t native_obj_type_uuid =  /* 2a6e0418-bfbb-11ce-b77b-08000948fbd9 */
   {0x2a6e0418, 0xbfbb, 0x11ce, 0xb7, 0x7b, 0x08, 0x00, 0x09, 0x48, 0xfb, 0xd9};

uuid_t legacy_obj_type_uuid =  /* 76f05606-bfbb-11ce-a68d-08000948fbd9 */
   {0x76f05606, 0xbfbb, 0x11ce, 0xa6, 0x8d, 0x08, 0x00, 0x09, 0x48, 0xfb, 0xd9};

uuid_t room_acl_mgr_uuid    =  /* 4e203958-47ac-11ce-8f8c-080009307c01 */
   {0x4e203958, 0x47ac, 0x11ce, 0x8f, 0x8c, 0x08, 0x00, 0x09, 0x30, 0x7c, 0x01};

static sec_acl_printstring_t room_acl_perms_printstrings[] =
{
/* token  description                    permset         */
   {"R",  "Reserve a room",              sch_acl_perm_reserve},
   {"C",  "Cancel any reservation",      sch_acl_perm_cancel },
   {"I",  "Inquire about a room",        sch_acl_perm_inq    },
   {"c",  "control a room ACL",          sch_acl_perm_control},
   {"t",  "test access for a room ACL", sch_acl_perm_test    }
};

#define N_ROOM_ACL_PERMS 5
```

```
static sec_acl_printstring_t room_acl_help_printstring =
  {"room_acl", "Room ACL Manager", 0};

/*
 * make_name()
 *    Constructs a name string by concatenating s1 and s2. This string must
 *    be deallocated after it is used.
 */
unsigned_char_p_t make_name(char *s1, char *s2)
{
   unsigned_char_p_t name;

   name = (unsigned_char_p_t) malloc(strlen(s1) + strlen(s2) + 1);
   if (name == NULL)
   {
      printf("Count not allocate name string\n");
      exit(0);
   }
   sprintf((char *) name, "%s%s", s1, s2);
   return(name);
}

/*
 * validate_identity()
 *    Completes the validation of the server's login context. Called when the
 *    server first sets up its identity, and later when the server refreshes
 *    its identity.
 */
void validate_identity(
   sec_login_handle_t *login_context)
{
   void                  *key_data;
   sec_login_auth_src_t authn_source;
   boolean32             reset_password;
   unsigned32            status;

      /*
       * Get the latest version of the password key for the server's
       * principal from the the server's keyfile.
       */
   sec_key_mgmt_get_key(
      rpc_c_authn_dce_secret,
      server_keyfile,
      server_principal,
      0,
      &key_data,
      (error_status_t *) &status);
   CHECK_DCE(status, "Cannot get server key from keyfile");

      /*
       * Validate the login context for the server with key from the keytab
       * file. This is equivalent to entering the password for a dce_login.
       */
   sec_login_validate_identity(
      *login_context,
      (sec_passwd_rec_t *) key_data,
      &reset_password,
```

```
        &authn_source,
        &status);
    CHECK_DCE(status, "Cannot validate identity for principal");

        /*
         * Certify that the authentication service is genuine.
         */
    sec_login_certify_identity(*login_context, &status);
    CHECK_DCE(status, "Cannot certify identity for principal");
}

/*
 * refresh_identity() thread
 *    Periodically refreshes the server's login context before it expires.
 */
pthread_addr_t refresh_identity(pthread_addr_t arg)
{
    sec_login_handle_t *login_context = (sec_login_handle_t) arg;
    struct timeval      now;
    struct timespec     sleep_time;
    signed32            expiration;
    unsigned32          status;

        /*
         * Loop indefinitely, for the life of the server.
         */
    while (true)
    {
            /*
             * Get the number of seconds until the context expires.
             */
        sec_login_get_expiration(*login_context, &expiration, &status);
        CHECK_DCE(status, "Cannot get login context expiration");

            /*
             * Compute the time 10 minutes before the context expires, and
             * wait in this thread until that time.
             */
        gettimeofday(&now, NULL);
        sleep_time.tv_sec  = expiration - now.tv_sec - 600; /* 10 minutes */
        sleep_time.tv_nsec = 0;
        if (sleep_time.tv_sec < 0)
        {
            fprintf(stderr,
                "Login context expires in less than the minimum 10 minutes." ;
            exit(0);
        }
        pthread_delay_np(&sleep_time);

            /*
             * Context will expire in 10 minutes. Refresh and revalidate the
             * context.
             */
        sec_login_refresh_identity(*login_context, &status);
        CHECK_DCE(status, "Cannot refresh server's identity");
        validate_identity(login_context);
    }
}
```

```
/*
 * key_mgmt() thread
 *    Periodically changes the server's key before it expires.
 */
pthread_addr_t key_mgmt(pthread_addr_t arg)
{
   unsigned32 status;

      /*
       * The thread will stay in this call for the duration of the server.
       */
   sec_key_mgmt_manage_key(
      rpc_c_authn_dce_secret,
      server_keyfile,
      server_principal,
      &status);
   CHECK_DCE(status, "Cannot manage server keys");
}

/*
 * signal_catcher thread
 *    This thread will catch termination signals and terminate the server's
 *    rpc_server_listen(), to allow cleanup before exit.
 */
pthread_addr_t signal_catcher(pthread_addr_t arg)
{
   sigset_t mask;
   unsigned32 status;

   sigemptyset(&mask);          /* Set of signals to catch:          */
   sigaddset(&mask, SIGTERM);   /*   software termination signal    */
   sigaddset(&mask, SIGINT);    /*   process interrupt - control-c  */
   sigaddset(&mask, SIGHUP);    /*   hangup                         */

   sigwait(&mask);

   rpc_mgmt_stop_server_listening(NULL, &status);
   CHECK_DCE(status, "Cannot stop server listening");
}

int main(int argc, char *argv[])
{
   rpc_binding_vector_t *binding_vector;
   unsigned_char_p_t     string_binding;
   pthread_t             refresh_id_thread;
   pthread_t             key_mgmt_thread;
   pthread_t             sigcatch_thread;
   rpc_if_id_t           if_id;
   sec_login_handle_t    login_context;
   unsigned32            status, ignored_st;
   char                  hostname[256];
   unsigned_char_p_t     ns_server_entry;
   void                 *loc_p;
   unsigned char        *loc_name;
   unsigned char        *loc_otype;
   unsigned char        *loc_admin;
   uuid_t               *loc_obj_uuid_p;
```

```
uuid_t               *loc_obj_type_uuid_p;
uuid_vector_t        *loc_obj_vector;
dce_db_handle_t       acl_db_h;
boolean32             initialize_acl_db;
unsigned32            db_create_flag;
int                   n_loc_obj;
int                   i;

   /*
    * Set up and display bindings (i.e. sockets) for all protocols
    * supported on this host.
    */
rpc_server_use_all_protseqs(rpc_c_protseq_max_reqs_default, &status);
CHECK_DCE(status, "Cannot get bindings for all protocols");

rpc_server_inq_bindings(&binding_vector, &status);
CHECK_DCE(status, "Cannot get server bindings");

printf("Using bindings: \n");
for (i = 0; i < binding_vector->count; i++)
{
   rpc_binding_to_string_binding(binding_vector->binding_h[i],
                                 &string_binding, &status);
   CHECK_DCE(status, "Can't convert binding to string");
   printf("   %s\n", string_binding);
   rpc_string_free(&string_binding, &ignored_st);
}

   /*
    * Construct the server's
    *    principal name: /.:/room-server.HOST_NAME
    *    keytab file:    room_keyfile.HOST_NAME
    *    NS entry:       /.:/subsys/sch/room_server.HOST_NAME
    */
if (gethostname(hostname, sizeof(hostname)) == -1)
{
   perror("Cannot get hostname: ");
   exit(1);
}
server_principal = make_name("/.:/room-server.", hostname);
server_keyfile   = make_name("room_keyfile.", hostname);
ns_server_entry  = make_name("/.:/subsys/sch/room_server.", hostname);

   /*
    * Set up and validate server's principal identity. This is the
    * equivalent of a dce_login.
    */
printf("Setting server identity to %s...\n", server_principal);
sec_login_setup_identity(
   server_principal,
   sec_login_no_flags,
   &login_context,
   &status);
CHECK_DCE(status, "Cannot setup identity for principal");

validate_identity(&login_context);

sec_login_set_context(login_context, &status);
```

```
CHECK_DCE(status, "Cannot set context for principal");

   /*
    * Start a thread to periodically refresh the server's identity.
    * This is the equivalent of a kinit or another dce_login.
    */
create_thread(
   refresh_identity,
   "refresh identity",
   &refresh_id_thread,
   (pthread_addr_t) &login_context);

   /*
    * Register the server's principal, authentication method, and password
    * retrieval method with the Security Runtime. This uses the default
    * keytab mechanism.
    */
rpc_server_register_auth_info(
   server_principal,
   rpc_c_authn_dce_secret,
   NULL,
   server_keyfile,
   &status);
CHECK_DCE(status, "Cannot register server authentication information");

   /*
    * Start a thread to periodically change the server principal's password
    * before it expires.
    */
create_thread(
   key_mgmt,
   "key management",
   &key_mgmt_thread,
   NULL);

   /*
    * Register the room interface with two managers: the (native) room
    * manager and the legacy manager.
    */

rpc_server_register_if(
   room_v1_0_s_ifspec,
   &native_obj_type_uuid,
   (rpc_mgr_epv_t) &native_mgr_epv,
   &status);
CHECK_DCE(status,
   "Cannot register room interface and room manager with RPC runtime");

rpc_server_register_if(
   room_v1_0_s_ifspec,
   &legacy_obj_type_uuid,
   (rpc_mgr_epv_t) &legacy_mgr_epv,
   &status);
CHECK_DCE(status,
   "Cannot register room interface and legacy manager with RPC runtime");

   /*
    * Register the rdaclif interface, used by the ACL library. The manager
```

```
     * implementation is also in the ACL library (in libdce.sl). Note that
     * this registration has to be done with both location object types
     */
  rpc_server_register_if(
     rdaclif_v1_0_s_ifspec,
     &native_obj_type_uuid,
     (rpc_mgr_epv_t) &dce_acl_v1_0_epv,
     &status);
  CHECK_DCE(status, "Cannot register rdaclif interface with RPC runtime");

  rpc_server_register_if(
     rdaclif_v1_0_s_ifspec,
     &legacy_obj_type_uuid,
     (rpc_mgr_epv_t) &dce_acl_v1_0_epv,
     &status);
  CHECK_DCE(status, "Cannot register rdaclif interface with RPC runtime");

    /*
     * Perform application-specific initialization, including reading
     * the room database into memory.
     */
  room_open();

    /*
     * Register the location objects with their manager types, using the
     * UUIDs read from the room database. This also counts the number of
     * location objects for the object vector below.
     */
  n_loc_obj = 0;
  room_loc_begin(&loc_p);
  while (loc_p != NULL)
  {
     room_loc_next(&loc_p, &loc_name, &loc_obj_uuid_p, &loc_otype, &loc_admin);

     if (strcmp(loc_otype, "native") == 0)
     {
        loc_obj_type_uuid_p = &native_obj_type_uuid;
     }
     else if (strcmp(loc_otype, "legacy") == 0)
     {
        loc_obj_type_uuid_p = &legacy_obj_type_uuid;
     }
     else
     {
        fprintf(stderr, "Object type %s for location %s is not supported\n",
           loc_otype, loc_name);
        exit(0);
     }

     rpc_object_set_type(loc_obj_uuid_p, loc_obj_type_uuid_p, &status);
     CHECK_DCE(status, "Cannot set object type");

     n_loc_obj++;
  }

    /*
     * Construct an object vector for the location objects, to be used
     * when registering with the Endpoint Map and exporting to CDS.
```

```
     */
loc_obj_vector = (uuid_vector_t *) malloc(sizeof(uuid_vector_t) +
                                n_loc_obj * sizeof(uuid_p_t));
loc_obj_vector->count = n_loc_obj;
i = 0;
room_loc_begin(&loc_p);
while (loc_p != NULL)
{
   room_loc_next(&loc_p, &loc_name, &loc_obj_uuid_p, &loc_otype, &loc_admin);
   loc_obj_vector->uuid[i] = loc_obj_uuid_p;
   i++;
}

   /*
    * Register the room interface, location objects and bindings with the
    * local host Endpoint Map.
    */
rpc_ep_register(
   room_v1_0_s_ifspec,
   binding_vector,
   loc_obj_vector,
   (unsigned_char_p_t) "Room Server",
   &status);
CHECK_DCE(status, "Cannot register room interface with Endpoint Map");

   /*
    * Register the rdaclif interface, used by the ACL library, the location
    * objects and bindings with the local host Endpoint Map.
    */
rpc_ep_register(
   rdaclif_v1_0_s_ifspec,
   binding_vector,
   loc_obj_vector,
   (unsigned_char_p_t) "Room ACL Manager",
   &status);
CHECK_DCE(status, "Cannot register rdaclif interface with Endpoint Map");

   /*
    * Export the room interface, location objects, and bindings to the
    * CDS entry for the room server.
    */

printf("Exporting bindings to CDS entry %s\n", ns_server_entry);
rpc_ns_binding_export(
   rpc_c_ns_syntax_default,
   ns_server_entry,
   room_v1_0_s_ifspec,
   binding_vector,
   loc_obj_vector,
   &status);
CHECK_DCE(status, "Cannot export binding to room_server entry");

   /*
    * Add the room server entry to the room group.
    */
printf("Adding %s to room_group\n", ns_server_entry);
rpc_ns_group_mbr_add(
   rpc_c_ns_syntax_default,
```

```
        (unsigned_char_p_t) "/.:/subsys/sch/room_group",
        rpc_c_ns_syntax_default,
        ns_server_entry,
        &status);
    CHECK_DCE(status, "Cannot add room_server member to room_group");

        /*
         * Add the room server entry to the cell profile.
         */
    rpc_if_inq_id(room_v1_0_s_ifspec, &if_id, &status);
    CHECK_DCE(status, "Cannot get room interface UUID");

    printf("Adding %s to cell-profile\n", ns_server_entry);
    rpc_ns_profile_elt_add(
        rpc_c_ns_syntax_default,
        (unsigned_char_p_t) "/.:/cell-profile",
        &if_id,
        rpc_c_ns_syntax_default,
        ns_server_entry,
        0,
        (unsigned_char_p_t) "Room Server",
        &status);
    CHECK_DCE(status, "Cannot add room_server element to cell-profile");

        /*
         * Now export each location object to its own CDS entry: /.:/subsys/
         * sch/room/LOCATION. Each CDS entry will have an object UUID vector
         * with one location UUID. There are two interfaces exported for each
         * location: our room interface and the rdaclif interface for the ACL
         * library.
         */
    room_loc_begin(&loc_p);
    while (loc_p != NULL)
    {
        unsigned_char_p_t loc_ns_server_entry;
        uuid_vector_t     one_loc_obj_vector;

        room_loc_next(&loc_p, &loc_name, &loc_obj_uuid_p, &loc_otype, &loc_admin);
        one_loc_obj_vector.count   = 1;
        one_loc_obj_vector.uuid[0] = loc_obj_uuid_p;

        loc_ns_server_entry = make_name("/.:/subsys/sch/room/", (char *)loc_name);
        printf("Exporting bindings to CDS entry %s\n", loc_ns_server_entry);
        rpc_ns_binding_export(
            rpc_c_ns_syntax_default,
            loc_ns_server_entry,
            room_v1_0_s_ifspec,
            binding_vector,
            &one_loc_obj_vector,
            &status);
        CHECK_DCE(status, "Cannot export binding to location server entry");

        rpc_ns_binding_export(
            rpc_c_ns_syntax_default,
            loc_ns_server_entry,
            rdaclif_v1_0_s_ifspec,
            binding_vector,
            &one_loc_obj_vector,
```

```
        &status);
    CHECK_DCE(status, "Cannot export binding to rdaclif server entry");
    free(loc_ns_server_entry);
}

    /*
     * Set up the ACL manager and the ACL database. First, check if the
     * ACL database already exists.
     */
if ((access("room_acl_db", R_OK) == -1) && (errno == ENOENT))
{
    printf("Creating Room ACL database and manager\n");
    initialize_acl_db = true;
    db_create_flag     = db_c_create;
}
else
{
    printf("Opening Room ACL database and manager\n");
    initialize_acl_db = false;
    db_create_flag     = 0;
}

    /*
     * Open the existing ACL database, or create a new ACL database,
     * indexed by the ACL UUIDs, and using the built-in conversion
     * function dce_rdacl_convert() to serialize the ACL structures.
     */
dce_db_open(
    "room_acl_db",
    NULL,  /* default backend_type - a hash table */
    db_c_index_by_uuid | db_create_flag,
    (dce_db_convert_func_t) dce_rdacl_convert,
    &acl_db_h,
    &status);
CHECK_DCE(status, "Cannot open ACL database");

    /*
     * Register the ACL manager, using the ACL database, the printstrings
     * array that define the ACL permissions, and the room_acl_resolve()
     * function for mapping room names to their ACL UUIDs. room_acl_resolve()
     * is in room_mgr.c
     */
dce_acl_register_object_type(
    acl_db_h,
    &room_acl_mgr_uuid,
    N_ROOM_ACL_PERMS,
    room_acl_perms_printstrings,
    &room_acl_help_printstring,
    sch_acl_perm_control,
    sch_acl_perm_test,
    room_acl_resolve,     /* resolver function        */
    NULL,                 /* no argument for resolver */
    0,                    /* no flags                 */
    &status);
CHECK_DCE(status, "Cannot set up room ACL manager");

    /*
     * If the ACL database has just been created, set up default ACL
```

```
     * entries for each room. room_acl_setup() is in room_mgr.c.
     */
   if (initialize_acl_db)
   {
      room_acl_setup(acl_db_h);
   }

      /*
       * Create a thread to catch termination signals. The signal_catcher
       * routine will kick the server out of its rpc_server_listen().
       */
   create_thread(
      signal_catcher,
      "signal catcher",
      &sigcatch_thread,
      NULL);

      /*
       * Listen for and execute incoming remote calls. The rpc_server_listen()
       * will exit only when the server receives a termination signal.
       */
   printf("\nRoom server listening...\n");
   rpc_server_listen(1, &status);
   CHECK_DCE_NONFATAL(status, "Server stopped listening");
   printf("Room server shutting down...\n");

      /*
       * Termination signal received. Kill the signal catcher thread.
       */
   kill_thread(sigcatch_thread, "signal catcher");

      /*
       * Perform application-specific termination processing, including
       * writing the room database to permanent storage (i.e. a disk file).
       */
   room_close();

      /*
       * DCE cleanup:
       *     - Remove the room_server element from the cell profile.
       *     - Remove the room_server member from the room_group.
       *     - Remove the interface, objects, and bindings from the server
       *       CDS entry.
       *     - Remove each location CDS entry.
       *     - Remove the interface, objects, and bindings from the local
       *       Endpoint Map.
       *     - Remove the interface and managers from the local RPC Runtime.
       *     - Kill the key management and refresh identity threads.
       *     - Destroy the server's login context.
       */
   printf("Removing %s from cell-profile\n", ns_server_entry);
   rpc_ns_profile_elt_remove(
      rpc_c_ns_syntax_default,
      (unsigned_char_p_t) "/.:/cell-profile",
      &if_id,
      rpc_c_ns_syntax_default,
      (unsigned_char_p_t) ns_server_entry,
      &status);
```

```
CHECK_DCE_NONFATAL(status,
   "Cannot remove room_server element from cell-profile");

printf("Removing %s from room_group\n", ns_server_entry);
rpc_ns_group_mbr_remove(
   rpc_c_ns_syntax_default,
   (unsigned_char_p_t) "/.:/subsys/sch/room_group",
   rpc_c_ns_syntax_default,
   (unsigned_char_p_t) ns_server_entry,
   &status);
CHECK_DCE(status, "Cannot remove room_server member from room_group");

printf("Removing bindings from CDS entry %s\n", ns_server_entry);
rpc_ns_binding_unexport(
   rpc_c_ns_syntax_default,
   (unsigned_char_p_t) ns_server_entry,
   room_v1_0_s_ifspec,
   loc_obj_vector,
   &status);
CHECK_DCE_NONFATAL(status,
  "Cannot unexport binding from server entry");

room_loc_begin(&loc_p);
while (loc_p != NULL)
{
   unsigned_char_p_t loc_ns_server_entry;
   uuid_vector_t     one_loc_obj_vector;

   room_loc_next(&loc_p, &loc_name, &loc_obj_uuid_p, &loc_otype, &loc_admin);
   one_loc_obj_vector.count    = 1;
   one_loc_obj_vector.uuid[0] = loc_obj_uuid_p;

   loc_ns_server_entry = make_name("/.:/subsys/sch/room/", (char *)loc_name);
   printf("Removing bindings from CDS entry %s\n", loc_ns_server_entry);
   rpc_ns_binding_unexport(
      rpc_c_ns_syntax_default,
      loc_ns_server_entry,
      rdaclif_v1_0_s_ifspec,
      NULL,                    /* Don't remove object quite yet. */
      &status);
   CHECK_DCE(status, "Cannot unexport binding from rdaclif server entry");

   rpc_ns_binding_unexport(
      rpc_c_ns_syntax_default,
      loc_ns_server_entry,
      room_v1_0_s_ifspec,
      &one_loc_obj_vector,     /* Remove object now. */
      &status);
   CHECK_DCE(status, "Cannot unexport binding from location server entry");
   free(loc_ns_server_entry);
}

rpc_ep_unregister(
   room_v1_0_s_ifspec,
   binding_vector,
   loc_obj_vector,
   &status);
CHECK_DCE_NONFATAL(status,
```

```
      "Cannot unregister room interface with Endpoint Map");

   rpc_ep_unregister(
      rdaclif_v1_0_s_ifspec,
      binding_vector,
      loc_obj_vector,
      &status);
   CHECK_DCE_NONFATAL(status,
     "Cannot unregister rdaclif interface with Endpoint Map");

   rpc_server_unregister_if(room_v1_0_s_ifspec, &native_obj_type_uuid, &status);
   CHECK_DCE(status,
      "Cannot unregister room interface and native obj type with RPC runtime");

   rpc_server_unregister_if(room_v1_0_s_ifspec, &legacy_obj_type_uuid, &status);
   CHECK_DCE(status,
      "Cannot unregister room interface and legacy obj type with RPC runtime");

   rpc_server_unregister_if(rdaclif_v1_0_s_ifspec, &native_obj_type_uuid,
       &status);
   CHECK_DCE(status,
      "Cannot unregister rdaclif interface/native obj type with RPC runtime");

   rpc_server_unregister_if(rdaclif_v1_0_s_ifspec, &legacy_obj_type_uuid,
       &status);
   CHECK_DCE(status,
      "Cannot unregister rdaclif interface/legacy obj type  with RPC runtime");

   dce_db_close(&acl_db_h, &status);
   CHECK_DCE(status, "Cannot close ACL database");

   kill_thread(key_mgmt_thread, "key management");
   kill_thread(refresh_id_thread, "refresh identity");

   sec_login_release_context(&login_context, &status);
   CHECK_DCE_NONFATAL(status, "Cannot release login context");

   rpc_binding_vector_free(&binding_vector, &status);
   CHECK_DCE_NONFATAL(status, "Cannot free binding vector");
}
```

B.6 schedule/obj/room_mgr.c

```
/*
 * room_mgr.c
 *
 * Implementation of the room interface operations for the room_server program.
 */

#include <stdio.h>
#include <time.h>
#include <pthread.h>
#include <dce/rpc.h>
#include <dce/id_base.h>
#include <dce/rgybase.h>
#include <dce/dce_cf.h>
#include <dce/dce.h>
#include <dce/dbif.h>
#include <dce/aclif.h>
#include "room.h"
#include "sch_util.h"
#include "room_mgr.h"

extern FILE *out_fd;
extern unsigned_char_p_t server_principal;
extern uuid_t            room_acl_mgr_uuid;


/*
 * Room Database File
 *    An character file holding the room and reservation information.  The
 *    format is:
 *
 *    location_record
 *      room_record
 *         ...
 *         event_record
 *         event_record
 *         ...
 *      room_record
 *         ...
 *         event_record
 *         event_record
 *         ...
 *    location_record
 *       room_record
 *       ...
 *
 *   Location record
 *      *loc_name|loc_object_uuid|loc_otype|loc_admin
 *
 *   Room record
 *      +room_name|max_people|room_description|acl_uuid|
 *
 *   Event record
 *       date_time|reserver|event_description|reserver_id|
 *
 *   Note that each record begins with a character that indicates its type,
 *   and that | is used as a delimiter at the end of record fields.  All
 *   records are terminated by a newline.
```

```
 *
 *   An example of some records:
 *
 *       *44M|21696160-c6bd-11ce-b35f-08000948fbd9|room|/.:/cell_admin|  loc)
 *       +Landmark|20|Col R3; audio teleconference|     (room_record)
 *        94-07-12 18:00-19:00|cwk|meeting|cwk_UUID|        (event_record)
 *
 *   The room database must be initially set up to include location and room
 *   records, but not event records.
 */

#define ROOM_DB_PATH "room_db.dat"

/*
 * Room Database Internal Structure
 *    An in-memory set of linked lists holding the current location, room,
 *    and event records.  When the room database is read, records are allocated
 *    and linked together for each location, room, and event.  As reservations
 *    are made and cancelled new event records are allocated and deallocated.
 *    When room_server terminates, the contents of the internal data structure
 *    are written back to the room database file.
 *
 *    The linkage of the internal data structure is shown below.  Records in
 *    a list are doubly-linked to the previous and next records, if any, in
 *    the list.  The head pointer for each list is contained in the next
 *    higher level record in the hierarchy.  The global loc_list variable
 *    points to the head of the location record list.
 *
 *       loc_list
 *       |
 *       v
 *       location_record
 *       ^   |
 *       |   v
 *       |   room_record
 *       |   ^   |
 *       |   |   v
 *       |   |   event_record<-->event_record<-->...
 *       |   v
 *       |   room_record
 *       |   ^   |
 *       |   |   v
 *       |   |   event_record<-->event_record<-->...
 *       |   v
 *       |   . . .
 *       v
 *       location_record
 *       ^   :
 *       |   v
 *       |   room_record
 *       |   ^   |
 *       |   |   v
 *       |   |   event_record<-->event_record<-->...
 *       |   v
 *       |   . . .
 *       v
 *       . . .
 *
```

```
 */

#define ID_LENGTH sec_rgy_name_t_size  /* from /usr/include/dce/rgybase.h */
#define UUID_STR_LENGTH 37
typedef unsigned_char_p_t reserver_id_p_t;

/*
 * event_rec_t
 *    Record for a reserved event, including the original event information
 *    (time_date, reserver, and description) and the starting and ending
 *    times of the event in Unix time_t format (see below).
 */

typedef struct EVENT_REC_T {
   struct EVENT_REC_T *prev;
   struct EVENT_REC_T *next;
   sch_event_t         event;
   reserver_id_p_t     r_id_p;
   time_t              start;
   time_t              end;
} event_rec_t;

/*
 * room_rec_t
 *    Record for a room, including the room information (location, name,
 *    max people, and description) and a pointer to the event list for the
 *    room. Also includes a mutex for protection during concurrent call
 *    execution. The mutex is locked when the event list is used. Since the
 *    room record itself is static (it won't be deleted), operations that
 *    just look at the record do not need to lock the mutex.
 */

typedef struct ROOM_REC_T {
   struct ROOM_REC_T *prev;
   struct ROOM_REC_T *next;
   pthread_mutex_t    mutex;
   event_rec_t       *event_list;
   sch_room_t         room;
   uuid_t             acl_uuid;
} room_rec_t;

/*
 * loc_rec_t
 *    Record for a location, with the location name and a pointer to the
 *    list of rooms in the location.  The global variable loc_list is the
 *    head of the list of locations.
 */

typedef struct LOC_REC_T {
   struct LOC_REC_T  *prev;
   struct LOC_REC_T  *next;
   room_rec_t        *room_list;
   sch_loc_name_t     loc;
   uuid_t             loc_obj_uuid;
   unsigned char      loc_otype[ID_LENGTH];
   unsigned char      loc_admin[ID_LENGTH];
} loc_rec_t;
```

```
loc_rec_t *loc_list;


/*
 * Transaction Log File
 *     Records room_reserve() and room_cancel(), transactions made after the
 *     room_server has input the room database.  Used to recover if the room
 *     server terminates without writing out the current contents of the room
 *     database.  During startup, room_server will apply the transactions to
 *     the database to bring the data up to date.  During (graceful) shutdown,
 *     room_server will erase the transaction log after it has written the
 *     updated database to disk.
 *
 * xn_rec_t
 *     Structure for one transaction log record.  The xn_type field is R
 *     for room_reserve(), C for room_cancel().  The other fields are the
 *     parameters from the original call.  Room_cancel() does not include
 *     and event description, but a blank description will be included to
 *     keep the record format consistent.
 *
 * fxn
 *     Global file descriptor for the opened transaction log.
 */

#define ROOM_XN_PATH "room_xn.dat"

typedef struct {
   char                xn_type;
   char                blank;
   sch_loc_name_t      loc;
   sch_room_name_t     room_name;
   sch_event_t         event;
   reserver_id_p_t     r_id_p;
} xn_rec_t;

FILE *fxn;

/*
 * *_EQ macros
 *     Determine if two character strings of a particular type are equal.
 */

#define ROOM_NAME_EQ(n1, n2) (strncmp((n1), (n2), sizeof(sch_room_name_t)) == 0)
#define LOC_NAME_EQ(n1, n2)  (strncmp((n1), (n2), sizeof(sch_loc_name_t))  == 0)
#define NAME_EQ(n1, n2)      (strncmp((n1), (n2), sizeof(sch_name_t))      == 0)

/*
 * OVERLAP macro
 *     Determines if a time interval lower2-upper2 overlaps with the time
 *     interval lower1-upper1. All times are in Unix time_t format (see below).
 */

#define OVERLAP(lower1, upper1, lower2, upper2) \
   ((lower1 <= lower2) && (lower2 <  upper1) || \
    (lower1 <  upper2) && (upper2 <= upper1))

/*
 * MALLOC macro
```

```
 *    Allocates memory for a specified type and returns a pointer to the
 *    allocated memory.  Checks if allocation failed.
 */

#define CHECK_MALLOC(p) \
   if ((p) == NULL) \
   { \
      fprintf(out_fd, "Out of memory."); \
      exit(1); \
   }

#define MALLOC(p, typ) \
   (p) = (typ *) malloc(sizeof(typ)); \
   CHECK_MALLOC(p);

#define COPY_STRING(copy, original) \
   (copy) = malloc(strlen((original) + 1)); \
   CHECK_MALLOC(copy); \
   strcpy((copy), (original));

/*
 * LINK macro
 *    Links a new record into a list between a previous and next record.  If
 *    there is no previous record, points the list head at the new record.
 */

#define LINK(new_p, prev_p, next_p, head) \
   if ((prev_p) != NULL) \
   { \
      (prev_p)->next = (new_p); \
   } \
   else \
   { \
      (head) = (new_p); \
   } \
   if ((next_p) != NULL) \
   { \
      (next_p)->prev = (new_p); \
   } \
   (new_p)->prev = (prev_p); \
   (new_p)->next = (next_p);

/*
 * LINK_NEW macro
 *    Links a new record at the end of a list, after a previous record.  If
 *    there is no previous record, points the list head at the new record.
 *    Note that this is a special case of the LINK macro, with next_p = NULL.
 *    A separate macro is needed because (NULL)->prev = (new_p) would
 *    (probably) not compile.
 */

#define LINK_NEW(new_p, prev_p, head) \
   if ((prev_p) != NULL) \
   { \
      (prev_p)->next = (new_p); \
   } \
   else \
   { \
```

```
      (head) = (new_p); \
   } \
   (new_p)->prev = (prev_p); \
   (new_p)->next = NULL;

/*
 * UNLINK macro
 *    Unlinks a record pointed to be p from its list.  Links the record's
 *    previous and next records together.  If there is no previous record,
 *    points the list head at the next record.
 */

#define UNLINK(p, head) \
   if ((p)->prev != NULL) \
   { \
      (p)->prev->next = (p)->next; \
   } \
   else \
   { \
      (head) = (p)->next; \
   } \
   if ((p)->next != NULL) \
   { \
      (p)->next->prev = (p)->prev; \
   }

/*
 * MUTEX macros
 */

#define LOCK_ROOM_MUTEX(room_p) \
   if (pthread_mutex_lock(&(room_p->mutex)) != 0) \
   { \
      fprintf(out_fd,"Cannot lock mutex for room %s record", room_p->room.name);\
      perror("Error: "); \
   }

#define UNLOCK_ROOM_MUTEX(room_p) \
   if (pthread_mutex_unlock(&(room_p->mutex)) != 0) \
   { \
      fprintf(out_fd,"Cannot unlock mutex for room %s record", room_p->room.name); \
      perror("Error: "); \
   }



/*
 * MK_TIME macro
 *    Computes a Unix time_t value for a given date and time.  Assumes day,
 *    mon, and year are defined in the calling procedure.  Unix time_t values
 *    are the number of seconds since the beginning of the so-called Unix
 *    Epoch, 0:00 January 1, 1970. Assumes we are in an area with a summer
 *    timezone adjustment (e.g. Daylight Savings Time).
 */

#define MK_TIME(hour, min, time) \
   tm.tm_sec  = 0; \
   tm.tm_min  = (min); \
```

```
   tm.tm_hour = (hour); \
   tm.tm_mday = day; \
   tm.tm_mon  = mon-1; \
   tm.tm_year = year; \
   tm.tm_wday = 0; \
   tm.tm_yday = 0; \
   tm.tm_isdst = 1; \
   (time) = mktime(&tm);

#define ERROR_EXIT(message, parm) \
   fprintf(out_fd, message, parm); \
   exit(1);

/*
 * Forward Procedure Declarations
 */

void find_room(sch_room_t, room_rec_t **, sch_status_t *);
void reserve(room_rec_t *, sch_date_time_t, sch_name_t, sch_event_desc_t,
     reserver_id_p_t, sch_status_t *);
void cancel (room_rec_t *, sch_date_time_t, sch_name_t, reserver_id_p_t,
     boolean32, sch_status_t *);
void process_xn_acl();

/*
 * convert_date_time()
 *    Converts a date and time interval (e.g. 94-07-18 13:00-14:00) into
 *    a start and end time in the Unix time_t format.
 */

void convert_date_time(
   sch_date_time_t  date_time,
   time_t           *start,
   time_t           *end,
   sch_status_t     *status)
{
   idl_long_int year, mon, day, shour, smin, ehour, emin;
   idl_long_int n_items;
   struct tm tm;

   /* yy-mm-dd hh:mm-hh:mm */
   n_items = sscanf((char *) date_time, "%2d-%2d-%2d %2d:%2d-%2d:%2d",
                     &year, &mon, &day, &shour, &smin, &ehour, &emin);
   if ((n_items != 7) ||
       (mon   < 1) || (mon   > 12) ||
       (day   < 1) || (day   > 31) ||
       (shour < 0) || (shour > 23) ||
       (smin  < 0) || (smin  > 59) ||
       (ehour < 0) || (ehour > 23) ||
       (emin  < 0) || (emin  > 59))
   {
      *status = sch_status_bad_date_time;
      return;
   }

   MK_TIME(shour, smin, *start);
   MK_TIME(ehour, emin, *end);
   if ((*start == (time_t) -1) || (*end == (time_t) -1) || (*start > *end))
```

```
    {
        *status   = sch_status_bad_date_time;
        return;
    }
    *status = sch_status_ok;
}

/*
 * convert_short_date_time()
 *     Converts a date and time (e.g. 94-07-18 13:00) into a time in the Unix
 *     time_t format.
 */

void convert_short_date_time(
    sch_short_date_time_t date_time,
    time_t                *time,
    sch_status_t          *status)
{
    idl_long_int year, mon, day, shour, smin;
    idl_long_int n_items;
    struct tm tm;

    n_items = sscanf((char *) date_time, "%2d-%2d-%2d %2d:%2d",
                     &year, &mon, &day, &shour, &smin);
    if ((n_items != 5) ||
        (mon   < 1) || (mon   > 12) ||
        (day   < 1) || (day   > 31) ||
        (shour < 0) || (shour > 23) ||
        (smin  < 0) || (smin  > 59))
    {
        *status = sch_status_bad_date_time;
        return;
    }

    MK_TIME(shour, smin, *time);
    if ((*time == (time_t) -1))
    {
        *status   = sch_status_bad_date_time;
        return;
    }
    *status = sch_status_ok;
}

/*
 * room_event_scrubber()
 *     Periodically deletes room events that are older than the current time.
 *     Runs as a thread created by room_open, and scans the location, room,
 *     and event data structures every hour.
 */

pthread_addr_t room_event_scrubber(pthread_addr_t arg)
{
    struct timeval   now;
    struct timespec  sleep_time;
    loc_rec_t       *loc_p;
    room_rec_t      *room_p;
    event_rec_t     *event_p;
```

```
   while (true)
   {
      gettimeofday(&now, NULL);

      for (loc_p = loc_list; loc_p != NULL; loc_p = loc_p->next)
      {
         for (room_p = loc_p->room_list; room_p != NULL; room_p = room_p->next)
         {
            LOCK_ROOM_MUTEX(room_p);

            for (event_p = room_p->event_list;
                 (event_p != NULL) && (event_p->end < now.tv_sec);
                 event_p = event_p->next)
            {
               UNLINK(event_p, room_p->event_list);
               free(event_p);
            }

            UNLOCK_ROOM_MUTEX(room_p);
         }
      }
      sleep_time.tv_sec  = 60*60; /* 1 hour from now */
      sleep_time.tv_nsec = 0;
      pthread_delay_np(&sleep_time);
   }
}

pthread_t scrubber_thread;

/*
 * room_open()
 *    Initializes the room database internal data structures.
 *
 *    - Opens the room database file for reading.
 *    - Reads each room database record, allocates an internal record
 *      for the data, and links the record into the internal data structure.
 *    - Closes the room database file.
 *    - Opens the transaction log file for reading.
 *    - Reads each transaction log record (if any) and applies the transaction
 *      to the room database internal data structure.
 *    - Closes the transaction log and reopens it for writing, which deletes
 *      the previous transactions in the log.
 *    - Starts up the room event scrubber thread, which deletes old events
 *      from the internal data structure.
 */

void room_open()
{
   FILE         *fdb;
   char          rec_type;
   char          blank;
   char          delim;
   char          newline;
   loc_rec_t    *prev_loc_p;
   loc_rec_t    *new_loc_p;
   room_rec_t   *room_p;
   room_rec_t   *prev_room_p;
   room_rec_t   *new_room_p;
```

```
    event_rec_t *prev_event_p;
    event_rec_t *new_event_p;
    char         r_id[ID_LENGTH];
    unsigned char obj_uuid_str[UUID_STR_LENGTH];
    unsigned char acl_uuid_str[UUID_STR_LENGTH];
    xn_rec_t     xn;
    sch_room_t   room;
    int          n_xn;
    sch_status_t status;
    unsigned32   dce_st;

    fprintf(out_fd, "Reading %s...\n", ROOM_DB_PATH);

    loc_list   = NULL;
    prev_loc_p = NULL;

    /*
     * Read in the room database.
     */
    fdb = fopen(ROOM_DB_PATH, "r");
    if (fdb == NULL)
    {
       fprintf(out_fd, "Can't open %s for reading\n", ROOM_DB_PATH);
       perror("Error: ");
       exit(1);
    }

    while (fscanf(fdb, "%c", &rec_type) != EOF)
    {
       switch (rec_type)
       {
       case '*':                                /* location record */
          MALLOC(new_loc_p, loc_rec_t);
          LINK_NEW(new_loc_p, prev_loc_p, loc_list);
          fscanf(fdb, "%[^|]%c%[^|]%c%[^|]%c%[^|]%c",
             new_loc_p->loc,       &delim,
             obj_uuid_str,         &delim,
             new_loc_p->loc_otype, &delim,
             new_loc_p->loc_admin, &delim);

          new_loc_p->room_list = NULL;
          uuid_from_string(obj_uuid_str, &(new_loc_p->loc_obj_uuid), &dce_st);
          if (dce_st != uuid_s_ok)
          {
             fprintf(stderr, "Cannot convert UUID %s in location record %s\n",
                obj_uuid_str, new_loc_p->loc);
             exit(0);
          }
          prev_room_p = NULL;
          prev_loc_p = new_loc_p;
          break;

       case '+':                                /* room record    */
          MALLOC(new_room_p, room_rec_t);
          LINK_NEW(new_room_p, prev_room_p, prev_loc_p->room_list);
          fscanf(fdb, "%[^|]%c%i%c%[^|]%c%[^|]%c",
                 new_room_p->room.name,        &delim,
                 &new_room_p->room.max_people, &delim,
```

```
            new_room_p->room.desc,         &delim,
            acl_uuid_str,                  &delim);
      strncpy(new_room_p->room.loc, prev_loc_p->loc,
              sizeof(sch_loc_name_t));
      uuid_from_string(acl_uuid_str, &(new_room_p->acl_uuid), &dce_st);
      if (dce_st != uuid_s_ok)
      {
         fprintf(stderr, "Cannot convert UUID %s in room record %s\n",
            acl_uuid_str, new_room_p->room.name);
         exit(0);
      }
      new_room_p->event_list = NULL;
      if (pthread_mutex_init(&(new_room_p->mutex),
           pthread_mutexattr_default) != 0)
      {
         fprintf(out_fd, "Can't create mutex for room %s record",
                  new_room_p->room.name);
         perror("Error: ");
         exit(0);
      }
      prev_event_p = NULL;
      prev_room_p  = new_room_p;
      break;

   case ' ':                                   /* event record    */
      MALLOC(new_event_p, event_rec_t);
      LINK_NEW(new_event_p, prev_event_p, prev_room_p->event_list);
      fscanf(fdb, "%[^|]%c%[^|]%c%[^|]%c%[^|]%c",
              new_event_p->event.date_time, &delim,
              new_event_p->event.reserver,  &delim,
              new_event_p->event.desc,      &delim,
              r_id,                         &delim);
      convert_date_time(new_event_p->event.date_time,
              &new_event_p->start,
              &new_event_p->end,
              &status);
      if (status != sch_status_ok)
      {
         ERROR_EXIT("Invalid date_time %s\n",
              new_event_p->event.date_time);
      }
      new_event_p->r_id_p = malloc(strlen(r_id) + 1);
      if (new_event_p->r_id_p == NULL)
      {
         ERROR_EXIT("Cannot allocate reserver id for room %s\n",
              prev_room_p->room.name);
      }
      strcpy(new_event_p->r_id_p, r_id);
      prev_event_p = new_event_p;
      break;

   default:
      ERROR_EXIT("Unexpected record beginning with %c\n", rec_type);
   }

   while ((blank = getc(fdb)) != '\n');  /* skip any extraneous chars */
}
```

```
    fclose(fdb);

    /*
     * Apply any new transactions to the room database. Note that it is not
     * necessary to lock the room record mutex during when applying a
     * transaction, since this is done before any remote calls can be
     * executed.
     */
    fxn = fopen(ROOM_XN_PATH, "r");
    if (fxn == NULL)
    {
       fprintf(out_fd, "Can't open %s for reading\n", ROOM_XN_PATH);
       perror("Error: ");
       exit(1);
    }

    n_xn = 0;
    while (fscanf(fxn, "%c", &xn.xn_type) != EOF)
    {
       if (n_xn == 0)
       {
          fprintf(out_fd, "Applying transactions from %s...\n", ROOM_XN_PATH);
       }
       n_xn++;

       fscanf(fxn, "%c%[^|]%c%[^|]%c%[^|]%c%[^|]%c%[^|]%c%[^|]%c%c",
              &blank,
              xn.loc,              &delim,
              xn.room_name,        &delim,
              xn.event.date_time,  &delim,
              xn.event.reserver,   &delim,
              xn.event.desc,       &delim,
              r_id,                &delim,
              &newline),
       strcpy(room.loc, xn.loc);
       strcpy(room.name, xn.room_name);
       xn.r_id_p = malloc(strlen(r_id) + 1);
       if (xn.r_id_p == NULL)
       {
         ERROR_EXIT("Cannot allocate reserver id for room %s\n",
                    xn.room_name);
         exit(1);
       }
       strcpy(xn.r_id_p, r_id);

       find_room(room, &room_p, &status);
       if (status == sch_status_ok)
       {
          switch (xn.xn_type)
          {
          case 'R':
              reserve(room_p, xn.event.date_time, xn.event.reserver,
                      xn.event.desc, xn.r_id_p, &status);
              break;

          case 'C':
              cancel(room_p, xn.event.date_time, xn.event.reserver,
                     xn.r_id_p, (xn.event.desc[0] == 'Y'), &status);
```

```
                break;

            default:
                ERROR_EXIT("Unknown transaction %c\n", xn.xn_type);
            }
        }
        if (status != sch_status_ok)
        {
            fprintf(out_fd, "Could not apply transaction %c %s %s %s %s %s %s\n",
                xn.xn_type, xn.loc, xn.room_name, xn.event.date_time,
                xn.event.reserver, xn.event.desc, xn.r_id_p);
            print_sch_status(status);
            exit(1);
        }
    }
    fclose(fxn);

    /*
     * Reopen the transaction log for writing of new transactions during
     * remote call execution.
     */
    fxn = fopen(ROOM_XN_PATH, "w");
    if (fxn == NULL)
    {
        fprintf(out_fd, "Can't open %s for writing\n", ROOM_XN_PATH);
        perror("Error: ");
        exit(1);
    }


    /*
     * Create the scrubber thread to delete old events.
     */
    create_thread(
        room_event_scrubber,
        "room_event_scrubber",
        &scrubber_thread,
        NULL);
}

/*
 * room_close()
 *    Updates the room database file from the internal data structures.
 *
 *    - Opens the room database file for writing.
 *    - Steps through all of the location, room, and event lists and writes
 *      each record to the room database file, including the room ACLs.
 *    - Closes the room database file.
 *    - Closes the transaction log and reopens it for writing, which deletes
 *      the transactions.
 */

void room_close()
{
    FILE            *fdb;
    loc_rec_t       *loc_p;
    room_rec_t      *room_p;
    event_rec_t     *event_p;
```

```
int             n_acl_entries;
unsigned char *obj_uuid_str;
unsigned char *acl_uuid_str;
unsigned32      ignored_st;
int             i;

kill_thread(scrubber_thread, "room_event_scrubber");

fprintf(out_fd, "Writing %s...\n", ROOM_DB_PATH);

fdb = fopen(ROOM_DB_PATH, "w");
if (fdb == NULL)
{
   fprintf(out_fd, "Can't open %s for writing\n", ROOM_DB_PATH);
   perror("Error: ");
   exit(1);
}

for (loc_p = loc_list; loc_p != NULL; loc_p = loc_p->next)
{
   uuid_to_string(&loc_p->loc_obj_uuid, &obj_uuid_str, &ignored_st);
   fprintf(fdb, "*%s|%s|%s|%s|\n",
           loc_p->loc,
           obj_uuid_str,
           loc_p->loc_otype,
           loc_p->loc_admin);
   rpc_string_free(&obj_uuid_str, &ignored_st);

   for (room_p = loc_p->room_list; room_p != NULL; room_p = room_p->next)
   {
      uuid_to_string(&room_p->acl_uuid, &acl_uuid_str, &ignored_st);
      fprintf(fdb, "+%s|%i|%s|%s|\n",      /* Write the room record. */
              room_p->room.name,
              room_p->room.max_people,
              room_p->room.desc,
              acl_uuid_str);

      for (event_p = room_p->event_list; event_p != NULL;
              event_p = event_p->next)
      {
         fprintf(fdb, " %s|%s|%s|%s|\n",    /* Write a reservation event. */
                 event_p->event.date_time,
                 event_p->event.reserver,
                 event_p->event.desc,
                 event_p->r_id_p);
      }
   }
}

fclose(fdb);

fprintf(out_fd, "Discarding transactions in %s...\n", ROOM_XN_PATH);
fclose(fxn);
fxn = fopen(ROOM_XN_PATH, "w");
if (fdb == NULL)
{
   fprintf(out_fd, "Can't open %s for writing\n", ROOM_XN_PATH);
   perror("Error: ");
```

```
        exit(1);
    }
    fclose(fxn);
}

/*
 * room_loc_begin()
 *     Initialize the next_loc cursor to point to the first location
 *     record.
 */

void room_loc_begin(
  /* [out] */ void **next_loc)
{
   *next_loc = (void *) loc_list;
}

/*
 * room_loc_next()
 *     Return the location name, object UUID, manager name, and admin user
 *     from the location record pointed to by next_loc. Then advance next_loc
 *     to the next location record. If there are no more records, set next_loc
 *     to NULL.
 */

void room_loc_next(
  /* [in/out] */ void           **next_loc,
  /* [out]    */ unsigned char **loc_name,
  /* [out]    */ uuid_t         **loc_obj_uuid,
  /* [out]    */ unsigned char **loc_otype,
  /* [out]    */ unsigned char **loc_admin)
{
  loc_rec_t *loc_p = (loc_rec_t *) *next_loc;

  *loc_name     =  loc_p->loc;
  *loc_obj_uuid = &loc_p->loc_obj_uuid;
  *loc_otype    =  loc_p->loc_otype;
  *loc_admin    =  loc_p->loc_admin;
  *next_loc     = (void *) loc_p->next;
}

/*
 * find_room()
 *     Searches the location and room lists for a specified room.  Returns
 *     a pointer to the room record.
 */

void find_room(
    /* [in ] */ sch_room_t      room,
    /* [out] */ room_rec_t    **room_p,
    /* [out] */ sch_status_t   *status)
{
   loc_rec_t   *loc_p;

   *room_p = NULL;
   for (loc_p = loc_list; loc_p != NULL; loc_p = loc_p->next)
   {
      if (LOC_NAME_EQ(loc_p->loc, room.loc))
```

```
      {
         for (*room_p = loc_p->room_list;
              *room_p != NULL;
              *room_p = (*room_p)->next)
         {
            if (ROOM_NAME_EQ((*room_p)->room.name, room.name))
            {
                 *status = sch_status_ok;
                 return;
            }
         }
         *status = sch_status_room_not_found;
          return;
      }
   }
   *status = sch_status_loc_not_found;
   return;
}



/*
 * call_is_secure()
 *    Determine if the remote caller represented by the binding handle has
 *    used sufficient security in making a remote call. Returns the privs
 *    from the binding handle.
 */

boolean32 call_is_secure(
   rpc_binding_handle_t h,
   unsigned32            expected_prot_level,
   rpc_authz_handle_t  *privs)
{
   char               *cell_name;
   char                expected_server_name[256];
   unsigned_char_p_t   server_name;
   unsigned32          protect_level;
   unsigned32          authn_service;
   unsigned32          authz_service;
   unsigned32          status;

   rpc_binding_inq_auth_client(
      h,
      privs,
      &server_name,
      &protect_level,
      &authn_service,
      &authz_service,
      &status);
   if (status == rpc_s_binding_has_no_auth)
   {
      return(false);
   }
   CHECK_DCE(status, "Cannot get client security info");

      /*
       * Construct the expected server name to be /.../cell_name/principal.
       * The server_principal set up in room_server.c is /.:/principal.
```

```
     */
   dce_cf_get_cell_name(&cell_name, &status);
   CHECK_DCE(status, "Cannot get local cell name");
   sprintf(expected_server_name, "%s/%s", cell_name, &server_principal[4]);
   free(cell_name);

   if ((strcmp((char *) server_name, expected_server_name) == 0) &&
       (protect_level >= expected_prot_level)              &&
       (authn_service == rpc_c_authn_dce_secret)           &&
       (authz_service == rpc_c_authz_dce))
   {
      return(true);
   }
   else
   {
      return(false);
   }
}

/*
 * client_is_authorized()
 *    Returns true if the client of the incoming remote call represented by
 *    the handle h has the required permissions in the room ACL represented by
 *    the ACL UUID.
 */
boolean32 client_is_authorized(
   rpc_binding_handle_t h,
   uuid_t              *acl_uuid,
   sec_acl_permset_t    required_perms)
{
   boolean32  authorized;
   unsigned32 status;

   dce_acl_is_client_authorized(
      h,
      &room_acl_mgr_uuid,
      acl_uuid,
      NULL,      /* no object owner */
      NULL,      /* no object group */
      required_perms,
      &authorized,
      &status);
   CHECK_DCE_NONFATAL(status, "Cannot check client authorization");
   if (status != error_status_ok)
   {
      return(false);
   }
   else
   {
      return(authorized);
   }
}

sch_room_t empty_room = {"", "", 0, ""};

/*
 * room_description()
 *    RPC manager: Searches the location and room lists for a specified
```

```
 *     room name.  Unlike find_room(), this will search all locations for
 *     the room name.
 *
 *     - Check if the caller used the right security.
 *     - For each location
 *        - For each room in the location
 *           - If the room matches the requested room name
 *              - Check if the caller is authorized to inquire about the room.
 *              - If so, return the sch_room_t part of the room record.
 *
 *     Does not lock the room record mutex, since it does not affect the
 *     room's event list.
 */

void room_description(
    /* [in ] */ handle_t        h,
    /* [in ] */ sch_room_name_t room_name,
    /* [out] */ sch_room_t      *room,
    /* [out] */ sch_status_t    *status,
    /* [out] */ error_status_t *call_status)
{
   loc_rec_t  *loc_p;
   room_rec_t *room_p;
   rpc_authz_handle_t privs;

   *call_status = error_status_ok;
   memcpy(room, empty_room, sizeof(sch_room_t)); /* in case of error */

   if (!call_is_secure(h, rpc_c_protect_level_pkt_integ, &privs))
   {
      *status = sch_status_not_secure;
      return;
   }

   for (loc_p = loc_list; loc_p != NULL; loc_p = loc_p->next)
   {
      for (room_p = loc_p->room_list; room_p != NULL; room_p = room_p->next)
      {
         if (ROOM_NAME_EQ(room_p->room.name, room_name))
         {
            if (!client_is_authorized(h, &room_p->acl_uuid, sch_acl_perm_inq))
            {
                 *status = sch_status_not_authorized;
                 return;
            }
            else
            {
                 memcpy(room, room_p->room, sizeof(sch_room_t));
                 *status = sch_status_ok;
                 return;
            }
         }
      }
   }

   *status = sch_status_room_not_found;
}
```

```
/*
 * reserve()
 *    Reserves a room for a date and time interval, for a reserver and an
 *    event.  This is the local routine called by the RPC manager
 *    room_reserve() and by room_open() when applying reserve transactions
 *    from the xn log.
 *
 *    - Convert the date_time to a start and end time.
 *    - Find the desired room.
 *    - Search the event list for the room for the first event not earlier
 *      than the start time.
 *    - Check if the next event conflicts with the desired start and end time.
 *    - Allocate, link, and initialize a new event record for the reservation.
 */

void reserve(
   /* [in ] */ room_rec_t       *room_p,
   /* [in ] */ sch_date_time_t  date_time,
   /* [in ] */ sch_name_t       reserver,
   /* [in ] */ sch_event_desc_t desc,
   /* [in ] */ reserver_id_p_t  r_id_p,
   /* [out] */ sch_status_t    *status)
{
   time_t       start;
   time_t       end;
   loc_rec_t   *loc_p;
   event_rec_t *prev_event_p;
   event_rec_t *next_event_p;
   event_rec_t *new_event_p;

   convert_date_time(date_time, &start, &end, status);
   if (*status != sch_status_ok)
   {
      return;
   }

   prev_event_p = NULL;
   for (next_event_p = room_p->event_list;
        ((next_event_p != NULL) && (next_event_p->end <= start));
        next_event_p = next_event_p->next)
   {
      prev_event_p = next_event_p;
   }

   if ((next_event_p != NULL) &&
       (OVERLAP(next_event_p->start, next_event_p->end, start, end)))
   {
      *status = sch_status_room_unavail;
      return;
   }

   MALLOC(new_event_p, event_rec_t);
   LINK(new_event_p,prev_event_p,next_event_p,room_p->event_list);
   strcpy(new_event_p->event.date_time, date_time);
   strcpy(new_event_p->event.reserver, reserver);
   strcpy(new_event_p->event.desc, desc);
   new_event_p->r_id_p = r_id_p;
   new_event_p->start  = start;
```

```
   new_event_p->end     = end;

   *status = sch_status_ok;
}

/*
 * room_reserve()
 *    RPC manager: Reserve a room for a specified date and time interval,
 *    reserver, and event.
 *
 *    - Check that the caller used the right security.
 *    - Find the desired room.
 *    - Check if the caller is authorized to reserve the room.
 *    - Lock the room record mutex to prevent other managers from
 *      altering the room's event list.
 *    - Call reserve() to set up the reservation.
 *    - Write a reserve transaction record to the xn log.
 *    - Unlock the room record mutex.
 */

void room_reserve(
   /* [in ] */ handle_t          h,
   /* [in ] */ sch_room_t        room,
   /* [in ] */ sch_date_time_t  date_time,
   /* [in ] */ sch_name_t        reserver,
   /* [in ] */ sch_event_desc_t desc,
   /* [out] */ sch_status_t     *status,
   /* [out] */ error_status_t   *call_status)
{
   room_rec_t        *room_p;
   reserver_id_p_t    r_id_p;
   unsigned_char_p_t  client_id;
   unsigned32         ret1, ret2;
   unsigned32         ignored_st;
   rpc_authz_handle_t privs;
#  define PAC          ((sec_id_pac_t *) privs)

   *call_status = error_status_ok;

   if (!call_is_secure(h, rpc_c_protect_level_pkt_integ, &privs))
   {
      *status = sch_status_not_secure;
      return;
   }

   r_id_p = malloc(UUID_STR_LENGTH+1);
   uuid_to_string(&(PAC->principal.uuid), &r_id_p, &ignored_st);

   find_room(room, &room_p, status);
   if (*status != sch_status_ok)
   {
      return;
   }

   if (!client_is_authorized(h, &room_p->acl_uuid, sch_acl_perm_reserve))
   {
      *status = sch_status_not_authorized;
      return;
```

```
    }

    LOCK_ROOM_MUTEX(room_p);

    reserve(room_p, date_time, reserver, desc, r_id_p, status);
    if (*status == sch_status_ok)
    {
       ret1 = fprintf(fxn, "R %s|%s|%s|%s|%s|%s|\n",
                 room.loc, room.name, date_time, reserver, desc, r_id_p);
       ret2 = fflush(fxn);
       if ((ret1 == -1) || (ret2 == EOF))
       {
          fprintf(out_fd, "Could not write transaction R %s %s %s %s %s\n",
              room.loc, room.name, date_time, reserver, desc, r_id_p);
          perror("Error: ");
          exit(1);
       }
    }

    UNLOCK_ROOM_MUTEX(room_p);
}

/*
 * cancel()
 *    Cancels a room reservation for a date and time interval.  The reservation
 *    must be canceled by the same reserver than made it.  This is the local
 *    routine called by the RPC manager room_cancel() and by room_open() when
 *    applying cancel transactions from the xn log.
 *
 *    - Convert the date_time to a start and end time.
 *    - Check if the canceler is the reserver, or is authorized to cancel
 *      any reservation for the room.
 *    - Search the event list for the room for the first event not earlier
 *      than the start time.
 *    - Check if the next event is the specified time interval.
 *    - Unlink and deallocate the event record for the canceled reservation.
 */

void cancel(
    /* [in ] */ room_rec_t      *room_p,
    /* [in ] */ sch_date_time_t date_time,
    /* [in ] */ sch_name_t      reserver,
    /* [in ] */ reserver_id_p_t r_id_p,
    /* [in ] */ boolean32       can_cancel,
    /* [out] */ sch_status_t   *status)
{
    time_t       start;
    time_t       end;
    event_rec_t *event_p;

    convert_date_time(date_time, &start, &end, status);
    if (*status != sch_status_ok)
    {
       return;
    }

    for (event_p = room_p->event_list;
         ((event_p != NULL) && (event_p->end <= start));
```

```
        event_p = event_p->next)
   {
   }

   if ((event_p->start == start) && (event_p->end == end))
   {
      if (can_cancel ||
          ((strcmp(event_p->r_id_p, r_id_p) == 0) &&
           (strcmp(event_p->event.reserver, reserver) == 0)))
      {
         UNLINK(event_p, room_p->event_list);
         free(event_p);
         *status = sch_status_ok;
      }
      else
      {
         *status = sch_status_not_reserver;
      }
   }
   else
   {
      *status = sch_status_event_not_found;
   }
}

/*
 * room_cancel()
 *    RPC manager: Cancel a room reservation for a specified date and time
 *    interval, and reserver.
 *
 *    - Check that the caller used the right security.
 *    - Find the desired room.
 *    - Determine if the caller has blanket cancellation authority.
 *    - Lock the room record mutex to prevent other managers from
 *      altering the room's event list.
 *    - Call cancel() to cancel the reservation.
 *    - Write a cancel transaction record to the xn log.
 *    - Unlock the room record mutex.
 */

void room_cancel(
   /* [in ] */ handle_t        h,
   /* [in ] */ sch_room_t      room,
   /* [in ] */ sch_date_time_t date_time,
   /* [in ] */ sch_name_t      reserver,
   /* [out] */ sch_status_t   *status,
   /* [out] */ error_status_t *call_status)
{
   room_rec_t        *room_p;
   reserver_id_p_t   r_id_p;
   unsigned_char_p_t client_id;
   boolean32         can_cancel;
   unsigned32        ret1, ret2;
   unsigned32        ignored_st;
   rpc_authz_handle_t privs;

   *call_status = error_status_ok;

   if (!call_is_secure(h, rpc_c_protect_level_pkt_integ, &privs))
```

```
   {
      *status = sch_status_not_secure;
      return;
   }

   r_id_p = malloc (UUID_STR-LENGTH+1);
   uuid_to_string(&(PAC->principal.uuid,
                   &r_id_p, &ignored_st);

   find_room(room, &room_p, status);
   if (*status != sch_status_ok)
   {
      return;
   }

   can_cancel = client_is_authorized(h, &room_p->acl_uuid, sch_acl_perm_cancel);

   LOCK_ROOM_MUTEX(room_p);

   cancel(room_p, date_time, reserver, r_id_p, can_cancel, status);
   if (*status == sch_status_ok)
   {
      ret1 = fprintf(fxn, "C %s|%s|%s|%s|%s|%s|\n",
                  room.loc, room.name, date_time, reserver,
                  (can_cancel ? "Y" : "N"), r_id_p);
      ret2 = fflush(fxn);
      if ((ret1 == -1) || (ret2 == EOF))
      {
         fprintf(out_fd, "Could not write transaction C %s %s %s %s\n",
             room.loc, room.name, date_time, reserver, r_id_p);
         perror("Error: ");
         exit(1);
      }
   }

   UNLOCK_ROOM_MUTEX(room_p);
}

/*
 * room_avail()
 *    RPC manager: Return an array of rooms that are available on a specified
 *    date and time interval and can accommodate a given number of people.  The
 *    rooms are ordered by one or more preferred locations.
 *
 *    - Check that the caller has used the right security.
 *    - Convert the date_time to a start and end time.
 *    - For each preferred location:
 *      - Search the location list for the preferred location.
 *      - For each room in the preferred location:
 *        - Check if the caller is authorized to inquire about the room.
 *        - Lock the room record mutex to keep other managers from altering
 *          the event list.
 *        - Search the room's event list for the first event not earlier than
 *          the start time.
 *        - If the next event does not conflict with the start and end times,
 *          add the room to the avail_rooms array.
 *        - Unlock the room record mutex.
 *        - If the avail_rooms array is full, return.
 */
```

```
void room_avail(
   /* [in ] */ handle_t        h,
   /* [in ] */ sch_date_time_t date_time,
   /* [in ] */ idl_long_int    n_people,
   /* [in ] */ idl_long_int    n_pref_locs,
   /* [in ] */ sch_loc_name_t  pref_locs[],
   /* [in ] */ idl_long_int    max_avail_rooms,
   /* [out] */ idl_long_int   *n_avail_rooms,
   /* [out] */ sch_room_t      avail_rooms[],
   /* [out] */ sch_status_t   *status,
   /* [out] */ error_status_t *call_status)
{
   time_t        start;
   time_t        end;
   idl_long_int i;
   loc_rec_t    *loc_p;
   room_rec_t   *room_p;
   event_rec_t *event_p;
   rpc_authz_handle_t privs;

   *n_avail_rooms = 0;
   *call_status = error_status_ok;

   if (!call_is_secure(h, rpc_c_protect_level_pkt_integ, &privs))
   {
      *status = sch_status_not_secure;
      return;
   }

   convert_date_time(date_time, &start, &end, status);
   if (*status != sch_status_ok)
   {
      return;
   }

   if (max_avail_rooms == 0)
   {
      return;
   }

   for (i = 0; i < n_pref_locs; i++)
   {
      for (loc_p = loc_list; loc_p != NULL; loc_p = loc_p->next)
      {
          if (LOC_NAME_EQ(loc_p->loc, pref_locs[i]))
          {
              for (room_p = loc_p->room_list;
                   room_p != NULL;
                   room_p = room_p->next)
             {
                if (!client_is_authorized(h, &room_p->acl_uuid,
                                             sch_acl_perm_inq))
                {
                   continue;
                }

                LOCK_ROOM_MUTEX(room_p);
```

```
                for (event_p = room_p->event_list;
                     ((event_p != NULL) && (event_p->end <= start));
                     event_p = event_p->next)
                  {
                  }

                if ((event_p != NULL) &&
                       (OVERLAP(event_p->start, event_p->end, start, end)))
                {
                   UNLOCK_ROOM_MUTEX(room_p);
                   continue;
                }

                memcpy(&(avail_rooms[*n_avail_rooms]), &room_p->room,
                        sizeof(sch_room_t));
               (*n_avail_rooms)++;

                UNLOCK_ROOM_MUTEX(room_p);

               if (*n_avail_rooms == max_avail_rooms)
                 {
                    *status = sch_status_ok;
                    return;
                 }
          }
       }
     }
   }

   *status = sch_status_ok;
}

/*
 * room_events()
 *    RPC manager: Returns a linked list of events for which a room is
 *    reserved between a beginning and an end date and time.
 *
 *    - Check that the caller used the right security.
 *    - Convert the begin and end date_times to a start and end time.
 *    - Find the specified room.
 *    - Check if the caller is authorized to inquire about the room.
 *    - Lock the room record mutex to prevent other managers from
 *      altering the room's event list.
 *    - Search the event list for the room for the first event not earlier
 *      than the start time.
 *    - For each event until an event later than the end time is found:
 *      - Allocate and initialize a sch_event_rec_t record for the event.
 *      - Link the record at the end of the room_event_list.
 *    - Unlock the room record mutex.
 */

void room_events(
   /* [in ] */ handle_t              h,
   /* [in ] */ sch_room_t            room,
   /* [in ] */ sch_short_date_time_t begin_date_time,
   /* [in ] */ sch_short_date_time_t end_date_time,
   /* [out] */ sch_event_rec_p_t    *room_event_list,
```

```
    /* [out] */ sch_status_t         *status,
    /* [out] */ error_status_t       *call_status)
{
    time_t            begin;
    time_t            end;
    room_rec_t       *room_p;
    event_rec_t      *event_p;
    sch_event_rec_t *prev_ev_p;
    sch_event_rec_t *new_ev_p;
    rpc_authz_handle_t privs;

    *room_event_list = NULL;
    *call_status = error_status_ok;

    if (!call_is_secure(h, rpc_c_protect_level_pkt_integ, &privs))
    {
       *status = sch_status_not_secure;
       return;
    }

    convert_short_date_time(begin_date_time, &begin, status);
    if (*status != sch_status_ok)
    {
       return;
    }
    convert_short_date_time(end_date_time, &end, status);
    if (*status != sch_status_ok)
    {
       return;
    }

    find_room(room, &room_p, status);
    if (*status != sch_status_ok)
    {
       return;
    }

    if (!client_is_authorized(h, &room_p->acl_uuid, sch_acl_perm_inq))
    {
       *status = sch_status_not_authorized;
       return;
    }

    LOCK_ROOM_MUTEX(room_p);

    for (event_p = room_p->event_list;
         ((event_p != NULL) && (event_p->end < begin));
         event_p = event_p->next)
    {
    }

    prev_ev_p = NULL;
    for ( ;
         ((event_p != NULL) && (event_p->end < end));
         event_p = event_p->next)
    {
       new_ev_p = rpc_ss_allocate(sizeof(sch_event_rec_t));
       LINK_NEW(new_ev_p, prev_ev_p, *room_event_list);
```

```
        memcpy(&(new_ev_p->event), &(event_p->event), sizeof(sch_event_t));
        prev_ev_p = new_ev_p;
    }

    UNLOCK_ROOM_MUTEX(room_p);

    *status = sch_status_ok;
}

/*
 * room_acl_setup()
 *     Creates default ACLs for each room:
 *         - For the admin user defined for the room's location, grants
 *             inquire, reserve, cancel, test, and control
 *         - For all other users, grants
 *             inquire, reserve, test
 */
void room_acl_setup(
    dce_db_handle_t acl_db_h)
{
    loc_rec_t         *loc_p;
    room_rec_t        *room_p;
    sec_rgy_handle_t  rgy_h;
    uuid_t            loc_admin_uuid;
    dce_db_header_t   std_header;
    sec_acl_t         acl;
    unsigned32        status;

#   define NORMAL_ROOM_PERMS \
        sch_acl_perm_inq | sch_acl_perm_reserve | sch_acl_perm_test
#   define ADMIN_ROOM_PERMS \
        NORMAL_ROOM_PERMS | sch_acl_perm_cancel | sch_acl_perm_control

    rpc_sm_enable_allocate(&status);  /* required by db_store_by_uuid() */
    CHECK_DCE(status, "Cannot enable allocation");

    sec_rgy_site_open((unsigned_char_t *) "", &rgy_h, &status);
    CHECK_DCE(status, "Cannot open Security Registry");

    for (loc_p = loc_list; loc_p != NULL; loc_p = loc_p->next)
    {
        sec_id_parse_name(rgy_h, loc_p->loc_admin, NULL, NULL, NULL,
                          &loc_admin_uuid, &status);
        CHECK_DCE(status, "Cannot convert admin principal to UUID");

        for (room_p = loc_p->room_list; room_p != NULL; room_p = room_p->next)
        {
            dce_acl_obj_init(&room_acl_mgr_uuid, &acl, &status);
            CHECK_DCE(status, "Cannot initialize location ACL");

            dce_acl_obj_add_user_entry(
                &acl,
                ADMIN_ROOM_PERMS,
                &loc_admin_uuid,
                &status);
            CHECK_DCE(status, "Cannot add admin ACL permissions");

            dce_acl_obj_add_obj_entry(
                &acl,
```

```
            sec_acl_e_type_any_other,
            NORMAL_ROOM_PERMS,
            &status);
        CHECK_DCE(status, "Cannot add normal ACL permissions");

        dce_db_store_by_uuid(
            acl_db_h,
            &(room_p->acl_uuid),
            &acl,
            &status);
        CHECK_DCE(status, "Cannot store room ACL in ACL database");

        dce_acl_obj_free_entries(&acl, &status);
        CHECK_DCE(status, "Cannot free ACL entries");
      }
   }

   sec_rgy_site_close(rgy_h, &status);
   CHECK_DCE(status, "Cannot close Registry");
}

/*
 * room_acl_resolve()
 *    Maps a room name (in the component_name parameter) into the UUID for
 *    the room's ACL. This is called by the ACL Library when it needs to
 *    resolve a component into an ACL.
 */
void room_acl_resolve(
   handle_t                  handle,
   sec_acl_component_name_t component_name,
   sec_acl_type_t            sec_acl_type,
   uuid_t                    *mgr_type,
   boolean32                 writing,
   void                      *resolver_arg,
   uuid_t                    *acl_uuid,
   error_status_t            *status)
{
   loc_rec_t   *loc_p;
   room_rec_t  *room_p;
   unsigned32   ignored_st;

   *status = error_status_ok;

   if (uuid_compare(mgr_type, &room_acl_mgr_uuid, &ignored_st) != 0)
   {
      uuid_create_nil(acl_uuid, &ignored_st);
      return;
   }

   if (sec_acl_type != sec_acl_type_object)
   {
      uuid_create_nil(acl_uuid, &ignored_st);
      return;
   }

   for (loc_p = loc_list; loc_p != NULL; loc_p = loc_p->next)
   {
      for (room_p = loc_p->room_list; room_p != NULL; room_p = room_p->next)
```

```
      {
         if (ROOM_NAME_EQ(room_p->room.name, component_name))
         {
            memcpy(acl_uuid, &room_p->acl_uuid, sizeof(uuid_t));
            return;
         }
      }
   }

   uuid_create_nil(acl_uuid, &ignored_st);
   *status    = db_s_key_not_found;
}

room_v1_0_epv_t native_mgr_epv =
{
   room_description,
   room_reserve,
   room_cancel,
   room_avail,
   room_events,
};
```

B.7 schedule/obj/legacy_mgr.c

```
/*
 * legacy_mgr.c
 */

#include <stdio.h>
#include "room.h"
#include "sch_util.h"

void legacy_description(
    /* [in ] */ handle_t        h,
    /* [in ] */ sch_room_name_t room_name,
    /* [out] */ sch_room_t      *room,
    /* [out] */ sch_status_t    *status,
    /* [out] */ error_status_t *call_status)
{
   *status = sch_status_unimplemented;
   *call_status = error_status_ok;
}

void legacy_reserve(
   /* [in ] */ handle_t         h,
   /* [in ] */ sch_room_t       room,
   /* [in ] */ sch_date_time_t  date_time,
   /* [in ] */ sch_name_t       reserver,
   /* [in ] */ sch_event_desc_t desc,
   /* [out] */ sch_status_t    *status,
   /* [out] */ error_status_t  *call_status)
{
   *status = sch_status_unimplemented;
   *call_status = error_status_ok;
}

void legacy_cancel(
   /* [in ] */ handle_t        h,
   /* [in ] */ sch_room_t      room,
   /* [in ] */ sch_date_time_t date_time,
   /* [in ] */ sch_name_t      reserver,
   /* [out] */ sch_status_t   *status,
   /* [out] */ error_status_t *call_status)
{
   *status = sch_status_unimplemented;
   *call_status = error_status_ok;
}

void legacy_avail(
   /* [in ] */ handle_t        h,
   /* [in ] */ sch_date_time_t date_time,
   /* [in ] */ idl_long_int    n_people,
   /* [in ] */ idl_long_int    n_pref_locs,
   /* [in ] */ sch_loc_name_t  pref_locs[],
   /* [in ] */ idl_long_int    max_avail_rooms,
   /* [out] */ idl_long_int   *n_avail_rooms,
   /* [out] */ sch_room_t      avail_rooms[],
   /* [out] */ sch_status_t   *status,
   /* [out] */ error_status_t *call_status)
{
   *status = sch_status_unimplemented;
```

```
    *n_avail_rooms = 0;
    *call_status = error_status_ok;
}

void legacy_events(
    /* [in ] */ handle_t              h,
    /* [in ] */ sch_room_t            room,
    /* [in ] */ sch_short_date_time_t begin_date_time,
    /* [in ] */ sch_short_date_time_t end_date_time,
    /* [out] */ sch_event_rec_p_t    *room_event_list,
    /* [out] */ sch_status_t         *status,
    /* [out] */ error_status_t       *call_status)
{
    *status = sch_status_unimplemented;
    *room_event_list = NULL;
    *call_status = error_status_ok;
}

room_v1_0_epv_t legacy_mgr_epv =
{
    legacy_description,
    legacy_reserve,
    legacy_cancel,
    legacy_avail,
    legacy_events,
};
```

B.8 schedule/obj/sch_util.c

```
/*
 * sch_util.c
 *
 * Utility routines used by room clients and servers.
 */

#include <stdio.h>
#include <errno.h>
#include <dce/dce_error.h>
#include "sch_util.h"
#include "sch.h"

void dce_error(
   unsigned32 status,
   char       *errmsg,
   boolean32  abort)
{
   unsigned char errstr[dce_c_error_string_len];
   int error_status;

   fprintf(stderr, "%s\n", errmsg);
   dce_error_inq_text(status, errstr, &error_status);
   if (error_status == error_status_ok)
   {
      fprintf(stderr, "%s\n", errstr);
   }
   else
   {
      fprintf(stderr, "Could not get error text for status 0x%8x\n", status);
   }
   if (abort)
   {
      exit(0);
   }
}

/*
 * print_sch_status()
 *    Prints a message corresponding to an sch status.
 */

void print_sch_status(
   sch_status_t status)
{
   switch (status)
   {
      case sch_status_ok:
         printf("Operation successful\n");       break;
      case sch_status_loc_not_found:
         printf("Location not found\n");         break;
      case sch_status_room_not_found:
         printf("Room not found\n");             break;
      case sch_status_room_unavail:
         printf("Room unavailable\n");           break;
      case sch_status_bad_date_time:
         printf("Invalid date or time\n");       break;
      case sch_status_event_not_found:
```

```
         printf("Event not found\n");            break;
      case sch_status_not_reserver:
         printf("Not reserver\n");               break;
      case sch_status_unimplemented:
         printf("Operation not implemented\n"); break;
      case sch_status_not_secure:
         printf("Operation not secure\n");      break;
      case sch_status_not_authorized:
         printf("Not authorized\n");             break;
      default:
         printf("Unknown status %i\n", status); break;
   }
}

/*
 * print_call_status()
 *    Prints the DCE error for a returned call status.
 */

void print_call_status(
   error_status_t call_status)
{
   unsigned char error_text[dce_c_error_string_len];
   int ignored_st;

   dce_error_inq_text(call_status, error_text, &ignored_st);
   printf("%s\n", error_text);
}

void create_thread(
   pthread_startroutine_t thread_routine,
   char                   *thread_name,
   pthread_t              *thread_id,
   pthread_addr_t          thread_arg)
{
   unsigned32 status;

   status = pthread_create(thread_id, pthread_attr_default,
                           thread_routine, thread_arg);
   if (status != 0)
   {
      fprintf(stderr, "Cannot create %s thread\n", thread_name);
      fprintf(stderr, "%s\n", strerror(errno));
      exit(0);
   }
   pthread_yield();
}

void kill_thread(
   pthread_t thread_id,
   char     *thread_name)
{
   unsigned32 status;

   status = pthread_cancel(thread_id);
   if (status != 0)
   {
      fprintf(stderr, "Cannot kill %s thread\n", thread_name);
```

```
        fprintf(stderr, "%s\n", strerror(errno));
    }
}

boolean32 is_server_there(
    rpc_binding_handle_t h,
    rpc_if_handle_t      ifspec)
{
    boolean32  listening;
    unsigned32 status;

    listening = rpc_mgmt_is_server_listening(h, &status);
    if (status == rpc_s_binding_incomplete)
    {
        /*
         * Binding is lacking an endpoint, so request that the server's
         * Endpoint Map provide an endpoint and try again. If the server
         * is not registered with the Endpoint Map, we assume it is not
         * active.  Also, if we can't even get to the Endpoint Map, we
         * assume we can't get to the server either.
         */
        rpc_ep_resolve_binding(h, ifspec, &status);
        if ((status == ept_s_not_registered) ||
            (status == rpc_s_comm_failure)   ||
            (status == rpc_s_connect_rejected))
        {
          return(false);
        }
        CHECK_DCE(status, "Cannot resolve binding");
        listening = rpc_mgmt_is_server_listening(h, &status);
    }

    if ((status == rpc_s_comm_failure) ||
        (status == rpc_s_connect_rejected))
    {
        return(false);
    }
    CHECK_DCE(status,"Cannot check if server is listening");
    return (listening);
}
```

B.9 schedule/obj/sch_util.h

```
/*
 * sch_util.h
 *
 * Defines function prototypes for the sch_util.c module.
 */

#ifndef SCH_UTIL_INCLUDED
#define SCH_UTIL_INCLUDED

#include <dce/rpc.h>
#include <pthread.h>
#include "sch.h"

#define CHECK_DCE(status, errmsg) \
   if (status != error_status_ok) dce_error(status, errmsg, true);

#define CHECK_DCE_NONFATAL(status, errmsg) \
   if (status != error_status_ok) dce_error(status, errmsg, false);

void dce_error(
   unsigned32 status,
   char      *errmsg,
   boolean32  abort);

void print_sch_status(
   sch_status_t status);

void print_call_status(
   error_status_t call_status);

void create_thread(
   pthread_startroutine_t thread_routine,
   char                  *thread_name,
   pthread_t             *thread_id,
   pthread_addr_t         thread_arg);

void kill_thread(
   pthread_t thread_id,
   char     *thread_name);

boolean32 is_server_there(
   rpc_binding_handle_t h,
   rpc_if_handle_t      ifspec);

#endif /* SCH_UTIL_INCLUDED */
```

B.10 schedule/obj/rgy_create.ksh

```
#
# rgy_create.ksh - script to create room server group
#
echo "Creating room-server-group"
echo "
domain group
add room-server-group
quit" | rgy_edit
```

B.11 schedule/obj/rgy_create_host.ksh

```
#
# rgy_create_host.ksh - script to create principal and
#                       keytab file for local room server
#
# rgy_create_host.ksh admin_password
#
ADMIN_PW=$1
if [[ -z $ADMIN_PW ]]
then
   echo "Expected your administrator's password in arg 1"
   exit
fi
S_HOST=`hostname`
echo "Creating room-server.$S_HOST and room_keyfile.$S_HOST"
echo "
domain principal
add room-server.$S_HOST
domain account
add room-server.$S_HOST -g room-server-group -o none -mp $ADMIN_PW -pw -dce-
ktadd -p room-server.$S_HOST -pw -dce- -f room_keyfile.$S_HOST
ktadd -p room-server.$S_HOST -a -r -f room_keyfile.$S_HOST
quit" | rgy_edit
```

B.12 schedule/obj/rgy_delete.ksh

```
#
# rgy_delete.ksh - script to delete the room-server-group
#
echo "Deleting room-server-group"
echo "
domain group
delete room-server-group
quit" | rgy_edit
```

B.13 schedule/obj/rgy_delete_host.ksh

```
#
# rgy_delete_host.ksh - script to delete server principal and
#                       keytab file used by the local room server
#
S_HOST=`hostname`
echo "Deleting room-server.$S_HOST and room_keyfile.$S_HOST"
echo "
domain principal
delete room-server.$S_HOST
ktdelete -p room-server.$S_HOST -v 1 -f room_keyfile.$S_HOST
ktdelete -p room-server.$S_HOST -v 2 -f room_keyfile.$S_HOST
quit" | rgy_edit
rm room_keyfile.$S_HOST
```

B.14 schedule/obj/cds_create.ksh

```
#
# cds_create.ksh - script to set up CDS entries for room application,
#                  used by all room servers
#
set -x
cdscp create dir /.:/subsys/sch
cdscp create obj /.:/subsys/sch/room_group
cdscp create dir /.:/subsys/sch/room
```

B.15 schedule/obj/cds_create_host.ksh

```
#
# cds_create_host.ksh - script to set up CDS entries for one room server on the
#                       local system
#
# cds_create_host.ksh loc1 loc2 ... locn
S_HOST=`hostname`
set -x
cdscp create obj /.:/subsys/sch/room_server.$S_HOST
for LOC in "$@"
do
   cdscp create obj /.:/subsys/sch/room/$LOC
done
acl_edit -e /.:/subsys/sch/room_server.$S_HOST -m user:room-server.$S_HOST:rwt
acl_edit -e /.:/subsys/sch/room_group -m user:room-server.$S_HOST:rwt
acl_edit -e /.:/subsys/sch/room -m user:room-server.$S_HOST:rwt
for LOC in "$@"
do
   acl_edit -e /.:/subsys/sch/room/$LOC -m user:room-server.$S_HOST:rwt
done
acl_edit -e /.:/cell-profile -m user:room-server.$S_HOST:rwt
```

B.16 schedule/obj/cds_delete.ksh

```
#
# cds_delete.ksh - script to delete CDS entries used by
#                  all room servers
#
set -x
cdscp delete obj /.:/subsys/sch/room_group
cdscp delete dir /.:/subsys/sch/room
cdscp delete dir /.:/subsys/sch
```

B.17 schedule/obj/cds_delete_host.ksh

```
#
# rgy_delete_host.ksh - script to delete server principal and
#                       keytab file used by the local room server
#
S_HOST=`hostname`
echo "Deleting room-server.$S_HOST and room_keyfile.$S_HOST"
echo "
domain principal
delete room-server.$S_HOST
ktdelete -p room-server.$S_HOST -v 1 -f room_keyfile.$S_HOST
ktdelete -p room-server.$S_HOST -v 2 -f room_keyfile.$S_HOST
quit" | rgy_edit
rm room_keyfile.$S_HOST
```

B.18 schedule/obj/Makefile

```
#
# Makefile for room schedule application
#
IDLFLAGS   = -keep all -cc_opt '-g'
CFLAGS     = -Aa -c -g -D_HPUX_SOURCE -D_REENTRANT
INCDIRS    = -I. -I$(SETUPDIR)  -I/usr/include/reentrant
LDFLAGS    = -Wl,-Bimmediate,-Bnonfatal
LIBS       = -ldce -lc_r
SERVER_OBJS= room_server.o room_mgr.o legacy_mgr.o room_sstub.o sch_util.o
CLIENT_OBJS= room.o room_cstub.o sch_util.o

all: room room_server

sch.h: sch.idl
idl $(IDLFLAGS) sch.idl

sch_util.o: sch_util.c sch_util.h
cc $(CFLAGS) $(INCDIRS) sch_util.c

room.h room_cstub.o room_sstub.o: room.idl room.acf sch.h
idl $(IDLFLAGS) room.idl

room.o: room.c room.h sch_util.h
cc $(CFLAGS) $(INCDIRS) room.c

room_server.o: room_server.c room.h
cc $(CFLAGS) $(INCDIRS) room_server.c
```

```
room_mgr.o: room_mgr.c room.h sch_util.h
cc $(CFLAGS) $(INCDIRS) room_mgr.c

legacy_mgr.o: legacy_mgr.c room.h sch_util.h
cc $(CFLAGS) $(INCDIRS) legacy_mgr.c

room_server: $(SERVER_OBJS)
cc $(LDFLAGS) -o room_server $(SERVER_OBJS) $(LIBS)

room: $(CLIENT_OBJS)
cc $(LDFLAGS) -o room $(CLIENT_OBJS) $(LIBS)

clean: ;
rm -f sch.h room.h *stub.c *aux.c *.o room room_server
```

B.19 schedule/obj/room_db.dat1

```
*44L|21689b0e-c6bd-11ce-b35f-08000948fbd9|native|/.:/cell_admin|
+Weibel|12|Col P4|d43995ee-d1c6-11ce-aedf-08000948fbd9|
+Stonegate|12|Col P4; audio teleconference|d43a5f4c-d1c6-11ce-aedf-08000948fbd9|
+Spring Mountain|12|Col P5|d43a7928-d1c6-11ce-aedf-08000948fbd9|
+Sycamore Creek|24|Col R2|d43a9124-d1c6-11ce-aedf-08000948fbd9|
*44M|21696160-c6bd-11ce-b35f-08000948fbd9|native|/.:/cell_admin|
+Sterling|20|Col E8; training|d43aa916-d1c6-11ce-aedf-08000948fbd9|
+Landmark|20|Col R3; audio teleconference|d43ac112-d1c6-11ce-aedf-08000948fbd9|
+Franciscan_A|16|Col R5|d43ad8b4-d1c6-11ce-aedf-08000948fbd9|
+Franciscan_B|24|Col R7|d43af0ce-d1c6-11ce-aedf-08000948fbd9|
+Diamond_Creek|22|Col R9; audio teleconference|d43b08d4-d1c6-11ce-aedf-08000948fbd9|
*44U|216983f2-c6bd-11ce-b35f-08000948fbd9|native|/.:/cell_admin|
+Inglenook|15|Col E2; audio teleconference|d43b20d0-d1c6-11ce-aedf-08000948fbd9|
+Beringer|20|Col R2; audio teleconference|d43b484e-d1c6-11ce-aedf-08000948fbd9|
+Mirassou|20|Col R9; audio teleconference|d43b60ea-d1c6-11ce-aedf-08000948fbd9|
*01L|21699c02-c6bd-11ce-b35f-08000948fbd9|legacy|/.:/cell_admin|
*01U|2169b37c-c6bd-11ce-b35f-08000948fbd9|legacy|/.:/cell_admin|
```

B.20 schedule/obj/room_db.dat1

```
*43L|c8f5db8c-c6d3-11ce-b79f-080009421b3c|native|/.:/cell_admin|
+Mt.Shasta|20|Col R3|fbaf6990-d40b-11ce-8f0b-080009421b3c|
+Mt.Rainer|20|Col E4|fbb4c85e-d40b-11ce-8f0b-080009421b3c|
*43U|c8f6be44-c6d3-11ce-b79f-080009421b3c|native|/.:/cell_admin|
+Mt.Rushmore|8|Col R9|fbb4ed5c-d40b-11ce-8f0b-080009421b3c|
+Mt.Kilimanjaro|20|Col E9|fbb50e9a-d40b-11ce-8f0b-080009421b3c|
```

Function and Command Index

A

B

C

D

F

G

I

K

L

M

P

R

S

T

U

V

General Index

A

D

E

K

L

M

N

O

P

R

S

T

V

W

X

LICENSE AGREEMENT AND LIMITED WARRANTY

READ THE FOLLOWING TERMS AND CONDITIONS CAREFULLY BEFORE OPENING THIS DISK PACKAGE. THIS LEGAL DOCUMENT IS AN AGREEMENT BETWEEN YOU AND PRENTICE-HALL, INC. (THE "COMPANY"). BY OPENING THIS SEALED DISK PACKAGE, YOU ARE AGREEING TO BE BOUND BY THESE TERMS AND CONDITIONS. IF YOU DO NOT AGREE WITH THESE TERMS AND CONDITIONS, DO NOT OPEN THE DISK PACKAGE. PROMPTLY RETURN THE UNOPENED DISK PACKAGE AND ALL ACCOMPANYING ITEMS TO THE PLACE YOU OBTAINED THEM FOR A FULL REFUND OF ANY SUMS YOU HAVE PAID.

1. **GRANT OF LICENSE:** In consideration of your payment of the license fee, which is part of the price you paid for this product, and your agreement to abide by the terms and conditions of this Agreement, the Company grants to you a nonexclusive right to use and display the copy of the enclosed software program (hereinafter the "SOFTWARE") on a single computer (i.e., with a single CPU) at a single location so long as you comply with the terms of this Agreement. The Company reserves all rights not expressly granted to you under this Agreement.

2. **OWNERSHIP OF SOFTWARE:** You own only the magnetic or physical media (the enclosed disks) on which the SOFTWARE is recorded or fixed, but the Company retains all the rights, title, and ownership to the SOFTWARE recorded on the original disk copy(ies) and all subsequent copies of the SOFTWARE, regardless of the form or media on which the original or other copies may exist. This license is not a sale of the original SOFTWARE or any copy to you.

3. **COPY RESTRICTIONS:** This SOFTWARE and the accompanying printed materials and user manual (the "Documentation") are the subject of copyright. You may not copy the Documentation or the SOFTWARE, except that you may make a single copy of the SOFTWARE for backup or archival purposes only. You may be held legally responsible for any copying or copyright infringement which is caused or encouraged by your failure to abide by the terms of this restriction.

4. **USE RESTRICTIONS:** You may not network the SOFTWARE or otherwise use it on more than one computer or computer terminal at the same time. You may physically transfer the SOFTWARE from one computer to another provided that the SOFTWARE is used on only one computer at a time. You may not distribute copies of the SOFTWARE or Documentation to others. You may not reverse engineer, disassemble, decompile, modify, adapt, translate, or create derivative works based on the SOFTWARE or the Documentation without the prior written consent of the Company.

5. **TRANSFER RESTRICTIONS:** The enclosed SOFTWARE is licensed only to you and may not be transferred to any one else without the prior written consent of the Company. Any unauthorized transfer of the SOFTWARE shall result in the immediate termination of this Agreement.

6. **TERMINATION:** This license is effective until terminated. This license will terminate automatically without notice from the Company and become null and void if you fail to comply with any provisions or limitations of this license. Upon termination, you shall destroy the Documentation and all copies of the SOFTWARE. All provisions of this Agreement as to warranties, limitation of liability, remedies or damages, and our ownership rights shall survive termination.

7. **MISCELLANEOUS:** This Agreement shall be construed in accordance with the laws of the United States of America and the State of New York and shall benefit the Company, its affiliates, and assignees.

8. **LIMITED WARRANTY AND DISCLAIMER OF WARRANTY:** The Company warrants that the SOFTWARE, when properly used in accordance with the Documentation, will operate in substantial conformity with the description of the SOFTWARE set forth in the Documentation. The Company does not warrant that the SOFTWARE will meet your requirements or that the operation of the SOFTWARE will be uninterrupted or error-free. The Company warrants that the media on which the SOFTWARE is delivered shall be free from defects in materials and workmanship under normal use

for a period of thirty (30) days from the date of your purchase. Your only remedy and the Company's only obligation under these limited warranties is, at the Company's option, return of the warranted item for a refund of any amounts paid by you or replacement of the item. Any replacement of SOFTWARE or media under the warranties shall not extend the original warranty period. The limited warranty set forth above shall not apply to any SOFTWARE which the Company determines in good faith has been subject to misuse, neglect, improper installation, repair, alteration, or damage by you. EXCEPT FOR THE EXPRESSED WARRANTIES SET FORTH ABOVE, THE COMPANY DISCLAIMS ALL WARRANTIES, EXPRESS OR IMPLIED, INCLUDING WITHOUT LIMITATION, THE IMPLIED WARRANTIES OF MERCHANTABILITY AND FITNESS FOR A PARTICULAR PURPOSE. EXCEPT FOR THE EXPRESS WARRANTY SET FORTH ABOVE, THE COMPANY DOES NOT WARRANT, GUARANTEE, OR MAKE ANY REPRESENTATION REGARDING THE USE OR THE RESULTS OF THE USE OF THE SOFTWARE IN TERMS OF ITS CORRECTNESS, ACCURACY, RELIABILITY, CURRENTNESS, OR OTHERWISE.

IN NO EVENT, SHALL THE COMPANY OR ITS EMPLOYEES, AGENTS, SUPPLIERS, OR CONTRACTORS BE LIABLE FOR ANY INCIDENTAL, INDIRECT, SPECIAL, OR CONSEQUENTIAL DAMAGES ARISING OUT OF OR IN CONNECTION WITH THE LICENSE GRANTED UNDER THIS AGREEMENT, OR FOR LOSS OF USE, LOSS OF DATA, LOSS OF INCOME OR PROFIT, OR OTHER LOSSES, SUSTAINED AS A RESULT OF INJURY TO ANY PERSON, OR LOSS OF OR DAMAGE TO PROPERTY, OR CLAIMS OF THIRD PARTIES, EVEN IF THE COMPANY OR AN AUTHORIZED REPRESENTATIVE OF THE COMPANY HAS BEEN ADVISED OF THE POSSIBILITY OF SUCH DAMAGES. IN NO EVENT SHALL LIABILITY OF THE COMPANY FOR DAMAGES WITH RESPECT TO THE SOFTWARE EXCEED THE AMOUNTS ACTUALLY PAID BY YOU, IF ANY, FOR THE SOFTWARE.

SOME JURISDICTIONS DO NOT ALLOW THE LIMITATION OF IMPLIED WARRANTIES OR LIABILITY FOR INCIDENTAL, INDIRECT, SPECIAL, OR CONSEQUENTIAL DAMAGES, SO THE ABOVE LIMITATIONS MAY NOT ALWAYS APPLY. THE WARRANTIES IN THIS AGREEMENT GIVE YOU SPECIFIC LEGAL RIGHTS AND YOU MAY ALSO HAVE OTHER RIGHTS WHICH VARY IN ACCORDANCE WITH LOCAL LAW.

ACKNOWLEDGMENT

YOU ACKNOWLEDGE THAT YOU HAVE READ THIS AGREEMENT, UNDERSTAND IT, AND AGREE TO BE BOUND BY ITS TERMS AND CONDITIONS. YOU ALSO AGREE THAT THIS AGREEMENT IS THE COMPLETE AND EXCLUSIVE STATEMENT OF THE AGREEMENT BETWEEN YOU AND THE COMPANY AND SUPERSEDES ALL PROPOSALS OR PRIOR AGREEMENTS, ORAL, OR WRITTEN, AND ANY OTHER COMMUNICATIONS BETWEEN YOU AND THE COMPANY OR ANY REPRESENTATIVE OF THE COMPANY RELATING TO THE SUBJECT MATTER OF THIS AGREEMENT.

Should you have any questions concerning this Agreement or if you wish to contact the Company for any reason, please contact in writing at the address below.

Robin Short
Prentice Hall PTR
One Lake Street
Upper Saddle River, New Jersey 07458